# SARASOTA & NAPLES

## JASON FERGUSON

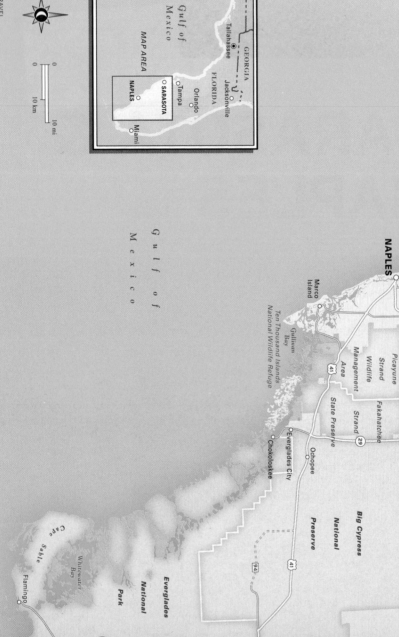

© AVALON TRAVEL

0 ——— 10 mi
0 ——— 10 km

**GEORGIA**

Tallahassee

**FLORIDA**

Jacksonville

Gulf of Mexico

MAP AREA

Orlando

Tampa

SARASOTA

NAPLES

Miami

Gulf of Mexico

**NAPLES**

NAPLES ZOO

41

846

Florida Panther National Wildlife Refuge

Picayune Strand Fakahatchee Strand

Wildlife Management Area

29

State Preserve

41

75

Marco Island

Gullivan Bay

Ten Thousand Islands National Wildlife Refuge

Ochopee

Everglades City

Chokoloskee

Big Cypress National Preserve

41

94

Cape Sable

Whitewater Bay

Everglades National Park

Flamingo

# SARASOTA AND NAPLES

# Contents

DISCOVER

# Sarasota & Naples

Close your eyes and picture soft, white sand merging into calm, blue waters. Welcome to the Paradise Coast, offering pleasures unlike anywhere else in Florida. This slice of heaven along the Gulf of Mexico doesn't boast theme-park attractions, spring-break bacchanalia, or glitz and glamour—and that's what makes it so great.

Even the little-known beaches here are idyllic, providing remote pastoral beauty, in-city access, or—amazingly—a combination of the two. The secret islands of Sanibel and Captiva are not so secret anymore—the bigger names like Siesta Key and Cayo Costa State Park routinely rank among the top choices of experts with the envious task of ranking beaches for awesomeness.

But the beaches are just the beginning. There are vast, open wildernesses here, ranging from rivers and forests ripe for exploration to undeveloped nature preserves ideal for bird-watching and hiking. And then you have the Everglades. Florida's most precious natural resource is made up of marshes, hardwood hammocks, mangrove copses, and a slow-moving "River of Grass" that provides a home to diverse wildlife and adventure to human visitors.

---

**Clockwise from top left:** the Sanibel shoreline; the John & Mable Ringling Museum of Art in Sarasota; signage on St. James Island; Fort Myers Beach; Marie Selby Botanical Garden; a swampy forest in the Ten Thousand Islands National Wildlife Refuge.

The gateways to the Paradise Coast offer their own attractions. Sarasota is an intimate city with a magnetism that makes all visitors potential future residents. It sustains a flourishing arts community of local creative types, moneyed snowbirds, and casual aficionados. Nearby, Naples similarly lays claim to a vibrant arts calendar and row of galleries that inspire envy in cities of similar size, as well as quirkier activities that will surprise you (swamp buggy races, anyone?).

Head for the Paradise Coast and make this vision of Florida your own.

**Clockwise from top left:** Big Cypress National Preserve; Caspersen Beach Park; sunset on the pier at Fort Myers Beach; *Unconditional Surrender*, by sculptor J. Seward Johnson II, on the Sarasota Bayfront.

# **8** TOP EXPERIENCES

**1** **A Day at the Beach:** Relax, play, or just admire the view at some of the best beaches in America (page 24).

**2** **Wilderness Walks:** Both well-manicured boardwalks and robust hiking trails are plentiful in the wildlife-rich parks of the Paradise Coast (page 31).

**3** **Go Fish:** Whether in rivers, lakes, or the Gulf of Mexico, the waters of southwest Florida are prime fishing destinations year-round (page 29).

>>>

 **4** **Edison & Ford Winter Estates:** Get a glimpse into the lives of these legendary inventors, both of whom spent winters in the warmth of Fort Myers (page 115).

**5** **Canoeing & Kayaking in the Everglades:** The wide-open wetlands and hemmed-in waterways of the Everglades make an ideal environment for paddling (page 227).

<<<

**6** **Art:** Visit renowned **museums** (pages 41 and 174), thriving **art colonies** (page 38), and top-notch **galleries** (pages 53 and 184)—or spend a weekend doing all of the above (page 27).

**7** **Bird-Watching:** Spot migratory birds at Charlotte Harbor Preserve State Park (page 95), Corkscrew Swamp Sanctuary (page 177), and especially at the J.N. "Ding" Darling National Wildlife Refuge on Sanibel Island (page 145).

**8** **Seafood:** The southwest coast of Florida offers an abundance of great seafood, from juicy gulf shrimp to fresh, wild-caught fish (page 30).

<<<

# Planning Your Trip

## Where to Go

The cities and sights of southwest Florida are in fairly close proximity; you can drive from southernmost Naples to northernmost Sarasota in less than three hours. However, despite the fact that I-75 and the Tamiami Trail make all the cities a short drive from each other, you'll seldom travel in a straight line between destinations. The Paradise Coast is full of nooks and crannies, with outlying wilderness areas, hard-to-access barrier islands, and communities that may be separated by just 20 miles as the crow flies but nonetheless require an hour or more of navigation to connect.

### Sarasota

Sarasota is the unofficial **gateway** to southwest Florida, with a pace that's both relaxed and refined. Sarasota is a slow-moving city, inhabited by cultured retirees, moneyed beach bums, and arts-and-classics-minded college students. That combination has yielded a unique demographic personality that not only appreciates the vibrant **visual and performing arts scene** but also takes advantage of the beautiful weather and stunning natural vistas. The **barrier islands** that hug the coastline—Siesta Key, Longboat Key, and Anna Maria Island—are home to some of the most **gorgeous beaches** in the world.

### Charlotte Harbor

Many visitors to southwest Florida zoom right past the Charlotte Harbor area on their way south from Sarasota. However, this area is one of my favorite places in the entire state. From the quiet and quaint riverfront town of **Punta Gorda** to the exclusive island enclave of **Boca Grande,** there are pockets of amazing beauty all

downtown Fort Myers

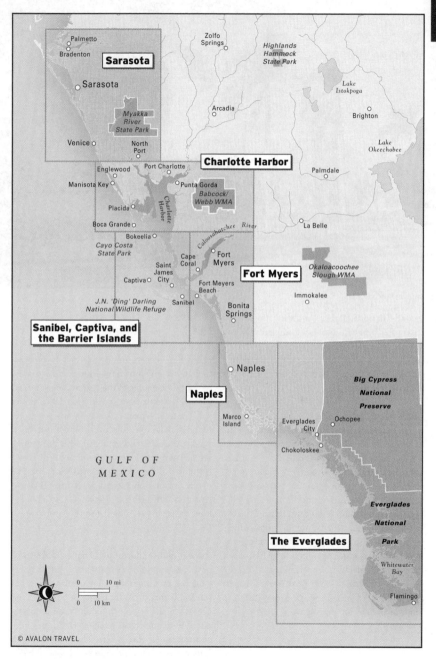

© AVALON TRAVEL

downtown Punta Gorda

around Charlotte Harbor. And while the coastal areas offer beautiful beaches and plenty of waterfront activities, the vast **palmetto prairies** and **swampy forests** inland provide ample opportunities for hikers, bird-watchers, and other outdoor explorers.

## Fort Myers

When Thomas Edison made Fort Myers his winter home, he was likely as attracted by the mild weather as he was by the fact that the city—then, not much more than a pioneer's backwater—would give him the mental and physical space he needed to focus on his work. These days, Fort Myers is considerably less sleepy. Edison's legacy weighs heavily on the city, not just at his winter estate, but also in Fort Myers's revitalized **downtown district,** which at night is lit up like one of the inventor's electrical experiments. Along the coast, the laid-back vibe at **Fort Myers Beach** and **Lovers Key State Park** evoke different kinds of Old Florida charm.

## Sanibel, Captiva, and the Barrier Islands

The names Sanibel and Captiva tend to be whispered like secrets among visitors to Florida, though it's well known that these connected sister islands are some of the best and most peaceful beach destinations in America. Once you've paid the toll to cross the Sanibel Causeway to get to the islands, you'll discover communities that, though exclusive and predominantly residential, are welcoming to tourists. From the **shell-filled beaches** to the incredible bird-watching and nature exploration in the **J. N. "Ding" Darling National Wildlife Refuge,** you'll find it hard to leave the beauty and quiet of Sanibel and Captiva.

## Naples

At first glance, downtown Naples looks to be devoted to **upscale restaurants,** exclusive art galleries, and other high-dollar attractions, but the fact is that there are plenty of beautiful and accessible places here that don't require taking out a second mortgage to enjoy. Heck, they have **swamp buggy races** here! The beaches are not only convenient to downtown, they also boast some of the most powdery white sand to be found in the state, and attractions like the **Naples Zoo at Caribbean Gardens** are affordable and enjoyable.

## The Everglades

For many people, the Everglades define Florida. The 'Glades have remained undeveloped, asserting the natural strength that comes from being nearly 4,000 square miles of **swampland, rivers, marshes, and forest.** For nature lovers, this part of the state is a seemingly infinite paradise. Hiking, **kayaking,** canoeing, and **wildlife spotting** are the main activities, and the solitude one experiences while here gives all of these activities additional poignancy.

# Know Before You Go

## High and Low Seasons

This part of the state fills up with snowbirds and frozen northerners during the winter. Unfortunately, although hotel rates go down in the summer (watch out for hurricanes!), many businesses simply close up shop between May and October, as it's not worth it for them to stay open to cater to the small number of tourists who visit. Also, many of the non-beach-oriented outdoor activities covered in this guide can be decidedly unpleasant during the oppressive heat and humidity of the summer months. So, if you're focusing on hitting the **beach** and getting **deals,** the best times to visit are **May and September,** when the weather (and the water) is warm but not devastatingly so, prices are lower, and the resorts aren't packed with families on summer vacation. For **outdoor recreation** such as hiking, kayaking, and exploring state and national parks (like the Everglades), the **cooler months** are best, as the weather is much more bearable, the bugs are less overwhelming, and the skies and trees are filled with scores of migratory bird species. Fans of the **arts** will also appreciate the winter months, as cultural season kicks into high gear from **January through March.**

## What to Pack

Unless you're visiting the Everglades, you'll be able to find almost anything you need within a 5- or 10-minute drive from nearly anywhere in the area, so if you forget something, don't sweat it, because you'll certainly be able to get it when you arrive.

Florida is a very casual state, so pack for comfort. **One dressy outfit** in a suitcase filled with sundresses or shorts and beachwear is probably plenty. Although some parts of southwest Florida, like Naples, are a little more buttoned-down than others, for the most part, as long as you don't look like a beach bum, you'll be fine. Be sure to pack at least one pair of **closed-toe shoes,** as the many non-beach outdoor activities in the area, such as hiking the Everglades, are not ideally done in flip-flops or sandals.

If you're going to be spending any time outdoors, pack **sunscreen,** as the tropical sun is merciless.

# The Best of the Paradise Coast

There's a lot to enjoy in southwest Florida, and even though a week in the area will only scratch the surface of what the Paradise Coast has to offer, this itinerary will help you explore the best of the region.

## Day 1: Sarasota

Sarasota is the most interesting and beautiful of all the cities covered in this guide, and you'll want to dedicate at least two days to taking in the best it has to offer. For your first day, spend the morning exploring the incredible **John & Mable Ringling Museum of Art** and taking in the **Circus Museum** and John Ringling's stunning (and stunningly ornate) mansion, **Ca' d'Zan,** which are also located on the grounds.

Afterward, grab lunch at **Nancy's BBQ** in downtown Sarasota, and allocate a couple of hours to stroll through the beautiful **Marie Selby Botanical Gardens,** wrapping the day up with some shopping and dinner among the upscale boutiques and restaurants of **St. Armands Circle.** Take in the sunset at nearby **Lido Beach.** Spend the night on Lido Beach, at the vintage and affordable **Gulf Beach Resort.**

## Day 2: Siesta Key

Give over a whole day to relaxing on the white sands of the famously **beautiful beaches** of Siesta Key. The calm blue waters and broad expanse of beach that are a hallmark of Siesta Key may be similar to other spots in southwest Florida, but Siesta Key is an exceptional example, and it's routinely acknowledged as one of the best beaches in the United States for a very good reason. Grab lunch, dinner, or drinks at the rowdy **Siesta Key Oyster Bar,** or, if you're here on a Sunday morning, hit the **Siesta Key Farmers Market** to stock up on locally sourced food.

the John & Mable Ringling Museum of Art

## Day 3: Punta Gorda

Take an early morning, hour-long drive from Sarasota to explore the small and friendly riverfront town of Punta Gorda. Afterward, head east for one of the exceptional (and accessible) ecotours offered by the folks at **Babcock Ranch Eco-Tours,** which will give you an excellent look at the many ecosystems in the area, as well as some historical perspective on how this part of the state has developed over the years. If ecotouring isn't your thing, head to **Gasparilla Island State Park** in the quaint and upscale island resort town of **Boca Grande.** Here, you can picnic on the beautiful grounds of **Boca Grande Lighthouse,** then relax for a few hours on the white-sand beach.

Head back to Punta Gorda for the evening and dine on the excellent, local seafood at **Peace River Seafood.** Spend the night downtown at the luxurious and surprisingly affordable **Wyvern Hotel.**

## Day 4: Fort Myers

Downtown Fort Myers is less than an hour away from Punta Gorda, so you can easily make the drive to get coffee and one of the fantastically decadent homemade doughnuts at **Bennett's Fresh Roast** before exploring the historic **Edison & Ford Winter Estates.** The expansive grounds and instructive exhibits are well worth at least a half-day visit.

Next, head to Fort Myers Beach and grab lunch from **Smokin' Oyster Brewery.** Make your way to the wildlife sanctuary at **Matanzas Pass Preserve** and fight off your food coma with a walk through some of the preserve's many nature trails. If you've got a kayak in tow, this is also a great place to get in the water: There's a launch area for the **Great Calusa Blueway** paddling trail here. After you've hiked or paddled yourself tired, drop your bags at the **Silver Sands Villas,** then have a relaxed seafood dinner at the **Beached Whale.**

## Day 5: Sanibel and Captiva

Stop for a bagel breakfast at **Tuckaway Bagel & Wafel** before making the half-hour drive to the islands of Sanibel and Captiva. Spend the morning taking a nature tour or bird-watching walk in the **J. N. "Ding" Darling National Wildlife**

Boca Grande Lighthouse

observation tower in the Everglades

**Refuge.** Then try the conch fritters at **Lazy Flamingo** in Sanibel village for lunch. Linger in Sanibel for a while, and browse the wares at one of the boutiques at **The Village Shops.**

Next, be sure to head for **Captiva Beach** for a lazy afternoon in the sun. Take in a beautiful sunset while you have dinner and drinks at **The Mucky Duck.** Make your way to Sanibel and splurge on a room at the upscale **Seaside Inn,** or settle in for the night on Captiva at the unique and rustic **'Tween Waters Inn.**

## Day 6: Naples

Head for Naples and start your day with coffee and a pastry at the European-style **Jane's Cafe** downtown. Afterward, explore the historic bayside area known as **Tin City,** as well as the upscale shops and art galleries situated along **5th Avenue South.** Stop in the well-known **New River Fine Art** and decide which masterwork is the best. Play a set or two of tennis at the **Arthur L. Allen Tennis Center** before enjoying lunch alfresco at the casual but upscale **Citrus.**

A stroll through the animal exhibits and lush landscapes of the **Naples Zoo at Caribbean Gardens** is a good way to work up an appetite for dinner at the stylish **Sea Salt** in downtown Naples. Stay the night at **The Naples Beach Hotel & Golf Club,** a classic, Old Florida resort that is homey, luxurious, and friendly in equal measure.

## Day 7: The Everglades

Spend your last day in the vast landscapes and rough natural beauty of the Everglades, only a short drive away from the luxurious environs of Naples. Stop into **Everglades City** for a lunch of fried gator at **Camellia Street Grill.** Use the rest of your day for canoeing, hiking, or just meandering through the River of Grass. If you're looking to kayak through the area, check out **Shurr Adventures** to set up a water-based tour.

Now it's time to say goodbye to the Paradise Coast and head home, though you're likely already planning your next trip here.

# Weekend Getaway to Sarasota

Sarasota makes for an excellent weekend getaway for first-time visitors and for area residents. For the former, it offers some of the best sights and experiences in the region; for the latter, it offers extensive opportunities to revisit, whether it's to more thoroughly explore the arts-and-culture scene, to suss out some of the less well-known outdoor opportunities, or to more deeply experience the subtle charms of this underappreciated urban oasis. This itinerary is for visitors who want to go beyond the highlights but only have about 48 hours in town.

## Friday

Drop your bags at **Hotel Ranola**, a boutique hotel downtown, and head over to **Centennial Park** to watch the boats float by. In the evening, check out the performance schedule for that night at the beautiful **Van Wezel Performing Arts Hall**, and stay for a show if something piques your interest. Afterward, explore the **Sarasota Bayfront.** Grab dinner at **Indigenous,** one of Sarasota's best restaurants, where you can feast on expertly prepared and locally sourced fare.

## Saturday

Start your day with a hearty meal at **The Breakfast House,** and follow it up with a stroll through the historic homes and sights of the **Central Cocoanut** district. Afterward, you can head over to Lido Shores, where you can explore one of the highest concentrations of legendary residential architecture in the country.

At this point, you're just five minutes from the **Mote Marine Laboratory & Aquarium** on City Island. Ogle the preserved giant squid and get close to marine life with the touch pools. Plan on spending the rest of the afternoon exploring the galleries of the **Ringling College of Art & Design.** A fresh, stylish seafood dinner

entrances to the Sarasota Bayfront

## SIESTA KEY

The gently curving coastline of Crescent Beach at Siesta Key is legendary for its white sand and remarkably wide and spacious stretches. It's quite popular, thanks to those expanses of sand and gentle, blue Gulf waters that are shallow and calm (page 70).

## FORT MYERS BEACH

The vibe in the town of Fort Myers Beach is overwhelmingly laid-back and neighborly. The large and beautiful white-sand beaches are easily accessible and family-friendly, and parking is a breeze (page 127).

## LOVERS KEY STATE PARK

Located between Fort Myers Beach and Bonita Springs, this quiet and isolated state park gained a reputation—and its name—for being a perfect place for couples to get away from the crowds. While it's definitely no longer a secret, the gorgeous beaches and splendid sense of being away from it all remain (page 133).

## BAREFOOT BEACH PRESERVE COUNTY PARK

Although it's situated at the end of a road that goes through a gated community, this beach is very much open to the public, but it never seems to be overwhelmed with visitors . . . unless you count the gopher tortoises who seem to love this beach nearly as much as the locals who flock to it (page 135).

## CAPTIVA BEACH

Beautiful beaches abound on the islands of Sanibel and Captiva, but the remote and quiet stretch of sand at the northern tip of Captiva Island is truly

Fort Myers Beach

special, thanks to its soft, white sand and relative quietude (page 153).

## CAYO COSTA STATE PARK

Routinely ranked by folks like "Dr. Beach" as one of the state's best beaches, the nine miles of white sand at Cayo Costa are, indeed, impossibly gorgeous. Accessible only by a private boat or ferry, and with only the most basic of amenities, this rustic, tropical island is a great place to get away from it all (page 166).

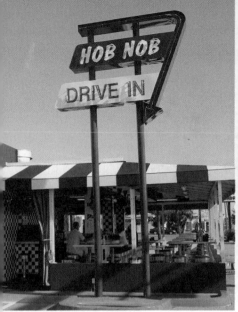

Sarasota's Hob Nob Drive In

St. Armands Circle near Sarasota

at **The Table—Creekside** or a decadent, meat-centered feast at **The Alpine Steakhouse and Karl Ehmers Quality Meats** should be followed up with an evening of drinks and music in the Gulf Gate area. Fans of handcrafted beer should settle in at **Mr. Beery's.**

### Sunday
Grab a great, old-school breakfast at the **Hob Nob Drive In,** then head to **St. Armands Circle** for souvenirs and retail therapy; those who want something to remember their trip by should make their way into **Uniquity,** a funky boutique offering jewelry and Sarasota-based knickknacks.

Check out of Hotel Ranola and get yourself to Siesta Key. Plan on spending the rest of your trip with your toes in the beautiful white sands of **Siesta Beach,** then head home with visions of sandy beaches and blue ocean dancing in your head.

# Weekend Getaway to Naples

### Friday
Check in to **Inn on 5th** for your weekend accommodations; it manages to be both luxe and friendly, and it's perfectly located in downtown on 5th Ave. Spend the afternoon exploring downtown **Old Naples** on foot; you'll be able to window shop the upscale boutiques as well as art galleries like **New River Fine Art** and **Four Winds Gallery**. In the evening, head over to the half-historic/half-kitschy **Tin City** lto get a feel for Naples' Old Florida roots, and enjoy dinner overlooking the water at Pinchers Crab Shack. Afterward, head grab some late-night drinks at **Shane's Cabana Bar.**

### Saturday
After breakfast at **Jane's Café**, head a few minutes north of downtown Naples to spend the morning enjoying the beautiful beach at **Delnor-Wiggins Pass State Recreation Area.**

hiking in the Pine Island Flatwoods Preserve

The outdoor opportunities in southwest Florida are truly unparalleled. The winter months are temperate and quite dry, making outdoor exploration something of a must. With rivers, swamps, forests, and beautiful Gulf waters, there's plenty outdoors to explore.

## KAYAKING

There are ample opportunities for kayakers here, from the mangrove thickets in **Edwards Islands Park** and the beautiful acres of **Myakka River State Park**, to the well-marked **Nine Mile Pond Trail** in the Everglades. Outfitters like **Almost Heaven Kayak Adventures** in Sarasota and **North American Canoe Tours** in Everglades City can set you up with rentals or lead you on a tour.

## BOATING AND SAILING

Almost all of the marinas in southwest Florida are home to tour companies and charters, so you don't need to tow your own boat to have a good time on the water. **Naples Sailing Adventures** can get you out on the water for a truly unique look at the area's waterways. Sunset sailing tours, like those offered by **Kathleen D Sailing Catamarans**, in Sarasota, are also quite popular.

## HIKING AND BIKING

Southwest Florida has a stunning amount of untouched, nearly pastoral land that is perfect for trail adventures. Even on tiny Pine Island, there are two great hiking experiences—in the **Pine Island Flatwoods Preserve** and the **St. James Creek Preserve**—that are only a mile long, but each offers its own unique challenges. Larger areas, like the **Myakka State Forest,** are even more impressive, with waterfront routes and forest trails that add to the diversity of opportunities in the area.

## BIRD-WATCHING

The winter months offer some incredible bird-watching opportunities. The **J. N. "Ding" Darling National Wildlife Refuge** on Sanibel Island is one of the best places for bird-watchers, featuring an astonishing diversity of species, thanks both to the ideal winter weather and the healthy ecosystems within the preserve. Near Naples, the Audubon Society-operated **Corkscrew Swamp Sanctuary** also offers some exceptional bird-watching opportunities, along one of the most pastoral and scenic boardwalk swamp trails you'll ever walk upon.

Afterward, head back toward central Naples, stopping by the **Baker Museum** to enjoy the exceptionally curated galleries of contemporary and classic art and then **Brooks Gourmet Burgers & Dogs** for lunch and an ice-cold beer. For the afternoon, drive a half-hour south to **Marco Island** where you can explore **Olde Marco Village** and, later, take a sunset river cruise with **Marco Island Princess Tours**. If you're feeling fancy, enjoy an upscale, European-style dinner at Marco Island's **Bistro Soleil**; if you're feeling the opposite of fancy, head to nearby Goodland, where the bar-and-grill/locals-only vibe at **Stan's Idle Hour** is welcoming and raucous, and the oysters and fried frog legs are perfectly prepared.

## Sunday

Get up early and head about a half-hour east of downtown Naples for the **Corkscrew Swamp Sanctuary**. An early arrival not only ensures cooler weather and a more peaceful (less-populated) walk along the swamp's boardwalks, it also increases the likelihood that you'll see a wide range of wildlife at this Audubon sanctuary. Afterward, if you still have some time before your flight home, take a couple of hours to explore **Naples Zoo** or **Naples Botanical Garden**.

# Arts and Architecture

Sarasota and Naples are cities that are known for their arts and cultural scenes, particularly during the winter snowbird season, when retirees "migrate" to Florida to enjoy the mild weather. This itinerary can be enjoyed any time of year, though, as southwest Florida's art scene is vibrant all year long.

## Day 1

The most notable and most often overlooked artistic attraction in **Sarasota** is the city's architecture. True architecture buffs will want to allocate a day searching out the scores of Sarasota School of Architecture buildings still standing, while casual enthusiasts can dedicate a morning to checking out the exceptional residences of Lido Shores.

After a morning of idle driving, a visit to the **Towles Court Artist Colony** in downtown Sarasota allows you to get a little more hands-on, with nearly two dozen studios, galleries, and shops situated in a scenic clutch of converted historic bungalows. Towles is also home to several restaurants, like the casual yet upscale **Indigenous.** Savor a glass of wine at the cottage that serves as their wine bar, then stay for a bite to eat, and take in the muted yet elegant decor of the restaurant.

After dinner, take in a concert at the **Van Wezel Performing Arts Hall,** a lavender-colored building that's as visually unique as it is architecturally significant: It was designed by William Wesley Peters, Frank Lloyd Wright's son-in-law, and is often described as "the purple seashell."

If you're lucky enough to get one of the four rooms at **Hotel Ranola,** you'll enjoy an elegant and luxurious stay at a bed-and-breakfast that features canopy beds and Turkish rugs.

## Day 2

You can—and should—spend an entire day exploring the **John & Mable Ringling Museum of Art** and its surrounding grounds. The museum itself is, obviously, the star attraction, with a range of exhibits featuring everything from the Old Masters and Asian sculpture to modern art. It's worth noting that, although the Ringling has quite a bit of historical cachet to it (including an actual *room* that John Ringling bought from a Du Pont mansion), it is a living museum, with frequent rotation of exhibits and a deft curatorial touch. The architecture of Ringling's mammoth house—the **Ca' d'Zan** mansion—is also notable for its Gilded Age excesses, and it can be accessed via the same admission ticket that got you into the museum. And, while you're on the grounds, you should also explore the **Circus Museum,** which, in addition to providing a surprising amount of historical context and information about the circus, also has a fascinating display of circus poster art, as well as a stunning scale model of an actual turn-of-the-20th-century circus. Just a few blocks away are the galleries of the **Ringling College of Art & Design,** which host numerous exhibits by student and faculty artists, as well as notable international artists. And, staying in the neighborhood will allow you to catch a performance at the **Asolo Repertory Theatre,** the largest repertory theater in the Southeast.

## Day 3

**Naples** is often thought of as southwest Florida's arts haven. Downtown Naples is well stocked with dozens of galleries, some of which are quite impressive. Plan on spending at least a morning browsing the offerings of Naples's **5th Avenue South,** like the **Shaw Gallery,** which features works from local and national artists in various mediums: sculpture, glass, and paint, to name a few. If you venture southward, you'll find another enclave of galleries on 3rd Street, like the **Darvish Collection of Fine Art,** which is Naples's second-oldest gallery. It appeals to lovers of 19th- and 20th-century art. Take a break from appreciating all that art to indulge in a glass of wine with an early lunch at **Ridgway Bar & Grill,** just down the way on 3rd Street.

After lunch, it's an easy and scenic two-hour drive through the **Everglades** to photographer Clyde Butcher's **Big Cypress Gallery,** where not only can you view and buy prints of the legendary photographer's work, but, if you're lucky, you may just get the chance to hear the man himself expound on the natural beauty of this part of the state. Stop in for dinner at **Joanie's Blue Crab Cafe** and sample some of the local swamp fare while you listen to live music from the bar.

Head back to Naples for the night, and treat yourself to a night at **The Naples Beach Hotel & Golf Club,** where you'll recognize the artwork: The hotel's rooms feature Clyde Butcher prints, as well as Naples artist Jim Rice's ceramics.

Van Wezel Performing Arts Hall in Sarasota

# Go Fish

Southwest Florida is an angler's paradise. Not only does the Gulf of Mexico provide ample opportunities for saltwater fishing, but the brackish waters in the coastal mangroves and estuaries, as well as the freshwater creeks and rivers that are abundant in the region, present a wide variety of options for fishing.

## COMMON SPECIES AND WHERE TO FIND THEM

The tidal creeks, estuaries, and mangroves in the region are home to redfish, snook, sea trout, and tarpon. The estuaries near **Pine Island** and **Charlotte Harbor** are particularly great if these are the species you're looking for, since the waters are generally clean and the marine ecosystems quite healthy. Snook, in particular, is abundant for flats fishing from late spring through autumn, but backcountry fishing is great all year round. Offshore fishing is even better, with grouper, kingfish, blackfin tuna, Spanish mackerel, bonita, permit, and more in the waters of the Gulf of Mexico; deepwater fishing off the coast of **Naples** is notably great.

fishing at Fort Myers Beach

For inland anglers, the **Myakka River** provides a surprisingly diverse array of fish, with bass and bluegill providing a challenge for fly-casters in the upper, freshwater sections near **Sarasota**; in the lower, brackish sections (approximately the last 20 miles before the river dumps into Charlotte Harbor), one can pursue saltwater species like snook and redfish, as well as largemouth bass.

A particularly great way to fish and explore the area is in a kayak on the **Great Calusa Blueway,** comprising 190 miles of paddling trails stretching from the southern end of Charlotte Harbor down to Bonita Springs. Trout, redfish, and snook are abundant in the mangroves and creeks. Bass fishing is best in the eastern freshwater of the **Everglades** near Naples.

## AQUATIC PRESERVES

Florida's Department of Environmental Protection (DEP) has established many aquatic preserves throughout the state, and eight of them are in the southwest region. The **Gasparilla Sound-Charlotte Harbor Aquatic Preserve** is the second-largest estuary in the state, and, according to the DEP, it's the "largest, deepest, and most diverse of the five Charlotte Harbor aquatic preserves." While the **Lemon Bay Aquatic Preserve** provides excellent fishing opportunities, the Gasparilla Sound-Charlotte Harbor Aquatic Preserve is definitely the best in the area, thanks to the range of habitats here: freshwater, saltwater, brackish waters, shoals, flats, mangroves, and reefs. It's not at all surprising that more than 200 different species of fish call the area home. Additionally, there are preserves in Rookery Bay (near Marco Island), Estero Bay (near Fort Myers), and in the Ten Thousand Islands area.

## GUIDES AND CHARTERS

**Everglades Kayak Fishing** provides one of the best ways to fish the narrow waterways of the Everglades. **Tarpon Bay Explorers** is located within the J. N. "Ding" Darling National Wildlife Refuge on Sanibel Island and offers guided kayak and canoe tours. **Magic Fishing Adventures** specializes in light-tackle fishing along the coastal flats around Sarasota, where you can hunt tarpon, kingfish, snapper, grouper, and other local inshore species. **Getaway Marina** in Fort Myers Beach provides half-day fishing charters aboard a 90-foot bus-on-the-water called *The Great Getaway*.

# Catch of the Day

The waters of the Gulf of Mexico contain a bounty of fresh seafood, and the restaurants along Florida's Gulf Coast definitely benefit from it. Many restaurants specialize in local seafood, and while the atmosphere can range from rustic waterfront fish shack to upscale surf-and-turf joint, the abundance of fresh, locally caught seafood means that you're sure to get a remarkable plate.

If you're in the area during the cooler months (Oct.-May), make sure to try **Florida stone crabs** (page 190) or check out a local seafood festival, like the January **Mullet Festival** or the March **Marco Island Seafood & Music Festival,** both in/near Naples (page 184).

Throughout the year, though, you'll be able to get great seafood at these restaurants, which are five of the best in the area.

Joanie's Blue Crab Cafe

- **Owens Fish Camp** (516 Burns Ln., Sarasota, 941/951-6936, 4pm-9:30pm Sun.-Thurs, 4pm-10:30pm Fri.-Sat., main courses from $10) boasts Old Florida decor and a friendly, slightly boozy vibe. Head straight for Owens's lowcountry boil, with crab claws, mussels, shrimp, potatoes, corn, and sausage delivered in copious quantities.

- **The Table—Creekside** (5365 S. Tamiami Trail, Sarasota, 941/921-9465, www.tablesrq.com, 4pm-10pm Sun.-Thurs., 4pm-10:30pm Fri.-Sat., main courses from $15) sits alongside Phillippi Creek and has a gorgeous outdoor deck overlooking the creek. The menu features exceptional takes on seafood (wahoo ceviche, lobster ceviche, Brazilian shrimp and grits).

- **Peace River Seafood & Crab Shack** (5337 Duncan Rd., Punta Gorda, 941/505-8440, 11am-7:30pm Tues.-Sat., main courses from $12) isn't actually on the Peace River (it's about a block away), but the renovated Florida cracker-style bungalow exudes charm from every corner of its cramped, cozy dining room. Seafood is incredibly fresh, as the owners are running an operation that's small enough to allow them to deal directly with local fishers to get some of the best stuff right off the boat.

- **Smokin' Oyster Brewery** (340 Old San Carlos Blvd., Fort Myers Beach, 239/463-3474, www.smokinoyster.com, 11am-11pm daily, main courses from $8) specializes in both oysters and beer. This is very much a casual, just-off-the-waterfront beach bar, complete with live music and potent cocktails, and the seafood is always super-fresh, well-chosen, and expertly prepared.

- **Joanie's Blue Crab Cafe** (39395 Tamiami Trail E., Ochopee, 239/695-2682, http://joanies-bluecrabcafe.com, 11am-5pm daily, from $12) is the best restaurant in Ochopee (granted, it's one of only two restaurants in Ochopee). The small menu focuses on true swamp fare, with frog legs, fried gator, garlic blue crabs, Indian fry bread, and a few other dishes. Everything on the menu is excellent and portions are huge.

Silence will be rewarded at Big Cypress National Preserve.

# Wilderness Walks

Southwest Florida has a tremendous bounty of wild, beautiful, and undeveloped land. It is, after all, the home of the Everglades. No matter where you're based during your stay here, you'll be able to escape into the wilderness. Most of the time, you'll be able to do it on foot. Thanks to mild winters and generally flat terrain, the biggest challenge for Florida nature-walkers is making sure to wear enough insect repellent while exploring the forests, swamps, and trails in the region.

## Sarasota

Head for **Myakka River State Park,** southeast of Sarasota. It's one of Florida's most beautiful inland state parks, covering a vast 37,000 acres of land. Here, you can hike the main **"backpacking trail"** for up to 36 miles of forest, marshland, and prairie. Those looking for a shorter distance should be sure to check out the **canopy walkway,** a treetop trail that gives you a literal bird's-eye view of your surroundings.

Birders and wildlife spotters should bring binoculars, as sightings of eagles, roseate spoonbills, wild hogs, and bobcats, among many others, are possible. Once you've gotten your fill on land, hop in a boat: The extensive river frontage makes it an excellent place for canoeing and kayaking, and airboat tours are also available.

## Charlotte Harbor

East of Charlotte Harbor, the Babcock/Webb Wildlife Management Area is home to both an active ranch and an ecotour outfitter. Riding around a in a "swamp buggy" (a repurposed, camouflage-painted school bus) may stretch the definition of wilderness solitude, but the ecotours at **Babcock Ranch Eco-Tours** are an excellent way to explore the varied ecosystems in this part of the state. A knowledgeable guide will teach you all about the swamp, grasslands, and forest around you. If swamp buggies aren't your thing, there's also a low-impact, 2.4-mile **walking trail** that takes you through much of the same terrain. Regardless of which mode of transport you employ, the chances are high that you'll see some alligators and a huge variety of birds. Keep your eyes peeled for wild hogs, and be sure to ask about the resident panther.

## Naples

An excursion to the **Corkscrew Swamp Sanctuary** is worth carving out an entire day for, mainly because the sanctuary is located, literally, in the middle of nowhere. The round-trip from Naples will take at least two hours of your day. Operated by the National Audubon Society, Corkscrew is a gorgeous and restful natural space, and one of the quietest natural spots outside of the Everglades.

Covering more than 11,000 acres of land, the sanctuary is a perfect place for bird-watchers, as it's a winter destination for numerous species of birds, like egrets, herons, and the endangered wood stork. Walk along the **2.5-mile boardwalk trail,** which takes you through a dense, swampy canopy filled with alligators, birds, and an arresting array of plant life.

## The Everglades

You can spend half of a day in the Everglades or you can spend half a year; the choice is yours. With hundreds of thousands of acres of protected land that's teeming with rivers, marshes, grasslands, swamps, and more, there's such an incredible variety of terrain and wildlife here that its vastness is both impossible to comprehend and impossible to avoid.

Make a point to avail yourself of the **scenic boardwalk trail** at **Fakahatchee Strand Preserve State Park;** it's one of the longest boardwalk trails in the Everglades, providing some great wildlife views. There are other, shorter boardwalk trails throughout the Everglades, which are wonderful, but more for taking in the views than for enjoying a robust hike.

If you're looking to break a sweat and get your boots a little dirty, there are other hiking trails in the region; most visitors head for the two loop trails at the **Royal Palm Visitor Center,** which are accessible but invigorating. Near the **Flamingo Visitor Center** there are more than a half-dozen hiking trails, ranging from the short loop **Eco Pond** trail to the six-mile **Coastal Prairie Trail**, which follows a route used by pioneer travelers.

# Sarasota

Look for ★ to find recommended
sights, activities, dining, and lodging.

# Highlights

★ **Towles Court Artist Colony:** Moss-draped oaks shade the historic buildings of this unique artist enclave, making for an experience that's as scenic as it is artsy (page 38).

★ **Marie Selby Botanical Gardens:** This pastoral oasis has an impressive and diverse display of flora. The smart curation of 20,000-plus plants—including more than 4,000 orchids—make exploration a breeze (page 40).

★ **Mote Marine Laboratory & Aquarium:** This research and conservation facility encourages visitors to engage with the vibrant Gulf Coast ecosystem and its wide variety of marine life (page 40).

★ **John & Mable Ringling Museum of Art:** John Ringling had an eye for fine art, resulting in one of the best-curated collections of masterworks in the state (page 41).

★ **Myakka River State Park:** This 37,000-acre state park is one of the most beautiful pieces of wilderness in Florida. The gorgeous Myakka River feeds marshes, wetlands, and forests—and provides an excellent environment for bird-watching (page 44).

★ **Siesta Key Beaches:** Routinely ranked among the best in the United States, these wide beaches boast a combination of snow-white sand, crystal-blue waters, and gentle wave action that's perfect for small kids and snorkelers (page 70).

★ **Longboat Key and Anna Maria Island:** Longboat Key and Anna Maria Island

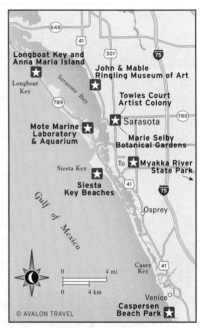

are home to a mixture of wild landscapes, isolated beaches, and an Old Florida atmosphere. Their slow pace and welcoming vibe manage to be visitor-friendly without being tourist-focused (page 74).

★ **Caspersen Beach Park:** You're likely to run across some prehistoric shark teeth at this quiet, isolated beach in Venice (page 83).

# t's rare to find world-class art in such close proximity to unspoiled nature.

There's a stunning amount of ecological diversity on display here—award-winning white-sand beaches, dense flatwood forests, the beautiful Myakka River, and, of course, the waters of Sarasota Bay itself—and, despite its reputation as a snowbird haven, quite a bit of social diversity as well. Although the Sarasota area doesn't have the same sort of multicultural vibe as some of Florida's bigger cities, the confluence of college students, moneyed yuppies, growing families, and art-loving retirees makes for an interesting mix indeed.

The artistic bent of this region is most pronounced in Sarasota, which is by no means a "big city." The Ringling College of Art & Design and the New College of Florida (the state's public honors college) draw a youthful crowd of students interested in the arts (both performing and fine). Residents are enthusiastic patrons of the arts: Just check out the crowds at the impressive John & Mable Ringling Museum of Art or at any local gallery opening. Even the ritzy shopping district of St. Armands Circle is punctuated by classical statues extolling the virtues of creativity and beauty. This love of the arts, combined with the abundant natural beauty of the area, ensures that visitors are likely to make Sarasota a repeat destination on future travels.

And then there are the beaches. Siesta Key's beaches are a work of art unto themselves, routinely awarded "best beach" status by whatever lucky judge it is who gets to make such designations. It's easy to understand why: The wide beaches boast soft, white sand that seamlessly merges into calm, crystal-blue waters that are largely unaffected by tidal action (this is the Gulf, after all). This beauty extends to the beaches on Longboat Key and Anna Maria Island as well, making the area around Sarasota one of the best in the state for beachgoers.

## HISTORY

Sarasota has the longest history of the major southern Gulf Coast cities, with European expeditions here dating back to the early 1500s; fishing camps were established in the mid-18th century, and by 1845, the U.S. Army had established Fort Armistead on Sarasota Bay. The town, like most of Florida, was a rural community defined by nearby ranches and a busy local fishing industry. It continued to grow, and by 1913, it was incorporated as a

**Previous:** Cortez Beach; Lido Beach. **Above:** a sign on Anna Maria Island.

# Sarasota County

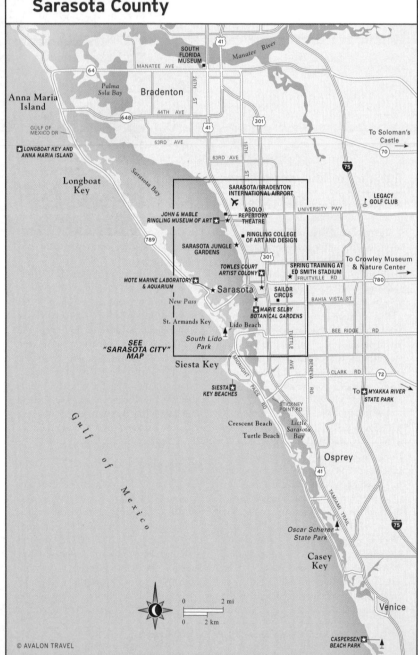

SOUTH FLORIDA MUSEUM

MANATEE AVE

Manatee River

64

26TH ST

Palma Sola Bay

Bradenton

44TH AVE

648

41

301

GULF OF MEXICO DR

53RD AVE

Anna Maria Island

63RD AVE

To Soloman's Castle

70

★ LONGBOAT KEY AND ANNA MARIA ISLAND

75

Longboat Key

Sarasota Bay

SARASOTA/BRADENTON INTERNATIONAL AIRPORT

LEGACY GOLF CLUB

789

UNIVERSITY PWY

JOHN & MABLE RINGLING MUSEUM OF ART

ASOLO REPERTORY THEATRE

RINGLING COLLEGE OF ART AND DESIGN

SARASOTA JUNGLE GARDENS

301

To Crowley Museum & Nature Center

TOWLES COURT ARTIST COLONY

SPRING TRAINING AT ED SMITH STADIUM

FRUITVILLE RD

780

MOTE MARINE LABORATORY & AQUARIUM

★ Sarasota

SAILOR CIRCUS

BAHIA VISTA ST

New Pass

MARIE SELBY BOTANICAL GARDENS

St. Armands Key

Lido Beach

BEE RIDGE RD

SEE "SARASOTA CITY" MAP

South Lido Park

Siesta Key

TUTTLE AVE

BENEVA RD

CLARK RD

72

SIESTA KEY BEACHES

MIDNIGHT PASS RD

To ★ MYAKKA RIVER STATE PARK

STICKNEY POINT RD

Crescent Beach

Turtle Beach

Little Sarasota Bay

Osprey

G u l f

o f

M e x i c o

41

Oscar Scherer State Park

TAMIAMI TRAIL

75

Casey Key

Venice

0        2 mi

0     2 km

© AVALON TRAVEL

CASPERSEN BEACH PARK

city. Development soon followed during the Florida Land Boom of the 1920s, and, with the development of the Tamiami Trail, the region was linked to the rest of Florida, making it easier for speculators and potential residents to get to Sarasota. It was during this time that several of the Ringling brothers began relocating to Sarasota, and in 1919, the Ringling Brothers Circus established Sarasota as its winter home. Like the rest of the state, Sarasota was hit hard by the combination of the imploding Florida real estate market and the Great Depression, but that didn't keep the city from experiencing rapid growth during the real estate booms that occurred in the 1950s and early 2000s.

## PLANNING YOUR TIME

It's possible—although certainly not recommended—to take in the highlights of Sarasota over the course of a long weekend. If sightseeing is your primary goal, make your home base in or near downtown Sarasota, as that will put you no more than a half-hour drive away from nearly every sight mentioned in this chapter, with most of them being substantially closer. However, it must be said that the real draw of places like Siesta Key and Anna Maria Island is their laid-back beach vibe, which should really be enjoyed over a much longer period of time.

Those with a weekend to spend should focus on the sights of Sarasota. Explore the John & Mable Ringling Museum of Art and the Marie Selby Botanical Gardens one day, then hit Lido Beach and stroll the shops of St. Armands Circle on another.

Travelers with a week or more should devote a day each to the beaches of Siesta Key and Anna Maria Island. Give a day over to taking a kayak out in Oscar Scherer State Park and visiting Venice's shops and beaches. Use the balance of your time to dig deeper into Sarasota by visiting the galleries at the Ringling College of Art & Design, the Towles Court Artist Colony, and the Mote Marine Laboratory & Aquarium.

# Sights

## HISTORIC DOWNTOWN SARASOTA

The unheralded heart of Sarasota is its historic downtown district. Although downtown proper is filled with mid-rise office buildings appropriate to a small city like Sarasota, the core business district is surrounded by decidedly more intimate neighborhoods, many of which have roots that date back to the early 20th century. Even in the business district itself, there are some buildings and businesses of interest; however, most visitors will want to focus their explorations on areas like the **Laurel Park** neighborhood, which is roughly bounded by Morrill Street on the north, Mound Street on the south, and Orange and Osprey Avenues on the west and east, with Laurel Street aptly cutting an east-west line through the center. Laurel Park, primarily a residential neighborhood, is on the National Register of Historic Places due to the high density of homes from the 1920s and 1930s, along with the fact that Sarasota's first mayor built a home and a nine-hole golf course here. (Please try to imagine, as you're bumping along the brick-lined streets, that you are meandering down a very rough fairway.) These bungalows and classic Florida homes are well maintained by their current residents—some with bright and beautiful color schemes.

To the north of Laurel Park is the **Central Cocoanut** district, which, in addition to a number of smaller, vintage residences from the early 20th century, is where you can find **Pioneer Park** (1260 12th St., sunrise-sunset daily, free). The park itself is a nice urban oasis, with a playground and plenty of running-around and picnicking space. It's also home to the 1882 **Bidwell-Wood House & Museum** (10am-2pm Mon.-Fri., free), the oldest residence in Sarasota County, and the 1901 **Crocker Memorial Church** (10am-2pm Mon.-Fri., free). Both of these are maintained and operated for the public by the **Historical Society of Sarasota County** (941/364-9076, www.hsosc.com, 10am-2pm Mon.-Fri.), which has its offices on the grounds of Pioneer Park.

**TOP** EXPERIENCE

# ★ TOWLES COURT ARTIST COLONY

One of the highlights of Sarasota's downtown area is the **Towles Court Artist Colony** (Adams Ln., between S. Links Ave. and Washington Blvd., www.towlescourt. com, 941/374-1988). Originally part of the golf course that Sarasota's first mayor built in Laurel Park, the property was purchased in the 1920s by William B. Towles and turned into a residential district. Many of the bungalows from that era are still part of Towles Court; however—given the vagaries of time and the ebb and flow of economics—they have been transformed from living spaces into galleries, studios, and restaurants. Covered by elegant and ancient oak trees dripping with

Spanish moss, the dozen or so cottages in Towles Court are both united in purpose and diverse in their flavor. There are upscale, modern dining establishments like **Indigenous** and **Lavanda**, but the many art establishments, like the **Elizabeth Stevens Gallery, Expressive Arts**, and a dozen others, are the heart of Towles. On the third Friday of every month, the district holds an art walk, with live music, drinks, and vendors holding forth with their wares. During the rest of the month, most of the establishments are reliably open between noon and 4pm, which makes afternoon the best time to visit.

# CENTENNIAL PARK

Running right along the waters of Sarasota Bay, **Centennial Park** (1075 N. Tamiami Trail, 941/955-2325, 5am-11pm daily, free) has a boat ramp, plenty of parking, shaded picnicking areas, and some outstanding waterfront views. The sight of the boats skipping along the waters of the bay is enticing. Centennial Park is almost directly across the street from the historical sights at Pioneer Park; it's also adjacent to the bright purple **Van Wezel Performing Arts Hall** and just a few blocks away from the **Sarasota Bayfront,** so it provides a good base of

Towles Court Artist Colony is located in the heart of Sarasota.

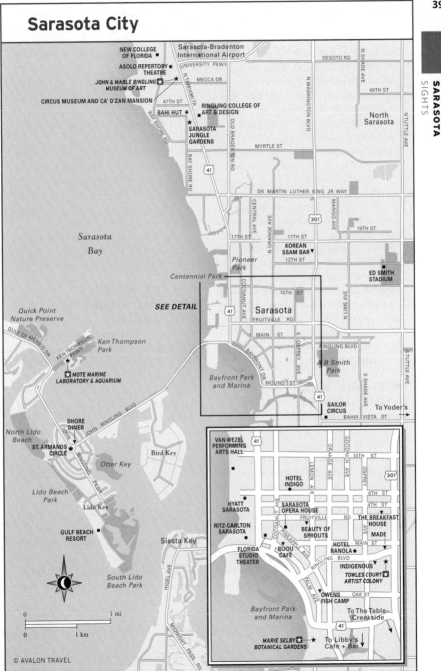

operations to help get you oriented for your day's activities.

## SARASOTA BAYFRONT

The **Sarasota Bayfront** (at Sunset Dr. and John Ringling Blvd.) is a great place to acclimate yourself to Sarasota's laid-back atmosphere. Watch the boats come in and out of the marina, and gawk at the downtown skyline. The calming waters of Sarasota Bay provide a great canvas for some spectacular sunsets; take advantage of the benches throughout the park. During the day, kids splash around in the playground fountains. For those brimming with energy, the park also offers a running/walking trail with exercise way stations; this being Sarasota, those trails are also decorated with stunning modern sculptures.

Speaking of sculptures, no visit to this park would be complete without a photo op in front of J. Seward Johnson's three-story-high *Unconditional Surrender* (known more commonly as *The Kiss*), a romantic homage to the end of World War II. Marina Jack, a restaurant that boasts some of the city's best views, offers waterfront dining and drinks.

## ★ MARIE SELBY BOTANICAL GARDENS

Just a couple of blocks away from the Bayfront area and downtown are the **Marie Selby Botanical Gardens** (811 S. Palm Ave., 941/366-5731, www.selby.org, 10am-5pm daily, $25 adults, $15 children, children 5 and under free). Despite being so close to the buzz of the business district and the busy marina, this beautiful, 13-acre estate is, quite literally, an urban oasis. The garden houses 20,000 plants, including over 4,000 orchids, in its eight greenhouses, as well as scores of tropical plants lining the garden pathways. There's an emphasis on tropical plants (obviously), but there are lots of Asian influences, too. The plants are curated and arranged smartly; however, due to the relatively limited space of the property, you will find several seemingly incongruous areas nestled directly next to one another.

There is a good bit of space given over to the massive banyan trees—you'll have trouble missing them. Only once you're up close can you truly understand how massive these twisted giants are; your kids, though, will take to them like monkeys, which is perfectly acceptable. (The little ones will also get a kick out of feeding the voracious koi, who move around their small pond in unison toward whoever's tossing the most food.)

The first floor of the former Selby mansion is now a small museum with art exhibits, and there's a great little café that overlooks the main lawn (with the banyans). It serves not only coffee, ice cream, sandwiches, and salads but also beer and wine. (There's free Wi-Fi, too.) The Marie Selby hosts events throughout the year, so make sure to check the calendar for a current listing of events.

## ★ MOTE MARINE LABORATORY & AQUARIUM

The **Mote Marine Laboratory & Aquarium** (1600 Ken Thompson Pkwy., 941/388-1720, www.mote.org, 10am-5pm daily, $20 adults, $19 seniors, $15 children, children 3 and under free) takes up almost the entirety of tiny City Island, out between Lido Key and Longboat Key. Inside the facility, which combines an open-to-the-public component with a working research operation, there are various marine habitats, including an enormous, 135,000-gallon saltwater shark tank, touch pools, a manatee exhibit, and, most mysteriously, the preserved 25-foot-long carcass of a giant squid. A 2011 addition to the Mote is undoubtedly cute: Penguin Island, home to six black-footed penguins. The seabirds are incredibly precocious and have taken quite well to their home in Florida; guests who fall in love with them while at the Mote can keep up with their exploits at home on the live penguin cam available on the aquarium's website.

There are some fantastic and informative displays at the Mote. Keep in mind that your ticket price is donation to some incredibly important work.

# SARASOTA JUNGLE GARDENS

Located north of downtown, near the Ringling College of Art & Design, **Sarasota Jungle Gardens** (3701 Bay Shore Rd., 941/355-1112, www.sarasotajunglegardens.com, 10am-5pm daily, $18 adults, $17 seniors, $13 children, children under 2 free) is a reminder of when Sarasota's tourist fortunes rested solely on Northerners making their way down the Tamiami Trail. It's a truly old-school Florida attraction, founded in 1936, and, amazingly, the 10-acre facility retains much of its original charm. If the Marie Selby Botanical Gardens are serene and meticulously curated, these botanical gardens, which are allowed to grow in a relatively wild state, are far more relaxed, with parrots, snakes, flamingos, and, somewhat incongruously, prairie dogs. The family-friendly atmosphere is welcoming, and the gardens are a great way to pass a half day or so.

# ★ JOHN & MABLE RINGLING MUSEUM OF ART

There are three museums on the grounds of the **John & Mable Ringling Museum of Art** (5401 Bay Shore Rd., 941/359-5700, www.ringling.org, 10am-5pm Fri.-Wed., 10am-8pm Thurs., $25 adults, $23 seniors, $5 children, children 5 and under free), and they couldn't be any more different. The primary attraction, of course, is John Ringling's impressive collection of masterworks in the massive, pink-tinted Museum of Art itself. Originals by El Greco, Velázquez, Titian, Rubens, and many others are displayed in a gorgeous (if overwhelming) environment meant to evoke Florence's Uffizi Gallery. There are several re-creations of classic sculptures in the courtyard, including, of course, Michelangelo's *David*, as well as re-creations of classic Italian fountains. The re-creations extend beyond the artwork, though; two of the galleries in the museum—a salon and a library—are entire rooms purchased by Ringling from the Astor mansion in 1926. But the museum is definitely not all reproductions and re-creations; in fact,

the Mote Marine Laboratory & Aquarium

it's the most active art gallery on the Gulf Coast. The curators keep most of the collections current, with new and notable exhibits rotating regularly. It's a fantastic art museum, well worth a day's visit.

## CIRCUS MUSEUM

John Ringling was, of course, the Circus King, so the collection of memorabilia at the **Circus Museum** (5401 Bay Shore Rd., 941/359-5700, 10am-5pm Fri.-Wed., 10am-8pm Thurs., admission included with Ringling Museum of Art admission) is both authentic and extensive. Everything from Ringling's private rail car to costumes, sketches, clown masks, and giant roller skates is on display. Interestingly, the most vital and engaging part of the Circus Museum isn't the actual memorabilia, but instead the massive scale model of a typical circus setup. The model is meticulous and incredibly detailed, including not just the three rings, menagerie, and sideshow but also the performers' quarters, food-prep areas, and even the public bathrooms. It's impressive how extensive and massive the circus's operations were, and this model does a great job of explaining how all of these elements come together for a single day's performance.

## CA' D'ZAN

Built in 1926, **Ca' d'Zan** (5401 Bay Shore Rd., 941/359-5700, 10am-5pm daily, admission included with Ringling Museum of Art admission; just tour of house $10) is an example of Gilded Age immensity. John and Mable Ringling's Venetian Gothic mansion has 56 rooms spread across 36,000 square feet, all adorned in marble, gold, dark woods, and crystal. While John Ringling surely felt that adding gold leaf and antiques by the ton to this house would somehow endear him to the upper class, looking at the mansion today, one can only be struck by just how little restraint went into it. A mishmash of global styles— Moroccan, French, Singaporean—were thrown into the decor in such a thoroughly ostentatious way that Ringling's elephant trainers probably would have revolted. It must be seen to be believed. Do not miss walking through this house.

## BIG CAT HABITAT AND GULF COAST SANCTUARY

About a half-hour drive from downtown Sarasota is the **Big Cat Habitat and Gulf Coast Sanctuary** (7101 Palmer Blvd., 941/371-6377, www.bigcathabitat.org,

The John & Mable Ringling Museum of Art contains a stunning selection of classic and modern art.

# The Ringling Brothers

The seven sons of Heinrich and Marie Ringling are, after the Jackson 5, perhaps the most popular siblings in American pop culture history. The small circus they started in Baraboo, Wisconsin, in 1884 eventually became one of the two most popular circuses touring the country, and with the 1907 purchase of the other most popular circus (the Barnum & Bailey Circus), it turned into a virtual three-ring monopoly. The circus's original winter home was in Bridgeport, Connecticut, but Sarasota, Florida, has been the cold-weather respite for the circus's animals, clowns, and equipment since the 1920s, a move inspired by both a tragic circus fire in Bridgeport and the fact that John Ringling and some of his brothers had been vacationing in the area.

As the "advance man" for the circus, John was responsible for a number of the promotional gambits that made the circus so successful, and his older brother Charles worked as the operations manager, keeping the circus running while it was on the road. These two had the most impact on Sarasota. Ringling Boulevard is named after Charles, who used his circus-derived wealth to invest in development and infrastructure projects throughout Sarasota. John wound up as the sole Ringling operating the circus after his six brothers died.

As you can imagine, one man running the nation's most popular circus amassed quite a bit of wealth, and though his **Ca' d'Zan** mansion is the most obviously ostentatious display of his wealth, Ringling was also convinced that art was a mark of true civilization. With the stunning galleries at the **John & Mable Ringling Museum of Art** and his co-founding of what is now known as the **Ringling College of Art & Design,** John Ringling's impact on Sarasota is still felt to this day, despite the fact that the circus that bore his name for decades is now out of business.

noon-4pm Wed.-Sun., $18 adults, $8 kids under 12). This is a tourist attraction founded on noble ideals. As a refuge and "safe haven" for lions, tigers, and bears that somehow make their way to Florida (some were exotic pets, others are "retired" performers), the Big Cat Habitat is home to a number of formerly mistreated animals. So, if you spy a lion or tiger that doesn't look like it's in the best shape, don't fret or call the wildlife department because these are the folks that the wildlife department would call to rescue them. The Rosarie family has more than three decades of experience rescuing big cats, and the Big Cat Habitat is more a labor of love than a money-making venture; in fact, the donations (and animal sponsorships) that visitors provide are barely enough to keep these felines fed and sheltered. In addition to being able to look at the animals, guests can watch "educational demonstrations" (training sessions), during which tricks are intertwined with a message of conservation and protection. It's clear that the Rosaries are completely invested in providing

refuge for these animals, and it's because of this that the Big Cat Habitat manages to be quite inspiring.

## CROWLEY MUSEUM & NATURE CENTER

The main attraction at the **Crowley Museum & Nature Center** (16405 Myakka Rd., 941/322-1000, www.crowleyfl.org, 10am-5pm Thurs.-Sun. Oct.-May, 10am-5pm Sat.-Sun. June-Sept., $5 adults, $2 children, children 5 and under free) isn't the quaint pioneer museum or the replica one-room cabin that shows how the area's early settlers lived; those things are nice, to be sure, but the most accurate way that Crowley helps transport visitors to mid-19th-century Florida is by putting them out in the middle of some beautiful, natural scenery. There's a walking trail that's part of the same wagon trail used by early settlers to move between towns, and there's also a gorgeous, half-mile-long boardwalk that allows you to traverse the Maple Branch Swamp without getting mud in your shoes. These walking paths, along with a two-story observation tower, provide plenty of opportunities for nature viewing, and bald eagles, wild hogs, and bobcats are just a few of the animals that have been spotted on the property. Located close to Myakka River State Park, the Crowley sometimes gets overlooked by more dedicated nature lovers, but it's definitely worth a half day of exploration.

## ★ MYAKKA RIVER STATE PARK

The 37,000 acres of the **Myakka River State Park** (13208 State Rd. 72, 941/361-6511, www.myakkariver.org, 8am-sunset daily, $6 vehicle 2-8 people, $4 single person or motorcycle) are some of the most treasured public park lands in all of Florida. Although the park is home to a museum and a few archaeological sites, the real draw is the diverse, abundant, and accessible wildlife. Native flora and fauna flourish throughout the park, and even though hiking trails and campsites are abundant, Myakka River State Park still manages to feel like a quiet, isolated, and ruggedly natural place. The waters of the Myakka River ensure that much of the property is wet, with marshes, swampland, and streams throughout. (Five of the six campsites even offer pitcher pumps

for campers to draw water from; please note that this water will still need to be sterilized before drinking.)

That plentiful water also means that there are lots of animals that call the park home; lucky and dedicated wildlife-spotters can—especially during the cool season—lay their eyes on wild turkeys, deer, bobcats, and wild hogs, and, if you look up, you'll likely catch a glimpse of an eagle, osprey, crane, or any of the other native (and nonnative) birds that call the park home. Roseate spoonbills—quite rare throughout Florida—have been seen here. However, your eyes are the only thing you'll be able to lay on them; even though only 7,500 acres of Myakka River State Park are officially designated as a wilderness preserve, all wildlife throughout the park is protected.

Hikers will enjoy heading out on the main "backpacking trail," which goes on for nearly 36 miles, with four main loops. The trail takes hikers through forests, marshlands, and some beautiful expanses of palmetto prairie. If you don't have a full day to commit to hiking, you should, at the very least, dedicate a half hour or so to traversing the gorgeous canopy walkway (the first public treetop trail in the United States), which will get you 25 feet above the ground for a stunning bird's-eye

Ca' d'Zan showcases the unique, ostentatious style preferred by the Ringlings.

# Sarasota's Colleges

Sarasota has something of a reputation as a retirees' haven. This is not entirely undeserved. However, it was interesting for me to note, on a visit during the height of the Occupy protests, that there was a phalanx of demonstrators lining the sidewalk of Bayfront Park hoisting Peace Not Profits and This Is What Democracy Looks Like signs, and not a single one of those demonstrators looked younger than 85 years old.

In fact, Sarasota is home to two of Florida's most innovative and creative colleges. Although the **Ringling College of Art & Design** and the **New College of Florida** don't necessarily define Sarasota, the impact of both of these schools on the city can't be understated.

New College is the smallest of all of Florida's public, four-year colleges, and is the state's honors college. Originally founded as a private school in 1964, New College offered a classical liberal arts education under a student-choice-focused model; rather than pursuing defined degrees under a requirements/electives model, students would propose a set of educational goals and work with the college's faculty to achieve those goals. This model still provides the foundation of New College's approach today, which means that the student body is a somewhat self-selected group of extremely bright young people who enjoy learning for the sake of learning.

Ringling College is a private school with roots that extend to the 1930s. Although the school was initially an arts-focused extension of the Orlando-based Southern College working in collaboration with the John & Mable Ringling Museum of Art, it didn't become fully accredited as a degree-granting institution until 1979. Over the past three decades, though, the Ringling has risen in stature to become one of the premier Southern arts schools, granting Bachelor of Fine Arts degrees in interior design, printmaking, computer animation, fine arts, game art, illustration, sculpture, and more.

Due to the selective and unique nature of their curricula, both schools have small student populations: Ringling's is about 1,400; New College has just over 800 students.

view. Canoeing, kayaking, and biking are also excellent. The park offers airboat tours too, for those who don't actually wish to hear any of the wildlife around them.

## SOLOMON'S CASTLE

An hour and a half east of Sarasota, in the swampy midsection of the state, is an homage to one man's vision of what housing grandeur should look like, and it's a vision that's decidedly different from John Ringling's. **Solomon's Castle** (4533 Solomon Rd., Ona, 863/494-6077, www.solomonscastle.org, 10am-3pm Tues.-Fri., 11am-4pm Sat.-Sun., closed Aug.-Sept., $12.50 adults, $5 children under 12) began taking shape in 1972, when sculptor Howard Solomon began building his dream home. That home has taken the shape of a medieval-styled castle, except rather than stone and iron, Solomon's Castle is crafted from recycled aluminum printing-press plates and stained glass. Each room within the castle is stacked with Solomon's whimsical sculptures (most of which, like the castle itself, are created from recycled materials). The sculptor is usually on hand to give tours himself, and it's an experience not to be missed; Solomon's pun-heavy narration is nearly as amusing as it is groan-inducing. But the truly unique perspective he puts on what is a truly unique piece of construction is enlightening. Though he lives in the castle, the building is less a domicile than it is a continuing art project. Make sure to have lunch at **The Boat on a Moat** restaurant, which is another of Solomon's creative endeavors.

# Beaches

When visitors talk about "the beach" in Sarasota, they're probably talking about hitting the famous stretches of white sand on nearby Siesta Key. Those beaches are consistently ranked at the top of "best beach" lists, and for good reason. However, for folks who are close to central Sarasota, the beaches on **Lido Key**—just a five-minute drive from downtown across the gorgeous John Ringling Causeway—are "the beach." The beaches on Lido Key aren't just convenient second-stringers, either: They're broad, calm, and beautiful, and, thanks to the relatively restricted parking options on Lido Key, they're often less crowded (that doesn't mean they're empty) than Siesta Key beaches.

## NORTH LIDO BEACH

Due to the beach's immediate proximity to the shopping district of St. Armands Circle, parking at **North Lido Beach** (1 John Ringling Blvd., sunrise-sunset daily, parking $2/hour) can be difficult. There's a small lot with about 25 spaces and streetside parking as well (you'll pay at a meter station for any of these); they all fill up fairly early in the day. Although this may make planning something of a pain, once you actually get the car parked and get to the beach, you'll be thankful it was so hard to find a place to put your automobile; the wide stretch of shell-filled sand is expansive enough that even a big crowd here never feels overwhelming, and the farther north you walk, the less crowded it gets (the northernmost points of North Lido Beach used to be popular nude sunbathing spots, but please note that nudity on the beach is illegal now). Dunes

and trees give the beach a wild and unspoiled feel, and the lack of facilities seems completely appropriate.

## LIDO BEACH PARK

**Lido Beach Park** (400 Ben Franklin Dr., sunrise-sunset daily, free parking) is the main beach destination on Lido Key, and the 400-space parking lot is a testament to that. Amazingly, even though a summer Saturday often sees the lot filled to capacity before lunch, the beach itself manages to maintain a sense of gentle calm, mainly because it's so huge. Nonetheless, this is a people-watching beach, not a silence-and-solitude beach, and the abundant facilities—which include a playground, showers, restrooms, a swimming pool, and (some surprisingly tasty) concessions—are all optimized for big crowds.

## SOUTH LIDO COUNTY PARK

**South Lido County Park** (100 Taft Dr., sunrise-sunset daily, free parking) splits the difference between the wild solitude of North Lido and the massive crowds of Lido Beach Park. There are a few facilities: restrooms, picnic tables, and a playground. The shady pine trees and walking trails provide ample opportunities for some alone time. The park is positioned at the lower tip of the key and is surrounded by four different bodies of water; the Gulf beach is the largest part, but boaters can dip their canoe or kayak into the waters of Sarasota Bay. Rip currents can be an issue for swimmers, so use caution. The free parking lot fills up quickly on weekends and holidays.

# Sports and Recreation

Surrounded as Sarasota is by water and wildlife, many of the activities here revolve around the ample opportunities to get out and about in a boat or on a trail.

## CANOEING AND KAYAKING

Between the calm waters of the Gulf of Mexico, the mangroves throughout Sarasota Bay, and the numerous smaller waterways in and around the city, small-boat-lovers will find plenty of places to explore in Sarasota. If you can't travel with your own boat, kayak, or stand-up paddleboard, rentals are available at **Economy Tackle** (6018 S. Tamiami Trail, 941/922-9671, www.floridakayak.com, kayaks from $35/day, SUPs from $45/day); they also offer diving gear, fishing tackle, and tours. Another good option for rentals is **Almost Heaven Kayak Adventures** (100 Taft Dr., 941/504-6296, www.kayakfl.com, kayaks and SUPs from $35/half-day). Both Economy and Almost Heaven offer multiday and weekly rates.

**Edwards Islands Park** (sunrise-sunset daily) is composed of three tiny islands in Roberts Bay, which is south of the Siesta Key bridge and is bounded by Siesta Key and the mainland. Although it is, technically, a park, there are zero facilities, and, in fact, the area is quite wild, dominated by oyster beds and rough and rocky beaches and frequently visited by seabirds and dolphins. Fishing is pretty good in the area, but most boaters prefer to visit to make their way through the mangroves and canopies, and to take a land break walking through the quiet island trails. The park is restricted to day use, so camping and fires are prohibited.

**South Lido Beach Park** (100 Taft Dr., sunrise-sunset daily, free parking) is a good spot for boating, thanks to the confluence of four major bodies of water and a preponderance of mangroves along the shoreline. The park itself is popular, and boating is definitely a reason for that. Those looking to hit the water away from the crowds may want to avoid this spot.

For a spot that's a little more isolated, head for **North Creek.** There's a reason that this narrow stretch of water—which runs roughly parallel to the Tamiami Trail before gradually widening and then dumping into Sarasota Bay near Osprey—isn't very busy: It's not only hard to find, it's also pretty tough to launch from. The best way to access it is to head to Vamo Drive (south of the Gulf Gate area of southern Sarasota) and trudge about a quarter mile south of Vamo Road until you can begin making your way through the mangroves with your eyes set on a line of condos (your only real visual landmark); eventually, you'll hit the water, but only after traversing a foot-slashing oyster bed. Again, I said it wouldn't be easy. You'll probably curse a lot on your way there, and you may very well get a little lost. But once you hit the water—which, after a good rain, can get quite fast—you'll forget your travails and simply be able to soak in the quiet run.

## SAILING AND FISHING CHARTERS

One look at the Sarasota Bayfront marina will let you know that this is a sailing city. And though you may not have the scratch to pull up to the marina with your own boat, there are nonetheless ample opportunities to sail around the bay. **Kathleen D Sailing Catamarans** (2 Marina Plaza, 941/896-6400, www.kathleend.net, call for reservations) offers charters aboard catamarans that can accommodate up to 20 guests. They have been plying the waters of Sarasota, Longboat Key, Siesta Key, and elsewhere around the region for over three decades. They offer trips ranging from two and three hours ($40/person and $50/person, respectively) to half-day trips ($70/person). Food and drinks are included.

**Sara-Bay Sailing School & Charter** (1505 Ken Thompson Pkwy., 941/914-5132, www.sarabaysailing.com, half day from $200/trip, full day from $300/trip, call for hours and rates) also offers charters. Additionally, they can provide rentals to qualified boaters, and, for those who aren't qualified but want to be, they offer sailing courses for beginners and intermediate sailors.

Captain Alan Routh has been fishing in Sarasota for more than 40 years and books charters on a 22-foot flats boat through **Magic Fishing Adventures** (multiple pickup locations, 941/345-7788, www.magic-fishing.com, average trip cost $450 for 1-4 anglers, multiboat charters available). Specializing in light-tackle fishing along the coastal flats, Routh can get anglers of varying skill levels into the areas where they can catch tarpon, kingfish, snapper, grouper, and other local inshore species.

## HIKING AND BIKING

Crossing over from downtown Sarasota to Lido Key on the Ringling Bridge Causeway, you'd be forgiven for thinking that the city had imposed some sort of mandatory provision that its residents walk or bike on a daily basis. The wide bike lanes and protected walkways are busy at almost any time of day, filled with pedestrians and cyclists taking advantage of the gorgeous views of the bay. This is not accidental; the **Ringling Bridge Causeway Park** (420 John Ringling Causeway, 941/365-2200, www.sarasotagov.com, 5am-11pm daily, free) was specifically designed for joggers and bikers (and anglers), a design that extends from the ample free parking on either side of the bridge to the various safety measures implemented to protect parkgoers from the busy traffic on the bridge.

Walkers and bikers looking for a more rustic and isolated experience should head to the bike trails of **Rothenbach Park** (8650 Bee Ridge Rd., 941/861-5000, www.scgov.net, 6am-6pm daily, call for summer hours,

free) and the hiking paths of **Pinecraft Park** (1420 Gilbert Ave., 941/861-5000, www.scgov.net, open 24 hours daily, parking closed midnight-6am, free). Both parks offer a good combination of well-marked entry points and natural beauty. The wildlife preserve of **Circus Hammock** (4572 17th St., 941/861-5000, www.scgov.net, 7:30am-8pm daily Apr.-Oct., 7:30am-6pm daily Nov.-Mar., free) is even more natural, with a wide variety of birds calling the dense tree canopy home; there are 1.5 miles of rough but easily accessible trails.

## GOLF

Of the numerous public courses in and around Sarasota, the best by far is the **Bobby Jones Golf Club** (1000 Circus Blvd., 941/955-8041, www.bobbyjonesgolfclub.com, greens fees $5-12 for 9-hole course), a highly rated municipal club with two 18-hole courses and one 9-hole course. The 9-hole Executive course is a tremendous bargain. It was apparently designed for overscheduled businesspeople and can be played in about two hours.

Another solid option is the 18-hole Red course at **Gulf Gate Golf Club** (2550 Bispham Rd., 941/921-5515, greens fees from $18).

## SPECTATOR SPORTS

For those with an eye to spectator sports, it's worth noting that baseball's **Baltimore Orioles** play their spring training games at **Ed Smith Stadium** (2700 12th St., 941/954-4101, $8-27) throughout the month of March. If you're looking for something more than Cracker Jacks and fly balls, you can also check out matches at the **Sarasota Polo Club** (8021 Polo Club Ln., 941/907-0000, www.sarasotapolo.com, $10). Matches are played every Sunday at 1pm from mid-December through early April.

## SPAS

The premier spa experience in Sarasota has long been had at **The Ritz-Carlton** (1111 Ritz-Carlton Dr., 941/309-2000, www.ritzcarlton.com, call for hours, massages from $135, spa treatments from $165). Offering an absurdly large menu of "rituals," ranging from a quick bath in essential oils to 80-minute massages, the spa at the Ritz is only available to rewards-program members and current hotel guests, which may be the exact incentive to book a room here.

For those not registered at the Ritz, exceptional spa experiences can still be had at **The Little Day Spa** (1990 Main St., #201, 941/363-9455, www.thelittledayspa.com, 9am-6pm Mon.-Fri., 9am-5pm Sat., massages from $45,

spa packages from $120), a downtown facility that offers multiple packages that include massage, skin care, facials, aromatherapy, and more.

The **L. Spa** (556 S. Pineapple Ave., 941/906-1358, www.lboutiques.com, 9am-7pm Mon.-Sat., massages from $85, spa packages from $185) is an expansion of the L. Boutique. The spa offers hair, makeup, and nail services, as well as massage and body treatments and a variety of packages for men and women.

# Entertainment and Events

## NIGHTLIFE
### Downtown Sarasota

The bar and club scene in downtown Sarasota has evolved and grown as more and more young professionals have begun calling the area home. Although this means that a lot of the action tends to cater to the bottle-service set, even the stylish spots still mostly emphasize comfort over velvet-rope requirements. That said, many of these places are not at all sheepish about charging sky-high prices for drinks, so you can expect some sticker shock.

**Pangea Alchemy Lab** (1564 Main St., 941/953-7111, www.pangealounge.com, 4pm-2am daily, no cover) is stylish and unique but still relatively intimate. Check out the pharmacological-looking "liquid spice cabinet" that the bar uses to concoct their one-of-a-kind drinks.

On the other end of the modernity spectrum is **The Starlite Room** (1001 Cocoanut Ave., 941/702-5613, www.starlitesrq.com, 4pm-12:30am Sun.-Thurs., 4pm-1:30am Fri.-Sat.), a split-level supper club and cabaret that serves decent enough food in the restaurant area and theatrical shows in the venue. It's a little pricey, but a definite experience.

The **Gator Club** (1490 Main St., 941/366-5969, 4pm-2am daily, cover charge varies) is loved by the cover-band-and-cosmos set, but the atmosphere is friendly, and the vintage

brick building that the club calls home provides its own ambience.

The environment at **Sarasota Lanes** (2250 Fruitville Rd., 941/955-7629, www.sarasotalanes.com, 9:30am-midnight Mon.-Thurs., 9:30am-1am Fri.-Sat., 9:30am-9pm Sun., games from $3.50) is down-to-earth. Even if bowling isn't your preferred evening recreation, you should still check in here, as this is one of the most fun places to catch some of the area's good local bands.

Just need a cool place to grab a pint downtown? Head for **Shamrock Pub** (2257 Ringling Blvd., 941/952-1730, 3pm-2am daily, no cover) and check out the incredible beer selection.

### Gulf Gate

A few miles south of downtown, and quite close to Siesta Key, is Gulf Gate, one of Sarasota's more concentrated dining and drinking areas. There is a wide variety of restaurants and bars. A popular spot is **Sarasota Brewing Company** (6607 Gateway Ave., 941/925-2337, 11am-midnight daily, no cover), worth stopping by for the selection of hand-crafted beers. There are usually a half dozen of the brewpub's beers on tap, and they're all exceptional. Brewmaster Vincent Pelosi does a particularly good job with richly flavored beers like IPAs and porters, but the light and tasty wheat beer can be mighty refreshing on a scorching Sarasota afternoon. They also serve above-average pub fare (wings, pizza, sandwiches).

**Mr. Beery's** (2645 Mall Dr, 941/343-2854, 3pm-1am daily) offers one of the best beer selections on the Gulf Coast, and it's staffed by a group of knowledgeable beer nerds who will enthusiastically guide you through their deep (and often changing) menu; make sure to avail yourself of their built-in-the-bar "Randall," which allows them to infuse your draft beer with various complementary flavors . . . or, you know, just more hops.

Spots like the **Paddy Wagon Irish Pub** (6586 Gateway Ave., 941/925-2344, noon-2am daily, no cover) offer both drinks and food, while sports bars like **Badda Bing** (6528 Superior Ave., 941/921-5109, 11am-2:30am daily, no cover) are great places to watch the game; this place is a haven for American football fans as well as those who want to shoot a few games of pool.

the legendary Bahi Hut

## Other Nightlife

Beyond these two main hubs of nightlife activity, there are still a good number of places in Sarasota worth exploring. About halfway between downtown and the Gulf Gate area is **Shakespeare's English Pub** (3550 S. Osprey Ave., 941/364-5938, www.shakespearespubsarasota.com, 11am-2am daily, no cover), an Irish pub with excellent food, a tremendous beer selection, and an overwhelmingly friendly staff. It's probably one of my favorite bars in all of Sarasota, likely because it feels more like a neighborhood hangout than a flavor-of-the-minute nightspot.

In a similarly classic vein is the **Bahi Hut** (4675 N. Tamiami Trail, 941/355-5141, 4:30pm-2am daily, no cover). Located in (dangerously) close proximity to New College of Florida and the Ringling College of Art & Design, the Bahi serves insanely, ridiculously, incredibly potent drinks. I would add more adjectives, but I really can't do much better than the "jet fuel" analogy many patrons make. This place has been slinging super-strong drinks for nearly 60 years, and has persisted in its location while the fortunes of the Tamiami Trail have gone through cycles of boom and bust. Accordingly, the staff has a vintage attitude toward bar culture: Drink as many hair-burning drinks as you please, but whatever you do, don't use any profanity.

If you've got a designated driver, make the 15- or 20-minute drive from downtown out to the **Cock & Bull Pub** (975 Cattlemen Rd., 941/341-9785, 8pm-2am Sat.-Tues., 5pm-2am Wed.-Fri., cover charge varies). Although it's all the way out near I-75, the European-style pub specializes in offering an enormous selection of beer (they call their beer menu a "bible") in a comfortable, rustic environment. They frequently host beer-tastings and occasionally have beer dinners. Pretzels and pizza are offered most nights. It's also a great spot to catch live music.

Also in the area is Sarasota's first craft brewery (and one of the best on the Gulf Coast), **Big Top Brewing Company** (6111 Porter Way, 800/590-2448, www.

bigtopbrewing.com, 2pm-10pm Mon.-Sat., noon-8pm Sun.). While their branding and theming nods toward the Sarasota area's long connection with the Ringling circus, these brewers aren't clowning around (sorry). The tasting room is warmly appointed, clean, and staffed by incredibly friendly and knowledgeable folks. Make sure to try one of their standards, like the Circus City IPA or the Trapeze Monk, but be prepared to have a flight or two of their rotating and experimental beers, too; they're always super-fresh (obviously, being brewed on-site) and often utilize unique local flavors.

Another good spot for live music (one that's quite a bit more centrally located) is **Growler's Pub** (2831 N. Tamiami Trail, 941/487-7373, 4pm-2am daily). Located near the campuses of Ringling and New College, it obviously draws a collegiate crowd, but as the kids at both of these schools are pretty unique, the live music they come to see can be a bit unpredictable as well; you may see a fumbling, nascent singer-songwriter, a knob-twisting electronic noise-monger, or, just maybe, your new favorite unknown indie rock band. Regardless of the quality of the music, the pub has a good selection of craft beer, so you'll muddle through for sure.

Located in the Burns Square district, **Burns Court Cinema** (506 Burns Ct., 941/955-3456, http://filmsociety.org) is operated by the Sarasota Film Society and is one of the best places in town to catch independent and under-the-radar films.

## PERFORMING ARTS

The **Van Wezel Performing Arts Hall** (777 N. Tamiami Trail, 941/953-3368, www.vanwezel.org) is the crown jewel of the Sarasota arts scene, hosting touring Broadway productions, classical music, and pop concerts firmly aimed at an older demographic. The building was originally designed by Frank Lloyd Wright Foundation architect William Wesley Peters (Frank Lloyd Wright's son-in-law). The lavender exterior is a sight to behold; as the Van Wezel folks say, it's "the world's only

purple seashell-shaped theater," and I have absolutely no reason to doubt them. Renovations undertaken in 2001 with the assistance of the original design team improved on the building without diminishing its unique character. Along the way, they have succeeded in heightening the impact of the near-flawless interior acoustics.

**Florida Studio Theatre** (1241 N. Palm Ave., 941/366-9000, www.floridastudiotheatre.org) is actually composed of three different on-site venues. The Keating Theatre is the main stage, where Broadway and Off-Broadway plays are performed. The slightly smaller Gompertz Theatre is dedicated to more cutting-edge live theater fare. Most unique among the three is the Goldstein Cabaret, which, as the name implies, is a great place to catch big and brash musical numbers.

Although it's not located in the cultural hub of central Sarasota, the **Asolo Repertory Theatre** (5555 N. Tamiami Trail, 941/351-8000, www.asolorep.org) is nonetheless an incredibly important component of the Sarasota arts scene. And, with neighbors like the Ringling museums and New College, it's probably best that the Asolo has staked out its own geographical turf outside of downtown. With seasons that often pack in more than a dozen productions, collectively attended by more than 100,000 people and supported by a partnership with Florida State University's Asolo Conservatory for Actor Training, the Asolo is the largest professional nonprofit theater in Florida. Surprisingly, that doesn't mean it's all hits all the time. Instead of focusing on pop-culture-driven Broadway rehashes, the Asolo resurrects classic musicals (such as *My Fair Lady* and *Yentl*), produces and promotes lesser-known quality works, and puts on the occasional piece of work that could be considered daring. The productions themselves are top-notch, benefiting from the innovations and boundary-pushing of conservatory students and the experience of the professionals who have been with the Asolo for decades.

Birthed in 1960 in the Asolo, the **Sarasota**

**Opera** moved downtown in 1979 to what is now the **Sarasota Opera House** (61 N. Pineapple Ave., 941/366-8450, www.sarasotaopera.org), a beautiful 1920s-era theater repurposed for the company's needs. Since then, the company has become one of the city's preeminent arts groups. The Sarasota Opera is probably best known for its ambitious, decades-spanning "Verdi Cycle" effort, during which the company performed every single one of Verdi's works, including alternate versions of his operatic works. Although the cycle concluded in 2016, the company still balances consistency and innovation under the steady hand of artistic director Victor DeRenzi, who has been with the company since 1983. The Sarasota Opera's season typically includes five productions.

The **Sarasota Ballet** (www.sarasotaballet.org, 941/359-0099) performs in multiple venues around town, primarily at the Sarasota Opera House, Van Wezel Performing Arts Hall, and FSU Center for the Performing Arts (on the grounds of the Asolo). With a season that usually includes a half-dozen performances, the repertoire of the Sarasota Ballet tends toward classics of relatively recent vintage. The quality of their performances of Frederick Ashton-choreographed pieces is particularly well regarded.

**McCurdy's Comedy Theatre and Humor Institute** (1923 Ringling Blvd., 941/925-3869, www.mccurdyscomedy.com) is a good place to grab a few laughs. Relocated in early 2014 from a small spot in the North Trail part of town to a roomy and modern space downtown, McCurdy's has evolved into a premier venue for touring and local comedians. If you've got the urge to try out some of your own material, the club has open-mic nights on Wednesdays and Thursdays.

For a performing-arts experience that's uniquely Sarasotan, be sure to check out a performance by the **Sailor Circus** (2075 Bahia Vista St., 941/361-6350, www.circusarts.org). "The Greatest 'Little' Show on Earth" has its roots in a high school gymnastics class, and, to this day, middle and high school students train here in the circus arts. The Sailor was operated for decades by the Sarasota County School Board but now operates as a private, nonprofit company, the Circus Arts Conservatory. Educating young people—and allowing them to perform—is the circus's primary emphasis. The Sailor holds performances at its school throughout the year, as well as special performances at venues across Sarasota.

# FESTIVALS AND EVENTS

One of the newest events on the Sarasota cultural calendar has also become one of the most popular. The **Ringling International Arts Festival** (RIAF, 5401 Bay Shore Rd., box office 941/360-7399, www.ringlingartsfestival.org, Oct.) is a five-day celebration of visual and performing art held on the grounds of the John & Mable Ringling Museum of Art. Launched in 2009 as a collaboration between the Ringling and the New York-based Baryshnikov Arts Center, the festival was an immediate hit, drawing more than 20,000 visitors over its first two years. There's an emphasis on surprisingly cutting-edge performances at the RIAF, with music, dance, and theater performances bringing out big crowds.

Despite the emergence of the RIAF, though, the **Sarasota Film Festival** (SFF, various locations, 941/364-9514, box office 941/366-6200, www.sarasotafilmfestival.com, Apr.) is still the preeminent cultural event in Sarasota. And for good reason: The SFF has grown considerably since its birth in 1999, not only in attendance and scope, but also in national acclaim. *Variety* magazine dubbed the festival "the acme of regional film festivals," based on the 10-day event's winning combination of independent film and marquee guests like Todd Solondz, Penelope Ann Miller, Olympia Dukakis, and Sophia Loren. Although the bulk of the festival is held at the downtown Regal Hollywood 20 multiplex, the SFF also includes beautiful locations like the Sarasota Opera House for various screenings and events.

The **Garden Music Series** (Marie Selby Botanical Gardens, 811 S. Palm Ave., 941/366-5731, www.selby.org, every third Sun., Feb.-July) is a great event. With jazz, classical, and even performing arts groups on the bill, and a biergarten/Oktoberfest atmosphere, the series provides a great finale for an afternoon at the gardens.

The **Sarasota Highland Games & Celtic Festival** (Sarasota County Fairgrounds, 3000 Ringling Blvd., www.sarasotahighlandgames.com, late Jan.) is a pretty big event, featuring a variety of athletic competitions (caber-tossing, stone-putting, hammer-throwing) as well as musical ones (solo and group bagpiping, Highland dancing). Throughout the day, there are folk musicians, pipe-and-drum corps, spinning and weaving demonstrations, and food and whisky.

Taking over the entirety of the Sarasota Fairgrounds, the **Sarasota Medieval Fair** (Sarasota County Fairgrounds, 3000 Ringling Blvd., 888/303-3247, www.sarasotamedievalfair.com, mid-Nov.) includes jousting, medieval music, medieval village re-creations, comedy shows, a kids' area, pony rides, and, yes, even a pub.

The **Forks & Corks Food & Wine Festival** (5401 Bay Shore Rd., 941/365-2800, www.dineoriginal.com, late Jan.) takes over the grounds of the John & Mable Ringling Museum of Art with more than 50 local, independent restaurants showing off their most creative (and paper-plate-portable) dishes and wine pairings.

# Shopping

Both of the main shopping districts in Sarasota are eminently walkable and quite beautiful, so even window-shopping in St. Armands Circle or downtown is a great experience.

## ART GALLERIES

Sarasota has a great arts scene that is driven by both deep-pocketed snowbirds and adventurous year-round locals. So although the winter definitely brings a sense of hyperactivity to the town's art scene, it manages to maintain itself quite well throughout the year.

The area around South Palm Avenue is where many downtown galleries are located. **Galleria Silecchia** (12 S. Palm Ave. and 20 S. Palm Ave., 941/365-7414, www.galleriasilecchia.com, 11am-5pm Mon.-Sat.) is Sarasota's largest gallery, and it has a pronounced focus on sculpture, art glass, and ceramics. The **Dabbert Gallery** (76 S. Palm Ave., 941/955-1315, www.dabbertgallery.com, 11am-5pm Tues.-Sat.) features works by sculptors and modernist and realist painters from throughout the United States.

A block or so off Palm Avenue is **Art Uptown** (1367 Main St., 941/955-5409, www.artuptown.com, 11am-5pm Mon.-Fri., 6pm-9pm Fri., 10am-4pm Sat.), a co-op gallery that features works from local member artists. Pieces range in style from abstract to realistic, with a large contingent of porcelain and ceramics pieces, too.

Combining the co-op vibe of Art Uptown and the community atmosphere of the Palm Avenue area, the tree-covered **Towles Court Artist Colony** (Adams Ln., between S. Links Ave. and Washington Blvd., www.towlescourt.com, most galleries open noon-4pm Tues.-Sun.) isn't just a great destination for arts lovers; it's a great destination period, with fantastic restaurants and shops complementing the works in the many intimate and friendly galleries here. There are more than 20 different galleries tucked into the bungalows that make up the Colony.

A few miles north of downtown is the **Ringling College of Art & Design** (2700 N.

# Arts Season

The arrival of winter heralds the arts season in most cities, and Sarasota is no different in that regard. However, like the rest of Florida—especially southern Florida—Sarasota also undergoes something of a population transformation during the colder months, as snowbirds make their way from the chilly climes of the north and the Midwest. In the case of Sarasota, many choose this city not just for its more temperate weather but also for its vibrant cultural scene. Many of these snowbirds are of the deep-pocketed species, but they also tend to be extremely engaged in the arts, providing a huge boost of both encouragement and funds during the winter months. That said, Sarasota is an incredibly respectable arts city during the warmer months, too, thanks to the presence of New College of Florida and Ringling College of Art & Design, as well as to the city's long history of support for the arts. It's just that, when the temperature drops—even if only a little—the city's cultural life noticeably perks up.

Tamiami Trail), home to six impressive galleries, including the **Selby Gallery** (941/359-7563, 10am-4pm Mon.-Sat., until 7pm on Tues., Sept.-Apr., closed second half of Dec.; 10am-4pm Mon.-Fri. May-Aug.), which is firmly focused on daring contemporary art. Exhibits rotate fairly frequently in these modern spaces, and the art on display is always superlative.

Nearby is the **Marietta Museum of Art & Whimsy** (2121 N. Tamiami Trail, 941/364-3399, 1pm-4pm Thurs.-Sat., free), a pleasant and personable place to visit, thanks to founder Mary Lee's ability to curate "happy" art. Some of the items verge toward kitschy (Lee even describes some of it as "goofy"), and all of the items are for sale. Expect to see sculptures of dogs in primary colors, brightly painted cuckoo clocks, and even Christmas trees.

## ST. ARMANDS CIRCLE

Shopaholics should head straight for Lido Key and the tony shops and boutiques of St. Armands Circle. Parking is something of a problem (especially on weekends, and especially on beach-worthy weekends), but thankfully, the layout of the circle is perfect for walking. Park your car at the first available spot and spend the rest of the day browsing the dozens of shops in the area. Clothing stores include chain operations like Fresh Produce, Lily Pulitzer, and

the Sarasota-based **Oh My Gauze** (352 St. Armands Circle, 941/388-1964, www.ohmygauze.com, 10am-9pm Mon.-Sat., noon-6pm Sun.), as well as local options like **Dream Weaver Collection** (364 St. Armands Circle, 941/388-1974, www.dreamweavercollection.com, 10am-8pm daily), a classy and sophisticated boutique firmly focused on an upscale and somewhat adventurous clientele, with its beautiful and expensive dresses and outfits; and **Casa Smeralda** (468 John Ringling Blvd., 941/388-1305, http://casasmeralda.com, 9am-8pm daily, extended hours on weekends), which features everything from wedding gowns to belly-dancing outfits.

Proprietor Cleon Dixon owns two interesting shops: **Binjara Traders** (327 John Ringling Blvd., 941/388-3335, 10am-8pm daily) and **Ivory Coast** (15 N. Blvd. of Presidents, 941/388-1999, 10am-8pm daily). Both feature fashion and accessories from around the world. Binjara emphasizes floral fabrics and accessories from South and Southeast Asia, and Ivory Coast focuses on African textiles, leathers, and decor items.

Jewelry stores range from traditional goldsmiths like **Armel Jewelers** (22 N. Blvd. of Presidents, 941/388-3711, www.armeljewelers.com, 10am-6pm Mon.-Sat.) to funky boutiques like **Uniquity** (21 Fillmore Dr., 941/388-2212, www.uniquityofstarmands.com, 10am-9pm Mon.-Sat.), which sells jewelry and interesting Sarasota-oriented gifts.

Garden Argosy (361 St. Armands Circle, 941/388-6402, www.gardenargosy.com, 10am-6pm daily) is also worth checking out for its selection of wind chimes, stationery, candles, and other easy-to-carry home goods.

## DOWNTOWN

While shopping downtown isn't quite as cohesive an experience as heading to St. Armands, the boutiques and shops in central Sarasota are a nice complement to the many art galleries in the area.

For clothing, try the eco-minded **Juno and Jove** (100 Central Ave., 941/957-0000, www.junoandjove.com, 10am-6pm Mon.-Sat.). **Toy Lab** (1529 Main St., 941/363-0064, 9am-9pm Mon.-Sat., noon-9pm Sun.) is a fantastic, independently owned toy store with lots of unusual items and a quirky, kid-centric vibe. There's even a gun store, the family-owned **Bullet Hole** (1576 Main St., 941/957-1996, www.bulletholeonline.com, 9:30am-5:30pm Mon.-Fri., 9:30am-2pm Sat.), which has been in downtown Sarasota

for more than three decades. **A. Parker's Books** (1488 Main St., 941/366-2898, 10am-5pm Mon.-Sat., noon-4pm Sun.) is remarkable for being not only a thriving independent bookstore but also one that specializes in rare and vintage used books, with an astounding selection of first editions and a focus on 20th-century American classics.

Antiques lovers will want to head to Sarasota's unofficial **Antique District** (Fruitville Rd., between Orange and Central Aves.), which skirts downtown. **American Pie Antiques & Collectibles** (1470 Fruitville Rd., 941/362-0682, 10:30am-5pm Mon.-Fri.) is jam-packed with books, glassware, furniture, artwork, miniatures, and lots more. **Antiques & Chatchkes** (1542 Fruitville Rd., 941/906-1221, www.antiquesandchatchkes.com, 10am-5pm Mon.-Fri.) feels like a miniature antiques mall. Although there are only three dealers, the variety of goods for sale, ranging from wall art and sculptures to furniture and, well, tchotchkes, is impressive.

# Food

## BREAKFAST AND QUICK BITES

★ **The Breakfast House** (1817 Fruitville Rd., 941/366-6860, 7am-2pm Mon.-Sat., 9am-2pm Sun., main courses from $7) is, literally, a little house, and even though it already gets points for its excellent and inviting setting, this restaurant does far more for breakfast than just a couple of eggs and a slab of bacon. With morning dishes that nod to both a Gulf Coast heritage (shrimp and grits) and the tropical weather (pancakes with pineapple, coconut, and macadamia nuts), the menu is a great combination of tradition and innovation. Combine that with the whimsical decor and a convenient downtown locale and this is one of the best spots in town to start your day.

Nearby is another great downtown breakfast option, **Toasted Mango** (430 N.

Tamiami Trail, 941/388-7728, 7am-3pm daily, breakfast from $5, lunch from $7). It takes a back-to-basics approach to the menu but focuses on making those bacon-and-egg plates, waffles, and breakfast wraps from fresh ingredients and serving them up in a service-forward, super-friendly, and unpretentious atmosphere. There's a great patio (that's dog-friendly) and a lunch menu as well.

It's hard to resist a waffle joint that proudly proclaims on its front window that ELVIS ATE HERE, and thankfully, downtown's **Waffle Stop** (660 S. Washington Blvd., 941/952-0555, main courses from $6, cash only) lives up to whatever expectations that front window sets. Super-kitschy and unapologetically trading on the fact that Elvis had breakfast here after playing a 1956 concert in Sarasota (check out the Burnin' Love omelet), the whole restaurant—from its straightforward diner fare to its surprisingly low prices—seems trapped in a bygone era.

Also downtown, the **Pastry Art Bakery Cafe** (1512 Main St., 941/955-7545, www.pastryartbakerycafe.com, 7am-6pm Mon.-Sat., 8am-2pm Sun., pastries from $3, lunch from $6) offers, predictably enough, freshly baked pastries and coffee drinks. Most of the pastries tend toward the sweet, dessert end of the spectrum.

The **Hob Nob Drive In** (1701 N. Washington Blvd., 941/955-5001, www.hobnobdrivein.com, 6am-8:30pm Sun.-Thurs., 6am-9pm Fri.-Sat., main courses from $5) doesn't seem to have changed all that much since it first started selling burgers, fries, and shakes back in 1957. Of course, the menu has expanded to include a full slate of standard breakfast fare, all of which is priced quite reasonably. You can get a good start to your day for less than four bucks with the basic morning menu: eggs, toast, bacon, potatoes, and pancakes. Plus, it's a classic drive-in, so if you can't make it for breakfast, you can still swing by and grab one of those burgers or shakes and sit outside and watch the traffic go by. There's even a car wash and a Laundromat on-site, so you can get your chores done while you eat.

If you're on Lido Key or getting an early start on your shopping in St. Armands, **Blue Dolphin** (470 John Ringling Blvd., 941/388-3566, 7am-3pm daily, main courses from $6) is a fantastic breakfast choice. Excellent homemade biscuits and cornbread—which are routinely afterthoughts at best at restaurants in this part of the state—emphasize this restaurant's country-style breakfast ethos, an approach that extends through other items like the home fries and corned-beef hash. The Blue Dolphin also does a bang-up job with standards (pancakes, omelets) as well as huevos rancheros and eggs Benedict. Portions are huge and reasonably priced.

## AMERICAN

Boasting a great location in the Towles Court Artist Colony, a casually upscale atmosphere, and a menu built around local ingredients, ★ **Indigenous** (239 S. Links Ave., 941/706-4740, www.indigenoussarasota.com, 5:30pm-9:30pm Mon.-Sat., main courses from $15) is justifiably regarded as one of the best restaurants in Sarasota. Chef Steve Phelps focuses on a combination of updated classics—grass-fed burgers, braised short ribs—with unique additions like parmesan beignets. Nearly everything is locally or regionally sourced—not only will your server tell you where your fish came from, but you'll also learn the name of the captain who piloted the boat that brought it in—so the menu is subject to frequent revisions. (Hopefully the roasted-peaches-and-lavender-crème biscuit that was on the dessert menu remains a permanent fixture.) The converted bungalow that houses the restaurant is decorated in a muted combination of rustic tones and cosmopolitan glamour, with a great patio and a separate cottage devoted to the wine bar. Service is unsurprisingly top-shelf.

A few blocks north of Towles Court is ★ **Made** (1990 Main St, 941/953-2900, 11:30am-2:30pm and 4:30pm-11pm Tues-Thurs, 11:30am-midnight Fri., 5pm-midnight Sat., 10am-3pm Sun., lunch from $8, dinner from $12, brunch from $13), one of the best and most unique restaurants in town. With a menu that's ostensibly "new Southern," Made nonetheless strips away much of the pretension that comes with that moniker. The kitchen enthusiastically serves up fried chicken, fried green tomatoes, mac-and-cheese, steak-and-eggs, meat loaf, and other standards that have been upgraded with fresh ingredients and creative recipe flourishes that do nothing to diminish these dishes' impact (on your taste buds or your waistline). The atmosphere is decidedly spirited, and the dining room is comfortable and cool but effortlessly so. Made also offers a fantastic brunch on Sunday mornings.

Just south of downtown is **Michael's on East** (1212 S. East Ave., 941/366-0007, lunch 11:30am-2pm Mon.-Fri., dinner 5:30pm-9pm Mon.-Fri. and 5:30pm-10pm Sat., main courses from $31), one of the essential fine-dining experiences in town (and Sarasota's only AAA-rated Four Diamond restaurant). Thoroughly upscale and boasting the appropriate level of attentive service, Michael's specializes in immaculately prepared classics like scallops, bone-in pork chops, and top-grade steaks, but the kitchen really shows its skills with a variety of excellent side dishes, like cumin-spiced chestnuts, yucca fries, roasted squash, and more. Keep in mind, though, that Michael's is not the place to go if you're looking for culinary adventures (or modern decor). The food and vibe are definitely old school, but it's still a satisfying splurge.

Another great spot for locally sourced and seasonal food is ★ **Libby's Cafe + Bar** (1917 S. Osprey Ave., 941/487-7300, www.libbyscafebar.com, lunch 11:30am-3pm and dinner 5pm-close Mon.-Sat., brunch 10:30am-3pm Sun., main courses from $18). Emphasizing a "fresh-from-market" menu that changes seasonally (with tweaks on a fairly regular basis), Libby's is a decidedly un-stuffy purveyor of local produce, meats, and seafood. The restaurant's two bars are often quite crowded with folks socializing or watching the game. Libby's also serves lunch, with a good selection of inventive sandwich interpretations rounding out small-plate versions of their dinner items.

The dining room at ★ **The Table— Creekside** (5365 S. Tamiami Trail, 941/921-9465, www.tablesrq.com, 4pm-10pm Sun.-Thurs., 4pm-10:30pm Fri.-Sat., main courses from $15) is stylish, boasting a retro-classic vibe, and there is a gorgeous outdoor deck overlooking the creek. But the views and decor are a distant second reason to come here; the menu features exceptional takes on seafood (wahoo ceviche, lobster ceviche, Brazilian shrimp and grits), meat dishes (short-rib pot roast, a lamb chop served with spinach chimichurri), and fantastic side dishes (farro risotto, yuca mozzarella roll).

Also on the southern end of town is **Mattison's Forty-One** (7275 S. Tamiami Trail, 941/921-3400, lunch 11:30am-2pm Mon.-Fri., dinner 4:30pm-9pm Mon.-Thurs.,

4:30pm-10pm Fri.-Sat., and 4:30pm-9:30pm Sun., main courses from $18), which hides a surprisingly excellent kitchen behind the facade of a fairly traditional midscale restaurant. A straightforward menu of beef, poultry, and pasta dishes is accented by seafood, grilled pizzas, and a handful of Italian appetizers (meatballs, bruschetta, beef ravioli), making the decision-making process pretty simple. However, the locally sourced ingredients and thoughtful preparations that go into these dishes more than make up for the lack of surprises on the menu. You may not write home about the off-the-shelf decor or the somewhat slow service, but like the other two Mattison's properties in town (City Grille downtown and Bayside at the Van Wezel Performing Arts Hall), this is a restaurant that seems most focused on kitchen excellence.

**Mozaic** (1377 Main St., 941/951-6272, www.mozaicsarasota.com, 5pm-10pm Mon.-Sat., main courses from $18) has a compact menu with less than a dozen Mediterranean-influenced entrées. Each of these dishes, however, is artfully prepared, including the roasted Cornish game hen with olives and lemon-saffron sauce, anise-infused duck breast, and even a simple vegetable couscous. Large windows provide ample views of downtown.

Don't be fooled by the name: ★ **Shore Diner** (465 John Ringling Blvd., 941/296-0301, 11am-10pm daily, lunch from $10, dinner from $14) is not some scruffy beachside meat-and-three. The locally sourced fare bends decidedly toward modern American, with the likes of lobster salad sandwiches and chicken salad flatbread for lunch and tuna-watermelon sashimi for dinner. Nonetheless, there are still diner classics on the menu, like fried chicken, meat loaf, and an excellent burger. Sunday brunch pulls the best of the lunch menu together with a collection of "brunchy" treats (French toast, pulled-pork hash, frittatas, eggs Benedict, etc.).

You can't get much more traditional than ★ **Yoder's** (3434 Bahia Vista St., 941/955-7771, 6am-8pm Mon.-Thurs., 6am-9pm

Fri.-Sat., main courses from $6), which has been going strong in Sarasota since 1975 as the premier (only?) place in town to get "Amish comfort food." Of course, the Amish find comfort in the same food as everyone else—excellent fried chicken, meat loaf, country fried steak, roast beef, burgers, fresh vegetables, and some of the best pies around. The restaurant is part of Yoder's "Amish Village," which also includes a deli where you can pick up everything from meats and cheeses to jellies and apple butter, as well as a produce stand and gift shop.

If the place's name isn't enough of a clue, the menu at **Munchies 4:20** (6639 Superior Ave., 941/929-9893, www.munchies420cafe. com, 4:20pm-4:20am daily, main courses from $7) is designed to appeal to late-night noshers. The huge selection of sandwiches, burgers, wraps, and hot dogs is actually a little daunting for those who stumble in after a night on the town, but the things you probably need to be most concerned about are the wings. Yes, they're good. Yes, they're cheap. But the "Fire in Your Hole" challenge Munchies offers up—eat 10 of their nuclear-hot wings and you get a shirt—could leave you in pretty rough shape. It's definitely not the highest quality food here, but it was good enough to get the attention of the *Man v. Food* show.

Although Sarasota is a great city for eating, there just aren't a whole lot of barbecue joints. Thankfully, one of them is **Nancy's Bar-B-Q** (301 S. Pineapple Ave., 941/366-2271, http:// nancysbarbq.com, 11:30am-9pm Mon.-Sat., sandwiches from $9). Nancy herself is often in the kitchen, and she *loves* North Carolina-style barbecue. (She also wittily notes on the menu that she's probably the only "white Jewish woman making pork barbecue." Well, she's definitely the only one in Sarasota.) Pork is the centerpiece, with pulled pork coming to you on a bun or on a fantastic taco with salsa and cucumber-dill sour cream, in addition to ribs and sausage. Beef brisket, cured salmon, chicken, and excellent sausages round out the menu, alongside sides, both standard (baked beans, coleslaw) and special (edamame succotash, cucumber salad), and desserts.

## STEAK

The smoker at ★ **The Alpine Steakhouse and Karl Ehmers Quality Meats** (4520 S. Tamiami Trail, 941/922-3797, www.alpinesteak.com, 9am-9pm Tues.-Sat., main courses from $9) produces a near-constant perfume that announces the meat-centric raison d'être here. This steakhouse doubles as a meat market (in the literal sense), and people are often coming and going picking up steaks and chops for home grilling. The casual, old-school vibe here is not to be missed. The Alpine has gotten a bit of attention for its turducken, turkey stuffed with duck stuffed with chicken, and it's attention they're certainly proud of, but the dry-aged steaks, Kobe beef burgers, roast pig, and German delicacies on the menu give diners plenty of other options.

For something a little more modern and upscale, head to downtown's **Hyde Park Prime Steakhouse** (35 S. Lemon Ave., 941/366-7788, 5pm-9:30pm Mon.-Thurs., 5pm-10pm Fri.-Sat., 5pm-9pm Sun., main courses from $20), one of two Florida outposts of this Ohio-based chain (the other is in Daytona Beach). There aren't too many surprises here, with the menu consisting primarily of the expected array of prime cuts, fish, seafood, and chops; however, the bar menu is pretty interesting, with a good selection of unique small plates built around many of the same ingredients found on the main menu but rendered in a much more creative fashion. Decor is, of course, quite nice, but surprisingly comfortable and welcoming, while service is pleasant and attentive without being obsequious.

## SEAFOOD

★ **Phillippi Creek Oyster Bar** (5353 S. Tamiami Trail, 941/925-4444, http://creek-seafood.com, 11am-10pm Sun.-Thurs., 11am-10:30pm Fri.-Sat., main courses from $9) is one of Sarasota's best seafood options. Though decidedly unpretentious, this creekside raw bar manages to serve up the freshest and most expertly prepared seafood in town. Those preparations are generally quite straightforward—fried, broiled, baked, or steamed—and mouthwateringly awesome. Big eaters or hungry couples should try a "combo pot," which piles oysters, shrimp, corn on the cob, onions, and celery into an unglamorous but highly appetizing container.

Another good upscale option is the **Crab & Fin** (420 St. Armands Circle, 941/388-3964, www.crabfinrestaurant.com, 11:30am-10pm Sun.-Thurs., 11:30am-10:30pm Fri.-Sat., main courses from $25) in St. Armands Circle. The ambience is modern and classy, and the menu is extensive, if not incredibly innovative.

A good nearby alternative that rests somewhere between creekside oyster bar and candlelit dinner is the **Lido Beach Grille** (700 Ben Franklin Dr., 941/388-2161, www.lidobeachresort.com, 6pm-10pm daily, bar opens at 5pm, main courses from $21). Yeah, it's in the Lido Beach Resort, but it manages to excel quite a bit beyond any expectations you may have of a hotel restaurant. Menu items are a little pricey, but the Grille gets incredibly fresh fish and prepares it well. The views of the Gulf don't hurt a bit.

Be forewarned: ★ **Owens Fish Camp**

(516 Burns Ln., 941/951-6936, 4pm-9:30pm Sun.-Thurs, 4pm-10:30pm Fri.-Sat., main courses from $10) is not an actual Florida fish camp. The real deal can be found all over the state, tucked away along docks and backwaters accessible only to boaters and boozers. Owens, however, is a pretty easy-to-find (but not so easy-to-find-parking-for) spot in the heart of downtown Sarasota. Nonetheless, from the Old Florida decor to the friendly, slightly boozy vibe of the place, the proprietors have done a pretty good job at creating a reasonable facsimile of the real thing. While steaks and grilled fish and fried seafood dominate the menu, you can just ignore everything and head straight for Owens's lowcountry boil, which is actually more South Carolina than Florida, but it hardly matters. With crab claws, mussels, shrimp, potatoes, corn, and sausage delivered in copious quantities, it's the quintessential way to eat seafood, and Owens does a near-perfect job with theirs. Make sure you get one of the fried fruit pies for dessert.

## ITALIAN

The upscale St. Armands Circle shopping district offers **15 South Ristorante Enoteca** (15 S. Blvd. of the Presidents, 941/388-1555, www.15southristorante.com, 4pm-11pm daily,

It's not on the water, but Owens Fish Camp is the best seafood spot downtown.

main courses from $14). Though dinner can be something of a buttoned-down affair, the atmosphere is surprisingly rustic and friendly; this is in keeping with the selection of traditional Italian country fare, like *pasticciata alla Bolognese,* risottos, stuffed cannelloni, and grilled veal chops. The dining room is beautiful and comfortable. Solo diners will definitely want to grab a seat at the marble-topped bar and let the bartender guide them through the selection of over 600 bottles of wine that 15 South offers.

**Mozzarella Fella** (1668 Main St., 941/366-7600, 10am-5:30pm Mon.-Sat., sandwiches from $7.50) eschews the pages and pages of pizza and pasta that most Italian restaurants go in for and instead focuses its menu on sandwiches. Potato-and-egg, fried calamari, salami, prosciutto, fried eggplant, and a dozen other amazing dishes-stuffed-into-bread sandwiches are the stars, along with a few appetizers and sides and, yes, a couple of pasta selections. The bread is always fresh, and the fillings are prepared with care, making for a different kind of Italian authenticity.

Combining an Italian market with casual, trattoria-style dining, **Cafe Epicure** (1296 N. Palm Ave., 941/366-5648, www.cafeepicuresrq.com, 11am-9pm Mon.-Sat., main courses from $7) is a great choice for a relaxed and reasonably priced meal. Basic pasta dishes are fantastic, and hearty dishes like their sausage-and-onion-topped penne pasta or the lasagna Bolognese are surprisingly affordable given the large portions and fresh ingredients. Cold-cut sandwiches and freshly baked pizza are also available.

## VEGETARIAN AND VEGAN

**Veg** (2164 Gulf Gate Dr., 941/312-6424, lunch 11am-2:30pm Mon.-Sat., dinner 5pm-8pm Mon.-Thurs. and 5pm-9pm Fri.-Sat., main courses from $8) calls itself "a vegetarian seafood eatery," and while that may strike hardcore vegans as a bit of blasphemy, those complaints will be silenced by the quality and variety of the truly vegan fare available,

ranging from cauliflower steak to a mouth-watering pan-seared tofu salad as well as the option to have tempeh or tofu added to basically any of their dishes. Coupled with the extensive selection of fresh seafood on offer, this makes Veg a fantastic option for mixed groups or even for solo diners who want to eat healthy but want more choices than a black-bean burger.

If you're looking for a strictly vegetarian option, ★ **Beauty of Sprouts** (1474 Fruitville Rd., 941/350-8449, 10am-8pm Mon.-Sat., main courses from $8) is an excellent choice. Although small (the restaurant seats only about a dozen people) and slow (everything is made by the owner from scratch out of a small kitchen), BoS is well worth whatever wait you may endure, with a stunning selection of fresh, vegan fare that's mostly raw and mostly organic. While one may expect items like the spring rolls, raw pizza, and the fennel-and-beet salad, the fact that this one-woman kitchen can produce a lavender crème brûlée that's not only vegan but that also holds its own against the most milk-thick dessert kitchen tells you all you need to know.

**The Granary** (1930 Stickney Point Rd., 941/924-4754, 8am-8pm Mon.-Sat., 10am-6pm Sun.) is an organic grocery located between Siesta Key and mainland Sarasota. The deli and salad bar are great for picking up a ready-made vegetarian meal to go, and the store has all you'll need to stock up on supplies for an organic beach picnic.

**Simon's Coffee House** (5900 S. Tamiami Trail, 941/926-7151, http://simonstogo.com, 8am-8pm Mon.-Sat., main courses from $6) has vegan and vegetarian options on its breakfast, lunch, and dinner menus. Though this place isn't strictly meat-free, tempeh and tofu form the cornerstone of several of their meals. Offering everything from crepes and breakfast wraps in the morning and soups and sandwiches for lunch to dinner dishes that include curry vegetables, panini pizza, tempeh meat loaf, shrimp fettuccine, and more for dinner, the "whole food"-oriented Simon's also serves coffee, smoothies, and even beer and wine.

# LATIN

★ **Darwin's Evolutionary Cuisine** (4141 S. Tamiami Trail, 941/260-5964, 5pm-10pm Mon.-Thurs., 5pm-11pm Fri.-Sat., main courses from $18) is one of the best restaurants in Sarasota, Latin or otherwise. Chef Darwin Santa Maria saddened Sarasota foodies when he closed his "Peruvian gastro brewpub" Darwin's on 4th, but soon made them smile again when he opened Darwin's Evolutionary Cuisine, which riffs on notes that recall his past hits. With a similar emphasis on tapas, ceviche, and other small plates (like poke bowls), the menu also has some entrée carryovers from the chef's previous venture, like the malbec-braised short ribs. And while Darwin's is notable for its marvelous food, the stylish, friendly, and festive environment makes it an equally great spot to grab a craft brew or a glass of a hard-to-find wine.

For another Darwin-esque experience in the event that Darwin's is booked up, **Selva Grill** (1345 Main St., 941/362-4427, 5pm-11pm Sun.-Thurs, 5pm-1am Fri.-Sat., main courses from $31) is a good option. Santa Maria was formerly the head chef, and the legacy he left is apparent, with a menu that emphasizes Peruvian seafood dishes and expertly prepared steaks. The vibe is more like that of a traditional restaurant, and although the bar serves up some mighty fine libations, there's no mistaking Selva for a gastropub.

# ASIAN

Located downtown, the **Drunken Poet Cafe** (1572 Main St., 941/955-8404, www.drunkenpoetsarasota.com, 11am-10pm Sun.-Thurs., 11am-midnight Fri.-Sat., main courses from $11) offers both Japanese *and* Thai food. The cozy café is kinda tiny, and service is sometimes hit-or-miss, but the dozen house rolls—including the Sexy Woman and the Chef Ginch—are exceptional. The kitchen menu is where the Thai flavors come forth, with well-known dishes alongside more unique preparations like salmon Panang and *gai bai teuy* (marinated chicken wrapped in leaves).

**Pacific Rim** (1859 Hillview St., 941/330-8071, http://pacificrimsarasota.com, lunch 11:30am-2pm Mon.-Fri., dinner 5pm-9:30pm Mon.-Thurs., 5pm-10:30pm Fri.-Sat., and 5pm-9pm Sun., sushi rolls from $6, main courses from $12) is a modern and stylish Japanese restaurant just south of downtown. The atmosphere is casual, and the martini menu is almost as popular as the sushi bar. The sushi rolls are uniformly excellent, drawing large (and sometimes loud) evening crowds to the open dining room.

Offering sushi and Korean dishes is the superb ★ **Korean SSAM BAR** (1303 N. Washington Blvd., 941/312-6264, 11am-2:30pm and 5pm-9pm Mon.-Sat., main courses from $13), which manages to excel at both. Despite the fact that some of the best sushi in Sarasota can be found here, you'll definitely want to tuck into the authentic Korean food on offer. Classics like bibimbap, galbi, and Korean fried chicken are cooked to near-perfection, whether at lunch or dinner. The atmosphere is friendly and casual, if a bit anonymous, but the food is some of the best in town.

**Pho Cali** (1578 Main St., 941/955-2683, http://phocalisarasota.com, 11am-4pm and 5pm-9pm Mon.-Thurs, 11am-4pm and 5pm-9:30pm Fri.-Sat., main courses from $13) is a solid choice for Vietnamese food downtown. In addition to standards like pho (in a dozen-plus varieties), *bún* (almost as many choices), barbecue, and broken rice dishes (*cơm tấm*), Pho Cali offers the option to create "do-it-yourself rolls" with rice paper rolls, sauce, vermicelli, and condiments aside a plate of protein (shrimp paste on sugarcane; pork meatballs; grilled pork, beef, or chicken), making for a fun (and sorta messy) way to have dinner. There's a handful of Thai dishes on the menu, as well as less-well-known Vietnamese fare such as clay-pot fish and pork, beef shank-and-tendon stew, and lotus stem salads.

# EUROPEAN

**Café L'Europe** (431 St. Armands Circle, 941/388-4415, www.cafeleurope.net, lunch 11:30am-3pm, dinner 5pm-10pm daily, main courses from $35) has been a St. Armands mainstay for nearly 40 years, and the way this place delivers a classy Continental dining experience leaves little doubt that it will probably be around for another few decades, at least. With white-linen service, an extensive wine list, and a menu of French and Italian fine-dining classics, Café L'Europe has an intimate and romantic environment that is as perfect for a date night as it is for a luxurious vacation splurge.

Located in Towles Court Artist Colony is **Lavanda** (1938 Adams Ln., #105, 941/366-0070, www.lavandasarasota.com, 11:30am-2pm and 6pm-9:30pm Tues.-Sat., main courses from $15), which offers a more traditional Continental fine-dining experience. Sitting on the beautiful wraparound porch provides great atmosphere, and the menu features artful interpretations of classic dishes like steak, fish, and duck.

Although it's almost halfway between downtown Sarasota and Venice, **Roessler's** (2033 Vamo Way, 941/966-5688, www.roesslersrestaurant.com, 5pm-10pm Tues.-Sun., main courses from $25) is well worth the drive. It's thoroughly upscale and traditional (they've been here since 1985), boasting a menu of Continental classics, but the welcoming and romantic atmosphere (with three acres of lush foliage and a beautiful outdoor dining patio) means that "upscale" definitely doesn't have to mean "stuffy." The service is attentive and knowledgeable, encouraging a leisurely and informed journey through veal scaloppine, crispy duck with a peppery bing cherry sauce, chicken Française, veal sweetbreads, schnitzels, filet mignon, and even meat loaf. Keep in mind there are two distinct areas of Roessler's; the main dining room is the fancier version, with a focus on those European classics, while the bistro area offers outdoor seating and a somewhat more affordable menu featuring shrimp scampi, veal piccata, burgers, salads, and a three-course, $29 tasting menu featuring the stars of the main dining room.

Next door to the Sarasota Opera House is **Bijou Café** (1287 1st St., 941/366-8111, http://bijoucafe.net, lunch 11:30am-2pm Mon.-Fri., dinner 5pm-10pm Mon.-Sat., lunch from $12, dinner from $20), which could certainly get by on just serving the most basic French fare to pre-show crowds but instead manages to provide a wide range of accessible and interesting dishes aimed at a wide cross-section of guests. The lunch sandwiches are excellent and satisfying (try the gravlax on rye or the roast-duck-and-mango-chutney on ciabatta), and dinner features fresh seafood, steaks, pasta dishes, and, notably, a South African mixed grill with lamb, steak, grits, and grilled tomatoes.

In the Gulf Gate area is a prime option for German food (and pre-drinks carbo-loading): **Schnitzel Kitchen** (6521 Superior Ave., 941/922-9299, www.schnitzelkitchen.com, 4:30pm-9pm Wed.-Sat., main courses from $12). The proprietors seem to be focused more on making sure the kitchen serves up authentic fare than on dressing up their dining room like a German biergarten, so while the decor may be bland, the food is substantial and flavorful, with an unsurprising focus on a variety of schnitzels complemented by spaetzle and cucumber salad.

# Accommodations

## $50-100

Cheap lodging options are plentiful in Sarasota. Just taking a drive down the Tamiami Trail between the John & Mable Ringling Museum of Art and downtown will reveal inexpensive motels that hearken back to the days when the Trail was the primary tourist route through the area. Unfortunately, quite a few of these motels are difficult to recommend; many are pretty rough around the edges. Nonetheless, there are a handful of national budget chains with outposts here, and your odds of getting a clean, safe room are quite a bit better at them than at some of the more "vintage" motels. A **Quality Inn** (4800 N. Tamiami Trail, 941/355-7091, www.choicehotels.com, doubles from $55) and a **Super 8** (4309 N. Tamiami Trail, 941/355-9326, www.super8.com, doubles from $59) near the Ringling College of Art & Design will suffice in a light-wallet pinch.

Boasting a little bit of character is the **Golden Host Resort** (4675 N. Tamiami Trail, 941/355-5141, www.goldenhostresort.com, doubles from $89), a Best Western property that's well-maintained despite its age. The rooms are outfitted with high-speed Internet, coffeemakers, and cable TV. The grounds (especially the area around the pool) are lush with foliage, providing a tiny bit of pastoralism alongside the busy Tamiami Trail. One big bonus to staying here: The legendary Bahi Hut—home of some of the most brutally strong drinks in Sarasota—is on the property, meaning you won't even have to think about driving home after experiencing one (or two) of their skull-knocking mai tais.

If you travel with your own hotel room, the **Sun-N-Fun RV Resort** (7125 Fruitville Rd., 941/342-6189, www.sunnfunfl.com, RV sites from $58) is a solid and inexpensive option. Although it's a half hour or so from downtown—a couple of miles east of I-75 on Fruitville Road—this resort has proven to be a preferred destination for motor home travelers. There are more than 600 RV sites, all of which include cable TV and 30- and 50-amp hookups. There are also sites for tent camping. Additionally, Sun-N-Fun offers rental homes in four different sizes and feature levels, with homes laid out close to one another. What the facilities may lack in architectural beauty, the resort more than makes up for in amenities: an Olympic-size pool, tennis and volleyball courts, a gym, and an activities center where guests can take classes in woodcarving, painting, or even computer skills. Obviously, this is a place optimized for folks who are going to be spending a big chunk of time here—most likely during the winter—so it's also got the basics like laundry facilities.

## $100-200

Although it's a breeze to find hotels in this price range during the low season in Sarasota, finding a midrange-cost place to stay during the Sarasota high season can be something of a challenge. There are some consistently priced hotels near the airport, ranging from the basic **Comfort Inn** (5000 N. Tamiami Trail, 941/351-7734, www.choicehotels.com, doubles from $100) to the nicer environs of a **Hampton Inn & Suites** (975 University Pkwy., 941/355-8140, www.hamptoninn.hilton.com, doubles from $159) and a **Hyatt Place** (950 University Pkwy., 941/554-5800, www.sarasotabradenton.place.hyatt.com, doubles from $179). As these are airport chain hotels, you already know exactly what you're getting, but if you need something at a reasonable cost during high season, and don't mind driving a bit to see nearly everything Sarasota has to offer, then these hotels offer a solid option.

For something more historically Sarasotan, the ★ **Gulf Beach Resort Motel** (930 Ben Franklin Dr., 941/388-2127, www.gulfbeach-sarasota.com, doubles from $160) is a much better choice. The fact that this place is as inexpensive as it is remains something of a mystery to me. It's the oldest hotel on Lido Beach, an area of Sarasota notably light on hotels already. And it sits right on a beautiful, quiet stretch of that beach. Sure, the TV only shows basic cable, and you have to get the remotes from the front desk, but, again, this is the oldest hotel on one of the Gulf Coast's best beaches. Who cares if you have to watch ESPN in standard definition? Go to the beach! Accommodations range from standard (and somewhat small) rooms to larger mini-apartments complete with kitchenettes. Each room is individually decorated, and many guests have favorites that they return to every year. There's a heated pool, a beachside picnic area, and you can even play shuffleboard. The staff here is exceedingly friendly and helpful, making this place feel more like a family affair than a beach "resort."

About half a block from the beach on Lido Key is **Beau Lido Suites** (139 Tyler Dr., 888/543-6539, www.beaulido.com, doubles from $150). This tiny, no-frills motel features somewhat outdated decor and no-frills rooms that range from their guest room, which holds a double bed and a TV, to a fully detached, two-bedroom house.

Conversely, the unassuming outside of the ★ **Hotel Ranola** (118 Indian Pl., 941/951-0111, doubles from $179) doesn't seem all that promising, but inside, this downtown boutique hotel is a real gem. Its nine rooms are all decorated in a hip, playful, and urban style, with hardwood floors, checkerboard tiles, and bold color schemes, and they feel less like hotel accommodations and more like tiny apartments. All of the rooms are kitted out with flat-screen plasma TVs, free Wi-Fi, decadently soft bedding, and full (if small) kitchens; the basic rooms are around 400 square feet, but a couple of deluxe suites top out at 600 square feet.

## $200-300

The **Lido Beach Resort** (700 Ben Franklin Dr., 941/388-2161, www.lidobeachresort.com, doubles from $219) is the largest beachfront property on Lido Key, but thanks to its somewhat labyrinthine layout, it feels surprisingly intimate. The waterfront tiki bar and restaurant are popular evening spots for guests and nonguests staying on the key who don't feel like braving the high-season crowds in St. Armands Circle. The pet-friendly resort sits right on the Gulf, with a private beach area reserved for hotel guests. Facilities include volleyball, a fitness center, and two heated pools. The rooms are incredibly spacious, ranging from standard hotel-style rooms to kitchenette rooms and one- and two-bedroom suites. All rooms have flat-screen TVs and safes, and there's Wi-Fi throughout the hotel.

Another good option on Lido Key is **Coquina on the Beach** (1008 Ben Franklin Dr., 941/388-2141, www.coquinaonthebeach.com, doubles from $209). Although it's lighter on the amenities than the Lido Beach Resort, the vibe is friendly, and the rooms are tidy and comfortable, if a little dated. The location provides great beach views from almost every room, and, if saltwater's not on the agenda, the heated pool is a nice option. In addition to standard rooms, one-bedroom apartments are also available.

Operated by the InterContinental conglomerate, the **Hotel Indigo** (1223 Blvd. of the Arts, 941/487-3800, doubles from $224) gamely attempts to pull off a boutique hotel vibe. The 95 small rooms are very brightly painted, and the corporate staff is well trained to provide fastidious service. There's a small pool and fitness center on-site.

Sarasota's **Ritz-Carlton** (1111 Ritz-Carlton Dr., 941/309-2000, doubles from $269) overlooks Sarasota Bay and is just a few blocks away from the Van Wezel Performing Arts Hall. Accommodations are typically Ritz-luxe, with feather beds, Egyptian-cotton linens, turndown service, and even complimentary shoeshine service. The property opens into a marble-floored foyer, and there are three tennis courts, a pool, a spa, and two fitness centers on-site. Guests also have access to the Members Beach Club on Lido Key.

Somewhat surprisingly, the hotel is also pet-friendly, permitting cats and dogs under 20 pounds to stay in specially designated rooms.

Literally standing in the shadows of Sarasota's Ritz-Carlton, the **Hyatt Regency** (1000 Blvd. of the Arts, 941/953-1234, www.sarasota.hyatt.com, doubles from $259) boasts a stupendous bayfront location, right next to the Van Wezel and Centennial Park. There's a fantastic, lagoon-style pool, and the hotel's own marina provides a great waterfront setting. It's not as upscale as the Ritz, but it's luxurious, and definitely the most affordable of all of downtown's upmarket accommodations.

If you've got reward points to burn, the **Holiday Inn Lido Beach** (233 Ben Franklin Dr., 941/388-5555, www.lidobeachholidayinn.com, doubles from $238) is conveniently located on Lido Key directly across the street from the beach. Views from the rooms' balconies are stupendous, and this is the closest hotel property on Lido to the shops and dining of St. Armands Circle. The on-site restaurant is mediocre.

## VACATION RENTALS

For longer visits, a good alternative to extended-stay hotels is **Timberwoods Vacation Villas** (8378 S. Tamiami Trail, 941/312-5934, www.timberwoods.com, villas $1,295 weekly). The two-bedroom/two-bath villas are reasonably priced, clean, and comfortable, providing fairly easy access to Siesta Key and the food and nightlife of the Gulf Gate area. The complex, which feels like a somewhat-dated planned community, is along the Tamiami Trail south of Sarasota.

# Information and Services

## VISITOR INFORMATION

The local visitors bureau operates the official **Sarasota County Visitor Information Center** (14 Lemon Ave., 941/957-1877, www.sarasotafl.org, 10am-4pm Mon.-Sat.), conveniently located in the downtown area near the Van Wezel Performing Arts Hall.

## MEDIA

Two daily newspapers are available throughout Sarasota. The *Herald-Tribune* (www.heraldtribune.com) is best for information about central Sarasota, while the smaller *Bradenton Herald* (www.bradenton.com) will be useful for those in the northern part of town, including Anna Maria Island. The *Herald-Tribune* also publishes **Ticket** (www.heraldtribune.com/ticket), a website devoted to entertainment, nightlife, and events in the area.

## MEDICAL AND EMERGENCY SERVICES

**Sarasota Memorial Hospital** (1700 S. Tamiami Trail, 941/917-9000) is just a few minutes south of downtown and is the closest hospital with a 24-hour emergency room. For prescriptions, there are dozens of branches of national chain pharmacies throughout the city, including **Walgreens** and **CVS,** and prescriptions can also be filled at many **Publix** grocery stores.

## POST OFFICES

The downtown **Sarasota Post Office** (1661 Ringling Blvd., 941/331-4200, 8am-5pm Mon.-Fri., 9am-noon Sat.) is one of several branches in the area.

## INTERNET ACCESS

Free Wi-Fi access is available at many cafés, bars, and restaurants in Sarasota, including chains like McDonald's and Starbucks, as well as at the eight branches of the **Sarasota County Library** (main branch: 1331 1st St.,

239/861-1100, http://suncat.co.sarasota.fl.us/ Libraries, 10am-8pm Mon.-Thurs., 10am-5pm Fri.-Sat.) located in Sarasota, Venice, and Englewood.

## BANKS

The banks most well-represented in the Sarasota area are **Wells Fargo, SunTrust, Regions Bank,** and **Fifth Third,** each of which has several branches with ATMs in town. ATMs are also available at **Publix** supermarkets.

# Getting There and Around

## GETTING THERE

The **Sarasota-Bradenton International Airport** (SRQ, 6000 Airport Circle, 941/359-2770, www.srq-airport.com) is located in northern Sarasota, near the John & Mable Ringling Museum of Art and the New College of Florida and about 15 minutes or so from downtown. The airport is serviced by Delta, United, American, JetBlue, and several charter services. Flights to SRQ are somewhat limited, and you'll definitely be able to find more flight options at the larger **Tampa International Airport** (TPA, 4100 George J. Bean Pkwy., 813/870-8700, www.tampaairport.com), which is about an hour away. SRQ is connected to downtown Sarasota by SCAT (see "Getting Around" below); use Bus Route 99. Taxi fare from SRQ to downtown is approximately $20-$25. Both SRQ and TPA offer a full range of car rental services.

By car, Sarasota is about 60 miles—or about an hour—south of Tampa Bay, via I-75 and I-275. The city itself is about 10 miles west of I-75. The historic Tamiami Trail runs through the city.

The nearest **Greyhound** station is the **Bradenton Greyhound Station** (3028 1st St. W., Bradenton, 941/747-2984, 8am-8:30pm daily).

## GETTING AROUND

Like most of the rest of Florida, Sarasota is a car city. Public parking throughout Sarasota is mostly metered, although there are many areas downtown where street-side parking is timed. Time violations earn a $15 parking citation.

The city government operates a decent bus system in the form of the unfortunately named **SCAT** (www.scgov.net), with fairly direct routes and a **transfer station** (1565 1st St.) downtown. SCAT, in conjunction with Manatee County's **MCAT** (www.mymanatee.org), also operates trolley service to Longboat Key and Anna Maria Island. Routes are limited on Sundays, and there is no service on major holidays. Single-ride fares for buses and the trolley are $1.25, but you can get unlimited-ride passes for $20 per week or $60 per month.

# Bradenton

Bradenton is actually the largest city in the Sarasota metro area, with a couple thousand more residents than Sarasota. However, while there may be more people living here, the city doesn't offer much for visitors. Most folks zip through town on their way to Anna Maria Island to the east or Sarasota to the south. Still, the city does get a bit of a tourist boomlet during spring training season—the Pittsburgh Pirates play their Grapefruit League home games downtown at McKechnie Field—and whether you're here for a game or just passing through, Bradenton offers a few sights worth seeing.

## SIGHTS

Bradenton, with its pleasant downtown, stands out among other small Florida cities due to its placement alongside the gorgeous Braden River. The **Village of the Arts** (14th St. W. at 12th Ave. W., www.villageofthearts. com) exhibits Bradenton's quirky character. Located just a few blocks outside of the main downtown area, this 10-square-block area is the sort of organic, locally oriented, creative community that municipalities everywhere try to summon into existence with development plans and incentive committees. Affordable housing and a spark of artistic vision from like-minded souls have created a unique enclave of colorfully painted galleries, studios, shops, and eateries nestled among small, older residences. It's only a few square blocks in size, but the area is incredibly walkable and quite welcoming: part laid-back neighborhood, part artistic oasis. There are more than two dozen galleries and artists, and whether you're enjoying the whimsical, audiovisual approach at **The Dude and Mary's Art of Life & Music** (1414 11th St. W., 315/281-7231, 11am-6pm Tues.-Sat., noon-4pm Sun.) or browsing the avian-vibed fine art prints at **The Dancing Crane Gallery** (1019 10th Ave. W., 941/744-1333, 11am-4pm Thurs.-Sat.), nearly every single business in this community manages to evoke a friendly and quirky atmosphere without being overbearing or cutesy about it.

As one of the few actual "sights" in downtown Bradenton, the **South Florida**

Tucked into a residential neighborhood, the Village of the Arts is quirky and unique.

# Tropicana Juice Train

It's impossible to talk about the history of Florida's citrus industry without discussing Bradenton. The city is where the Tropicana company was founded in 1947. For nearly a decade, Tropicana was a local delicacy, as the freshly squeezed juice was primarily delivered to local residents and businesses in jars toted by delivery boys. Eventually though, demand in the northern United States required a way for Tropicana to get its product to places like New York. Starting in 1957, the S.S. *Tropicana* made a weekly delivery of juice to New York. After a search for a more efficient (and faster) way to get the fresh juice to northern customers, in 1971 a string of 150 custom-insulated boxcars began making the round-trip on rail lines between Florida and New Jersey. Painted bright orange with the Tropicana logo emblazoned on the side, these boxcars carry millions of gallons of fresh orange juice every week and serve as a powerful visual reminder of Florida's premier agricultural product.

**Museum** (201 10th St. W., 941/746-4131, www.southfloridamuseum.com, 10am-5pm Tues.-Sat., noon-5pm Sun., $19 adults, $17 seniors, $14 children 4-12, children under 4 free) is actually three museums in one, with a main museum area focused on ancient Florida history, an aquarium focused on manatees (with feedings several times a day), and a planetarium. The building the museum is housed in is gorgeous, and situated right next to the river. The Montague Tallant Gallery in the museum features artifacts gathered by collector Montague Tallant, while the Parker Manatee Aquarium was home to one of Florida's most famous manatees (and the world's oldest-known), Snooty, whose death in 2017 sparked an outpouring of homage from across the state.

Also downtown is the **Riverwalk** area, which, like most other "Riverwalk" areas in small cities across America, provides a scenic mile-and-a-half stroll alongside the marinas and docks that line the Manatee River, with benches, public art, and great views all along the way.

Just outside of downtown, on the way toward Anna Maria Island, is **De Soto National Memorial** (8300 De Soto Memorial Hwy., 941/792-0458, 9am-5pm daily, free), which marks the spot where, in 1539, an expedition led by Hernando de Soto became one of the first to extensively interact with native cultures in the southern part of the United States. (These interactions were not pleasant, it must be said; de Soto's team stole the natives' food and enslaved many of them.) A visitors center on-site does a remarkable job of balancing the historical importance of de Soto's expedition with the calamitous impact it had on native people. There are also extensive kayak trails through the mangrove coastline, and park rangers lead free guided tours during the summer. Additionally, the park has a couple of small beaches, some picnic areas, and a short hiking trail.

## FOOD

While in the downtown area, one of the best spots for coffee is **The B'Town Coffee Co** (440 12th St. W., 941/745-3100, 7am-8pm Mon.-Thurs., 7am-2am Fri.-Sat.), on Bradenton's old main street. There's great outdoor seating, and, in addition to coffee, they also serve breakfast and lunch.

For a more diner-style meal, head to **Robin's Downtown Cafe** (427 12th St. W., 941/747-8899, 7am-2:30pm Mon.-Fri., 7:30am-noon Sat., breakfast from $4, lunch from $6), just a half block away. Robin's also offers outdoor seating. The food and coffee menus feature standard eggs-and-meat breakfast dishes, hearty burgers and sandwiches, and other solid diner fare.

Dinner plans should definitely include **Ortygia** (1418 13th St. W., 941/741-8646, www.ortygiarestaurant.com, 11:30am-8:30pm

Tues.-Sat., main courses from $15), a fantastic Sicilian-inspired restaurant located in the Village of the Arts, with an extensive menu of authentic pasta, seafood, and meat dishes, and an appropriately wide selection of antipasti.

If you're looking for something a little more laid-back, check out **3 Keys Brewing & Eatery** (2505 Manatee Ave. E., 941/218-0396, 3keysbrewing.com, noon-10pm Mon.-Thurs., noon-midnight Fri., 11am-midnight Sat., 11am-10pm Sun., main courses from $11), located just outside of downtown. The brewery offers excellent beer brewed on-site (the menu changes regularly, so plan on getting a flight, which is served on an awesome Florida-shaped paddle) and a decent (if limited) selection of food. Their standard burgers are exceptional, but decadent treats like a chicken-and-bacon waffle sandwich are great, too.

## ACCOMMODATIONS

Located in the more historic area of Bradenton's downtown, **The Londoner Bed and Breakfast & Tearooms** (304 15th St. W., 941/748-5658, www.thelondonerinn.com, doubles from $150) is situated in a gorgeous 1926 house with a relaxing front porch. The rooms are named after stops on the London tube, and afternoon tea is a daily staple. It's a great place to stay, with six comfortable and reasonably spacious rooms, furnished with a minimum of fussiness.

Need to burn some loyalty points? The **Courtyard by Marriott** (100 Riverfront Blvd., 941/747-3727, www.courtyardbradenton.com, doubles from $149) is probably one of the best-located hotels in all of Bradenton, with great views of the river and just a few blocks' walk to downtown.

## GETTING THERE AND AROUND

Downtown Bradenton is about 30 minutes north of Sarasota, via the Tamiami Trail (U.S. 41), although there's little clear indication as to where Sarasota ends and Bradenton begins. (For the record, once you pass New College of Florida and the Sarasota-Bradenton International Airport, you're pretty much in Bradenton, though you'll have a good 15 minutes until you get to the city's core.) Downtown Bradenton is quite pedestrian-friendly, with a concentrated core along the waterfront and easily navigable streets with a surprising sidewalk culture. However, to get to the Village of the Arts, you'll need a car; even though it's not all that far, you'll have to traverse a few very busy streets that are sadly lacking in sidewalks.

# The Keys

Three main Gulf islands hug the coast of Sarasota: Siesta Key, Longboat Key, and Anna Maria Island. Siesta Key is to the south of downtown Sarasota and boasts some of the most beautiful beaches in the United States. Of the three, Siesta Key is definitely the most popular, drawing big crowds of out-of-town visitors during the winter and locals throughout the year, all of whom are lured by the spectacular white-sand beaches.

Just north of Siesta Key, the southern tip of Longboat Key is an easily accessible, 10-minute drive from downtown Sarasota and stretches all the way north to Anna Maria Island (AMI), which is home to the residential communities of Bradenton Beach, Holmes Beach, and Anna Maria. Multistory condominiums line the Gulf Coast on Longboat Key, and the wilder, somewhat rougher beaches are quite a bit harder to access. Once you make it up to Anna Maria, though, with its bungalows and Old Florida atmosphere, you'll feel a whole lot more welcome.

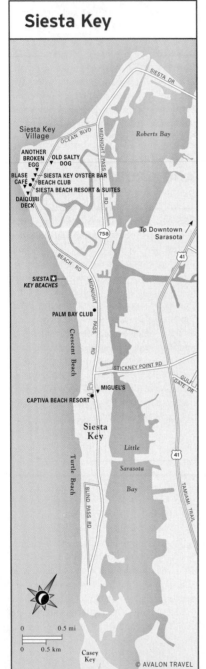

Siesta Key

Siesta Key Village
OCEAN BLVD
ANOTHER BROKEN EGG ▼
OLD SALTY DOG ▼
BLASE CAFÉ ▼
SIESTA KEY OYSTER BAR ▼
BEACH CLUB
SIESTA BEACH RESORT & SUITES
DAIQUIRI DECK
Roberts Bay
MIDNIGHT PASS RD.
758
To Downtown Sarasota
41
BEACH RD
SIESTA KEY BEACHES
MIDNIGHT PASS RD
PALM BAY CLUB
Crescent Beach
STICKNEY POINT RD
GULF GATE DR
MIGUEL'S
CAPTIVA BEACH RESORT
Siesta Key
Little
Sarasota
Bay
41
TAMIAMI TRAIL
Turtle Beach
BLIND PASS RD
0        0.5 mi
0    0.5 km
Casey Key
© AVALON TRAVEL

## SIESTA KEY
### ★ Beaches

The biggest issue with the marvelous beaches on Siesta Key is access. There are numerous beach access points; however, very few of them have dedicated parking. The main beach park has an epically huge parking lot, and it often fills up early on summer days and on almost every sunset-worthy evening. Still, since most visitors to Siesta Key are likely staying on the island, it's worth noting that the island is eminently walkable, and even if you're not staying right on the water, it's usually a none-too-challenging hike to get you and your stuff onto the sand.

The main beach is **Siesta Beach** (948 Beach Rd., sunrise-sunset daily, free). You'll find copious free public parking, bathroom and shower facilities, concessions, and lots and lots of people. Amazingly, the parking lot can feel like cars are stacked on top of one another, but the beach itself somehow still feels spacious. That wide-open beach vista is one of the biggest appeals of Siesta Key: The soft, white sand stretches out in all directions, providing ample space for all comers.

That said, those looking for a *little* more quietude might want to hit **Turtle Beach** (8918 Midnight Pass Rd., sunrise-sunset daily, free), a good option for some relative peace. It's still a pretty popular destination, thanks to the fact that it's got a free, public parking lot. But the lot is pretty small, there are no lifeguards, and the somewhat rougher and narrower beach (and its out-of-the-way location on the south part of the island) self-imposes its own form of population control.

A great destination for snorkelers and divers is **Crescent Beach** (at the western end of Point of Rocks Rd., sunrise-sunset daily, free). Parking is a living nightmare—you're restricted to a tiny handful of unmarked roadside spots. Everything else in this residential neighborhood is emblazoned with No Parking signs, so your best bet is to make your way here on foot or by bike (keeping in mind to be respectful of the folks who actually live here). Once you make it to the beach—which is expansive and smooth—snorkelers should head to the southernmost tip. That's the titular "point of rocks," an outcropping of coral formations that's home to a wide variety of fish and marine life. The water is gentle and easy to navigate, making it a prime destination for those who want to explore beneath the surface. If you didn't bring your own snorkeling gear, rentals are available nearby at **Siesta Sports Rentals** (6551 Midnight Pass Rd., 941/346-1797, www.siestasportsrentals.com, 9am-5pm daily, snorkel rentals from $12/day).

## Sports and Recreation

**Siesta Key Parasailing** (1265 Stickney Point Rd., 941/586-1972, www.siestakeyparasailing.com, $75/person) and **Siesta Key Water Sports** (1536 Stickney Point Rd., 941/921-3030, http://siestakeywatersports.com, $75/person) both offer parasailing experiences over the beautiful Gulf waters. Siesta Key Water Sports also has Jet Skis and kayaks available for rent.

There are a half-dozen boats available for rent at **CB's Saltwater Outfitters** (1249 Stickney Point Rd., 941/349-4400, http://cbsoutfitters.com, half-day fishing charters from $350, half-day boat rentals from $95). Those folks who don't want to bother with piloting their own boat should definitely avail themselves of CB's many fishing charters; they offer four-, six-, and eight-hour trips both into Sarasota Bay as well as inshore, near-shore, and reef trips. Full-day trips into Charlotte Harbor (about 40 miles southeast) to hunt for snook, redfish, and more are also available.

## Entertainment and Events

### NIGHTLIFE

Most of the nightlife on the island is limited to a standard selection of beach bars and a few restaurants that have a relatively lively after-hours scene. **Daiquiri Deck** (5250 Ocean Blvd., 941/349-8697, http://daiquiri-deck.com, no cover) is one of the more popular, with daily drink specials, a party-hearty atmosphere, and a none-too-shabby menu. (There's also a location in St. Armands Circle in Sarasota.) More low-key (and comfortably divey) is **Crescent Club** (6519 Midnight Pass Rd., 941/349-1311, 10am-2am daily, no cover), which opens early and stays up late, serving strong and inexpensive drinks in a friendly, boozy, locals-focused environment.

If you're hankering for live music on Siesta Key, the **Beach Club** (5151 Ocean Blvd., 941/349-6311, www.beachclubsiestakey.com, 11am-2am daily, no cover) is pretty much your

The beach at Siesta Key is world-renowned.

only option. The bands tend to play covers and crowd-friendly dance numbers. When there's not a band on stage, there's usually a DJ on the decks so people can dance the night away. The vibe is decidedly laid-back and unmistakably "beachy."

With a somewhat more upscale (but still casual) environment, the **Blasé Café & Martini Bar** (5263 Ocean Blvd., 941/349-9822, http://theblasecafe.com, 4pm-midnight daily, no cover) has a martini bar that serves up a dozen-plus "designer" drink concoctions, making it a popular spot for after-dinner drinks. Blasé Café also offers a menu of steak, seafood, and sandwiches.

### FESTIVALS AND EVENTS

Every November, kids and adults (but mostly adults) descend on the beach at Siesta Key to compete in the **Siesta Key Crystal Classic** (www.crystalsand.org), a massive sand-sculpting contest that's also a benefit for sea turtle conservation. The contest has been featured on several cable travel shows, and for good reason; the soft, white sand at Siesta Key packs quite well but is also malleable enough to allow for considerable detail. These are no ordinary sandcastles. If you don't have the patience to watch folks pack, wet, carve, and repeat for hours upon end, the judging usually takes place around lunchtime. In addition to the breathtaking creations made on the sand, there are food and beverage vendors on-site.

If you've rented a condo or beach cottage and need to fill the refrigerator, hit the **Siesta Key Farmers Market** (5124 Ocean Blvd., www.siestafarmersmarket.com, 8am-1pm Sun.). The market brings local produce and craft vendors out to the heart of Siesta Key Village every Sunday morning and is a great way to stock your rental's pantry with unique and locally sourced food.

## Shopping

Most of the shopping on Siesta Key is in the Siesta Key Village area. There, you can find shops like **Created Gems** (5212 Ocean Blvd.,

941/349-2748, www.siestakeygems.com, hours vary seasonally), a jewelry store that specializes in "diamond alternatives," alongside a selection of beachwear and beach-gear stores.

## Food
### BREAKFAST

The friendly breakfast joint **Another Broken Egg** (140 Avenida Messina, 941/346-2750, www.anotherbrokenegg.com, 7am-9pm daily, main courses from $6) has a great patio area for dining, as well as a spacious inside dining room with lots of local artwork on the walls. It's a great choice for breakfast on Siesta Key, with standards supplemented by a selection of originals like an Egg Largo (a Benedict-style plate that substitutes sour cream, scallions, and tomatoes for hollandaise sauce), as well as massive omelets, blintzes, and Tex-Mex-style breakfasts.

If you're sleeping on Siesta Key but headed into Sarasota or other eastward points for the day, **Word of Mouth** (6604 Gateway Ave., 941/925-2400, 7am-2pm daily, main courses from $7) is often considerably less crowded than the Broken Egg, and it's in the Gulf Gate area just beyond the bridge that connects Siesta Key and the mainland. The breakfast menu is rounded out with blintzes, crepes, fresh-fruit plates, and a truly decadent croissant-based French toast.

Located in the heart of Siesta Key Village, **Meaney's Mini Donuts** (201 Canal Rd., no phone, 8am-9pm daily) is a morning must-stop for many longtime Siesta Key vacationers. While they also serve some lunch options like hot dogs, the main reason there's usually a line at this little shack throughout the day is that these half-size doughnuts are freshly fried before your eyes and flavored with everything from cinnamon and chocolate to strawberry, peanut butter, key lime, and whatever concoction they've come up with that day. These doughnuts are also super cheap; you can grab a bag of nearly 20 donuts for less than five bucks.

## FRENCH

Everyone who makes it out to **Miguel's** (6631 Midnight Pass Rd., 941/349-4024, www.miguelsrestaurant.net, 5pm-10pm Tues.-Sat., main courses from $18) thinks they've discovered a secret little beachside treasure. But this French restaurant, stuck in a hidden corner of a nondescript strip mall, has been a Siesta Key staple for years, serving up a somewhat lighter take on French standards. Almost half of the entrée selections are seafood-based, and even the sauces employed for many of the meat and poultry dishes—lemon-butter, madeira, balsamic vinegar—shy away from the decadent, creamy richness one most often associates with French food. (Fear not, milk-and-butter fans—the kitchen can still whip up a rich béarnaise or cream champagne sauce.)

## SEAFOOD

There's a much higher density of restaurant choices in the Siesta Key Village area, and one of the most popular is the **Siesta Key Oyster Bar** (5238 Ocean Blvd., 941/346-5443, www.skob.com, 9am-midnight daily, main courses from $12, sandwiches from $6), renowned almost as much for its massive bivalves as it is for its raucously friendly atmosphere. Superfresh seafood and super-cold beers have made SKOB an essential stop, especially for oyster fans and partiers.

## BURGERS & PIZZA

The **Old Salty Dog** (5023 Ocean Blvd., 941/349-0158, www.theoldsaltydog.com, 11am-9:30pm daily, bar open until midnight daily, main courses from $15, sandwiches from $7) is another quintessential beach spot to hit while in Siesta Key. The menu includes burgers, seafood, and other pub grub. More importantly, the views are great, the staff is quite friendly, and the beer selection is exceptional. Beer fans who want pizza with their brew should head a few blocks over to **3.14 Pi Craft Beer & Spirits** (5263 Ocean Blvd., 941/346-1188, siestapi.com, noon-2am daily, main courses from $12), where you can get good pizza, great wings, and an astounding array of craft beers (on tap and in the bottle). The vibe here is super laid-back (there are typically surf videos playing on the TVs), despite the fact that they take their beer (and pizza) quite seriously.

## Accommodations
### $100-200

Despite being more than 50 miles from Captiva Beach, the ★ **Captiva Beach Resort** (6772 Sara Sea Circle, 941/349-4131, http://captivabeachresort.com, doubles from $219) is one of the better places to stay on Siesta Key. The affordable units are available in one- and two-bedroom configurations, and also as efficiencies equipped with full kitchens. Though within walking distance of several nearby restaurants, the resort is set off of the main road in a private circle that gives it a comfortable, secluded feel. While it doesn't offer many of the typical upscale amenities folks may associate with resort stays, the semi-private beach, heated pool, and foliage-draped grounds combine with the clean (but somewhat dated) rooms and friendly, family-oriented staff to make a stay quite pleasant.

Considerably less intimate is the **Palm Bay Club** (5960 Midnight Pass Rd., www.palmbayclub.com, 941/349-1911, doubles from $185); however, the wide variety of rooms on offer provides considerable choice, with studios and one-, two-, and three-bedroom suites in the Grande Tower building, as well as more town-house-like accommodations in the two Club complexes (one overlooks the bay, the other the Gulf). All the rooms are clean and relatively contemporary, though they're all individually owned, so decor varies from room to room.

### $200-300

Right next door to the Captiva Beach Resort is the three-resort property enclave of **Tropical Beach Resorts** (617 Sara Sea Circle, 941/349-3330, www.tropicalbeachresorts.com, doubles from $209). All three resorts—the Tropical Shores, the Sara Sea, and the Tropical Sun—share an enviable location right at one of the most beautiful stretches of beach on Siesta Key. They all feature updated rooms in varying sizes (from standard double rooms to efficiency apartments) and are generally similar beyond their themes of decor.

## VACATION RENTALS

A great option for Siesta Key, given all of the gulf-front condominium complexes, is to rent a condo for your stay. **Siesta-4-Rent** (941/349-5500, www.siesta4rent.com) has scores of units, ranging from studios and one-bedrooms to four- and five-bedrooms. Almost all units require a one-week rental minimum, and quite a few require at least a monthlong contract. High-season rental rates can vary from $700 a week for a tiny one-bedroom a half block from the beach to $3,500/week for a five-bedroom unit that sleeps a dozen people.

## CAMPING

**Turtle Beach Campground** (8862 Midnight Pass Rd., 941/349-3839, www.scgov.net/turtlebeachcampground, from $45) is a former RV park that was purchased by Sarasota County and turned into a versatile campground with 40 sites catering to RV campers and tent campers who want to get *right* on the beach. The 14-acre park features 2,600 feet of beach, and, for those who drive up in their camper, the sites feature electricity and cable TV hookups. Wi-Fi is available throughout the campground, but why check email with the beautiful vistas of the Gulf of Mexico stretched out in front of you? Sarasota County residents can reserve campground spots up to nine months in advance; out-of-area guests can reserve up to six months in advance.

## ★ LONGBOAT KEY AND ANNA MARIA ISLAND
### Sights
#### HISTORIC BRIDGE STREET

Historic Bridge Street on Anna Maria Island is primarily a commercial district in Bradenton Beach, but the combination of cute shops and vintage island architecture makes it well worth a stroll. The brightly colored, low-slung buildings that line the lushly landscaped street house a wide variety of businesses, from tchotchke shops and beach-bum eateries to art galleries, jewelry shops, and fine-dining establishments. Make sure to check out the **Bridge Street Pier,** which is all that remains of the wooden bridge that originally connected Bradenton Beach to the mainland. It is currently beloved by anglers, and it makes for a great walk. The clock tower is a fantastic photo op.

## COQUINA BAYWALK

Although most folks in the area head straight for the white sands of Coquina Beach, nature lovers will want to dedicate a couple of hours to exploring the trails and boardwalk of **Coquina Baywalk** (across from Coquina Beach on East Bay Dr., Anna Maria Island). Winding along the waterfront, the boardwalk not only offers great sunset views but also gives walkers an opportunity to soak in the quietude of the wooded areas and mangroves. There are multiple walking paths off the boardwalk as well. During the spring and summer months, copious amounts of insect repellent are recommended.

## ANNA MARIA BAYFRONT PARK

**Anna Maria Bayfront Park** (310 N. Bay Blvd., Anna Maria Island, sunrise-10pm daily, free) has great views, picnic pavilions, picnic tables, grills, a playground, and shower/toilet facilities, right along the waterfront.

## ANNA MARIA ISLAND HISTORICAL MUSEUM

The small main building of the **Anna Maria Island Historical Museum** (402 Pine Ave., Anna Maria Island, 941/778-0492, www.amihs.net, 10am-1pm Tues.-Sat., free, donations encouraged) is somewhat deceptive. The museum complex actually houses three separate buildings, all of which are worth checking out. The main museum lives in a 1920s-era building that was originally the island's icehouse, constructed by the city's first mayor. The few exhibits are smartly curated and well arranged, giving visitors a look at memorabilia, clothing, and archival records from throughout the island's history. Nearby is the **Belle Haven Cracker Cottage,** which was moved intact from its original location a couple of blocks away. The 1920s-era building was originally a fish-packing plant, but, by the late 1990s, it was a dilapidated rental cottage, nearly stripped of its vintage beauty. The Anna Maria Island Historical Society moved the building and restored it to its original charm; it houses even more period antiques, and although not all of them hail from the island, the cottage does give good insight into how some of the island's earliest cracker settlers lived. And then there's the jail: It had bars but no windows. Currently, thanks to a fire in the 1940s, it doesn't have a roof or doors either (and no bars), but it makes a fantastic backdrop for a family photo.

## Beaches

The parking and public access issue on Longboat Key is almost hilariously frustrating. There are nearly a dozen public access points, but they're poorly marked and parking is limited to a small handful of spaces (and they're usually on the opposite side of the road from the actual beach). Do not park along the

road. On the northern side of the island, the **Broadway** (100 Broadway St., Longboat Key) beach access provides the most parking and the easiest access, providing a boardwalk over the dunes to the waterfront. The beach itself is very nice, if a bit crowded.

Almost all of the other public beach accesses are numbered to correspond with their addresses on Gulf of Mexico Drive. (Numbers increase going south to north.) On-site parking is available for **#3175** and **#3355,** and the accesses at **#3495, #4711,** and **#4795** offer on-site disabled parking as well. Please keep in mind that, although these beaches offer parking, it is *very* limited. Nonetheless, if you get here early enough to snag a spot, you'll be rewarded with a beach that's somewhat wilder than the ones found elsewhere in the area. Although the famed white sand and calm blue waters are in abundance, these are dune beaches, bounded by tall lines of sea oats that provide something of a barrier between you and the traffic whizzing by on the road.

Also on the north part of Longboat Key— right before you cross the bridge onto Anna Maria Island—is **Beer Can Island** (sunrise-sunset daily, free). Not so much an actual island as an isolated spit of gorgeous white sand and swaying pine trees, Beer Can Island is a

Beaches on Longboat Key aren't easy to access, but they're worth it.

popular party spot for boaters, and is only accessible by boat.

Beach access on Anna Maria Island—especially in the town of Bradenton Beach—is a breeze. Almost as soon as you cross the bridge from Longboat onto Anna Maria, you'll be greeted by the sight of the massive parking lot that serves **Coquina Beach** (sunrise-sunset daily, free). This lot also provides parking for the many anglers that come to the site to fish on the bayside, so even if the lot seems crowded, the beautiful gulf-side beach is often blissfully low-density. Amenities include lifeguards, a small concession stand, and bathroom/shower facilities.

Coquina Beach segues somewhat seamlessly into the more northerly **Cortez Beach** (sunrise-sunset daily, free), which doesn't provide such a singularly large parking area but instead offers multiple access points with generous and easily found lots. Both of these beaches are a little rougher than some of the other Gulf beaches—the sand is packed tighter and doesn't have the same "snowdrift" quality of the beaches on Siesta Key and Longboat Key. Regardless, the sky-scraping pine trees and expansive swaths of sand provide a spectacular backdrop.

Getting to the beach is a little tougher in the towns of Anna Maria and Holmes Beach, thanks to the increased number of residences that line the Gulf. **Manatee Beach Park** (400 State Rd. 64, Holmes Beach, Anna Maria Island, sunrise-sunset daily, free) is a popular and easily accessed park. It can get very crowded, thanks to its copious amenities—there are bathrooms and showers, of course, but also a playground, a café and gift shop, and lots of picnicking space.

For something far more isolated, head to the very northern end of Anna Maria Island, where **Bean Point** (N. Shore Dr., Anna Maria Island, sunrise-sunset daily, free) awaits you. There is marked foot access at Fern Street and Gladiolus Street, and only limited roadside parking is available. Bean Point marks the intersection of Tampa Bay and the Gulf of Mexico, and normally such a confluence of bodies of water would mean a tempestuous and rip-current-prone area, but the waters of Bean Point are remarkably calm, especially close to the shore. The sands are dense with shells, and the rough foliage of the dunes provides plenty of nesting opportunities for birds and other small wildlife. It's a beautiful and calm beach spot.

## Sports and Recreation
### BOATING
For full-service boat rentals, head for **Cannons Marina** (6040 Gulf of Mexico Dr., Longboat Key, 941/383-1311, http://cannons. com, half-day rentals from $175). It has half-day, full-day, and multi-day rentals of a wide variety of fishing boats as well as sport and ski boats.

**Anna Maria Sailing and Boat Rides** (Anna Maria Island, 941/580-1502, www.annamariasailing.com, from $50/person) departs from Bradenton Beach's Municipal Pier on Bridge Street with five different types of sailing excursions. Their most popular are their two sunset cruises, a three-hour cruise designed for larger groups ($40/person, drinks included) and another, more intimate, four-hour trip for couples ($150/couple, meal included). They also offer full-day tours ($110/ person, meal included) and a more economical three-hour trip in the daytime ($30/ person).

### GOLF
The only option for golf on Longboat Key is the **Longboat Key Club & Resort** (220 Sands Point Rd., Longboat Key, 941/387-1632, $82 for greens and cart fees). The course is private and only available for use by resort guests.

### BIKE RENTALS
Longboat Key is an ideal spot for long bike rides, and the friendly folks at **Backyard Bike Shop** (5610 Gulf of Mexico Dr., Longboat Key, 941/383-5184, from $25/day) have bike rentals available. (If you've brought your own

bike, they also service bicycles.) Additionally, kayaks are available for rent.

## Entertainment and Events
### NIGHTLIFE

Due to the overwhelmingly residential nature of Longboat Key, there's not much in the way of nightlife on the island. However, **The Haye Loft** (5540 Gulf of Mexico Dr., Longboat Key, 941/387-0495, www.euphemiahaye.com, 6pm-11pm daily, no cover) is the "bar and dessert room" of the Euphemia Haye restaurant, offering a limited selection of noshes from the main restaurant's menu (flatbreads, appetizers) and desserts, as well as a full liquor bar and live jazz on the weekends. It's a tiny space, with seating preference given to customers from the restaurant.

The sidewalks on Anna Maria Island tend to roll up around 10pm. (Please keep in mind that drinking on the beach is strictly verboten.) Still, **Slim's Place** (9701 Gulf Dr., Anna Maria Island, 941/567-4056, http://slimsplaceami.com, 11am-2am daily, no cover) tends to stay open a bit later. There are pool tables and a ton of TVs, making it a good option for watching the game or starting a game of your own. The drink menu is beer and wine only.

### FESTIVALS AND EVENTS

There are two main annual festivals on Anna Maria Island, and both of them are arts festivals. **Winterfest** (941/778-2099, www.islandartleague.org) happens in December, and **Springfest** (941/778-2099, www.islandartleague.org) occurs in March. Dozens of local and regional arts vendors turn out for both festivals, offering handcrafted goods and a wide variety of visual art. Both festivals feature music, entertainment, and food, with proceeds supporting the local arts center and a scholarship fund.

## Shopping

A handful of locally owned boutiques, restaurants, and art galleries make up **The Centre Shops** (5370 Gulf of Mexico Dr., Longboat

Key). For necessities, the **Avenue of Flowers** (525 Bay Isles Pkwy., on the southern end of Longboat Key) has a large and well-stocked Publix grocery store, a drugstore, and a couple of clothing stores.

The best shopping on Anna Maria Island can be found in the Historic Bridge Street area of Bradenton Beach. **The Back Alley** (121 Bridge St., Anna Maria Island, 941/778-1800, http://backalleygifts.com, 8am-5pm Mon.-Thurs., 8am-7pm Fri.-Sat., 10am-5pm Sun.) is a local artists' haven, with work on display (and for sale) as well as a gift shop; they also offer classes and have a coffee shop on-site.

## Food
### CAFÉS

**Ginny & Jane E's Bakery Café** (9807 Gulf Dr., Anna Maria Island, 941/778-3170, www.annamariacafe.com, 7am-4pm daily, main courses from $6) is exactly what it sounds like—an old grocery store repurposed into a comfortable, casual café. Breakfast and coffees are the specialty, with excellent homemade pastries on offer as well as standard eggs-and-bacon dishes. And, as it's located in the old IGA grocery store building, there's even a store here, selling AMI artisans' goods, making it something of a locals-only version of a Cracker Barrel.

### AMERICAN

**Slim's Place** (9701 Gulf Dr., Anna Maria Island, 941/567-4056, http://slimsplaceami.com, 11am-2am daily, main courses from $7) is more of a bar with a great menu than it is a restaurant with a good bar. The pool tables and TVs make that pretty clear when you walk in. Still, dishes like lobster macaroni-and-cheese, thick portobello mushroom burgers, and fish tacos mean it's exactly the right sort of casual dining spot folks often feel the need for when at the beach.

### EUROPEAN

Restaurant options in Longboat Key are somewhat limited, but the choices that are there are generally excellent. ★ **Maison Blanche**

(2605 Gulf of Mexico Dr., Longboat Key, 941/383-8088, www.maisonblancherestaurants.com, 5:30pm-9:30pm Tues.-Sun., main courses from $31) is a superlative French restaurant, boasting a Michelin-starred chef and a beautiful, minimalist dining room. Unsurprisingly, the fare tends toward modern interpretations of French classics, with an emphasis on local seafood. Reservations are imperative, even in the slow season, as foodies from downtown Sarasota are frequent visitors.

Vegetarians won't have much luck at **Old Hamburg Schnitzel Haus** (3246 E. Bay Dr., Anna Maria Island, 941/778-1320, 5pm-9pm Tues.-Sat., main courses from $16). Veal, beef, pork, and schnitzels, along with bratwurst and other sausages, make up the bulk of the (obviously) German menu, alongside standard sides like sauerkraut and spaetzle. Portions are atypically moderate for those who may be used to gorging themselves in biergartens elsewhere. There's a decent selection of German wines and beers, as well as desserts.

### NEW AMERICAN

**Euphemia Haye** (5540 Gulf of Mexico Dr., Longboat Key, 941/383-3633, www.euphemiahaye.com, 6pm-11pm daily, main courses from $23) is situated in a repurposed cottage

that dates back to the 1940s, resulting in an atmosphere that's instantly inviting and comfortable. Though cozy, Euphemia Haye still delivers an exceptional dining experience, building "standard" dishes—filet mignon, chicken Florentine, beef noisettes, fettuccini al pesto—out of high-quality, locally sourced ingredients. All the fish and seafood on the menu is from the area, and Euphemia Haye makes all of its bread, desserts, stocks, and soups in-house.

**Eat Here** (5315 Gulf Dr., Anna Maria Island, 941/778-0411, www.eathere-ami.com, 5pm-10pm daily, main courses from $13) dishes up fine-dining fare in a casual, gastropub atmosphere, making for a fantastic addition to Holmes Beach's dining scene. Located in an off-beach commercial district, the restaurant features an inventive menu that combines classic meat and seafood preparations with bistro selections like "lobstercargot" (lobster chunks prepared in a butter sauce à la escargot) and foie gras on brioche bread pudding. Dishes are available as small plates and standard entrée-size, which makes it possible for a small group to dig into a variety of different dishes, although such sampling can get pricey.

In the town of Anna Maria, **The Sign of**

Euphemia Haye is a cozy, upscale dining option on Longboat Key.

the **Mermaid** (9707 Gulf Dr., Anna Maria Island, 941/778-9399, www.signofthemermaidonline.com, 7am-10pm Wed.-Sun., 5pm-10pm Mon.-Tues., main courses from $14) is one of the best dining options, open for breakfast, lunch, and dinner (and brunch on Sundays). The menu is diverse and extensive, incorporating Asian, European, and Floridian specialties. Seafood and steak are the go-to items, but make sure to try some of the specialty appetizers, like the baked brie with orange blossom honey.

### SEAFOOD

For something on the casual side, check out the **Lazy Lobster** (5530 Gulf of Mexico Dr., Longboat Key, 941/383-0440, www.longboatkeylazylobster.com, 4pm-9pm daily, main courses from $24) for seafood dinners and early-bird specials.

With stunning views of the Gulf, the **Beachhouse** (200 Gulf Dr. N., Anna Maria Island, 941/779-2222, 11:30am-10pm daily, lunch from $9, dinner from $15) specializes in fresh seafood, but it's really the views of the Gulf that make this place so special. Heck, you won't even notice your table is plastic when the sunset happens.

More incredible vistas can be had at the **Bridge Street Bistro** (111 Gulf Dr. S., Anna Maria Island, 941/782-1122, www.bridgestreetbistroonline.com, 5pm-9pm daily, main courses from $14), which also focuses on seafood, boasting inventive preparations and an intimate atmosphere.

### BARBECUE

Holmes Beach is home to one of my favorite restaurants on Anna Maria Island. ★ **Mr. Bones** (3007 Gulf Dr. N., Anna Maria Island, 941/778-6614, www.mrbonesbbq.com, 11am-9pm daily, main courses from $7) solves the age-old quandary faced in my house—when you love barbecue, but the rest of your family members are vegetarians exhausted by the corn-on-the-cob and french fries that function as the "meat-free selections" at most 'cue joints. Mr. Bones serves up ribs, wings, and

brisket sandwiches, but they also have a dizzying selection of other items such as Tex-Mex, Indian dishes, subs, salads, and curried rice. They also have takeout.

## Accommodations

If you're a golfer, you'll want to book a room at the **Longboat Key Club & Resort** (301 Gulf of Mexico Dr., Longboat Key, 941/383-8821, www.longboatkeyclub.com, doubles from $237), as its golf course is the only one on the island, and is only available for use by club members and resort guests. There's much more to the 218-room resort than the links, though: The accommodations and amenities are fairly upscale, from the six restaurants and private beach to the enormous spa facilities. All of the rooms have modern and classy furniture that echoes the waterfront locale. Flatscreen TVs, marble-topped kitchenette areas, in-room music players, and private balconies are standard in all guest rooms, and there are also one- and two-bedroom suites available.

Far more cozy and laid-back are the 11 efficiency-style rooms at the **Sandpiper Inn** (5451 Gulf of Mexico Dr., Longboat Key, 941/383-2552, www.sandpiperinn.com/FL, doubles from $125 with significant rate reductions for non-peak season or stays longer than one night), on the southern end of the key. Two of the rooms are two-bedroom units, while the rest are one-bedrooms with king-size beds. Only two of the rooms are gulf-front, but all are clean and quiet, with relatively new furnishings and appliances.

The absolute best way to experience Anna Maria Island is by renting a cottage or apartment. Although there are several great hotel-style options on the island, settling into a house for a week or so really allows you to fall into the laid-back pace of the island. **Anna Maria Island Accommodations** (5604B Marina Dr., Holmes Beach, Anna Maria Island, 941/779-0773, www.annamariaparadise.com, from $800/week) has an extensive selection of rental properties in Bradenton Beach, Holmes Beach, and Anna Maria. Cute and character-rich one-bedroom rentals with a pool are available for as little as $700/week, or you can splurge on a beachfront five-bedroom for $7,000/week. (Just remember: Even though you may not be right *on* the beach, you're never very far from the water on AMI.) Anna Maria Island Accommodations offers incredible discounts of up to 20 percent for rentals longer than 28 days.

If you're going to be on the island for less than a week, the **Harrington House Bed and Breakfast** (5626 Gulf Dr., Anna Maria Island, 941/778-5444, www.harringtonhouse. com, doubles from $179) in Holmes Beach is a great option, offering 26 uniquely appointed guest rooms right on the beach.

## INFORMATION AND SERVICES
### Visitor Information

The local visitors bureau operates the official **Sarasota County Visitor Information Center** (14 Lemon Ave., 941/957-1877, www. sarasotafl.org, 10am-4pm Mon.-Sat.) in downtown Sarasota, and they provide information for all of the local islands.

### Media

The Sarasota *Herald-Tribune* (www.herald-tribune.com) and *Bradenton Herald* (www.bradenton.com) are the two daily newspapers, with the *Herald-Tribune* offering the most extensive coverage.

## GETTING THERE AND AROUND
### Getting There

Siesta Key is about 15 minutes south of downtown Sarasota via a six-mile drive along the Tamiami Trail, while the southern tip of Longboat Key is about 10 minutes away from downtown, via the John Ringling Causeway, which takes you through St. Armands Circle and Lido Key. County Road 789 is the main road that runs through the entirety of Longboat Key as Gulf of Mexico Drive; once you cross onto Anna Maria Island, its name gets shortened to just Gulf Drive. You can also access Anna Maria Island via Bradenton on Manatee Avenue or Cortez Road.

### Getting Around

Bus and trolley service offered by Sarasota County via **SCAT** (www.scgov.net) covers Siesta Key and Longboat Key, albeit in relatively limited fashion. Manatee County Area Transit operates **MCAT** (www.mymanatee. org) on Anna Maria Island, and, yes, service is also limited. Thankfully, all three islands are quite well set up for bikers and pedestrians, and for those in cars, the tiny number of roads means getting lost is very nearly not an option. (Parking, however, especially near the beaches, is something of a nightmare.) **Lightning Bugz** (http://lightningbugzlsv. com, from $100/day) offers electric-golf-cart rentals on both Siesta Key (5253 Ocean Blvd., 843/478-7945) and Anna Maria Island (5347 Gulf Dr., Holmes Beach, 843/478-7945).

# Venice

Located about a half hour south of Sarasota is the quaint and quiet town of Venice. Many of the buildings are built in a Northern Italian style of architecture, but the visual theme is subtle, and is really only noticeable if you're looking for it. Instead, the excellent, easily accessible beaches and the small-town atmosphere of the downtown area are what draw most visitors. Nearby state parks offer plenty of opportunities for bird-watchers, hikers, and kayakers.

## SIGHTS
### Downtown Venice

Besides the nearby beaches, the biggest attraction in Venice is its cute and compact downtown district. Downtown Venice (www.venicemainstreet.com) manages to radiate small-town charm without draping itself in some sort of hokey sense of nostalgia. Although visitors are warmly welcomed, strolling around the area you definitely get the sense that this small, vibrant area is bustling with the energy of local (and wintertime) residents. Barely three blocks long and one block wide, the downtown area doesn't pack in any sights, per se, but exploring stores like **Venice Olive Oil** (101 W. Venice Ave., 941/483-4200, http://veniceoliveoil.com, 10am-6pm Mon.-Sat.), checking the near-kitschy and tourist-friendly shark teeth and dried coral on display at **Sea Pleasures & Treasures** (255 W. Tampa Ave., 941/488-3510, 10am-6pm Mon.-Sat.), or browsing the "shabby chic" decor, attire, and jewelry at **Posh on Palm** (327 W. Venice Ave., 941/786-1008, www.poshonpalm.com, 10am-5pm Mon.-Sat.) is good for a half-day stroll. Grab a bite to eat at one of the local eateries, and maybe you'll want to stick around for a performance at the **Venice Theatre** (140 W. Tampa Ave., 941/488-1115, www.venicestage.com), one of the largest community theaters in the United States.

### Oscar Scherer State Park

Near the town of Osprey, about halfway between Venice and Sarasota, is **Oscar Scherer State Park** (1843 S. Tamiami Trail, Osprey, 941/483-5956, www.floridastateparks.org/oscarscherer, 8am-sunset daily, $5/car with

Downtown Venice offers shopping and strolling.

# Venice

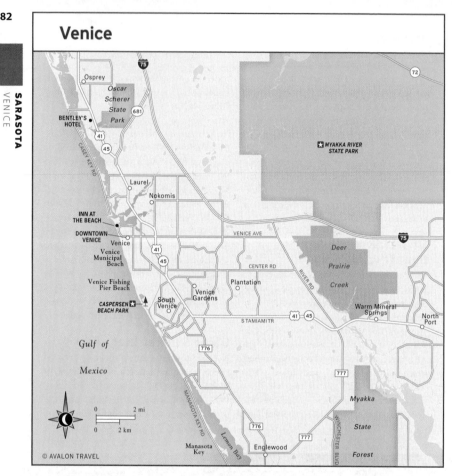

2-8 people, $4/single-occupant vehicle). With beautiful Lake Osprey as the heart of the park, Oscar Scherer is blissfully underdeveloped. Although there are picnic areas (the one at Lake Osprey is usually the busiest), a playground, and a visitors center with an interpretive nature exhibit, the real reason folks come here is for the trails that wend through the dense expanses of scrub-pine forest. There are six different hiking trails, 15 miles of bike trails, and excellent kayaking and canoeing opportunities along South Creek. Fishing and swimming in Lake Osprey are also popular activities. Primitive and RV campsites are available. It can get a little crowded in parts during the busy season and on weekends, but it's incredibly easy to leave the people behind and head out for some scrub jay viewing.

## Myakka State Forest

There are nearly 8,600 acres of flatwood forest in the **Myakka State Forest** (2000 S. River Rd., Englewood, 941/460-1333, 8am-sunset daily, $2/person), making it an ideal destination for hikers, trail bikers, and campers. (Horseback riders and even hunters are welcome, too.) The developed areas of the park are nice and accessible, but they are dwarfed by the sheer expanse of the wild acreage that falls within the forest's boundaries. The forest's two loop trails are part of the state's equestrian Trailtrotter and hiking Trailwalker programs, and are well marked and maintained. Thanks to the 2.5 miles of the Myakka River that cut through the forest, there's also ample opportunity for canoeing and kayaking. Registration is required for all campers (sites are primitive).

## BEACHES

Venice is home to several excellent beaches, all but one of which are very easy to access. The Gulf waters are beautiful and clear blue, and although the sand isn't of the same white-powder consistency as at many other Gulf beaches, it's still soft and clean.

### Venice Municipal Beach

The city-owned **Venice Municipal Beach** (westernmost end of W. Venice Ave., sunrise-sunset daily, free) is incredibly close to downtown and has ample parking. Amazingly, though, it never seems to get overcrowded, due mainly to the vast and wide expanse of sand that's available for sunbathing. There are volleyball courts, a picnic area, and a concession area. Bonus: It's a nonsmoking beach, with the city ordinance enforced both by lifeguards and local beach cops.

### Venice Fishing Pier Beach

South of downtown is the **Venice Fishing Pier Beach** (1600 Harbor Dr. S., sunrise-sunset daily, free), located, logically enough, alongside the city's scenic 740-foot fishing pier, in Brohard Park. It can get pretty crowded, but the beach is beautiful, and there are restaurants and shops nearby catering both to beachgoers and anglers. There's also a dog-friendly beach at the park.

### ★ Caspersen Beach Park

**Caspersen Beach Park** (4100 Harbor Dr. S., sunrise-sunset daily, free) is the most natural and secluded beach in the Venice area. There are no lifeguards, although there are restrooms, a picnic area, and a gorgeous boardwalk/nature trail. This is one of the best spots in the area to hunt for prehistoric shark teeth and shells, thanks to the relatively vital tidal action. ("Relatively" is the operative term. This is the Gulf, after all, where tides are much calmer than either the Atlantic or Pacific Ocean.) Despite its beauty, Caspersen is one of the less-popular beaches in the area, probably due to its somewhat isolated location south of town; still, it's well worth the 15-minute drive from downtown Venice.

## FESTIVALS AND EVENTS

The beaches in Venice are well-known as good places to find shark teeth, and the **Venice Shark's Tooth Festival** (120 E. Airport Ave., 941/412-0402, www.sharkstoothfest. com, Apr.) is an appropriate celebration of that fact. The three-day festival takes place at the Airport Festival Grounds, with live music; arts, crafts, and food vendors; and, of course, folks showing off fossils and shark choppers.

There's something of a tradition in South Florida of communities hosting big local festivals just before or just after "Snowbird Season." In Venice, the **Venice Sun Fiesta** (941/416-5267, http://sunfiesta.net, mid-Oct.) happens downtown just before the northern retirees arrive for the winter, and the three-day festival—a 40-year tradition, sponsored by the Venice Women's Sertoma Club—features such wholesome activities as a pancake breakfast, bed races, a parade, and the Miss Sun Fiesta Pageant.

The **Sarasota Chalk Festival** (Venice Airport Fairgrounds, www.chalkfestival. com, early Nov., free) may sound like the sort of quaint, family-friendly event that peppers the calendar of small cities across America, but this temporary outdoor exhibition has become a weeklong highlight of the area's cultural calendar, bringing in street artists from all over the world and drawing more than 200,000 visitors. The festival, relocated from downtown Sarasota to Venice, focuses mainly on internationally renowned street artists, who craft elaborate and often quite huge works (some as big as 180 square feet), all of which disappear at the end of the festival in a massive washdown. Beyond the chalk art, there are also arts and craft vendors, food, and live music.

## FOOD

**Luna Ristorante** (200 St. Augustine Ave., 941/412-9898, http://lunapizzavenice.com, 11am-9pm daily, pizzas from $12, main courses from $18) is best known for its pizza, but this Italian restaurant is also a popular before-theater spot (the Venice Theatre is just around the corner), and it boasts some great alfresco seating and an extensive menu of Italian standards. Service can sometimes lag, and the restaurant is cash-only, but the portions are family-style huge. There's also a location near the beach.

A great café experience can be found at **Upper Crust Cafe & Bakery** (213 W. Venice Ave., 941/244-0430, 8am-5pm Mon.-Sat., 8am-noon Sun., main courses from $7). Although their selections are a little pricey—probably due to their use of organic ingredients—this is one of the best places in Venice to grab breakfast. Omelets, French toast, bagels, and eggs-and-bacon dishes are available. But it's the pastries and scones that come out of the bakery that make Upper Crust worth the high-season wait. Lunch is also available.

Despite Venice's proximity to the beach, the best meal-with-a-view in town can be had at **Dockside Waterfront Grill** (509 N. Tamiami Trail, 941/218-6418, 11am-9pm Sun.-Thurs., 11am-10pm Fri.-Sat., main courses from $14), which sits among the marinas on the south end of Roberts Bay. Seafood and pasta dishes are superb here, but the views and lively bar scene are even better.

## ACCOMMODATIONS
### Venice

The best hotel option in Venice is the ★ **Inn at the Beach** (725 W. Venice Ave., 941/484-8471, www.innatthebeach.com, doubles from $219). It's very conveniently located right next to the Venice Municipal Beach, which also makes downtown highly accessible. There are only about 50 rooms at this reconstituted motel, but all of them are incredibly clean and well-maintained. Room rates are reasonable in high season and amazingly affordable in low season, making it a great option for families visiting the beach during the summer. (In addition to standard rooms, they have a handful of suites.) Getting a decent beachfront motel room for a song is probably enough for

The Inn at the Beach is a great option if you want to be near the coast.

most folks, but the staff is extremely friendly, and amenities like continental breakfast and Internet access are thrown in for free, making the Inn at the Beach a no-brainer first choice for most visitors to the area.

If the beach isn't on your agenda, the **Island Breeze Inn** (340 S. Tamiami Trail, 941/488-4417, www.islandbreezeinn.com, doubles from $109) is right on the Tamiami Trail very close to downtown. This 1950s-era motel is well-maintained and clean, although its public areas are somewhat cluttered. Still, that clutter is more charming than bothersome, and the guest rooms—standard rooms and efficiencies—are tidy and tropical, if not huge. All the rooms have microwaves and mini-fridges, and Internet access is available. There's a nice pool area, and the grounds are lushly landscaped.

## Outside Venice

Out near Oscar Scherer State Park is **Bentley's Hotel** (1660 S. Tamiami Trail, Osprey, 941/966-2121, www.bentleyssarasota. com, doubles from $119), a great option for those planning on spending most of their time in the area exploring the park or wanting to split their time between Venice and Sarasota. This family-owned property offers spacious rooms with modern decor and comfortable beds. It's a surprisingly stylish place, given its relatively out-of-the-way location and affordable room rates. The hotel restaurant, Morgan's, is quite good, and the poolside tiki bar is a great spot to relax.

About a half hour east of downtown, right on the Myakka River, is **Camp Venice Retreat** (4085 E. Venice Ave., 941/488-0850, www.campvenice.com, RVs from $73/night, tents from $46/night, cabin rentals from $85/ night). The blissfully quiet waterfront location makes it an ideal getaway for campers— of both the primitive and RV-driving style. There are more than 100 RV hookup sites, all of which are situated in a gorgeously tree-shaded area, and some of which are right on the water; all sites offer electricity, water, and waste facilities. Nested in its own isolated

and shaded waterfront spot is the tent-camping area, which offers sites with water/electric hookups as well as a handful of primitive sites. There are also basic cabins available (no kitchen or bathroom in the cabins); the cabins have beds but you must bring your own linens. Showers and bathrooms are nearby. Almost all of the public areas of the park have Wi-Fi access, and there's also a main recreational area with a heated pool. Most guests are here to enjoy the natural solitude, taking to the nature trails or renting a canoe to explore the Myakka River. Even though Camp Venice is popular among RVers, the retreat has a much more relaxed and pastoral vibe than most RV parks.

## INFORMATION AND SERVICES

The **Venice Area Chamber of Commerce** (597 S. Tamiami Trail, 941/488-2236, www. venicechamber.com) is a good resource for information on local shops and events, although it's not a visitors bureau per se.

The Sarasota *Herald-Tribune* (www.heraldtribune.com) is the best and biggest newspaper in the area. More local news can be found in the *Venice Gondolier Sun* (www. yoursun.com), which has a coverage area that also extends south to Englewood and Punta Gorda.

## GETTING THERE AND AROUND
### Getting There

**Sarasota-Bradenton International Airport** (SRQ, 6000 Airport Circle, 941/359-2770, www.srq-airport.com) is in northern Sarasota and is the largest airport close to Venice, with limited service from Delta, United, American, JetBlue, and several charter services. Both **Southwest Florida International Airport** (RSW, 11000 Terminal Access Rd., Fort Myers, 239/590-4800, www.flylcpa.com) in Fort Myers and **Tampa International Airport** (TPA, 4100 George J. Bean Pkwy., 813/870-8700, www. tampaairport.com) offer a much wider array of airlines, but each is nearly 90 minutes away from Venice. (The drive to RSW is prettier, if that helps you make up your mind.) **Venice Municipal Airport** (VNC, 150 Airport Ave. E., 941/486-2711) is a general aviation facility just about a mile or so from downtown.

By car, Venice is about a half hour south of Sarasota. The easiest access to Venice is the Tamiami Trail, which runs right through the heart of town. Via I-75, Venice is about two hours from Naples.

Although the historic **Venice Train Depot** (303 E. Venice Ave.) is beautiful to look at, it no longer functions as a train station—the last public train pulled in in 1971—but instead as a bus depot for the county. The nearest Amtrak station is in Tampa, and there are Greyhound depots in Tampa and Fort Myers.

## Getting Around

Downtown Venice is compact and built for pedestrians. However, to get to the beaches or any of the sights beyond the tiny downtown area, you'll probably need a car. Parking is limited downtown, and timing is strictly enforced. Although Sarasota County's bus service **SCAT** (www.scgov.net) operates here, routes are limited. Single-ride rates are $1.25, but you can get unlimited-ride passes for $20/week or $60/month.

# Charlotte Harbor

Look for ★ to find recommended sights, activities, dining, and lodging.

# Highlights

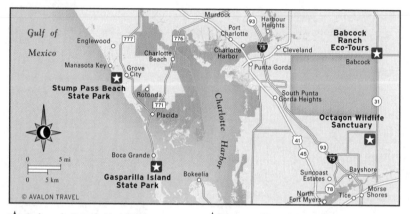

★ **Babcock Ranch Eco-Tours:** There's a lot of ground to cover in the 90,000 acres of the Babcock/Webb Wildlife Management Area, but, thankfully, you can take a tour to get an informative look at the various ecosystems and natural life (page 92).

★ **Octagon Wildlife Sanctuary:** This volunteer-run sanctuary rehabilitates abandoned, abused, and rescued animals. Permanent residents include lions, tigers, horses, monkeys, and bears (page 93).

★ **Gasparilla Island State Park:** The beaches that line the Gulf coast of Gasparilla Island are so beautiful and so unspoiled that there is a whole state park dedicated to them (page 103).

★ **Stump Pass Beach State Park:** This state park is a beach-of-all-trades. You can surf-fish, search for shells along the shoreline, or hike a beautiful trail where you can spot birds and other wildlife (page 103).

# A
s the wide and sparkling Peace River flows into Charlotte Harbor, which itself opens up into the Gulf of Mexico, this portion of southwest Florida is blessed with an abundance of wild and natural beauty.

The small city of Punta Gorda, with its historic downtown area, stands as an example of an ideal waterfront town. Cobblestone streets combined with angler-friendly access to the harbor and the Gulf of Mexico make the city charming and appealing to both upscale travelers and more salt-of-the-earth visitors. Meanwhile, just beyond the city limits are extensive wildlife preserves beloved by bird-watchers and outdoorspeople. Out on Gasparilla Island, the upscale waterfront community of Boca Grande manages to retain its historical, small-town atmosphere while offering a lifestyle—and vacation style—that's both ritzy and low-key, along with some of the best beaches in the state. Englewood gives visitors access to similarly beautiful beaches, but with a much more down-to-earth, beach-town vibe.

## HISTORY

Although Charlotte Harbor is named after Queen Charlotte of 18th-century England, the area's history stretches much further back, and the impact of early settlers and colonists is still felt today.

Some of the earliest residents in the area—from 3,000 years ago—were the Calusa people, who were one of the more dominant tribes along the southwest coast of Florida. Some of the canals that the Calusa dug are still visible in the southern parts of Charlotte Harbor. The Timucua tribe was also present in the area. In the early 16th century, Ponce de León landed in the area, opening the area to Spanish colonization, an effort that was spearheaded by Menéndez de Avilés, who pioneered commercial fishing in the area. In the mid-18th century, the Spanish lost control of Florida to the British (that's when Charlotte Harbor got its name), but it wasn't until after the Civil

---

**Previous:** a dock near Cape Haze; downtown Punta Gorda. **Above:** Fishermen's Village Waterfront Mall in Punta Gorda.

# Charlotte Harbor

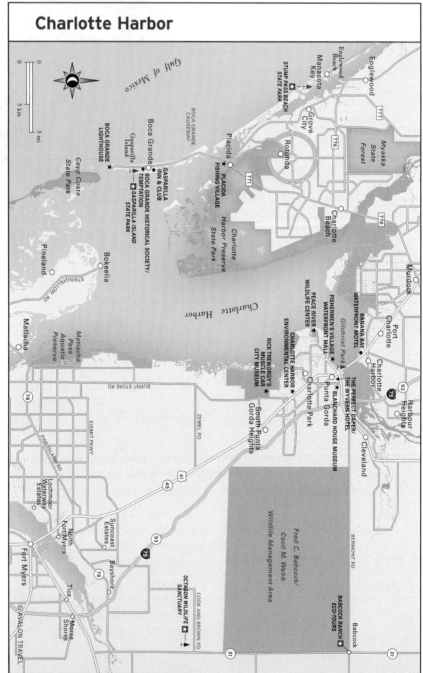

War—some 50 years after the U.S. gained control of Florida—that the region really began to develop.

Initially, the area was developed by pioneering cattle ranchers and brave homesteaders, and by the 1890s, both Punta Gorda and Englewood were established as towns. Along with ranching, fishing and shipbuilding were some of the primary economic drivers of the area, a trend that continued until railroads began bringing visitors who sought to escape the wintry cold of the northern United States. It wasn't until the 1920s, though, when Charlotte County separated from Desoto County, that the area really began to grow. Developer Joel Bean, founder of the El Jobean community, encouraged circuses to make the county their winter home base, a move that helped promote Charlotte County as a unique and fun place to live.

In 2004, during a season of unusually high hurricane activity, Hurricane Charley made landfall in Charlotte County, bringing winds upward of 140 miles per hour and widespread destruction to the area. Much of the region has recovered from this cataclysmic event after a slow but steady process.

## PLANNING YOUR TIME

Most of your time in the Charlotte Harbor area should be focused on the Punta Gorda area and the beach communities in Boca Grande and Englewood. Plan on making Punta Gorda your home base. With a few days, you can take in most of the city's historical waterfront charm and make easy excursions out to Babcock Ranch Eco-Tours and Octagon Wildlife Sanctuary.

For those staying a week or so, give a couple days to the sights of Punta Gorda, and then relax even more by spending the rest of your time in Boca Grande. Birders and hikers should devote a day or so to exploring the natural beauty of Charlotte Harbor Preserve State Park. Baseball fans here for spring training will want to stay close to Port Charlotte.

# Punta Gorda

In 2004, Hurricane Charley nearly wiped Punta Gorda off the map. However, even before then, the small city of about 10,000 people wasn't really in the best of shape. Although the city had always benefited from its enviable position along Charlotte Harbor, the small downtown and general lack of commerce meant that if visitors came, they were probably just interested in fishing and not much more. These days, fishing is still a big draw for folks who come to the area, but thanks to the massive and concentrated rebuilding and revitalization that Punta Gorda underwent in the recovery from Charley, the city is a charming and beautiful vacation spot, with plenty of opportunities for outdoor activities.

## SIGHTS
### Downtown Punta Gorda

Downtown Punta Gorda is only a few blocks wide and a few blocks long, but that compact size makes it quite accessible. Primarily home to restaurants, shops, and, of course, the law firms and offices that make a downtown a "downtown," it doesn't really radiate the sort of idyllic and nostalgic on-the-nose charm that many small-town cores do, but that's part of what makes it so interesting. Punta Gorda doesn't try to be charming—it just is. Take to the pedestrian-friendly sidewalks that line the cobblestone streets and check out the murals depicting various Old Florida scenes on the sides of the downtown buildings; peek into some of the boutiques and shops on the main drags of Marion Avenue and Olympia Avenue (both are one-way streets); and maybe head over to **Laishley Park** (100 Naisbit St.), where there's a beautiful municipal marina, at which you can watch boats come and go along the Peace River.

## Blanchard House Museum of African-American History and Culture of Charlotte County

Located just a few, easily walkable blocks from the heart of downtown is the **Blanchard House Museum** (406 Martin Luther King Blvd., 941/575-7518, www.blanchardhousemuseum.us, 10am-4pm Tues.-Fri. late Sept.-late May, free). Originally built in 1925 as a home for Joseph Blanchard, an African American steamboat pilot who was heavily involved in Punta Gorda's early-20th-century growth, the museum houses a small collection of material relating to the history of African Americans throughout Charlotte County, as well as, of course, Blanchard himself. The house itself—a beautiful blue bungalow—is the star attraction.

## Fishermen's Village Waterfront Mall

One of the few truly touristy spots in Punta Gorda, **Fishermen's Village Waterfront Mall** (1200 W. Retta Esplanade, 800/639-0020, http://fishville.com, 10am-8pm Mon.-Sat., noon-6pm Sun.) is an open-air shopping center right on Charlotte Harbor. There are probably two dozen businesses, with the majority focused on selling gifts, crafts, and boutique-type items that toe right up to the line of tourist chintz but still manage to avoid being completely tacky. There are also several good, if predictable, restaurants. The main attraction at the mall is window-shopping and maybe grabbing a bite to eat or a drink while taking in some fabulous views of the harbor, but **King Fisher Fleet** (941/639-0969, http://kingfisherfleet.com, same hours as the mall) is based here, and offers sightseeing cruises of the harbor and out to Cabbage Key and Cayo Costa State Park (from $36.95/person) as well as fishing charters (from $350/half-day for 1-3 people). Additionally, **Holidaze Boat Rentals** (941/505-8888, http://holidazeboatrental.com) offers kayak rentals (from $15/hour) and motorboat rentals (from $60/hour).

## Peace River Wildlife Center

Nestled into a blink-and-you'll-miss-it corner of the parking lot of City Beach Park, the **Peace River Wildlife Center** (3400 Ponce de Leon Pkwy., 941/637-3830, www.peaceriverwildlifecenter.com, 11am-4pm daily, tours free, donations accepted) is a must-visit for bird lovers. The nonprofit, donations-dependent center is primarily a facility for caring for and rehabilitating wild birds and other small animals. More than 2,000 animals are admitted into the facility annually, cared for, and released back into the wild. There are also more than 200 animals who call the center their permanent home. A couple of regal bald eagles, red-tailed hawks, owls, pelicans, and other impressive birds live in cages in the tiny, walk-through area of the center. It's a quick stop—you can be in and out in less than five minutes. By visiting (and donating!), you'll be helping the staff maintain not just the viewing facilities but also the all-important work they do in their hospital.

## ★ Babcock Ranch Eco-Tours

It's quite a drive to get to **Babcock Ranch Eco-Tours** (8000 State Rd. 31, 800/500-5583, www.babcockranchecotours.com, 9am-4pm Tues.-Sat. Jan.-Apr., call for summer hours, tours from $24 adults, $23 seniors, $16 children 3-12). No matter where you're coming from, it's out in the middle of nowhere. But, of course, this isolation is intentional. The **Fred C. Babcock/Cecil M. Webb Wildlife Management Area** is a massive, 90,000-acre tract of land, originally cleared in the early 20th century for use by E. V. Babcock's (Fred Babcock's father) timber company. However, unlike many timber barons' clear-cut-then-bail ethos, Babcock's methodology was far more environmentally prescient. After all the sellable timber was harvested from a property Babcock bought, he would turn the land over to the relevant government authorities for use as a nature preserve. The acreage is protected, although it has been used for decades as a cattle ranch.

That ranch is still an active concern, but staring at cows isn't why visitors trek out here every day. The Babcock/Webb Wildlife Management Area includes a variety of ecosystems—from swamp to grassland to flatwood forest. By climbing aboard one of the repurposed (in camouflage) school buses used for ecotours of the ranch, you can see the ecological diversity and also get a well-versed and amiable tour guide to put it all into context. Now, to be clear, guide-driven bus tours are about the last thing on any of our bucket lists, but the folks at Babcock are incredibly knowledgeable about the land, its history, and its two- and four-legged inhabitants. You'll almost certainly see lots of alligators, a huge variety of birds, the ranch's heirloom cattle, and Babcock's resident panther, and maybe even get a peek at some wild hogs. You'll also leave with a much better sense of how wild Florida once was—and, in many places, still is—and why the combination of flora and fauna here is unique.

## ★ Octagon Wildlife Sanctuary

The work that the all-volunteer staff at **Octagon Wildlife Sanctuary** (41660 Horseshoe Rd., 239/543-1130, www.octagon-wildlife.org, 11am-4pm Sat.-Sun., $10 adults, $5 seniors and children, children under 7 free, cash/check only) does is, quite simply, amazing. Although there are many (too many, honestly) places around the state of Florida that take care of abandoned and abused animals, there aren't that many that take on the Herculean task of rehabilitating and housing lions, tigers, monkeys, panthers, horses, and bears. Octagon works closely with animal welfare agencies to rescue exotic critters that are in terrible situations. Almost all of the animals have been subject to some form of abuse. The staff does a marvelous job with their limited resources, is knowledgeable about the animals, and does its best to make Octagon pleasant and comfortable both for visitors and their many permanent residents. Small tables are set up throughout the sanctuary, lining the trails that wind through the animals' cages, so you can have a little picnic with a tiger breathing over your shoulder if you so desire. (Still, it must be said, the smell can get pretty intense; there are a lot of big animals here who eat a *lot* of food.) With its friendly, all-volunteer staff, quirky environment, and obvious dedication to animal welfare, Octagon more than deserves the donation (the price of admission) they ask for at the gate.

Lulu the (stuffed) three-horned cow is the unofficial mascot of Babcock Ranch Eco-Tours.

## Charlotte Harbor Environmental Center

The 20-minute or so trek out to the **Charlotte Harbor Environmental Center** (10941 Burnt Store Rd., 941/575-5435, http://chec-florida.org, 8am-3pm Mon.-Sat., 11am-3pm Sun., free) is well worth the detour for nature lovers or those heading south toward Fort Myers or Cape Coral. The nature center's facilities are pleasant, with a butterfly garden, interpretive center, and a picnic area. But the real attraction is the access to more than 3,000 acres of **Charlotte Harbor Preserve State Park.** There are four miles of well-cleared hiking trails throughout the preserve, and the isolation of the area provides plenty of opportunity for bird-watching.

## Rick Treworgy's Muscle Car City Museum

Also on the way south, **Rick Treworgy's Muscle Car City Museum** (10175 Tamiami Trail, 941/575-5959, www.musclecarcity.net, 9am-5pm Tues.-Sun., $12.50 adults, $6 children, children 2 and under free) is really just about the only truly touristy thing in all of Punta Gorda. Located in a Tamiami Trail strip mall south of downtown, the museum very much lives up to its name, with nearly 200 gas-guzzling, asphalt-chewing reminders of when America built the brawniest and fastest cars in the world. Treworgy is a longtime aficionado and collector of muscle cars, and his love of these vehicles is apparent from their mirror-bright wax jobs to the intelligent way they're displayed. The museum is well stocked with classic GTOs, Corvettes, and Mustangs. Its purview stretches all the way back to the cars of the early 20th century. There's even a 1960s-style diner on-site, serving up breakfast and lunch.

# SPORTS AND RECREATION

The Charlotte Harbor area offers plenty of opportunities for hiking, bird-watching, hunting, or just relaxing in a park.

## Parks

Downtown, **Gilchrist Park** (400 W. Retta Esplanade, 941/575-5050, www.ci.punta-gorda.fl.us, dawn-dusk daily, free) is a truly beautiful park, and a great spot to watch the sun set over Charlotte Harbor. During the day, the 11-acre park is a good destination for active visitors, with tennis courts, a basketball court, and jogging and biking along its sidewalks. Although there's a beach, it's more for

The trails at Charlotte Harbor Preserve State Park are great for day hikes.

# Birding in Charlotte Harbor

**Charlotte Harbor Preserve State Park** is one of the best destinations in Florida for bird-watchers to do their thing, but there are many other excellent birding spots in Charlotte Harbor. In fact, there are more than seven sections of the **Great Florida Birding Trail** (www.floridabirdingtrail.com). The varying ecology in the area—everything from flatwood forests and mangrove swamps to coastal brush and wetlands—means lots of different bird species are year-round residents. But it's the mild winters that bring even more birds here when the temperatures drop up north. January and February are some of the best months to view birds, and dedicated spotters can lay eyes on more than six dozen different species, ranging from vultures and herons to owls, warblers, hawks, and ospreys. Other good birding spots are **Amberjack Environmental Park** (6450 Gasparilla Pines Blvd., Rotonda, 941/764.4360, www.charlottecountyfl.com), **Tippecanoe Environmental Park** (2300 FL- 776, Port Charlotte, 941/625-7529, www.charlottecountyfl.com), and the **Babcock/Webb Wildlife Management Area** (open daily 1.5 hours before sunrise to 1.5 hours after sunset, $3 per person daily-use permit).

strolling than for sunbathing. In 2017, an impressive renovation of the park brought a new seawall, improved walking paths, a dedicated pet area, and upgraded pavilion areas.

**Ponce de Leon Park** (3400 Ponce de Leon Pkwy., 941/575-5050, www.ci.punta-gorda.fl.us, dawn-dusk daily, free) is a pretty great park, thanks to a quarter-mile boardwalk that wends through a thick natural wetland area, a good playground for kids (complete with No Smoking signs—don't smoke, kids!), picnic areas, and fishing piers. Peace River Wildlife Center is directly adjacent, and sunsets here are fantastic. The beach at Ponce de Leon Park is a small sandy area, right next to the Ponce de Leon Inlet, and it's primarily an extension of a boat launch.

## Hiking and Biking

Punta Gorda is currently in the process of developing a trail project dubbed "Ring Around the City." It's been in the works for a few years, and sort of moves along in fits and spurts as money becomes available. The concept behind the Ring is to link various parks and multi-use trails with connectors, so that, eventually, an 18-mile loop around Punta Gorda will be walkable/rideable with no interruption. Currently, the biggest completed elements of the Ring are part of a **Harborwalk** that

connects Fishermen's Village and the downtown area, a **Linear Park** trail in downtown, and two multi-use trails south of downtown.

For a less urban trail experience, head for **Charlotte Harbor Preserve State Park** (12301 Burnt Store Rd., 941/575-5861, http://floridastateparks.org/charlotteharbor, 8am-sundown daily, free). This is one of the best birding spots in all of southwest Florida, and, during the winter, it's almost impossible to not bump into a gaggle of bird-watchers with their binoculars. The preserve itself covers more than 43,000 acres and includes flatwood forests, marshland, and harbor shoreline. Although fishing is allowed, hunting is not. There are three primary trails, each of which is about two miles long and offers a unique look at the varying ecology of the preserve. There are an additional six miles of marked trails at the nearby **Charlotte Harbor Environmental Center** (10941 Burnt Store Rd., 941/575-5435, http://chec-florida.org, 8am-3pm Mon.-Sat., 11am-3pm Sun., free). Although the state park's main entrance is in Punta Gorda, there are also access points in Cape Coral, Cape Haze, El Jobean, Little Pine Island, and Rotonda.

## Fishing

**King Fisher Fleet** (1200 W. Retta Esplanade,

# Spring Training in Charlotte County

Even though the **Tampa Bay Rays** play their home games just an hour or so north in equally temperate St. Petersburg, when spring training time rolls around and the Grapefruit League gets rolling, the Rays pack up all their equipment and head down to play their spring training games in Port Charlotte's **Charlotte Sports Park** (2300 El Jobean Rd., 941/206-4487, http://charlottecountyfl.com, call for event info). Just a 10-minute drive from Punta Gorda, the park is an impressive facility, thanks to a massive renovation project that wrapped up in 2009. The stadium seats more than 7,000 people. When the Rays aren't taking on other MLB teams in the preseason, baseball lovers can catch the Charlotte Stone Crabs, the Rays' Class A Advanced minor-league team.

941/639-0969, http://kingfisherfleet.com, sightseeing cruises from $36.95, fishing charters from $350/half-day for 1-3 people) offers sightseeing cruises and fishing charters. King Fisher operates out of Fishermen's Village with two charter boats designated specifically for deep-sea fishing, a few flats boats for fishing in the shallows, and a big ol' double-decker harbor cruiser for sunset tours and jaunts out to Cayo Costa and other remote beaches.

## ENTERTAINMENT AND EVENTS
### Nightlife

While Punta Gorda isn't much of a party town, a few restaurants, once the dinner hour is over, transform into semi-raucous drinking establishments.

**Celtic Ray** (145 E. Marion Ave., 941/916-9115, http://celticray.net, 11am-2am daily) is, as you probably guessed, an Irish pub, and they serve exceptional food. But if you're not hungry, the Ray is a great place to pop in for a drink; the staff is super-friendly, there are some cool beach-swing seats out front, and they have a craft-beer selection that extends far beyond the expected Guinness and Harp. Similarly, the **Ice House Pub** (408 Tamiami Trail N., 941/575-0866, www.theicehousepub. com, 11am-2am Mon.-Sat., noon-11pm Sun.) is known almost as much for its drinking culture as it is for its skilled kitchen. (In this case, the grub is British, rather than Irish.) While the Ice House is pretty huge—it used to be an

ice factory—the vibe is friendly and surprisingly intimate, although it can get loud.

Live music options in Punta Gorda are fairly limited, but the **Orange House Wine Bar** (320 Sullivan St., 941/305-8233, http://theorangehousewinebar.com, 11am-9pm Tues.-Wed., 11am-10pm Thurs.-Fri., 5:30pm-10pm Sat.) does occasionally host jazz nights (typically on the softer, cooler side of the jazz spectrum), but the main attraction is a small but solidly curated menu of wines by the glass as well as a selection of tapas and appetizer-type dishes that are perfect accompaniments. It's friendly and decidedly un-stuffy.

There is food served at **TT's Tiki Bar** (33 Tamiami Trail, 941/637-6770, 11am-10pm Sun.-Thurs., 11am-midnight Fri., 10am-midnight Sat.), but those sandwiches and pub grub are little more than overpriced rationales to just hang out at this sandy, outdoor seating area, have a couple more drinks, and watch the sunset. It can get fairly crowded during high winter season when sunset happens to fall right at the junction of happy hour and dinner hour, and even though the facilities aren't much to write home about, the location can't be beat and the full bar and cold beer make them easy to overlook.

The cramped and convivial environs of **Shorty's Place** (306 W. Marion Ave., 941/639-2337, 11am-2am daily) don't look like they'd be home to one of the best beer bars in southwest Florida, but that is indeed the case. The selection is dizzyingly awesome; it's not a huge selection, but it's well curated. If the smoking inside gets to you, there's a fantastic covered patio outside, with its own bar, TV, and seating options.

## The Arts

The **Visual Arts Center** (210 Maud St., 941/639-8810, http://visualartcenter.org, 9am-4pm Mon.-Fri. and 10am-2pm Sat. Sept.-May, 10am-2pm Mon.-Fri. June-Aug.) showcases local talent in its galleries and offers classes in multiple disciplines.

The **Charlotte Performing Arts Center** (701 Carmalita St., 941/637-0459, www.thecpac.net, call for ticket info) is the main venue for theater in the area, putting on shows by local performing-arts groups. In addition to groups like the Charlotte Chorale, several local public schools use the center to put on music and theater productions.

## Festivals and Events

The big event on Punta Gorda's annual calendar is the **Punta Gorda Wine & Jazz Festival,** which brings smooth jazz and endless wine and beer to Laishley Park in February. Although jazz snobs may sneer at the festival's lineup, nobody can argue with the beautiful weather and unlimited wine and beer your ticket buys you.

The holidays kick off in Punta Gorda with the **Festival of Lights** (mid-Nov.-Dec. 31) and more than a million lights and holiday decorations at Fishermen's Village.

## SHOPPING

There are plenty of shops in the **Fishermen's Village Waterfront Mall** (1200 W. Retta Esplanade, 800/639-0020, http://fishville.com, 10am-8pm Mon.-Sat., noon-6pm Sun.), and many of them are aimed at tourists. However, there are quite a few clothing stores that may be worth exploring, from the resort flavors of **Caribongo** (941/575-9180) and **Palms on the Pier** (941/575-0361) to the somewhat more elegant styles of **In High Cotton** (941/575-0700). The mall also has gift shops like **Naples Soap Company** (941/916-9260) and **Bella Balsamic & the Pressed Olive** (941/249-3571) alongside the expected kitsch and tchotchke purveyors.

Downtown's business district isn't all that busy, but there are quite a few interesting stores and boutiques worth exploring. **Pomegranate and Fig** (117 W. Marion Ave., 941/205-2333, 10am-5pm Mon.-Fri., 10am-4pm Sat.) is low-key and offers a somewhat whimsical selection of decor items, along with baby clothes, accessories, and gifts. **Sea

Shorty's Place

**Grape Gallery** (113 W. Marion Ave., 941/575-1718, 10am-5pm Mon.-Fri., 10am-4pm Sat.) is a co-op art gallery downtown, displaying paintings, sculptures, jewelry, and other works by local artists.

Just a mile or so south of downtown is **Funkie Junkies** (204 E. McKenzie St., 941/575-9633, http://shopfunkiejunkies.com, 10am-5pm Mon.-Sat., 11am-4pm Sun.), a fantastic and unsurprisingly quirky take on your everyday thrift/consignment store. While there's certainly plenty of weird junk, it's all *interesting* weird junk, and lots of weird non-junk, too. Neither the goods nor the staff are overly precious, and the prices are kept pleasingly low. While you may not find much that you actually need, chances are you'll walk out the door with the perfect thing you'd have never imagined having.

## FOOD
### Quick Bites

One of the best spots in town for a hearty (if not heart-friendly) breakfast is **John Ski's House of Breakfast & Lunch** (502 King St., 941/347-7645, 6am-3pm Mon.-Sat., 7am-2pm Sun., main courses from $7), which, as you may have surmised, also serves lunch. Neither delicacy nor restraint is shown with this menu, which features massive portions of French toast, pancakes, hash browns, bacon (and the other essential breakfast-meat groups), and biscuits-and-gravy, as well as mammoth omelets and any other egg dish you can imagine. Lunch is similarly calorie-dense, with piled-high Reubens and other sandwiches.

For a sweet treat, head to the family-friendly **Cubby's Homemade Ice Cream** (264 W. Marion Ave., 941/637-9600, call for hours). They offer 22 flavors of fresh, hand-dipped ice cream served in a retro-heavy atmosphere. Cubby's also serves a limited selection of sandwiches.

For sundries, beer, wine, snacks, and some surprisingly decent deli fare, head to **Old Town Convenience & Deli** (311 W. Marion Ave., 941/639-3115, oldtownconvenience.com, 6am-6pm daily).

### Seafood

Like so many other cities on the Gulf Coast, Punta Gorda is a haven for seafood lovers. Downtown, the **Laishley Crab House** (100 E. Retta Esplanade, 941/205-5566, www.laishleycrabhouse.com, 11am-9pm Sun.-Thurs., 11am-10pm Fri.-Sat., main courses from $14) is right at Laishley Park Marina, so it

Peace River Seafood & Crab Shack

offers incredible views of Charlotte Harbor. The restaurant itself is enormous, and it can get quite busy on weekend evenings (again, those views!), so you can expect service to be slower then. The menu is quite expansive, with a standard array of boiled/grilled/fried seafood platters alongside sushi, pasta, steak, and sandwiches.

Over at the Fishermen's Village Waterfront Mall is another very popular local seafood joint, **Harpoon Harry's Lounge & Raw Bar** (1200 W. Retta Esplanade, #55, 941/637-1177, http://harpoonharrys.com, 11am-10pm Sun.-Thurs., 11am-2am Fri.-Sat., main courses from $15). Despite the fact that it's the biggest and most popular attraction in a heavily trafficked tourist attraction, Harpoon Harry's manages to deliver decent food and decent service. The vibe is friendly and decidedly of the dockside sports-bar variety.

For a more cozy and authentic seafood experience, head to **Peace River Seafood & Crab Shack** (5337 Duncan Rd., 941/505-8440, 11am-7:30pm Tues.-Sat., main courses from $12). Although it's a few minutes away from downtown and isn't actually on the Peace River (it's about a block away), the renovated Florida cracker-style bungalow exudes charm from every corner of its cramped, cozy dining room. (You'll probably want to grab a table on the covered back porch.) Seafood is incredibly fresh, as the owners are running an operation that's small enough to allow them to deal directly with local fishers to get some of the best stuff right off the boat. From the paper towels on your table to the plastic forks you'll use to eat, Peace River Seafood is a down-home establishment serving up the best seafood.

### New American

★ **The Perfect Caper** (121 E. Marion Ave., 941/505-9009, http://theperfectcaper.com, 4:30pm-9pm Mon.-Tues., 11:30am-9pm Wed., 11:30am-10pm Thurs.-Fri., 4:30pm-10pm Sat., 4pm-10pm Sun., main courses from $25) is one of the best fine-dining experiences in Punta Gorda—and probably in all of Charlotte County. Although the restaurant technically has a "smart casual" dress code, the atmosphere is upscale all the way. Yet, although it's fancy down to its jazzy soundtrack, the staff is friendly and welcoming, and the menu is an accessible blend of American classics, contemporary European cuisine, and Asian spice. Chef Jeanie Rowland is a James Beard Award nominee, and the freshness and diversity of the food show why. Leaning heavily on organic and locally grown ingredients, Rowland whips up a menu that offers everything from fried chicken and filet mignon to pork belly tacos and curried shrimp.

If you feel like getting out of the downtown core but not too far away, **Torch Bistro** (2113 Tamiami Trail, 941/575-3505, http://torchbistro.com, lunch 11:30am-2pm Mon.-Fri., dinner 4:30pm-9pm Mon.-Sat., main courses from $17) is just a five-minute drive away, located in a commercial area surrounded by car dealerships. Whatever Torch is lacking in external atmosphere, however, is more than made up for once you step through the doors. The ambience is modern and stylish, and the menu is an appropriate combination of forward-looking preparations and well-plated classics. Grab a drink at the martini bar first—they specialize in rumtinis. Then decide if you want to indulge in Torch's sushi bar selections or their dinner menu, which ranges from chicken potpie and pot roast to osso bucco and roast duck. Sides like yucca fries and brown-sugar-glazed plantains help add even more diversity to the selections.

## ACCOMMODATIONS

Conveniently enough, most of the choices for accommodations in the area are centrally located in the compact downtown core of Punta Gorda. Even better? They all command fantastic waterfront views of Charlotte Harbor.

★ **The Wyvern Hotel** (101 E. Retta Esplanade, 941/639-7700, www.thewyvernhotel.com, doubles from $249) is both the newest and the nicest of the batch. Standing six stories high, it may not be the tallest building in Punta Gorda, but when you're in the rooftop bar/pool area, it sure feels that way, as you'll be able to take in uninterrupted vistas of either the harbor or downtown Punta Gorda. It is, without a doubt, the best place in town to watch the sunset. Rooms are crisply modern and incredibly comfortable, with flat-screen TVs, broadband access, luxurious bathrooms (with tubs and showers separated from each other), and ridiculously comfortable beds. Minibars, in-room safes, and customized bathrobes round out the upscale touches, which makes it all the more surprising how affordable the rooms are.

Another stylish addition to downtown Punta Gorda is the **Four Points by Sheraton Punta Gorda Harborside** (33 Tamiami Trail, 941/637-6770, www.fourpointspuntagordaharborside.com, doubles from $149). The rooms are decorated in a clean and contemporary fashion, with European-style furnishings and a bright and open feel. There are flat-screen TVs and free Wi-Fi in every room. Although the standard king-size rooms are quite spacious, the one-bedroom suites offer lots of room to stretch out. Make sure to spring for a room with a view of the marina.

Just a couple of blocks away is the **PG Waterfront Hotel & Suites** (300 W. Retta Esplanade, 941/639-1165, http://pgwaterfront.com, doubles from $110). After spending decades as a typical, budget-range motel from Punta Gorda's pre-revitalization era, this former Best Western property got new owners and a new look in 2013. While the motel is still, well, a motel—the low-slung, midcentury architecture will be instantly familiar—it's modern enough, with flat-screen TVs, mini-fridges, microwaves, and reasonably stylish furnishings. The property is right on the river, and it features an on-site restaurant, and free Wi-Fi.

For a better budget option, cross the bridge from downtown Punta Gorda to Port Charlotte. Just on the other side of Charlotte Harbor is the **Banana Bay Waterfront Motel** (23285 Bayshore Rd., 941/743-4441, doubles from $135), a family-owned resort, known almost as much for its cozy and affordable rooms and friendly staff as it is for its tiki parties and karaoke nights. If you're here in the winter, prepare to share the pool with flocks of partying snowbirds. The rooms are small, tidy, and well maintained; all are efficiencies with kitchenettes. Pets are welcome (for a small surcharge), and impressive discounts are available on weekly stays.

The Wyvern Hotel offers upscale lodging in Punta Gorda.

## INFORMATION AND SERVICES

The **Southwest Florida Visitors Center** (26600 Jones Loop Rd., 941/639-0007, 6am-11pm daily) is an unofficial source for information, reservations, and discounts. It's right off of I-75.

For an official source, visit the **Punta Gorda/Englewood Beach Visitor and Convention Bureau** (1700 Tamiami Trail, 941/743-1900, www.charlotteharbortravel.com, 8am-5pm Mon.-Fri.).

There is a **post office** (130 E. Marion Ave.) in downtown Punta Gorda. There are branches of Bank of America and SunTrust conveniently located in the downtown core, both with ATMs. There are no drugstores in the downtown area, although there are quite a few just across the bridge in Port Charlotte, as well as along the Tamiami Trail heading south from downtown.

## GETTING THERE AND AROUND

### Getting There

As is the case with almost every other city in this guide, the Tamiami Trail runs right through Punta Gorda, connecting the city with Tampa and Sarasota to the north and Fort Myers, Naples, and Miami to the south. Punta Gorda is also accessible via I-75; take the Jones Loop Road exit to access the southern parts of the city and the U.S. 17 exit to get to downtown.

The closest major airport is **Southwest Florida International Airport** (RSW, 11000 Terminal Access Rd., Fort Myers, 239/590-4800, www.flylcpa.com), about a half hour away in Fort Myers. There is nonstop service into RSW from most major U.S. hubs, and several international charters fly into it as well. Southwest, Delta, United, American, Spirit, Frontier, and JetBlue all fly into RSW.

Bus service via **Greyhound** comes into Port Charlotte at a Mobil station (909 Kings Hwy., Port Charlotte, 941/391-5593, station office open 8am-8pm daily). There is no train service to Punta Gorda.

### Getting Around

TEAM Punta Gorda, a community group founded during the city's post-Charley recovery, has put together a great **bike loaner program** that makes bikes available—for free—all around Punta Gorda. The yellow bikes are pretty easy to spot, and all you need to do to borrow one is check in at one of the host locations (the Wyvern Hotel, Fishermen's Village, Laishley Marina, Charlotte Regional Medical Center, and others), show an ID and a credit card, and return the bike a half hour before sunset. This loaner program is great, because although central Punta Gorda is eminently walkable, the bikes make it very easy to get out of the downtown core without using your car.

However, many of the destinations in the Charlotte Harbor area are beyond the range of a bike, and there's no real public transit to speak of, so a car will be necessary.

# Boca Grande and Englewood

This part of the southwest coast is as wild and barren as it is ritzy and charming as it is sporty and casual. As you head toward Gasparilla Island from Punta Gorda via Port Charlotte, you'll first pass through the tiny fishing village of Placida, a rustic slice of Old Florida. And, within a few minutes after that, as you cross over onto the island itself, you'll be in the enchanting environs of Boca Grande, a low-slung, century-old community that's as thick with moneyed residents as it is blessed by beautiful beaches and early-20th-century charm.

Moving north, away from Gasparilla Island, the empty and quiet expanses of the marshes, beaches, and forests of Cape Haze give way to Englewood, a town that is pleasant and low-key along the beach, where you'll encounter white-sand waterfront and bungalow beach living that almost (almost!) makes you consider relocating here.

## SIGHTS
### Boca Grande Historical Society & Museum

One could make the argument that downtown Boca Grande is something of a history museum of its own. The dusty streets and clapboard buildings give the core downtown area a rustic vibe. Of course, some of those buildings house upscale boutiques and restaurants, and much of the rest of this part of Gasparilla Island is dotted with contemporary condo complexes and vacation homes, but the folks at the **Boca Grande Historical Society** (170 Park Ave., Boca Grande, 941/964-1600, http://bocagrandehistoricalsociety.com, 10am-4pm Mon.-Fri., 10am-2pm Sat., free) are doing their part to preserve and display artifacts and memorabilia that give an impressive perspective of how much—and how little—life on Gasparilla Island has changed over the past century. The museum is located in a building that's something of a museum piece itself. The Teacherage House was part of the Island School, built in the 1920s—it was where the school's teacher lived—and the rest of the school is now the Boca Grande Community Center. As far as exhibits go, the museum is somewhat limited, but the friendly and knowledgeable staff can help put the videos, photographs, and other displays into context.

### Boca Grande Lighthouse

The most prominent historical spot on Gasparilla Island is, logically enough, the **Boca Grande Lighthouse** (880 Belcher Rd., Boca Grande, 941/964-0060, 10am-4pm Mon.-Sat., noon-4pm Sun., call for summer hours, $3 per vehicle), located on the southernmost tip of the island, where Charlotte Harbor opens into the Gulf of Mexico. (There is a beach, but swimming is strongly discouraged due to extremely strong rip currents.) The lighthouse was built in 1890 as a navigational aid for the numerous boats entering and exiting Charlotte Harbor during a period when phosphate mining was one of the dominant industries along the Peace River. In time, a rail line opened to speed the transit of phosphate from inland areas directly to Port Boca Grande, and by the 1960s, the port was one of Florida's busiest, supplying more than half of the nation's phosphate. Eventually, the

the Boca Grande Lighthouse

phosphate industry consolidated its shipping efforts into Tampa Bay, and by the 1980s, most of the boats coming through Port Boca Grande were fishing boats and cruisers.

Conservation efforts led to the lighthouse's complete renovation in the mid-1980s, and a small museum opened in 1998. When most people think of lighthouses, they think of towering beacons reaching into the coastal sky; here, there are two identical, squat buildings set on stilts—one was the keeper's quarters, while the other has an extra little turret on top with the lamp in it. The grounds and picnic area are beautiful, the beach provides incredible vistas, and the museum gives a good overview of the history of the lighthouse and the island.

## Placida Fishing Village

**Placida Fishing Village** (13000 Fishery Rd., Placida) is a great place to catch a sunset, rent a kayak, or charter a fishing boat. Make sure to come by on a Saturday, when the village hosts an arts-and-crafts market, featuring local vendors. But even if you miss the market, this is still a great spot to soak in some Old Florida atmosphere. The village isn't much more than some low-slung houses that are now home to art galleries, a ramshackle marina, and a fish-packing warehouse that splits duty as a seafood shop (Placida Fish Market) and restaurant (The Fishery).

# BEACHES
## ★ Gasparilla Island State Park

Unlike many of the other state park beaches in Florida, **Gasparilla Island State Park** (880 Belcher Rd., Boca Grande, 941/964-0060, 6am-sunset daily, $3 per vehicle, payable in cash at honor box) doesn't actually feel like a state park. There are several different entrances for the park along Boca Grande's Gulf Boulevard, and each offers limited parking, often across the street from a private residential area. So, while some other state park beaches offer seclusion and natural solitude, the beaches of Gasparilla Island State Park feel

more like part of the fabric of the town of Boca Grande. But whatever you may be giving up in pastoral quietude, you're more than making up for in huge, white-sand beaches, gorgeous blue waters, and devastatingly beautiful sunsets. And, thanks to those tiny parking lots and the relatively low population density of Boca Grande, the beaches never really even feel that crowded. The park property also includes the **Boca Grande Lighthouse** (880 Belcher Rd., Boca Grande, 941/964-0060, 10am-4pm Mon.-Sat., noon-4pm Sun., call for summer hours).

## ★ Stump Pass Beach State Park

The three islands that make up **Stump Pass Beach State Park** (900 Gulf Blvd., Englewood, 941/964-0375, www.floridastateparks.org/stumppass, 8am-sunset daily, $3 per vehicle, payable in cash at honor box) offer quite a bit more than just some beautiful beachfront. Surf-fishing is great, and there's a short but beautiful and diverse hiking trail that gets you into areas where it's easy to spot gopher tortoises and different bird species. But, in the end, the beach is the main attraction, and it's easy to understand why. With more than a mile of secluded and quite unspoiled waterfront, Stump Pass offers great shelling opportunities along its coastline. While the beach itself has sand that's a little more brown and coarse than the powdery white stuff commonly associated with this part of the state, the rough and wild surroundings make it a pleasant and peaceful beach escape. There's a pretty big parking lot right next to the main beach, which makes for easy access.

## Englewood Beach

**Englewood Beach** (2100 N. Beach Rd., Englewood, 941/681-3742, 6am-9pm daily, pier open 24 hours, parking $0.75/hr) is one of four beaches in the beach town of Englewood (Stump Pass is one of the others). All four are connected, with their locations on Manasota Key giving each a bit of geographical separation from the others. In reality, you can make your way all along the gulf-front on Manasota Key and always be on "Englewood Beach," but technically speaking, the one bearing the actual name is the main and most accessible of the four. Although it still offers the same combination of white sand and blue waters, it is much busier than the others.

## SPORTS AND RECREATION
### Boating

The last thing you see before you cross the bridge onto Gasparilla Island is **Placida Park Boat Launch** (6499 Gasparilla Rd., Placida, 941/681-3742, parking $0.75/hr). The park, consisting of an ice machine, a dock, and a pretty big parking lot, is the best public place to put in to the water without having to pay to cross the bridge.

**Eldred's Marina** (6301 Boca Grande Causeway, Placida, 941/697-1431) is also on this side of the bridge, offering full services for boaters, a launch ramp, and bait and other supplies.

On Boca Grande proper, several fishing charters depart from the tiny, five-slip **Public Docks** (5th St. and Bayou Ave.), but **Boca Boat Cruises** (888/416-2628, www.bocaboat.com), in addition to full-boat charters (from $590 per half day) also offers tour-guided cruises ranging from 90-minute sunset cruises ($39) to half-day jaunts to Cabbage Key or Useppa Island ($59 with lunch).

### Fishing

There are three fishable aquatic preserves in this area: the **Lemon Bay Aquatic Preserve,** a narrow, mangrove-thick waterway near Englewood; the dense thicket of islands and creeks that make up the **Cape Haze Aquatic Preserve;** and the churning shoals and flatwaters of the **Gasparilla Sound-Charlotte Harbor Aquatic Preserve.** All three areas allow noncommercial fishing and, thanks to their designations as preserves, are fairly wild, allowing anglers to treat

a heron at Stump Pass Beach State Park

themselves to a rustic, backwater retreat. Of course, with three such diverse fishing areas, the kind of fish that are caught vary as well, and one can put everything from trout and redfish to snook and grouper to shark and snapper on a line in this area.

### Hiking and Biking

The **Cape Haze Pioneer Trail** is an eight-mile-long paved multi-use trail that runs along a stretch of a former railroad line that brought phosphate from inland Florida to Port Boca Grande. That sounds like a terrible environment to hike or bike in, but in reality, this trail provides some exceptional views and, in parts, some relative quietude. The main trailhead is at the **Cape Haze Pioneer Trail Park** (941/627-1628), near the intersection of FL-776 (S. McCall Rd.) and Charlotte County CR-771 in Englewood, and runs south, roughly parallel to CR-771 until it intersects with Harness Road, just a few miles north of Placida.

Temptation

CHARLOTTE HARBOR
BOCA GRANDE AND ENGLEWOOD

# FOOD
## Boca Grande

Not only does **The Pink Elephant** (491 Bayou Ave., 941/964-0100, www.the-gasparilla-inn. com, 5pm-9:30pm Mon.-Thurs., 11:30am-9:30pm Fri.-Sun., lunch from $14, dinner from $22) have the best name of any restaurant in Boca Grande, it also may just be the best restaurant on Gasparilla Island. Located in the gorgeous and historic Gasparilla Inn & Club, the Pink Elephant is a visual trip back to Old Florida. The food, on the other hand, comes from an extensive and incredibly modern menu that ranges from Italian seafood stews and thoughtful vegetarian selections to more standard items like barbecue brisket sandwiches and a semi-legendary wedge salad. The inside dining room is a pretty old-school and upscale affair. The patio dining is a little more casual and has beautiful views. Make sure to try "The Hummer," an ice-cream cocktail that easily serves as both nightcap and dessert. There is a dress code.

Running neck and neck with the Pink Elephant as a contender for best restaurant on the island is ★ **Temptation** (350 Park Ave., 941/964-2610, www.temptationbocagrande. com, 11:30am-9:30pm Mon.-Sat., lunch from $11, dinner from $30), a classy, 1950s-styled restaurant that evokes the boozy, white-napkin, steak-and-potato places that used to be shorthand for "upper middle class night on the town." The restaurant wears its retro suit as effortlessly as Don and Betty Draper. Go for some of the ridiculously fresh seafood. Even if you're not hungry, make sure to come by for a drink at the bar; the people-watching is priceless.

For a more casual dining experience, hit up the **Loose Caboose** (434 W. 4th St., 941/964-0440, www.loosecaboose.biz, 11am-4:30pm daily, main courses from $9), a family-friendly, Southern-style restaurant that serves classic dishes like filet mignon and chicken and dumplings in addition to a lobster mac-and-cheese dish that will make you swear off your diet forever. It also has burgers, pasta dishes, fish sandwiches, and an extensive selection of homemade ice cream.

The **Fishery** (13000 Fishery Rd., Placida, 941/697-2351, www.fisheryrestaurantplacida. com, 11:30am-9pm Mon.-Sat., 11:30am-8pm Sun., main courses from $15), just on the other side of the bridge in Placida, has a spectacular, Old Florida, dockside setting. Obviously, if you're coming to a dockside restaurant called "The Fishery," you'd be out of your mind to not get some seafood. The straightforward preparation of the seafood is appropriate for the setting and complements the super-freshness of the food. Of course, you can also dig into a basket of fried this or sandwiched that, but you'd be much better off trying one of the sautéed or grilled catches as you soak in the view. Service can be relaxed, so come when you've got some time to spare.

On the southernmost end of Gasparilla Island, near the lighthouse, is the aptly named **South Beach Bar & Grille** (760 Gulf Blvd., 941/964-0765, www.southbeachbarandgrille. com, 11:30am-9:30pm daily, main courses from $8), and while the decent pub grub and adequate seafood dishes won't be earning any Michelin stars soon, the atmosphere is decidedly low-key and friendly (especially in comparison to the upper-crust vibe that dominates Boca Grande), the beers are cold, and the location can't be beat come sunset time. Parking is a challenge.

## Englewood

There are two restaurants right near the beach—and right near each other—that are probably going to be your best bets while in Englewood. **Lock & Key Restaurant & Pub** (2045 N. Beach Rd., 941/474-1517, www. lockandkeyrestaurant.com, 11am-10pm Sun.-Thurs., 11am-11pm Fri.-Sat., lunch from $9, dinner from $16) offers a little bit of everything from surf-and-turf plates, steaks, and chops to a seafood menu featuring fresh catches available fried, broiled, or steamed. They even dish up early-bird specials. On the weekends, the bar is open late.

**The Gulf View Grill** (2095 N. Beach Rd., 941/475-3500, www.thegulfviewgrill.com, 11am-9pm Sun.-Thurs., 11am-10pm Fri.-Sat., lunch from $6, dinner from $13) is right on Englewood Beach and has incredible sunset views for happy-hour drinkers and early-evening eaters. Obviously, they offer a good deal of seafood, but the menu actually emphasizes various steak and poultry dishes. The menu is a little more dialed in and the vibe is just a little bit more upscale (while still being beach-casual) than Lock & Key Restaurant. Given their combination of specialty martinis and a pub grub selection that's pretty interesting (fried green beans, orange ginger chicken, homemade potato chips covered in blue cheese and tomatoes), you may find yourself heading for the far more vibrant bar area instead of the dining room.

# ACCOMMODATIONS
## Boca Grande

The ★ **Gasparilla Inn & Club** (500 W. Palm Ave., 941/964-4500, www.the-gasparilla-inn. com, doubles from $385) is a member of the Historic Hotels of America (www.historichotels.org), and it's easy to understand why. Originally opened in 1913, the hotel oozes Old Florida grandeur and charm, from its white columned entryway to the airy and expansive porches that surround it. The 141 rooms vary from standard (if luxurious) king- and queen-size rooms to suites and private cottages. The cottages are pricey—with rates up to $950 a night—but well worth it if you're in the market for an indulgent splurge, as they're

the upscale Gasparilla Inn & Club

incredibly private and comfortable; some even have the oddly un-Floridian presence of a fireplace. Guests have access to the inn's Pete Dye-designed golf course, a heated pool, tennis courts, and the 220-slip marina.

For a hotel experience that's nearly as historic but far more intimate, **The Anchor Inn** (450 4th St. E., 941/964-5600, www.anchorinnbocagrande.com, doubles from $265) dates from 1925. Instead of presenting itself in grand style, the inn has an atmosphere that is much more cozy. After all, there are only four rooms: a one-bedroom suite, a small efficiency, and two two-bedroom town houses. The Anchor Inn splits the difference between B&B and boutique hotel, as the property itself was built as a hotel, yet feels more like a converted residence. All rooms are nonsmoking, and they have full kitchens, central air-conditioning, and all the conveniences you'd need to settle in for an extended stay or just be comfortable for a couple of nights.

Although **The Palmetto Inn** (381 Palm Ave., 941/964-0410, www.thepalmettoinn.com, doubles with private bath from $175, doubles with shared bath from $145) is as old as the Gasparilla Inn and older than the Anchor Inn, it doesn't feel quite as steeped in historic charm as either of those two places. Still, it possesses its own sort of charm, with six basic suites, five of which have kitchenettes, and two of which have a shared bathroom.

Don't let the name fool you: **The Innlet on the Waterfront** (1251 12th St. E., 941/964-4600, www.theinnlet.com, doubles from $145) is on the water; however, the water that it's on is the Boca Grande bayou, and not the Gulf of Mexico. So, no beautiful sunset views, but you are just a short walk from the Gulf beaches. It has two different types of rooms: 24 efficiencies (20 of which open up to the bayou), each with two queen beds and a small kitchenette area; eight standard hotel-style rooms, and one junior suite. These latter nine room types face the courtyard area. All the rooms are clean and have standard conveniences.

There's also a restaurant on-site where you can grab breakfast or lunch.

## Englewood

For a short stay, the super-inexpensive **Beach Croft Motel** (2230 N. Beach Rd., 941/474-6509, www.beachcroftmotel.com, doubles from $129) is a good option. It has single rooms, suites, and efficiencies that are decent and clean, and you'll be just steps from the beach.

For stays longer than a few days, you should definitely look into vacation rentals, as many of the cottages and bungalows near Englewood Beach are cute and affordable. **Island Attitude Realty** (941/474-3939, www.islandattituderealty.com) is a good source for information and rentals, with houses, condos, and cottages for rent all along Manasota Key.

## INFORMATION

The best place for visitor information on Boca Grande is the **Boca Grande Chamber of Commerce** (471 Park Ave., 941/964-0568, www.bocagrandechamber.com, 10am-3pm Mon.-Fri.). It's about the closest thing to a visitors bureau on Gasparilla Island.

For the Englewood and Cape Haze area, the visitors center run by **Englewood and Cape Haze Chamber of Commerce** (601 S. Indiana Ave., 941/474-5511, www.englewoodchamber.com, 9am-5pm Mon.-Fri.) is an excellent resource. For more extensive planning information on the entire area, get in touch with the **Charlotte Harbor Visitor & Information Bureau** (18500 Murdock Circle, B104, Port Charlotte, 941/743-1900, www.charlotteharbortravel.com).

## GETTING THERE AND AROUND

Boca Grande is on the southern end of Gasparilla Island, which is only accessible via the Boca Grande Causeway bridge, about 20 minutes southwest of Port Charlotte via CR-771. It's a cash-only toll bridge that costs $6 for cars and, get this, $3 for bikes! Englewood is about 20 minutes north/northwest of Gasparilla Island, via CR-775/Placida Road.

Driving in Boca Grande is easy and slow; parking is a challenge. Most residents utilize golf carts to get around. There are wide sidewalks designed for bikers and walkers, and biking around the small island is both safe and encouraged. The area around Englewood Beach is incredibly walkable. However, the town of Englewood itself is something of a victim of sprawl, and a car is essential when traveling beyond the bucolic surroundings of the beach area.

# Fort Myers

Look for ★ to find recommended
sights, activities, dining, and lodging.

# Highlights

★ **Downtown Fort Myers River District:** After a decades-long rehabilitation, these roughly 25 square blocks have been transformed into a beautiful and pedestrian-friendly district of cool shops, restaurants, and cultural attractions (page 112).

★ **Edison & Ford Winter Estates:** Thomas Edison was so taken by Fort Myers that he not only built a large permanent winter residence here and equipped the city with an electrical grid, but he also convinced his friend Henry Ford to build his own winter home. The two estates are, conveniently enough, next door to each other and can be visited together (page 115).

★ **Lovers Key State Park:** Formerly only accessible by a backwater boat trip, Lovers Key State Park still feels like a secret, with secluded and quiet beaches, nature trails, and out-of-the-way canoe and kayak opportunities (page 133).

★ **Koreshan State Historic Site:** In some states, the site of a utopian cult community would be a footnote; in Florida, it's a state park. The Koreshan Unity Settlement was founded in 1894 by Dr. Cyrus R. Teed. The grounds are a well-preserved look at Florida in the late 19th century, seen from a thoroughly unique perspective (page 134).

The Fort Myers area is steeped in history—but the historical atmosphere here is unique. While some areas may boast of their past with pirates, conquistadors, and railroad barons, in this part of the state, the discussion is about Thomas Edison, a utopian cult, and Native American shell mounds.

Fort Myers Beach is one of the best beach towns in all of Florida, with a low-key and welcoming vibe that's decidedly unsophisticated but tremendously relaxing. Despite being a tourist-friendly destination, the town never feels "touristy." Plus, the beach is absolutely gorgeous.

To the east are the bedroom communities of Bonita Springs and Estero, where you'll be able to explore places like the Koreshan State Historic Site, at which the grounds of a turn-of-the-20th-century utopian cult are well preserved, giving visitors a unique look into a strange time in the state's history.

## HISTORY

With its position right along the Caloosahatchee River, it's no surprise that Fort Myers was considered an optimal location for the U.S. military to construct a fort. In fact, the recognition of its strategic benefits predates the U.S. Army's arrival; the Calusa and Seminole Indians both chose these riverbanks as settlement locations as the slight rise in elevation along the river and the river's opening into San Carlos Bay allowed excellent visibility of oncoming threats. This area was home to several military forts in the early 19th century, but it was the construction of Fort Harvie in the 1840s on the site of what is now downtown Fort Myers that marked the beginning of the area's military importance. Fort Harvie was renamed after Army colonel Abraham Myers, and was central in the United States' efforts to diminish the role of Seminole Indians in the area. It was at Fort Myers that the legendary Seminole chief Billy Bowlegs surrendered in 1858. The fort wasn't used for several years, until it became an important bastion for the Union Army's limited Florida campaigns during the Civil War; however, Union troops abandoned the facility as

---

**Previous:** Lovers Key State Park; downtown Fort Myers. **Above:** a pelican on Fort Myers Beach.

the war wound to a close. Soon after the Civil War, the area began to be settled by non-military pioneers, and was one of the earliest gateways to this part of the state; by the late 19th century, the city was not only incorporated but was also home to one of the premier upscale winter resorts for wealthy Northerners, the Royal Palm Hotel. It was Fort Myers's reputation as a cold-weather getaway that first drew Thomas Edison here, and it could fairly be said that his arrival put Fort Myers on the map and helped introduce it to the modern age.

## PLANNING YOUR TIME

The first decision you have to make when planning your visit to the Fort Myers area is if you want a beach vacation with a couple of sights thrown in, or if you want to take in the area's sights with an occasional respite on the white sands.

If it's the former, head straight for Fort Myers Beach and make that your base of operations; if it's the latter, pick a room near downtown Fort Myers, which puts you less than a half hour away from the beaches and any of the sights in the area. If you can't make up your mind, position yourself on the land side of the Sanibel Causeway; you won't really be super-close to anything, but you won't be more than a few minutes away, either.

If you have a weekend during the summer, spend it all at Fort Myers Beach. The friendly locals and low-key atmosphere can make a two-day jaunt as restorative as one that's twice as long. Make sure to set aside at least a half day to sneak in a visit to the Edison & Ford Winter Estates.

With more time, visitors should make sure to explore Fort Myers's River District and some of the museums downtown. Block off a day to take advantage of the ecotours offered by Everglades Day Safari. A day spent in the Bonita Springs area will let you take in the gorgeous beaches and natural beauty of Lovers Key State Park and the sublime weirdness of Koreshan State Historic Site.

# Fort Myers

When coming into central Fort Myers via McGregor Boulevard, it's easy to understand why the city has been dubbed the "City of Palms": The majestic, sky-scraping palms that line the street seem to go on forever. The neat block houses give way to progressively larger and more unique abodes, and by the time you arrive at the city's proudest property—the Edison & Ford Winter Estates—there's little doubt as to why Thomas Edison was so enthusiastic about living in the city. From this vantage point, it's hard to imagine the city as being anything but perfect.

Beyond that somewhat idyllic stretch of road, Fort Myers is a little rough around the edges. The economy has struggled, and crime in the area is consistently above the national average. Nonetheless, the historic core of the city has undergone some spectacular revitalization in the last decade, and between the city's beautiful River District, some well-worth-visiting sights in the city's downtown area, and, of course, the Edison & Ford Winter Estates, Fort Myers offers plenty of reasons to visit.

## SIGHTS
### ★ River District

Fort Myers's downtown area—referred to as the **River District** (www.myriverdistrict.com)—has undergone a massive transformation over the past few decades. Previously a fairly desolate and lifeless area, the River District today is the heart of the city, with dozens of restaurants, vintage boutiques, and art galleries. Covering roughly 25 square blocks along the Caloosahatchee River, the area is quite walkable, thanks to a redevelopment

# Fort Myers and Bonita Springs

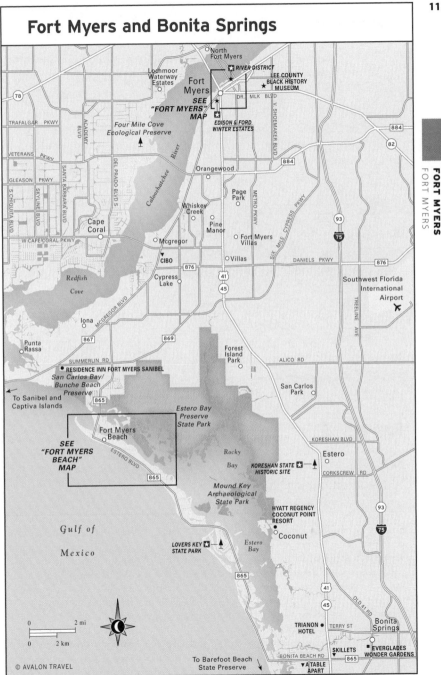

North Fort Myers

RIVER DISTRICT

LEE COUNTY BLACK HISTORY MUSEUM

Lochmoor Waterway Estates

Fort Myers

SEE "FORT MYERS" MAP

DR. MLK BLVD

V. SHOEMAKER BLVD

EDISON & FORD WINTER ESTATES

ACADEMY

78

TRAFALGAR PKWY

Four Mile Cove Ecological Preserve

Caloosahatchee River

884

82

VETERANS PKWY

DEL PRADO BLVD S

Orangewood

884

GLEASON PKWY

SANTA BARBARA BLVD

SKYLINE BLVD

S CHIQUITA BLVD

Page Park

METRO PKWY

SIX MILE CYPRESS PKWY

93

75

Cape Coral

Whiskey Creek

Pine Manor

Fort Myers Villas

W CAPE CORAL PKWY

Mcgregor

CIBO

Villas

DANIELS PKWY

876

Redfish Cove

Cypress Lake

876

41

45

Southwest Florida International Airport

MCGREGOR BLVD

Iona

867

869

Forest Island Park

ALICO RD

TREELINE AVE

Punta Rassa

SUMMERLIN RD

RESIDENCE INN FORT MYERS SANIBEL

San Carlos Bay/ Bunche Beach Preserve

865

San Carlos Park

To Sanibel and Captiva Islands

Estero Bay Preserve State Park

KORESHAN BLVD

SEE "FORT MYERS BEACH" MAP

Fort Myers Beach

ESTERO BLVD

Rocky Bay

KORESHAN STATE HISTORIC SITE

Estero

CORKSCREW RD

865

Mound Key Archaeological State Park

HYATT REGENCY COCONUT POINT RESORT

93

75

Gulf of

Mexico

LOVERS KEY STATE PARK

Estero Bay

Coconut

865

41

45

OLD 41 RD

0    2 mi

0    2 km

TRIANON HOTEL

TERRY ST

Bonita Springs

SKILLETS

EVERGLADES WONDER GARDENS

865

BONITA BEACH RD

To Barefoot Beach State Preserve

A TABLE APART

© AVALON TRAVEL

# Fort Myers

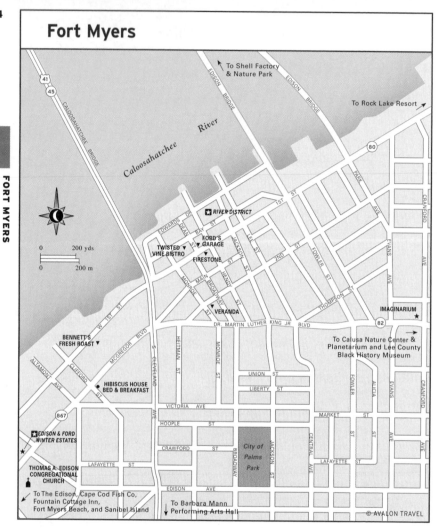

To Shell Factory & Nature Park

To Rock Lake Resort

River

Caloosahatchee

RIVER DISTRICT

TWISTED VINE BISTRO

FORD'S GARAGE

FIRESTONE

VERANDA

BENNETT'S FRESH ROAST

DR. MARTIN LUTHER KING JR BLVD

To Calusa Nature Center & Planetarium and Lee County Black History Museum

IMAGINARIUM

HIBISCUS HOUSE BED & BREAKFAST

City of Palms Park

EDISON & FORD WINTER ESTATES

THOMAS A. EDISON CONGREGATIONAL CHURCH

To The Edison, Cape Cod Fish Co, Fountain Cottage Inn, Fort Myers Beach, and Sanibel Island

To Barbara Mann Performing Arts Hall

0   200 yds
0   200 m

© AVALON TRAVEL

plan that wisely understood that active pedestrian traffic is integral to engendering a vibrant sense of community, especially within a quiet downtown. There are a couple of sights worth checking out, like a small but wonderfully maintained butterfly conservatory that's appropriately named **The Butterfly Estates** (1815 Fowler St., 239/690-2359, www.thebutterflyestates.com, 10am-3pm Tues.-Sun., $8 adults, $5 children, children 3 and under free) and the **Burroughs Home & Gardens** (2505 1st St., 239/337-0706, www.burroughshome.com, tours available Tues. at 10:30am and Wed. at 10:30am and 2pm, tours are $15 adults, $13 seniors, $8 children, children 5 and under free), an early-20th-century Georgian Colonial Revival house that often functions as a wedding venue but also offers docent-led tours a couple days a week. The way that this part of town maintains its friendly, semi-hip, but still historic atmosphere is admirable, and makes for an area that's well worth exploring.

## Lee County Black History Museum

The **Lee County Black History Museum** (1936 Henderson Ave., 239/332-8778, www.leecountyblackhistorysociety.org, 10am-4pm Mon.-Fri., $5 adults, $2 children) is a testament to challenges and perseverance, both in the exhibits that line its walls and in its own existence. For years, the museum struggled with poor funding, suboptimal organization, and little attention from the city or from visitors. For nearly a year, the museum was closed due to unpaid bills. However, in 2011, the museum reopened with an enthusiastic new team of volunteers and a refocused mission. The small museum is located in a two-room schoolhouse that once was Williams Academy, the first public school in Fort Myers for African Americans. The exhibits are primarily photographic in nature, with some visual memorabilia as well. The Lee County Black History Society is currently sifting through and organizing artifacts and other materials that document the difficult road that African Americans traveled in Fort Myers.

## Imaginarium

The **Imaginarium** (200 Cranford Ave., 239/337-3332, 10am-5pm Mon.-Sat., noon-5pm Sun., $12 adults, $8 students, children under 2 free) is a city-owned, kids-oriented science center. Much like other such municipal science centers, the Imaginarium is a collection of interactive exhibits intended to pique children's interest. The hands-on philosophy extends to several animal exhibits: Kids can touch different species of marine life in the "Sea to See" touch tanks.

---

**TOP** EXPERIENCE

## ★ Edison & Ford Winter Estates

Although there are dozens of historic and pedigreed homes throughout Florida, none captures the imagination or evokes an era as completely as the **Edison & Ford Winter Estates** (2350 McGregor Blvd., 239/334-7419, www.edisonfordwinterestates.org, 9am-5:30pm daily, admission to lab/museum $12 adults, $5 children, children 5 and under free; home/gardens tour $20 adults, $11 children, children 5 and under free; guided botanical tour $24 adults, $10 children, children 5 and under free). Guests to the estates can explore the gardens, grounds, and houses themselves, as well as a 15,000-square-foot

FORT MYERS
FORT MYERS

Kids will love the hands-on science exhibits at the Imaginarium.

museum filled with various inventions and memorabilia from both Thomas Edison's and Henry Ford's illustrious pasts. While Edison's house and labs are available to tour, Ford's house is not; however, there is a Model T in the museum area. The museum area is positively packed with inventions and educational displays, so much so that, at one point in your visit, you're likely to say, "Okay, I get it. Edison was a genius." And he certainly was. The museum exhibits go a long way to shed light on not only just how prodigious an inventor Edison was but also how adept he was in business; for every cool thing Thomas Edison created, it seemed that he also invented a heavily branded, vertical approach to marketing that ensured that his copyrights and patents would pay off handsomely. (Did you know that there was an Edison baby furniture company? An Edison concrete company? Or that Edison was the very first record-business mogul? No? Neither did I.)

## Thomas A. Edison Congregational Church

Amazingly, the gorgeous **Thomas A. Edison Congregational Church** (1619 Llewellyn Dr., 239/334-4978, www.taecc.com) is often completely overlooked by visitors to the Edison & Ford Winter Estates. It's right next door, and although it's very much an active church, the history behind the building and its religious community is quite interesting. The church's founding pastor was friends with Thomas Edison, and Edison's wife, Mina, wanted there to be a church next to their home in Fort Myers. The land next door to the estate was purchased in 1930, and in 1931—just two weeks after Thomas Edison's death—the church held its first services. Interestingly, even though Mrs. Edison was a Methodist, she was a regular attendee at this Congregational church. The church building is beautiful, as are the grounds. Visitors should be respectful of the fact that they're on the grounds of an active congregation.

## Calusa Nature Center & Planetarium

Primarily an educational and rescue facility, the **Calusa Nature Center & Planetarium** (3450 Ortiz Ave., 239/275-3435, www.calusa-nature.org, 9am-5pm Mon.-Sat., 11am-5pm Sun., $10 adults 13 and up, $8 children, children 2 and under free) sits on more than 100 acres near I-75 and has a butterfly garden, an aviary, and a small nature museum. The best reason to make the trek out here is to take in

This statue of Thomas Edison (by D. J. Wilkins) keeps an eye on his estate.

# Edison and Ford

Thomas Edison's lab has been kept "as-is," reflecting its state during the inventor's final days, and is included as part of the museum-style tour of the main house. The area of the lab that's open for guests provides a feel for just how expansive the room was and how wide a variety of experiments were undertaken.

From the period furnishings and Edison's swimming pool (one of the first concrete swimming pools in Florida) to the impressive banyan trees and verdant gardens, it's certainly worthwhile splurging for the full guided tour of the entire estate.

Edison bought 13 acres of riverfront land in Fort Myers in 1885, and the next year he began construction on the property where he and his new wife, Mina, would retreat to during most of the following winters. From the day that Edison first moved into the estate, the city of Fort Myers has fairly fallen over itself to honor his part-time residence (after all, if it weren't for Edison bringing his own electric dynamo to town, the city likely wouldn't have been electrified for another couple of decades). Edison's winter home in what was then a swampy hinterland inevitably brought other high-profile guests, including Teddy Roosevelt, John Burroughs, Herbert Hoover, and Henry Firestone; however, when Henry Ford arrived in Fort Myers in 1914, he was so impressed with the area he bought a home right next door to Edison's. Sixteen years after Edison's death in 1931, his widow, Mina, deeded the estate to the city of Fort Myers. In 1988, the neighboring Ford Estate was purchased, and today, the combined properties are the primary attraction in Fort Myers.

one of their many daily educational programs, which allow kids (and adults) to get up close with butterflies, manatees, reptiles, and other animals. Make sure to allow enough time to walk along the rarely crowded, pine-shaded nature trails.

## Shell Factory & Nature Park

With a history that stretches back more than 70 years, the **Shell Factory & Nature Park** (2787 N. Tamiami Trail, 800/282-5805, www.shellfactory.com, 10am-5pm daily, free) is a Fort Myers-area institution. While the original founders probably wouldn't recognize the evolution of their business—which began with a couple of northern transplants selling seashells from their front porch—the Shell Factory nonetheless manages to balance Old Florida tourist charm with New Florida spectacle overload. Yes, there's still a substantial part of this place that's given over to seashells in a wide variety of permutations (jewelry, art, tchotchkes), but there's also a petting zoo, a nature park with a huge aviary, a natural history museum (touted as the largest free private natural history museum), bumper boats, a seafood restaurant (and a Subway),

an arcade, a bar, and probably a half-dozen other things I'm somehow forgetting. It's all incredibly corny, and it's all incredibly awesome. Although admission to much of the site is free, the arcade and its attractions charge a separate pay-per-use fee.

# SPORTS AND RECREATION
## Golf

The course at **Shell Point Golf Club** (17401 On Par Blvd., 239/433-9790, greens fees from $55) was designed by Gordon Lewis and opened in 2000; the course is a par-72, at 6,546 yards. Another Gordon Lewis-designed course is the par-72, 6,538-yard course at **Eagle Ridge** (14589 Eagle Ridge Dr., 239/768-1888, greens fees from $45); this course is considered one of the more challenging ones in the area, and is known for its beautiful, well-maintained greens.

The city of Fort Myers owns and operates two municipal public golf courses. **Fort Myers Country Club** (3591 McGregor Blvd., 239/321-7488, 6:30am-6pm daily, greens fees from $35) was designed by Donald Ross in 1916, making it one of the oldest courses in the region. It's also one of the prettiest and, according to *Golf Digest,* one of the top public courses in the United States. It is an 18-hole, 6,421-yard, par-72 course. The city also runs the less historical **Eastwood Golf Course** (4600 Bruce Herd Ln., 239/321-7487, 7am-6pm daily, greens fees from $30), which is outside of the city center, closer to the airport. This is also a par-72, 18-hole course.

## Tennis

The city-owned **Racquet Club** (1700 Matthew Dr., 239/321-7550, 8am-8pm Mon.-Fri., 8am-2pm Sat., 8am-noon Sun., daily rates $10 for nonmembers, $5 for juniors) has eight lighted clay courts and two hard-surface courts. Daily admission charges are incredibly reasonable. This is a well-maintained and clean facility with lockers, showers, and a snack bar. Lessons are also available.

## Fishing

If you're staying in central Fort Myers and don't feel like heading out to Fort Myers Beach to go fishing, the **Tarpon Street Fishing Pier** (700 Tarpon St.) is a quiet (and free!) option near downtown.

## Spring Training

Two major league baseball teams have their Grapefruit League spring training games in Fort Myers. The **Boston Red Sox** play at **JetBlue Park** (2201 Edison Ave., tickets from $10). The **Minnesota Twins** play at Hammond Stadium at the **CenturyLink Sports Complex** (14100 Six Miles Cypress Pkwy., tickets from $12).

## Everglades Tours

In southwest Florida, any number of eco-tour companies will take you out into the Everglades. One of the best is **Everglades Day Safari** (pickups at four locations in the Fort Myers area, 239/472-1559, www.ecosafari.com, 7:30am-5:30pm daily, full-day all-inclusive safari adults $159, children 5-11 $139), which bases its west coast operations just outside of Fort Myers. Although Fort Myers isn't typically thought of as a launching point into the 'Glades, they're but a short drive away. Everglades Day Safari focuses primarily on full-day tours, giving customers the opportunity to take in the varied ecosystems of the Everglades via boat, swamp buggy, airboat, and on foot. Lunch is included. The 1.5-hour boat cruise is one of the best parts of the company's tours, as it offers a unique vantage

The kitschy Shell Factory & Nature Park still draws tourists.

point to how important the Everglades are to the area's aquatic health. While most tours tend to focus on the swamps, this is one of the few Everglades explorations that give a more well-rounded view of these ecosystems.

## ENTERTAINMENT AND EVENTS
### Nightlife

The after-hours scene in Fort Myers is limited and somewhat uninspired. There are plenty of sports pubs and anonymous dive bars, but outside of that the choices are pretty slim, although the downtown River District is pretty vibrant on weekend nights. **Firestone** (2224 Bay St., 239/332-7425, martini bar open 9pm-2am Fri.-Sat., Skybar open 4pm-2am Tues.-Sat.), in the compact downtown area, is primarily a restaurant but also has an upscale lounge and martini bar, as well as a rooftop bar where DJs spin "South Beach style." Also downtown is a similarly dance-oriented venue, the small but stylish two-floor **Celsius** (2213 Main St., 239/980-7630, 6pm-2am Wed.-Sun.). A nice, down-to-earth option is the **Indigo Room** (2219 Main St., 239/332-0014, 11am-2am Mon.-Fri, 6pm-2am Sat., 7pm-2am Sun.), which boasts a decent beer selection, pool tables, and a friendly atmosphere; likewise, downtown's decidedly unpretentious **Hideaway** (1418 Dean St., 239/337-9966, 11am-2am Mon.-Sat., 11am-midnight Sun.) bills itself as a sports bar, but it's really a super-friendly dive bar with TVs that show sports.

Gamblers should undertake the 45-minute drive out to the **Seminole Casino—Immokalee** (506 S. 1st St., Immokalee, 239/658-1313, open 24 hours daily). Poker, blackjack, table games, and lots and lots of slot machines are awaiting your open wallet. The casino has a small counter-service deli, a café, and a lounge area.

### The Arts

As in other cities in the rest of southwest Florida, Fort Myers's arts scene gets a little boost in the winter, and it's then that most local performing groups ramp up

their schedules. The **Southwest Florida Symphony** and **Gulf Coast Symphony** both stage concerts at the **Barbara Mann Performing Arts Hall** (8099 College Pkwy., 239/481-4849), which also hosts a slate of touring Broadway musicals and pop concerts.

Musical theater is also the main attraction at the **Broadway Palm Dinner Theatre** (1380 Colonial Blvd., 239/278-4422), which hosts touring versions of shows like *All Shook Up* and *Guys and Dolls*. The **Sidney & Berne Davis Art Center** (2301 1st St., 239/333-1933, www.sbdac.com) downtown also hosts classical concerts, dance performances, and lectures by authors and artists.

The community-oriented **Alliance for the Arts** (10091 McGregor Blvd., 239/939-2787, www.artinlee.org, 10am-4pm Mon.-Fri., 10am-1pm Sat.) is primarily a facility for classes, camps, and other arts-education events. It's also home to a gallery where local artists' works are displayed.

Of the handful of interesting galleries in Fort Myers, the most notable is the **Arts for ACT Gallery** (2265 1st St., 239/337-5050, 11am-5pm Mon.-Sat., 1pm-4pm Sun.). Owned and operated by Abuse Counseling and Treatment, Inc., a nonprofit group that assists victims of domestic violence and sexual assault, the gallery is in a beautifully repurposed space, with small sub-areas, each with its own unique focus. It's a modern and funky gallery with a serious mission, with art ranging from surrealism to sculpture.

### Festivals and Events

Sponsored by a local Kiwanis club, the annual **Medieval Faire** brings jugglers, jousting, turkey legs, and a human-sized chess match to the Lakes Regional Park every January.

In February, the city of Fort Myers honors its most famous part-time resident with the **Edison Festival of Light,** a month-long celebration that includes weekends with live music, craft shows, a parade, and even a bed race. Also in February, the **Southwest Florida Wine & Food Fest** finds more than 20 chefs and nearly a dozen vintners at the

Miromar Lakes Beach & Golf Club for a weekend of upscale but accessible tastings. The festival also features chef dinners held in various homes in the area.

## SHOPPING

Downtown's River District is mostly offices and restaurants, but there are a few local shops as well. By far the most interesting is **The Franklin Shops** (2200 1st St., 239/333-3130, 10am-8pm Mon.-Sat., 11am-6pm Sun.), which provides local artisans and small-scale retailers a place to sell their goods; it's like an antiques mall . . . for everything. There are nearly 100 different shops doing business, and the cast of characters does rotate, although they almost all tend toward the artsy end of the spectrum (books, crafts, clothes, jewelry, etc.), with a few home-goods stores as well. It's a unique shopping experience in a unique building (the circa-1937 Franklin Hardware building) that is well worth exploring.

## FOOD
### Breakfast

Although they do serve meals besides breakfast and brunch, the main reason you'll want to stop into the tiny **McGregor Cafe** (4305 McGregor Blvd., 239/936-1771, 10am-3pm Mon.-Tues., 10am-4pm Wed., 11am-8pm Thurs.-Sat., 8am-4pm Sun., main courses from $6) is for a morning meal. The outdoor seating, friendly locals-centric vibe, and historical atmosphere make it a great starting point for the rest of your day. Expect the standard eggs-and-bacon menu.

For a ridiculously decadent way to start your day, ★ **Bennett's Fresh Roast** (2011 Bayside Pkwy., 239/332-0077, www.bennetts-freshroast.com, 6am-6pm Mon.-Fri., 7am-3pm Sat.-Sun., breakfast from $6, lunch from $8) offers an insane menu of fresh doughnuts and breakfast pastries. Yeah, you can get a pita bread breakfast sandwich stuffed with eggs, ham, and cheese, or maybe even a fruit salad or some fresh yogurt. But when there are maple-bacon doughnuts and peanut butter-chocolate doughnuts and orange-coconut

doughnuts available, why would you take the healthy route? (You're on vacation, remember?) Of course, given this place's name, it shouldn't be all that surprising that the coffee is exceptional; all of it was roasted within the past 24 hours, and ground and brewed within the last hour or so. Bennett's also serves a frequently updated selection of sandwiches and salads for lunch. There is also a location on Sanibel Island.

### American

**Crave** (12901 McGregor Blvd., 239/466-4663, 8am-9pm Mon.-Sat., 8am-2pm Sun., main courses from $11) is a great, cooked-to-order modern diner that nails the standards of breakfast, lunch, and dinner, and also manages to add more than a few impressive touches of flair throughout. So, yes, you can get a plate of eggs and sausage, a stack of fluffy pancakes, or some stupendous biscuits and gravy for breakfast, but you can also tuck into a tremendous omelet stuffed with shrimp, crab, asparagus, and shiitake mushrooms. Lunch and dinner are similarly exceptional, with an entire menu of classics available from noon that includes such blue-plate specials as chicken potpie, meat loaf, roast chicken, and pot roast. Those classics are augmented by an extensive selection of sandwiches, salads, and pub grub that manages to consistently include fresh and innovative ingredients. Even if you're not all that hungry, make sure you order a basket of their homemade bread, a light and crispy French bread seasoned with sea salt and black pepper. Crave's Sunday brunch is incredibly popular, and for very good reason.

The best—and most popular—restaurant downtown is **Ford's Garage** (1415 Dean St., 239/332-3673, www.fordsgaragefl.com, 11am-midnight Mon.-Thurs., 11am-2am Fri.-Sat., 11am-10pm Sun., main courses from $10). The specialty is burgers, and Ford's will cook them perfectly, whether in a classic, straightforward style or as one of their special versions (try the Kobe burger). The craft beer selection is exceptional (with lots of local specialties), as are sides like fried pickles, and the atmosphere—loud, convivial, and decorated to look like a Model T garage—is definitely fun.

If you're downtown and need a no-frills meal, stop into **Oasis** (1661 Estero Blvd., #7, 239/334-1566, www.oasisatfortmyers.com, breakfast from $6, lunch from $7), a nice, diner-style café that's been feeding Fort Myers office workers for more than a quarter century. Focusing on the basics—omelets, waffles, and eggs-and-bacon for breakfast; burgers, sandwiches, and salads for lunch and dinner—Oasis doesn't try to be fancy (one of their specialties is a fried chicken wrap), and that approach serves them well. Prices are quite reasonable and service is ridiculously fast and friendly.

Another option for straightforward and super-filling grub is **Fancy's Southern Cafe** (8890 Salrose Ln., 239/561-2988, www.fancyssoutherncafe.com, 11am-9pm daily, main courses from $8), near the airport and I-75. Unapologetically serving up heaping helpings of chicken and waffles, shrimp and grits, chicken potpies, meat-loaf sandwiches, and more, Fancy's uses fresh ingredients and a made-from-scratch ethos that puts most meat-and-three spots to shame.

## Barbecue

It's sort of hard to describe where to find the best barbecue in Fort Myers. At the corner of Dr. Martin Luther King Jr. Boulevard and Cranford Avenue is a completely nondescript house with a smoker outside and a screen-porch extension. There's no outdoor signage. There doesn't appear to be an actual name for the business either, but a placard inside says it's called **McCarter's BBQ & Catering** (2675 Dr. Martin Luther King Jr. Blvd., 239/690-0356, hours vary, main courses from $9). To the cars zooming by, it's not even clear it's a business in the commonly accepted sense of the word. However, when the smoker's on, this corner is bustling with folks stopping in to pick up some masterfully rubbed and smoked St. Louis-style ribs and some incredible tomato-based sauce. Needless to say, this is a cash-only enterprise, and to-go boxes are definitely available, which is good, since there is pretty much nowhere to sit except on the ground.

## Fine Dining

Located in a turn-of-the-20th-century building in downtown Fort Myers, ★ **Veranda** (2122 2nd St., 239/932-2065, lunch 11:30am-2:30pm Mon.-Fri., dinner 5:30pm-9:30pm Mon.-Thurs., 5:30pm-10:30pm Fri.-Sat., lunch from $9, dinner from $28) has been one of the city's top dining destinations since it opened in 1978. The menu is traditional American fare (steaks, chops, and seafood) prepared with a unique touch that combines Italian seasonings and Southern flair. The Veranda's Chicken Orleans combines shrimp, crab, and chicken breast with a spicy, Cajun-styled beurre blanc, while the decadent, bread-crumb-coated veal chops are stuffed with buffalo mozzarella and prosciutto. All of it is served in an opulent, historical atmosphere by an attentive and friendly waitstaff.

## New American

**Christof's on McGregor** (10231 McGregor Blvd., 239/791-8473, 11am-9pm Sun.-Wed., 11am-10pm Thurs.-Sat., main courses from $19) is hard to classify. There's a decidedly "modern Southern" tinge to the menu, thanks to the presence of items like fried green tomatoes and shrimp and grits, but they also serve burgers and sandwiches. Oh yeah, there's also a wide selection of Italian dishes. And steak. And seafood. Still, it seems that Christof's does a pretty good job with most of what they serve. And, given the interesting atmosphere—the restaurant is actually a "complex" of several 1950s-era residences, and the stylish decor is tempered by the casual, jeans-wearing waitstaff—a meal here can be quite exceptional.

**Twisted Vine Bistro** (2214 Bay St., 239/226-1687, www.twistedvinebistro.com, lunch 11am-2pm Mon.-Fri., dinner 4:30pm-11pm daily, lunch from $12, dinner from $29) is downtown and has a great selection of wine (and a staff knowledgeable enough to make a good recommendation). The dinner menu includes filet mignon, chicken breast, and pan-seared snapper as well as promising small plates. Twisted Vine's cheese plate—which comes with a selection of eight domestic and foreign cheeses, olives, prosciutto, bread, fruit, and even a little piece of honeycomb—is a fantastic way to do dinner.

## Seafood and Sushi

True sushi aficionados should head directly for downtown's **Blu Sushi** (13451 McGregor Blvd., 239/489-1500, 11am-10pm Sun.-Wed., 11am-2am Thurs.-Sat., sushi rolls $5-15). The sushi rolls are expertly prepared and served in a modern, stylish environment that's unique in Fort Myers. The hip, urban vibe extends to Blu's drinks menu, which features treats like the Frank Zappacino (coffee-infused rum, dulce de leche liqueur, Frangelico), Zenergy (vodka, green tea liqueur, Red Bull), saketinis, and "saktails."

There are quite a few places in Fort Myers to get an expertly grilled piece of fresh fish, but if you're looking for a down-to-earth and tremendously filling seafood experience, head directly to **Clam Bake** (16520 S. Tamiami Trail, 239/482-1930, www.clambakefortmyers.com, 11:30am-8pm daily, main courses from $8), an utterly unpretentious, family-owned seafood joint that specializes in fresh seafood that they'll be glad to serve you raw, broiled, steamed, baked, or fried. The dishes tend to have a New England-style slant to their preparations, so you can grab a lobster roll, clam chowder, and even stuffed quahog. Shellfish (obviously) is a specialty, with great mussels, oysters, and clams. If they've got fresh grouper in, make sure to order their grouper Reuben, and then plan on taking a nap afterward.

The beachy, tin-walled vibe at **Cape Cod Fish Co** (15501 Old McGregor Blvd., 239/313-6462, www.capecodfishco.com, noon-8pm daily, main courses from $10) is meant to imply a sort of loose, vacation-minded casualness that extends to the relaxed, super-friendly vibe of the staff and the open-air seating arrangements. But don't be fooled; this kitchen is serious business, focusing on serving up only the best and freshest seafood (especially clams and lobster rolls) in a way that's both classic and contemporary. Mouthwatering treats like a grilled pimiento-cheese-and-crab sandwich and blackened salmon tacos dominate the menu, allowing for plenty of pescatarian adventures as well as a journey through the fried-basket basics.

## European

The Italian menu at ★ **Cibo** (12901 McGregor Blvd., 239/454-3700, 5pm-9pm Mon.-Thurs., 5pm-10pm Fri.-Sat., main courses from $16) is kept simple and straightforward—a handful each of classic pasta, meat, and fish dishes, as well as an extensive antipasti menu—which allows the kitchen to focus their efforts on doing a few things excellently, rather than dishing up a wide range of mediocrity. Portions are reasonably sized, and presentation is exceptional. And, to the owners' credit, once you step inside the cozy restaurant, the strip mall exterior melts away to reveal a stylish and comfortable interior that's definitely classy and intimate.

**Austrian-German Restaurant** (1400 Colonial Blvd., 239/936-8118, 11am-9pm Mon.-Sat., main courses from $12) is a small, family-owned restaurant that is far and away one of the best German restaurants in all of Florida. The menu is simple and classics-based, with a selection of schnitzels, spaetzle, and potato salad served in massive portions. All of it is prepared from scratch by chef Helga, one-half of the husband-and-wife team that owns and operates this restaurant. Ingredients are fresh and authentic (Helga uses Austrian pumpkinseed oil as a salad dressing), and the atmosphere is incredibly convivial, making diners feel less like customers and more like houseguests.

# ACCOMMODATIONS
## $50-100

Although generally accommodations in the Fort Myers area aren't all that expensive, finding cheap and safe budget lodging that's conveniently located can be a challenge. Fortunately, the **Fountain Cottages Inn** (14621 McGregor Blvd., 239/481-0429, www.fountaincottagesinn.com, doubles from $80) is a clean and affordable option.

## $100-200

Stepping up just a tiny notch into slightly more costly digs affords a better selection of inexpensive lodging. There are at least a dozen affordable chain hotels with outlets in and around Fort Myers. If you're looking for something more unique, the **Rock Lake Resort** (2937 Palm Beach Blvd., 239/332-4080, www.rocklakeresort.com, doubles from $129) is where you should look first. Located just outside of downtown, Rock Lake is right on Palm Beach Boulevard and less than a block away from the Caloosahatchee River. The property is quite a nice destination in and of itself. The actual lake is kinda tiny, but the way these duplex-style units are ringed around it makes it feel like a private and pastoral spot, where every room has a beautiful view. Rooms are spacious and clean, with all basic necessities accounted for: comfortable beds, well-equipped kitchenettes, nice bathrooms, and tile floors. On the property, there's a heated pool, a tennis court, and even a horseshoe pitch. A nature trail, boardwalk, and shaded gazebo make it easy to find a peaceful moment to yourself. Easy access to the river is a godsend for those who want to go canoeing or kayaking.

Another great, reasonably priced option is **Hotel Indigo** (1520 Broadway, 239/337-3446, www.hotelindigo.com, doubles from $144), which is fancier than Rock Lake Resort and more conveniently located in the downtown area. As with other Indigo locations (the brand is InterContinental's "boutique" chain), the room count is low (74) and the style quotient is high. The smallish rooms have all modern conveniences, with fresh bedding, modern furnishings, flat-screen TVs, and some pretty luxe bathrooms.

The **Hibiscus House Bed & Breakfast** (2135 McGregor Blvd., 239/332-2651, www.thehibiscushouse.net, doubles from $139) is situated on a beautiful stretch of historic McGregor Boulevard, close to the Edison & Ford Winter Estates. While it may not have quite the historical cachet of its nearby neighbor, the tree-covered property and small rooms inside are charming and beautiful. All five rooms have private bathrooms, and each is decorated in a unique style that largely eschews the frills and lace one might expect from a B&B this close to the Edison house.

A fantastic choice for families who want to explore Fort Myers, Fort Myers Beach, and the islands of Sanibel and Captiva is the ★ **Residence Inn Fort Myers Sanibel** (20371 Summerlin Rd., 239/415-4150, www.marriott.com, doubles from $129). Located on the Fort Myers side of the Sanibel Causeway (which means you'll only need to pay the sky-high toll when you want to head out to Sanibel) and about a 15-minute drive to Fort Myers Beach or downtown Fort Myers, the hotel is located next to a strip mall and across the street from outlet stores. Within the mall is a very nice Publix grocery store, which will come in handy for stocking the full kitchen that's in each of these rooms. As at all Residence Inns, your room will be less like a standard hotel room and more like a tiny one-bedroom apartment. By some miraculous organizational feat, the designers managed to cram a comfortable living room, dining area, office, and kitchen into the non-bedroom space, leaving the sleeping area fairly spacious and comfortable. The staff is quite friendly and helpful. All expected site amenities—pool, fitness center, free breakfast, Wi-Fi—are available.

The **Sanibel Harbour Marriott Resort & Spa** (17260 Harbour Pointe Dr., 239/466-4000, www.marriott.com, doubles from $249) can boast of a location that's similarly convenient to that of the Residence Inn, although it's right at the base of the Sanibel Causeway in the relative isolation of Punta Rassa, which means that if you need anything that's not available on the resort property, you're going to need to get in your car. That said, there's a lot available on the resort property. Nearly 350 rooms—278 standard rooms, 69 suites—are stacked atop one another in giant, imposing towers, and it seems like nearly every one has a gorgeous view. There are five (!) restaurants on site, and if that's not enough to choose from, you can also splurge on a dinner cruise aboard the resort's 100-foot yacht. A full-service spa and fitness center, three heated pools, tennis courts, volleyball, and a jogging trail mean you won't need to leave the property to get your exercise.

## INFORMATION AND SERVICES

The **Lee County Visitor & Convention Bureau** (2210 2nd St., Ste. 600, 239/338-3500, www.fortmyers-sanibel.com) can help with information on Fort Myers, Fort Myers Beach, Sanibel and Captiva Islands, and any other destination in Lee County.

Fort Myers is a modern, midsize city, so you should have no problem tracking down banks, pharmacies, or grocery stores. Most every bank that operates throughout Florida has a branch in downtown Fort Myers, and there are Walgreens and CVS pharmacies throughout town. For groceries, your best bet is always Publix, which has more than a dozen stores in the area, many of which also have pharmacies.

## GETTING THERE AND AROUND
### Getting There

The largest airport in the entire south-

west Florida region is **Southwest Florida International Airport** (RSW, 11000 Terminal Access Rd., 239/590-4800, www.flylcpa.com), which, conveniently enough, is just a few minutes' drive from downtown Fort Myers. It's serviced by most major American carriers, including Southwest. **Greyhound** offers bus service into a **Fort Myers bus station** (2250 Widman Way, 239/334-1011).

By car, the nearest major highway is I-75, which connects the south Gulf Coast with the Midwestern United States. Running roughly parallel to I-75 is the Tamiami Trail (U.S. 41), which runs through Tampa, Sarasota, Fort Myers, Naples, and Miami.

### Getting Around

Lee County operates **LeeTran** (239/533-8726, www.rideleetran.com), a bus service with decent route service throughout the county and the Fort Myers core. Their **Trollee** service can easily get you right to Fort Myers Beach from the heart of the city. Fares start at $0.75 per ride.

If you choose not to avail yourself of public transportation, you will need to have a car to get around central Fort Myers. Other than within the River District, this is not a pedestrian-friendly city, and attempting to bike around it would be inefficient and dangerous, thanks to the not-insubstantial distances between sights and the lack of dedicated bike lanes along some of the busiest corridors.

# Fort Myers Beach

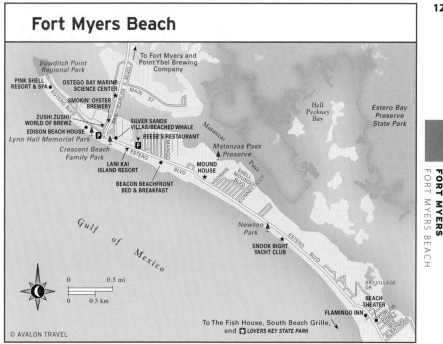

# Fort Myers Beach

I have a preference when it comes to beach towns: I like when they act like they're glad (or at least surprised) to see me. Fort Myers Beach is one of those towns. Of course, Fort Myers Beach acts like it's glad to see *everyone;* the vibe here is overwhelmingly laid-back and neighborly. It doesn't hurt that the town of FMB is, itself, pretty small and self-contained, but if I lived in a spot that had such large and beautiful beaches, I'd probably be pretty mellow and friendly, too. And when folks came over the bridge to escape the sprawl of Fort Myers, I'd be glad to welcome them; after all, what good is a gorgeous beach without plenty of people enjoying it?

## SIGHTS
### Ostego Bay Marine Science Center

The **Ostego Bay Marine Science Center** (718 Fisherman's Wharf, 239/765-8101, www. ostegobay.org, 10am-4pm Mon.-Sat., $5 adults, $3 children 6 and up) is a small, somewhat dated marine research facility located on the causeway right as you're about to enter Fort Myers Beach on its northern end. The center's primary function is educational, and on weekdays during the school year, groups of students are often found here. However, the educational message extends beyond the groups here for field trips, and the knowledgeable and friendly staff seems to take a lot of pride in showing guests around the facility and teaching about the various kinds of marine life. There's a touch tank that kids love, and although you can take in most of the actual center in about an hour or so, you'd do well to set aside a half day to go out on one of Ostego Bay's shrimp boat tours, which not only gives guests a good overview of the aquatic ecology of the area but also illuminates how shrimping actually gets done.

## Matanzas Pass Preserve

Although Fort Myers Beach is one of the most laid-back and friendly beach towns along the southwest Florida coast, it's also an extremely popular place to vacation, and sometimes—well, sometimes you might want to get away from your fellow visitors. **Matanzas Pass Preserve** (199 Bay Rd., 239/229-0649, www.leeparks.org, 7am-dusk daily, historic cottage open 10am-noon Wed. and Sat.) makes it pretty easy to do that. The county-owned property is a 60-acre wildlife sanctuary that opens right onto Estero Bay. The park has a mile or so of nature trails that take you through mangroves and one of the last maritime oak hammocks in this part of the state. Fishing in the bay is allowed with a saltwater fishing license, and if you've got a kayak or a canoe, the preserve has a launch area that can take you right into the Great Calusa Blueway paddling trail. At the entry for the preserve

is a "historic cottage" that was built in 1921 and was, at one time, a kindergarten; today it's the **Estero Island Historic Society and Nature Center,** and it's definitely worth exploring before or after your time in the preserve.

## Mound House

For an even more in-depth historical experience on Fort Myers Beach, take some time to explore the **Mound House** (289 Connecticut St., 239/765-0865, www.moundhouse.org, 9am-4pm Tues.-Sat. Jan.-Apr., 9am-4pm Tues., Wed., Sat. May-Dec., $10 adults, $8 students, $5 children). The house was a casino during the 1920s, but even more fascinatingly, it was later the site of an "experimental station" where restless scientists and researchers brainstormed various wild ideas, occasionally emerging with some practical results (like, for instance, frozen orange juice). The house—called the "Mound House" because it was originally built atop a Calusa Indian shell mound—is actually a full-featured museum open for tours and visitors. For amateur archaeologists, this is a must-visit, but anyone with an interest in old Floridiana will enjoy a visit here.

the Mound House

## BEACHES

The beaches here are easily accessible and marked well, and there are two large **municipal parking lots** (1661 Estero Blvd. and 200 San Carlos Blvd., $2/hour) on the northern end of the island. All along Estero Boulevard are numerous, well-marked public beach access points with small parking lots that fill up rather quickly. The farther south you go, the easier it is to find a parking spot; the access points are numbered in ascending order from south to north, and the best ones to head for are those with numbers lower than 20.

### Crescent Beach Family Park

**Crescent Beach Family Park** (1100 Estero Blvd., 239/765-6794, www.leeparks.org, sunrise-sunset daily, free) is the first beach park you'll encounter coming onto Fort Myers Beach from the Matanzas Pass Bridge. The park has plenty of facilities, with restrooms, volleyball courts, and a picnic area. Needless to say, given its prime location, this is one of the busiest beach spots on all of Fort Myers Beach. There is no parking here (the closest public lot is two blocks away at Lynn Hall Memorial Park and Fort Myers Beach Pier).

### Lynn Hall Memorial Park

If you come off the Matanzas Pass Bridge and *don't* follow the flow of traffic heading left toward the busier, southern parts of Fort Myers Beach, and instead turn right, you'll come across **Lynn Hall Memorial Park** (950 Estero Blvd., sunrise-sunset daily, free), which is in the heart of downtown Fort Myers Beach. This park is quite popular and busy, and the parking lot fills up pretty early. Still, the beach here is great, and if you enjoy sharing your beach day with crowds, this is the spot for you. The iconic **Fort Myers Beach Pier** is well loved by anglers *and* by a colony of Brazilian free-tailed bats that lives underneath it, which makes sunsets here not only beautiful but also kind of exciting.

### Newton Park

Located at about the midway point of Fort Myers Beach is **Newton Park** (4650 Estero Blvd., sunrise-sunset daily, free), one of the newest and most distinctive public beach parks in the area. In addition to offering easy access to one of the quietest stretches of beach, the park is on the former grounds of Seven Seas, the beachfront residence of the late Jim Newton, a wealthy real estate developer who is actually best known as the author of *Uncommon Friends,* a book that detailed his relationships with the likes of Thomas Edison, Charles Lindbergh, Harvey Firestone, and other notable well-to-dos. Newton was friends with many of them during the 1930s, but he hosted several of them (and many others) at Seven Seas during the 1950s.

## SPORTS AND RECREATION
### Boating and Fishing

Almost a dozen different boats are available for rent from **Snook Bight Yacht Club & Marina** (4765 Estero Blvd., 239/765-4371, pontoon rentals from $199/half-day), ranging in size from a 17-foot Aquasport to a leisurely 24-foot pontoon.

**Getaway Marina** (18400 San Carlos Blvd., 239/466-3600, half-day fishing charters from $70/person, four-hour boat rentals from $160/half-day, kayak rentals from $40/half-day) provides half-day fishing charters aboard a 90-foot bus-on-the-water called *The Great Getaway.* For a less crowded experience, you can also book one of several boats that are available for full-day charters. Getaway also offers nighttime fishing trips, sunset tours, and boat rentals.

### Kayaking

There are a half-dozen places on Fort Myers Beach where kayakers can put in and begin exploring the **Great Calusa Blueway** paddling trail (www.calusablueway.com). If you brought your own canoe or kayak, head for the Mound House or **Bowditch Point Regional Park** (50 Estero Blvd., 239/765-6794). If you need a rental, **Holiday Adventure Tours & Boat Rental** (250 Estero Blvd., 239/463-8661, kayak rentals from $30/hour) and **Salty Sam's Waterfront Adventures** (2500 Main St., 239/463-7333, kayak rentals from $50/three hours) can set you up; both businesses also offer guided tours.

## Bowling

Just on the mainland side of the Matanzas Pass Bridge is **Beach Bowl** (17651 San Carlos Blvd., 239/466-3033, 7am-11pm Mon.-Fri., noon-11pm Sat.-Sun.), a bowling alley and arcade with incredibly reasonable lane-rental rates.

# ENTERTAINMENT AND EVENTS
## Nightlife

There are dozens of places to grab a drink in Fort Myers Beach, and pretty much all of them are of the beach-bar-and-grill variety, like **Cottage Beach Pub & Grill** (1250 Estero Blvd., 239/765-5440, 11am-2am daily), which often has live music upstairs but is mainly a great place to drink and watch the sunset; the food is not great here, but the drinks and the view are superb. The top-floor lounge at the **Lani Kai Island Resort** (1400 Estero Blvd.,

239/463-3111, www.lanikaiislandresort.com, 11am-midnight Mon.-Thurs., 10am-2am Fri.-Sat.) is another bar-and-grill place. If you can beat (or outlast) the dinner crowd, you can grab one of their gliding table/bench combos to sip on a cold one while watching the sunset from one of the best (and highest) vantage points on Fort Myers Beach. Downstairs at the same hotel is a beach bar that stays pretty busy throughout the day and picks up at night with DJs and occasional cover bands. Open containers are only allowed on the beach if it's right at the place that served them. For a down-and-dirty dive bar experience, head to **The Mermaid Liquors and Lounge** (1204 Estero Blvd., 239/765-9100, 9am-2am Mon.-Sat., 9am-midnight Sun.), a combination package store and bar, filled with regulars who have learned to tolerate the bewildered tourists who occasionally stumble in here and staffed by some of the friendliest bartenders around. **World of Brewz** (201 Old San Carlos Blvd., 239/463-9874, 11:30am-10pm Sun.-Thurs., 11:30am-10:30pm Fri.-Sat.) is a good choice for craft beer in downtown Fort Myers Beach; they also have a full bar and are conveniently located in the same space as a sushi restaurant (Zushi Zushi), so you can eat, too. However, just a mile or so over the bridge in

The downtown River District in Fort Myers is lively at night.

beach, shrimp dinners, and the crowning of the Shrimp Festival Queen.

## FOOD
### Breakfast

For breakfast, **Reese's Restaurant** (1661 Estero Blvd., 239/463-3933, 7am-2pm daily, main courses from $6) is a dependable choice. The food is uniformly excellent in a greasy-spoon kind of way. Portions are laughably huge (don't order more than one pancake unless you're a glutton for griddle-fried dough), and though you may not see the bottom of your plate, working your way through Reese's biscuits and gravy or home fries is well worth the effort.

**Tuckaway Bagel & Wafel** (1740 Estero Blvd., 239/463-5398, 7am-2pm daily, menu items from $4.50) serves extraordinary steamed bagels in a variety of flavors and with a seemingly endless array of fillings. Bagels are available for breakfast and lunch. The French owners also make some exceptional Belgian-style waffles in both sweet and savory editions. (Beware that if you say "Yes" to whipped cream here, you are really saying "Yes, lots!") In addition to its titular dishes, Tuckaway serves pastries and fresh coffee in the morning and a good selection of sandwiches and salads in the afternoon. There's outdoor, pet-friendly seating.

### American

The building that houses the **Gulf Shore Grill** (1270 Estero Blvd., 239/765-5440, www.gulf-shoregrill.com, 8am-2am daily, main courses from $9) has been right on Fort Myers Beach for nearly a century. The all-day dining here is appropriately classic. Breakfast is a selection of traditional American standards, while the lunch menu is a typical array of burgers (yes, they have a Cheeseburger in Paradise option, like just about every other beach restaurant in Florida), sandwiches, and wraps, with a small selection of Mexican dishes. Dinner gets a little more interesting with filet mignon, prime rib, and seafood platters. The main reason to

The rocking chairs on the roof at Lani Kai are a great spot to watch the sunset.

Fort Myers proper is ★ **Point Ybel Brewing Company** (16120 San Carlos Blvd., 239/603-6535, 4pm-9pm Mon. and Wed.-Thurs., 4pm-10pm Tues. and Fri.-Sat., noon-7pm Sun.), a local microbrewery with expertly crafted beers that are served up super-fresh in a clean, beautiful tasting room that occasionally features some great local and regional live music.

### Cinemas

The tiny, four-screen **Beach Theater** (6425 Estero Blvd., 239/765-9000, www.fmbtheater. com, $12 adults, $9.50 seniors and children) shows first-run movies in a comfortable environment. In addition to popcorn and soda, you can order pizza, beer, wine, and dessert.

### Festivals and Events

For more than 50 years, the **Fort Myers Beach Shrimp Festival** (950 Estero Blvd., www.fortmyersbeachshrimpfestival.com, March) has been an institution in the area. The festival is a weekend-long event, with a huge food-and-crafts-vendors area on the head for the Gulf Shore is for a quick, beach-side bite or a cocktail as the sun sets.

The comfortable environment and rooftop dining area at the ★ **Beached Whale** (1249 Estero Blvd., 239/463-5505, 11am-2am daily, main courses from $9) makes it a popular spot around sunset time, but it's a great place to grab a quick bite or a drink any time of day. In addition to fresh fish and massive sandwiches, the Whale's relatively diverse menu also has some impressive flatbread pizzas and fall-off-the-bone barbecue dishes.

## Fine Dining

"Upscale" in Fort Myers Beach is a somewhat relative term. This is a beach town that takes "casual" pretty seriously, and really, there are only a handful of restaurants that successfully attempt to move beyond the sandy-shoes vibe. Of them, **South Beach Grille** (7205 Estero Blvd., 239/463-7770, 4:30pm-10pm daily, main courses from $13) does it best. Near the marina, but incongruously located in the Santini Marina Plaza strip mall, this is one of the few—if not the only—fine-dining options in Fort Myers Beach. The atmosphere is in keeping with the area's friendly, low-key vibe, and the service here is unpretentious. The food is classic fare, with steaks, chops, and fresh seafood prepared in a classic but thoughtful manner. If you brought good clothes to the beach, this is where you should wear them.

## Seafood

You're at the beach, so seafood is definitely on the menu. And while nearly every restaurant in the American cuisine categories will have a pretty good selection of fresh seafood on the menu, **The Fish House** (7225 Estero Blvd., 239/765-6766, 11am-10pm daily, main courses from $8) is probably your best bet for a seafood-centric dining experience. Located right on the marina, this unpretentious, open-air restaurant specializes in stone crab claws, fried seafood baskets, and ice-cold beer. Get here early if you want a chance at getting a table, or even a barstool. And yes, it's worth it.

Another good choice is the **Smokin' Oyster Brewery** (340 Old San Carlos Blvd., 239/463-3474, www.smokinoyster.com, 11am-11pm daily, main courses from $8), which, yes, specializes in both oysters and beer, two of the most essential ingredients for a successful beach vacation. This is very much a casual, just-off-the-waterfront beach bar, complete with live music and potent cocktails, but the food is actually quite exceptional for a joint like this. The seafood is always super-fresh,

the Smokin' Oyster Brewery in Fort Myers Beach

well-chosen, and expertly prepared, and other menu items like the burgers, sandwiches, and salads utilize fresh, local ingredients as much as possible.

## International

International options on Fort Myers Beach are somewhat limited, but there are a few places to go to get beyond the burgers-and-shrimp-baskets offered at so many spots. **Zushi Zushi** (201 Old San Carlos Blvd., 239/463-9874, www.zushizushi.com, 11:30am-11pm daily, sushi rolls from $6) is a reliable sushi joint in the heart of downtown that doesn't offer much in the way of surprises but does have decent rolls as well as Japanese and Thai kitchen food. It has a full bar and an extensive selection of craft beers, thanks to the fact that it shares space (and a kitchen) with World of Brewz.

**Yo Taco** (1375 Estero Blvd., 239/463-9864, 11am-3am daily, menu items from $2.50) isn't a food truck, but it kinda feels like one, as the walk-up stand offers window service and a few tables in the parking lot. Fillings here are ultra-fresh, and the tacos and burritos are generously stuffed and surprisingly inexpensive, making this an essential lunchtime spot on a beach day.

**Heidi's Island Bistro** (2943 Estero Blvd., 239/765-8844, www.heidisislandbistro.com, 7am-9pm daily, main courses from $7) offers authentic German and European food for breakfast, lunch, and dinner. Portions are huge, sandwiches (especially the Reuben) are fantastic, and you need to make sure to try their from-scratch strudel, no matter what time of day you stop by.

## ACCOMMODATIONS
### $100-200

There are plenty of accommodations to choose from on Fort Myers Beach, and among the best is ★ **Silver Sands Villas** (1207 Estero Blvd., 239/463-6554, doubles from $149). The casual, colorful, and semi-residential atmosphere here definitely makes it feel like a home away from home. Twenty rooms are scattered about the property in cottage-style buildings. Some are basic hotel-type accommodations; others are like tiny houses, complete with living rooms, multiple bedrooms, and kitchens. All of them are brightly painted and have beach-friendly hardwood or tile floors. Flat-screen TVs, soft towels, and deluxe bedding add a surprising touch of luxury. But from the neighborhood cats that roam the property to the super-friendly staff, this choice spot is rather down-to-earth.

The **Beacon Beachfront Bed & Breakfast** (1240 Estero Blvd., 239/463-5264, www.thebeaconmotel.com, doubles from $134) offers an economical and comfortable option very close to the heart of the action in Fort Myers. With 13 individually decorated rooms in various bedding configurations, two suites (one of which has a full kitchen), and a freestanding beach cottage, the Beacon is actually less of a proper bed-and-breakfast than it is a repurposed beachside motel. Although the rooms may not have the same sort of visual style as the pink-and-purple exterior of the building, they do all offer comfortable bedding, clean kitchenettes, and Wi-Fi.

Even more economical—but far from the action in downtown Fort Myers, while being more convenient for Lovers Key—is the **Flamingo Inn** (6090 Estero Blvd., 239/463-9194, http://je-hotels.com/flamingo-inn, doubles from $99), a small, clean, and friendly place with just 14 rooms. It has all the basics, like cable TV, microwaves, fridges, Wi-Fi, and window-unit air conditioners, and the beds are super-comfortable. There's a 7-Eleven across the street, but not much else around, except the beach, which is just a few steps away.

The **Neptune Resort** (2310 Estero Blvd., 239/463-6141, doubles from $159) is a traditional beachfront hotel, complete with two swimming pools, shuffleboard courts, and barbecue grills. There are 70 rooms divided between two wings; if you like crisp and clean, by all means, reserve your room in the newer north wing. Rooms have mini-kitchens, which may account for the popularity of the Neptune among families on a budget.

## $200-300

The all-suite **Edison Beach House** (830 Estero Blvd., 239/463-1530, doubles from $270) is a great option for couples or families. Rooms are large, apartment-style accommodations, with full kitchens, dining areas, sitting areas that feature 47-inch (!) flat-screen TVs, and balconies. The management is pretty fastidious about their cleanliness standards, extending all the way out to the beach, which is raked every morning.

## Over $300

The expansive grounds of the 12-acre **Pink Shell Beach Resort & Marina** (275 Estero Blvd., 239/463-6181, http://pinkshell.com, suites from $329) pack a lot of amenities onto the property, with two restaurants, a spa, an enormous pool, and a specially designated kids' area. Reasonably modern and well-maintained suites and villas range in size from 650 square feet to over 1,000. There's even a private, old-fashioned beach cottage for rent. All the accommodations have full kitchens, dining areas, and separate bedrooms. The best bets here are the Captiva Villas; although they're not the largest, they boast the nicest furnishings and appointments and are in their own, quiet building.

## Vacation Rentals

As with most other beach locales covered in this guide, I can't stress enough how much better of an option vacation rentals are than hotels when you're planning on staying for more than a couple of nights. I love a great hotel and the carefree existence that goes with it. But vacation rentals are both cheaper (in terms of tariff and food expenditures) and more immersive, allowing you to live like a local, even if it's just for a week. With that in mind, there are a few companies on Fort Myers Beach that specialize in getting you into the right property for your visit. Contact **Fun in the Sun Rentals** (1661 Estero Blvd., 239/463-6400, www.funinthesunrentals.com), **TriPower Vacation Rentals** (2001 Estero Blvd., 800/806-4586, www.tripowervacation-rentals.com), or **Beach Accommodations** (1335 Santos Rd., 239/765-1998, www.beachaccommodations.com) to find just the right spot.

The **Bahama Beach Club** (5370 Estero Blvd., 239/463-3148, www.bahamabchclub.com, rentals from $1,200/weekly) offers a unique take on the typical condo-on-the-beach rental. Instead of a shadow-casting tower of identical units, the buildings here are freestanding duplexes, built on stilts right on the sand. There are three rows of gulf-facing units and a collection of units near the pool. The entire property has a low-key, tropical feel, and all the units are modern, clean, and individually decorated by their respective owners. Rentals are on a weekly basis, not nightly, making it a tremendously affordable option for those who intend on staying in the area for more than a few nights.

## INFORMATION AND SERVICES

The **Lee County Visitor & Convention Bureau** (2210 2nd St., Ste. 600, 239/338-3500, www.fortmyers-sanibel.com) can help with information on Fort Myers, Fort Myers Beach, Sanibel and Captiva Islands, and any other destination in Lee County.

Fort Myers Beach has one **Publix** grocery store (4791 Estero Blvd.), which is your best bet for stocking up on supplies. For booze, there's **Nicola's Liquors** (7205 Estero Blvd.). There is also a **CVS Pharmacy** (7001 Estero Blvd.) on the southern end of town. SunTrust, Bank of America, BB&T, and Wells Fargo all have branches and ATMs on the island.

## GETTING THERE AND AROUND
### Getting There

The town of Fort Myers Beach is on an island that's connected to Fort Myers by San Carlos Boulevard and the Matanzas Pass Bridge. The largest airport in the entire southwest Florida region is **Southwest Florida International Airport** (RSW, 11000 Terminal Access Rd., Fort Myers, 239/590-4800, www.flylcpa.com), about a half-hour drive from Fort Myers Beach. It's serviced by most major American carriers, including Southwest. **Greyhound** offers bus service into Fort Myers only, with a station at 2250 Widman Way (239/334-1011).

By car, the nearest major highway is I-75, which connects the southern Gulf Coast with the Midwestern United States. Running roughly parallel to I-75 is the Tamiami Trail (U.S. 41), which runs through Tampa, Sarasota, Fort Myers, Naples, and Miami. Fort Myers Beach can be reached on its northern end via central Fort Myers and on its southern end via Bonita Springs and County Highway 865 (Estero Blvd.).

## Getting Around

Lee County operates **LeeTran** (239/533-8726, www.rideleetran.com), a bus service with decent route service throughout the county and the Fort Myers core. Its **Trollee** service can easily get you right to Fort Myers Beach from the heart of Fort Myers. Fares start at $0.75 per ride, and the trolley runs up and down Estero Boulevard, the main drag in Fort Myers Beach.

The heart of Fort Myers Beach is readily walkable and compact enough so that you really don't need a car if you're anywhere near the main downtown part of the city on the island's northern tip. If you're farther south, biking is a good alternative to having to start up the car.

# Bonita Springs and Estero

Bonita Springs and Estero are both bedroom communities with some interesting sights that are probably best experienced as day trips from Naples and Fort Myers, respectively. However, the beaches and waterfront area around Bonita Springs are quite nice, and make for a pleasant base of operations if beach-going and sightseeing are all that's on your agenda.

## SIGHTS
### ★ Lovers Key State Park

For a rustic beach trip, **Lovers Key State Park** (8700 Estero Blvd., Fort Myers Beach, 239/463-4588, 8am-sundown daily, $8 per vehicle) is a fantastic option. Lovers Key initially gained its reputation and name because it was only accessible by boat, making its beach, um, extra-private. Even though you can now pull into a parking lot and walk a few hundred meters to the beach, this park still has the feel of an isolated and secret location. Even during peak seasons, when there are concessionaires right at the boardwalk, you'll struggle to stifle a giggle that it's not any more crowded than it

is. The beach is two miles long, with the natural barrier-island setting and calm gulf waters instantly relaxing. Renting a canoe or kayak from the concessionaire (from $32/half-day for kayaks and $47/half-day for canoes) allows one to traverse the intimate backwaters, while a bike rental (from $18/half-day) makes the nature trails more easily accessible.

### Everglades Wonder Gardens

The small tropical gardens that comprise **Everglades Wonder Gardens** (27180 Old 41 Rd., Bonita Springs, 239/992-2591, 9am-5pm daily, $12 adults, $10 seniors, $7 children ages 3-12, children under 3 free) are lush and pretty during blooming season. Animal enclosures are somewhat small, so while you may get a chance to lay eyes on a wide variety of beasts—everything from deer and panthers to parrots and, of course, alligators—it's likely you may feel a twinge of sympathy for them. But don't worry: The friendly, longtime staff here is clearly enamored with the beasts. Be sure to listen in as they spin stories about the history of the animals and the property. It's important to keep in mind that many of the animals here are rescue animals, getting a new lease on life, and their keepers are obviously invested in making sure they're well cared for.

## ★ Koreshan State Historic Site

In 1894, Cyrus Teed moved to Estero, Florida. However, unlike many other late-19th-century pioneers in southwest Florida, Teed's mission was not about homesteading or enjoying the subtropical weather. No, Teed—aka Koresh—was the leader of a utopian community called the Koreshans, and they established a small village at what is now the **Koreshan State Historic Site** (3800 Corkscrew Rd., Estero, 239/992-0311, www.floridastateparks.org/koreshan, 8am-sundown daily, $5 per vehicle, $2 pedestrians and bicyclists). While modern-day eyes may see the Koreshans as a cult, the 19th century was something of a prime time for such utopian communities; the Amana Colonies in Iowa and the Oneida Community in New York both left behind legacies (appliances and silverware) that are still with us today. The Koreshans, unfortunately, left little beside some buildings, because thanks to the celestial aspirations of community members, celibacy was one of the group's central tenets, a practice (or lack thereof) that due to sheer mathematics, helped lead to the Koreshans' eventual dwindling. It also didn't help that the group's political aspirations—they incorporated the city of Estero—made locals highly suspicious of their intentions.

Cyrus Teed died in 1908, unable to bring forth his vision of a devout, utopian village of 10 million believers. By 1961, the Koreshan community was down to a single member, Hedwig Michel, who deeded a substantial portion of the grounds of the community to the state of Florida under the precondition that it be used as a state park. (The remaining Koreshan land is controlled by the College of Life Foundation, which is historically connected to the original Koreshan community but has nothing to do with any Koreshan teachings.)

the boardwalk at Lovers Key State Park

Walking through the grounds today is fascinating, because thanks to the upkeep of the buildings by the state of Florida, one is able to get a fairly good picture of what life was like not just for Koreshan followers, but also for many of the early settlers to the area. On top of that, the actual grounds are beautiful, with walking trails and dense natural areas that, while maybe not quite "utopian" (one can easily hear the whooshing of cars on the adjacent Tamiami Trail), are still very pastoral.

## Mound Key Archaeological State Park

The **Mound Key Archaeological State Park** (3800 Corkscrew Rd., Estero, 239/992-0311, www.floridastateparks.org/moundkey, free) is a small island in Estero Bay that's accessible only by boat. The island takes its name from the shell mounds built by the original Native American settlers, and it is said that Mound Key was an incredibly important ceremonial site for the Calusa Indians and was the capital of the Calusa nation. Spanish settlers took over the island, and, for a few years, it was the site of the first Jesuit mission in North America. The Calusa were not okay with this, and there were frequent battles between the new settlers and the area's oldest residents. Eventually, Mound Key was abandoned by the Spanish and the Calusa. There is little left here from either the Spanish or Calusa settlements, but the interpretive exhibits on the nature trail do a good job at explaining the history of the site. That trail is the main thing to see on this largely undeveloped island; there are no facilities, but anglers enjoy fishing the waters of Estero Bay. The best way to access Mound Key is by using the boat launch at the Koreshan State Historic Site; park rangers there can also advise the best ways to explore the island.

## BEACHES

If you're in the area with your four-footed best friend, there is a great dog beach just past the southern end of Lovers Key State Park. Officially known as the **Lee County Off-Leash Dog Area** (8800 Estero Blvd., Bonita Springs, 239/533-7275, www.leeparks.org, sunrise-sunset daily, free), it's not much more than a sandbar with a parking lot—but it's one of the few places in the area where you can let Fido splash around without having to worry about him bothering other beachgoers.

Closer to the heart of Bonita Springs is **Barefoot Beach Preserve County Park** (2 Barefoot Beach Blvd., Bonita Springs, 239/591-8596, 8am-sundown daily, $8 entrance fee per vehicle or free for Collier County residents with a beach parking permit). Although the name may have you picturing an isolated and rustic nature preserve in the middle of nowhere, the reality is somewhat stranger. To get to the park, you'll need to make your way through a gated community of expensive and large houses (don't worry; there's a pass-through lane for beach-bound visitors), rumbling along a private road at the end of which is the park. There, you'll pay the entrance fee for the park and be treated to a somewhat rough and shell-strewn beach that is somewhat narrow, but also quite beautiful. The waters are very calm, and the development (and traffic) is kept to a minimum due to the large number of gopher tortoises that call this preserve home.

Adjacent to Barefoot Beach—but much more directly accessible, as you don't have to drive through a neighborhood to get there—is **Bonita Beach Park** (27954 Hickory Blvd., 239/949-4615, 7am-sundown), which is a

Koreshan State Historic Site

much more typical municipal beach park, with a metered parking lot ($2/hour), bathrooms, a playground, picnic areas, and lots and lots of people.

## SPORTS AND RECREATION

There are more than a dozen golf courses in the area around Bonita Springs and Estero; however, most are private clubs. A good open-to-the-public option is Bonita Springs' **Raptor Bay Golf Club** (23001 Coconut Point Resort Dr., Bonita Springs, 239/390-4610, greens fees from $70 in summer to $179 in winter), an 18-hole, par-71, Raymond Floyd-designed course that's open year-round.

## FOOD

For breakfast, head to **Skillets** (9174 Bonita Beach Rd., Bonita Springs, 239/992-9333, 7am-2pm daily, main courses from $7), a southwest Florida micro-chain that also has two restaurants in Naples (and one in Charlotte, North Carolina, of all places). The menu is highlighted (obviously) by skillet breakfasts, with eggs, potatoes, and various fillings like mushrooms, ham, steak, cheese, and more served in, well, a skillet. Imagine an omelet with its component parts separated and dumped into a pan, and that's a skillet. Skillets also serves waffles, blintzes, crepes, omelets, and other standard breakfast fare. All their bread is freshly baked, and definitely a highlight. The restaurant also serves lunch, with sandwiches, salads, flatbreads, and wraps.

One of the best restaurants in Bonita Springs is **A Table Apart** (4295 Bonita Beach Rd., Bonita Springs, 239/221-8540, www.atableapart.com, 5pm-9pm daily, main courses from $22), which has a kitchen that serves up some remarkable dishes. Unsurprisingly, daily fish specials are ultra-fresh, and menu mainstays like pork chops, rack of lamb, and scallops are paired with unique sauces and side dishes built out of fresh, mostly local ingredients. And hey, how many other restaurants do you know that serve both boiled peanuts and escargot sautéed in coconut milk?

**C-Level Wine Bar** (4450 Bonita Beach Blvd., Bonita Springs, 239/221-7046, 5pm-11pm daily, main courses from $15) has a wide selection of tapas on offer. The best reason to come here is to explore the excellent wine list while noshing on cheese-and-antipasti plates (or even escargot). Desserts include ice cream and pastries.

## ACCOMMODATIONS

If you're going to be staying in the area, you'll likely want to stay in Bonita Springs. The **Trianon Hotel** (3401 Bay Commons Dr., Bonita Springs, 239/948-4400, www.trianon.com, doubles from $155) is where most visitors head, as it's elegant and affordable. It's close to the upscale Shops at the Promenade mall and the Bonita Bay residential community, and it's not too far from the beaches and sights in the area. Rooms are spacious, clean, and well maintained. In addition to standard guest rooms, the Trianon also has one-bedroom suites. All rooms have desks, coffeemakers, and free continental breakfast from the downstairs restaurant.

The nicest hotel in the area is a chain: The **Hyatt Regency Coconut Point Resort** (5001 Coconut Rd., Bonita Springs, 239/444-1234, http://coconutpoint.hyatt.com, doubles from $369) is a luxurious and isolated property, with lush landscaping that gives it a decidedly tropical vibe. That said, it is a huge resort, with four restaurants, shops, a rental-car desk, business center, kids' area, pools, and a spa, so it can feel a little busy. Still, the rooms are quite nice, the staff is friendly, and the availability of canoe and kayak rentals makes it pretty easy to get away from the thrumming crowds and out onto the relative calm of Estero Bay.

If you want to be near the beach, **Lovers Key Resort** (8771 Estero Blvd., 239/765-1040, www.loverskey.com, doubles from $249) is right at the northern boundary of Lovers Key State Park, and technically within the city limits of Fort Myers Beach. It's a pretty anonymous high-rise hotel, but it's nice enough, with clean, modern rooms, a friendly staff, and a restaurant on-site. However, be advised that it's not actually *on* the beach; you'll still have to walk, drive, or take the trolley to get to the park entrance.

## INFORMATION

The **Bonita Springs Area Chamber of Commerce** (25071 Chamber of Commerce Dr., Bonita Springs, 239/992-2943, www.bonitaspringschamber.com) is a good source of information on area attractions, accommodations, and restaurants. The office can supply a glossy, magazine-style guide with lots of ads for local businesses, maps, and more.

## GETTING THERE AND AROUND

Bonita Springs is almost equidistant from Fort Myers in the north and Naples in the south;

it's about 30 minutes via U.S. 41 (Tamiami Trail) or I-75 from either; however, Lovers Key State Park and the rest of Hickory Island are only about 10 minutes from downtown Fort Myers Beach via Estero Boulevard. Estero is slightly north of Bonita Springs, about 20 minutes from downtown Fort Myers via U.S. 41 and I-75.

Lee County operates **LeeTran** (239/533-8726, www.rideleetran.com), a bus service with decent route service throughout the county, with connections between Bonita Springs, Estero, and Fort Myers. Fares start at $0.75 per ride. If you choose not to avail yourself of public transportation, you will need to have a car to get around these two decidedly pedestrian-unfriendly cities; traffic corridors here are huge and merciless.

# Sanibel, Captiva, and the Barrier Islands

**D**espite their multimillion-dollar homes and high-priced hotels and resorts, Sanibel and Captiva Islands are a beach bum's paradise, surprisingly low-key in atmosphere and attitude. Both islands—but Sanibel in particular—are

excellent for shelling and bird-watching, and the beaches are absolutely stunning.

For a more rustic feel, barrier islands like Pine Island and Cayo Costa provide a beautiful glimpse of Old Florida; in the case of the former, it's an Old Florida of fishing villages and friendly charm, while the latter offers absolutely unspoiled nature and gorgeous beaches nearly untouched by human development.

## HISTORY

Six thousand years ago, Sanibel and Captiva were one island, and a few millennia after that, the Calusa Indians arrived. As is the case throughout most of southwest Florida, the Calusa reigned relatively undisturbed in the region until Spanish explorers arrived. By the late 1800s, early American pioneers had begun settling the area, and the Sanibel lighthouse was constructed in 1884. However, for the next 80 years, the islands were sparsely populated, and viewed primarily as an

isolated and private retirement and vacation destination until the Sanibel Causeway was built in 1963, replacing a ferry as the main way to get to the islands. This not only resulted in considerably more visitors and residents, but also led to some wise planning decisions; the city of Sanibel was incorporated in 1974 and immediately went about implementing tight zoning ordinances that prohibited the construction of new chain or fast-food restaurants (the Dairy Queen on the island was grandfathered in).

## PLANNING YOUR TIME

If you only have a couple of days, set yourself down on Sanibel Island and do not leave. Between the beaches, the friendly village atmosphere, and the balance of solitude, beauty, and *just enough* activity, you can make a weekend here exactly the vacation you need.

With more time, plan on spending at least

**Previous:** the Bailey-Matthews Shell Museum; the Sanibel Causeway. **Above:** Sanibel Island Light.

# Highlights

★ **Bailey-Matthews Shell Museum:** Visitors are often said to walk with "the Sanibel stoop," as they bend down to pull shells from the sand. So, it shouldn't be much of a surprise that there's an entire museum devoted to the natural beauty of shells (page 142).

★ **J. N. "Ding" Darling National Wildlife Refuge:** This wildlife refuge, named after one of the early 20th century's most notable (and ecologically minded) political cartoonists, welcomes thousands of guests for the best bird-watching in the entire state (page 145).

★ **Captiva Beach:** There is no shortage of postcard-worthy beaches on these islands. A wide, long, and nearly private expanse of soft white sand makes Captiva Beach one of the best (page 153).

★ **Matlacha:** This salt-of-the-sea fishing village has roots that go back nearly 100 years. It's also an eclectic and vibrant artists' colony (page 161).

★ **Cayo Costa State Park:** Accessible only by boat, this park is home to nine miles of beautiful and peaceful white-sand beaches, five miles of hiking trails, and not much else. And that's just the way it should be (page 166).

# Sanibel, Captiva, and the Barrier Islands

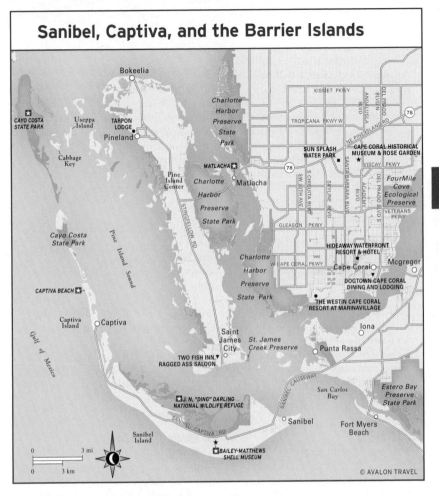

four days on Sanibel and Captiva Islands. You can make your home base on either and explore the sights and beaches of both islands easily. Take a day trip to Pine Island or Cayo Costa to round out your visit.

# Sanibel Island

Sanibel is the larger, more populous, and busier of the twin islands of Sanibel and Captiva. However, all of these definitions are incredibly relative. Just because there are more people and things on Sanibel, well, that doesn't mean that there are a lot of either. The quiet, secluded island feels like a beach town that has only hesitantly embraced its identity as a beach town. From the wide bike paths that straddle all of the main roads in town and the shops and restaurants of the main village area to the numerous residential enclaves, there are parts of Sanibel that feel positively quotidian; however, after just a few minutes of mastering the "Sanibel stoop"—that unique position brought on by continually combing the sands for the numerous shells found here—you'll realize quickly that Sanibel is something special indeed. Welcoming and warm without morphing into a tourist trap, upscale without being exclusionary, and also managing to find the right balance between maintaining its natural beauty and still being a fine place to live (and visit), Sanibel is a truly unique place along the Florida coast.

## SIGHTS
### Sanibel Island Light

First lit in 1884, the **Sanibel Island Light** (112 Periwinkle Way, 239/472-3700, www.nps.gov/maritime/light/sanibel.htm, sunrise-sunset, parking $2/hour) is a stark iron structure that has little of the architectural grace of many lighthouses, and instead projects a tough, industrial visage appropriate for the era of its provenance. The grounds are open to the public, and visitors are more than welcome to roam around, but there's no (legal) way to scale the 98-foot-high tower. Still, there's a great boardwalk nearby that can take you along a nice nature trail, and a stop at the lighthouse is a great side trip for anglers coming to visit the nearby fishing pier.

## Sanibel Historical Village & Museum

The ironic thing about the **Sanibel Historical Village & Museum** (950 Dunlop Rd., 239/472-4648, www.sanibelmuseum.org, 10am-4pm Tues.-Sat. mid-Oct -Apr., 10am-1pm Tues.-Sat. May-July, closed Aug.-mid-Oct., $10 adults, children free) is that the "village" itself has only been around since 1984. Although the eight buildings date from between 1898 and 1926, they were all at different places on the island until the 1980s, when they began to be relocated to this central location, refurbished, and opened as a historical attraction. Despite the relatively young vintage of the village, the buildings themselves are quite interesting, ranging from a blue "kit" house bought from the Sears Roebuck catalog for $2,200 in 1925 and a gas-station-turned-tearoom to a one-room schoolhouse and a tiny post office. There's a small museum in the Rutland House with a collection of antiques and artifacts from around the area. The best way to get a feel for Sanibel's history is to go on one of the docent-guided tours of the village.

## ★ Bailey-Matthews Shell Museum

Shelling is a hugely popular pastime along the barrier islands of the southern Gulf Coast. The **Bailey-Matthews Shell Museum** (3075 Sanibel-Captiva Rd., 239/395-2223, www.shellmuseum.org, 10am-5pm daily, $15 adults, $9 children 12-17, $7 children 5-11, children 4 and under free) goes a long way to putting a serious tilt on an activity many folks undertake as a way to pass the time on a leisurely holiday. The large, modern building on the outskirts of the town of Sanibel has more than two dozen displays of shells, as well as informative mini-exhibits on their various uses throughout history. It may seem somewhat odd to devote so much attention to these temporary marine-life homes, but as

# Sanibel and Captiva Islands

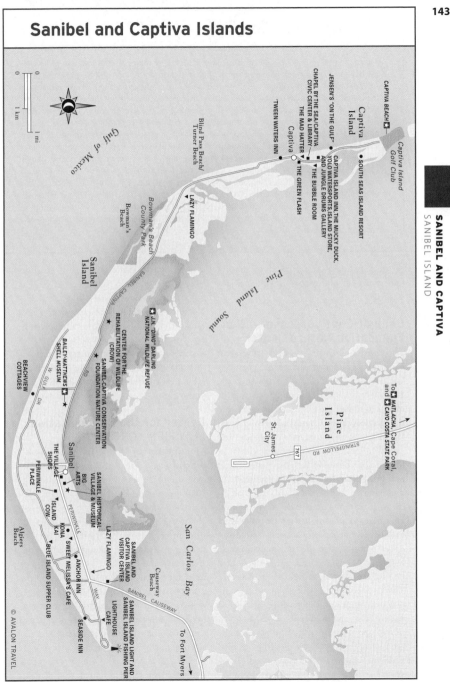

CAPTIVA BEACH

Captiva Island

Captiva Island Golf Club

Gulf of Mexico

CHAPEL BY THE SEA/CAPTIVA CIVIC CENTER & LIBRARY
JENSEN'S "ON THE GULF"
THE MAD HATTER
'TWEEN WATERS INN
Captiva

● SOUTH SEAS ISLAND RESORT

CAPTIVA ISLAND INN, THE MUCKY DUCK, YOLO WATERSPORTS, ISLAND STORE, AND JUNGLE DRUMS GALLERY
▼ THE BUBBLE ROOM
THE GREEN FLASH

Blind Pass Beach/Turner Beach

▲ LAZY FLAMINGO

Bowman's Beach

Bowman's Beach County Park

Sanibel Island

Pine Island Sound

SANIBEL-CAPTIVA

★

⊞ J.N. "DING" DARLING NATIONAL WILDLIFE REFUGE

CENTER FOR THE REHABILITATION OF WILDLIFE (CROW)

SANIBEL-CAPTIVA CONSERVATION FOUNDATION NATURE CENTER

Pine Island

To ✚ MATLACHA, Cape Coral, and ✚ CAYO COSTA STATE PARK

BEACHVIEW COTTAGES ●

BAILEY-MATTHEWS SHELL MUSEUM ⊞

W GULF DR

RD

St. James City

767

STRINGFELLOW RD

Sanibel

THE VILLAGE SHOPS
PERIWINKLE PLACE

BIG ARTS
★
ISLAND COW
KONA KAI
SWEET MELISSA'S CAFE
ANCHOR INN
BLUE ISLAND SUPPER CLUB

SANIBEL HISTORICAL VILLAGE & MUSEUM

PERIWINKLE

LAZY FLAMINGO ▲

SANIBEL AND CAPTIVA ISLAND VISITOR CENTER

San Carlos Bay

Causeway Beach

WAY

SANIBEL CAUSEWAY

To Fort Myers

Algiers Beach

SEASIDE INN

LIGHTHOUSE CAFE

SANIBEL ISLAND LIGHT AND SANIBEL ISLAND FISHING PIER

© AVALON TRAVEL

0 ___ 1 km
0 ___ 1 mi

## The CIA and Sanibel

After a career in espionage, it's easy to imagine that, on retirement, one might want to while away the days on a small, quiet island devoid of international intrigue. For many Central Intelligence Agency officers, Sanibel Island was that small, quiet island, and for decades, Sanibel was known in government circles as one of the preferred retirement destinations for those leaving the CIA. In fact, Sanibel was so popular among retired spooks that, upon retiring from the agency's Directorate of Operations in 1971, Porter Goss moved to Sanibel. Goss's retirement was a medical necessity—he came down with a potentially fatal staph infection—and the urging of fellow retired CIA officers and the beautiful weather of Sanibel made it an easy choice for him to move here. In 1974, Goss was elected to Sanibel's first city council—Goss was a prime motivator behind the city's incorporation—and from 1975 to 1977, he served as the city's mayor. (All the while, he also was the publisher of a community newspaper on the island.) Goss's roles in Sanibel politics ultimately led to his election as the district's representative to the U.S. House of Representatives, and, in something of a full circle, he was appointed director of the CIA by President George W. Bush in 2004. There are probably still quite a few retired CIA operatives living on Sanibel—but you'll never know it.

the museum makes clear, there are extensive bio-science and anthropological implications to shells.

### Sanibel-Captiva Conservation Foundation Nature Center

The **Sanibel-Captiva Conservation Foundation Nature Center** (3333 Sanibel-Captiva Rd., 239/472-2329, www.sccf.org, 8:30am-4pm Mon.-Fri., 10am-3pm Sat.) is the most prominent part of the great work that the Sanibel-Captiva Conservation Foundation (SCCF) does on the islands of Sanibel and Captiva. The 6,900-square-foot facility is the foundation's headquarters, but it also serves as a great place for visitors to acclimate to, and educate themselves about, the ecological and environmental history of the islands. Four miles of well-marked nature trails wend through several different habitats. You're welcome to head out on the trails on your own, but you'd do well to go on one of the guided tours offered daily by the knowledgeable staff. There's also a touch tank and a kid-friendly play area. However, the nature center is just part of what the foundation does. In addition to operating a marine laboratory on the grounds of the J. N. "Ding" Darling National Wildlife Refuge, the foundation also is responsible for the preservation and restoration

of several historic and ecologically sensitive sites on the islands. You'll see SCCF signs at various locations; some—like the Bailey Homestead, home to the Native Landscapes & Garden Center—are open to the public, others are active restoration projects with an eye toward tourism, while still others are primarily lands that have been removed from the development pool with an eye toward ecological preservation.

### Center for the Rehabilitation of Wildlife (CROW)

The **Center for the Rehabilitation of Wildlife** (CROW, 3883 Sanibel-Captiva Rd., 239/472-3644, www.crowclinic.org, 10am-4pm Mon.-Sat. Jan.-Apr., 10am-4pm Mon.-Fri. May-Dec., $12 adults, $7 children, children 3 and under free) has a visitors education center that highlights the center's work in rescuing and rehabilitating the native wildlife of Sanibel. The center treats more than 4,000 animals annually, and the primary role of the popular visitors center is to raise awareness in order to bring that number down. Most of the displays are designed to simultaneously impress upon guests the diversity of the area's wildlife and teach them what they can do to reduce the number of animals injured or threatened by human development.

# ★ J. N. "Ding" Darling National Wildlife Refuge

The **J. N. "Ding" Darling National Wildlife Refuge** (1 Wildlife Dr., 239/472-1100, education center 9am-5pm daily Jan.-Apr., 9am-4pm daily May-Dec., free; Wildlife Drive 7:30am-sunset Sat.-Thurs., $5 per vehicle) is named after Jay Norwood "Ding" Darling, a political cartoonist in the early 1900s whose primary interests were political corruption and environmental conservation. As a hunter and angler, Darling was a fierce advocate for wise land use, and he understood that intelligent regulations could ensure the viability of wildlife for generations to come. His cartoons earned him three Pulitzer Prizes, but perhaps one of his greatest accomplishments was being tapped by Franklin Roosevelt to head up the U.S. Biological Survey (the predecessor of today's U.S. Fish & Wildlife Service). In that position, Darling focused squarely on habitat preservation and restoration, as well as game management, all of which led to the establishment of national wildlife refuges throughout the United States.

Darling often wintered on Sanibel and Captiva, so it was only appropriate that one of the earliest national wildlife refuges—the Sanibel National Wildlife Refuge—was renamed in his honor. The J. N. "Ding" Darling National Wildlife Refuge is a permanent home or migratory stopover for more than 50 species of birds, and in the winter, the mudflats and waterfront trees are thick with spoonbills, oystercatchers, storks, ibis, and other birds. There is also a diversity of mammal and reptile life within the refuge, but bird-watching is one of the primary activities.

The refuge's Wildlife Drive, a five-mile circuit that's open to automobiles, is quite popular, especially during the winter. It allows visitors a leisurely route through the park's mangrove forests and mudflats in their own vehicles. A tour company also provides tram tours along the drive. There are also several hiking trails and two canoe trails for those who wish to explore on their own. The visitors center is also an impressive sight, with exhibits that give perspective on Darling's career as well as the variety of wildlife within the refuge. There's a pronounced sense of mission at the refuge; the staff and volunteers are exceedingly friendly and helpful, and their enthusiasm is contagious.

**SANIBEL AND CAPTIVA**
SANIBEL ISLAND

the J. N. "Ding" Darling National Wildlife Refuge

# BEACHES

**Causeway Beach** (sunrise-sunset daily), along the road between Sanibel and Fort Myers is, despite the traffic zooming by, quite nice. Parking is free, and bathrooms and picnic tables are at the main beach area right before the toll gate. The water is a bit rougher than on the island, but it's shallow, and the sandy beaches are stocked with shells.

Once on the island, beach lovers should head directly for **Algiers Beach** (Algiers Ln. at W. Gulf Rd., sunrise-sunset daily, parking $2/hour). This isolated beach is named after a steamboat that ran aground and was used as a home for a while. A favorite of locals, it has facilities (picnic tables, restrooms, a paid parking lot), but the beach itself is seldom very crowded. The sand has a lot of shells and the water is smooth and shallow; leashed pets are allowed.

Another quiet option is **Bowman's Beach** (end of Bowman's Beach Rd., sunrise-sunset daily, parking $2/hour); to get here, head northwest on Sanibel-Captiva Rd. and then left on Bowman's Beach Rd. The parking lot is a bit of a hike from the actual beach, and the general isolation of the location (it's quite a ways from any hotels or residences) gives it an insider's secret feel. However, the beach itself is fairly popular (the parking lot can fill up quickly). The white sand spreads out quite a distance from the entry point, so it's pretty easy to find a quiet spot. It's a very nicely equipped park, with picnic tables, barbecue grills, restrooms, a fitness trail, a playground, and an outdoor shower.

# SPORTS AND RECREATION
## Boating and Fishing

**Tarpon Bay Explorers** (900 Tarpon Bay Rd., 239/472-8900, fishing charters from $175/two people, nature cruises from $23, kayak/canoe/stand-up paddleboard rentals from $25/two hours) is within the J. N. "Ding" Darling National Wildlife Refuge, and is the company that provides the tram tours of the refuge's wildlife trail. The company also offers a couple of guided kayak and canoe tours; fishing supplies; and kayak, canoe, and pontoon rentals. At the company's main location, they have a gift shop and visitors center with a touch tank that allows kids (and adults) to get hands-on with hermit crabs, urchins, sea stars, and more.

Anglers interested in throwing a line in close to shore should head for the **Sanibel Island Fishing Pier** (112 Periwinkle Way, 239/472-3700, parking $2/hour). From there, you'll be able to land redfish, snook, sea trout, snapper, and grouper year-round, while the spring and summer months bring tarpon, cobia, and pompano. Heavier tackle is recommended here. You can pick up any necessary supplies at **The Bait Box** (1041 Periwinkle Way, 239/472-1618, www.thebaitbox.com, opens 7am daily), in the heart of Sanibel village.

## Golf and Tennis

There's not much golfing to be found on Sanibel, but this being Florida, it's not exactly nonexistent. The **Beachview Golf & Tennis Club** (1100 Par View Dr., 239/472-2626, greens fees from $40) and the top-rated **Dunes Golf & Tennis Club** (949 Sand Castle Rd., 239/472-3355, greens fees from $25) both offer 18 holes of golf. The Dunes has 13 tennis courts, and the Beachview has 5 courts.

## Biking

There are ample bike trails throughout Sanibel, and the flat surfaces make biking on the island far preferable to driving. **Billy's Rentals** (1470 Periwinkle Way, 239/472-5248, bike rentals from $5, scooter rentals from $40) has bikes, surreys, and scooters for rent, and offers Segway tours of the island, too. Another good option for bike rentals and repairs is **Finnimore's Cycle Shop** (2353 Periwinkle Way, 239/472-5577, www.finnimores.com, bike rentals from $13/day), which offers singles, tandems, and surreys, as well as beach gear, paddleboards, and kayak rentals.

# Shells Abound

Shells are numerous on the beaches of Sanibel Island.

Shelling on Sanibel Island goes far beyond the casual, exploratory pickings of a lazy day at the beach. No, shells are serious business; Sanibel and Captiva are known as the "Shell Islands," and there's even the **Bailey-Matthews Shell Museum** on Sanibel dedicated to them. Thanks to a peculiar confluence of Gulf of Mexico currents, and the geographical position of the island, Sanibel sees a large number of empty marine-life homes washing up on its shores. Sanibel itself is positioned on an unusual east-west trajectory (rather than the north-south of most barrier islands in the Gulf), and more than 400 different species of shells—from bivalves to conchs—can be found on the beaches, being dug up by visitors of all ages who, by the end of their vacation, are suffering from what's known as "the Sanibel stoop."

## ENTERTAINMENT AND EVENTS
### Nightlife

There's not much in the way of dedicated nightlife spots on Sanibel, but there's plenty of fun to be had at **Doc Ford's Rum Bar & Grille** (South Sea Islands Resort, 2500 Island Inn Rd., 239/472-8311, www.docfordssanibel. com, 11am-10pm daily). Founded by noted Florida author Randy Wayne White (and named after the star of his series of area-located crime novels), it's much more of a restaurant-cum-sports-bar kind of place, with good food and a festive bar area beloved by locals and tourists alike.

### The Arts

The arts scene on Sanibel pretty much falls under the umbrella of **Big Arts** (900 Dunlop Rd., 239/395-0900, www.bigarts.org, gallery hours 9am-4pm Mon.-Fri., 9am-1pm Sat.), the island's main (and only) dedicated cultural center. The center has a 400-seat performance hall, art gallery, sculpture garden, and classrooms. It's an impressive facility for such a small island, and Big Arts maintains a pretty robust cultural calendar throughout the year, one that greatly expands during the high-season winter months. Classical music, theater, dance, jazz concerts, art exhibits, and more make their way here, and the offerings consistently manage to produce a comfortable, community-oriented atmosphere that's respectful without being stuffy.

### Festivals and Events

For almost a quarter century, the **Sanibel Shell Fair & Show** (Mar.) has drawn beachcombers and shell aficionados to the island. Taking place over three days at the Sanibel Community House, there's an outdoor fair with shell-themed crafts and vendors. Inside, there's a show ($3 admission), where rare shells, jewelry, and juried exhibits are on display.

In November, local restaurants strut their stuff at the CROW-sponsored **Taste of the Islands.** Live music and local craft vendors round out the offerings at this one-day fundraiser/family-friendly event in Sanibel Community Park.

## SHOPPING
### Periwinkle Place

**Periwinkle Place** (2075 Periwinkle Way) is about as close as Sanibel gets to having a mall. This is the largest concentration of stores on the island, with a half-dozen clothing boutiques, like **Island Pursuit** (239/472-4600) and **Fresh Produce** (239/395-1800); a couple of jewelry stores; and gift shops like **Sanibel Olive Oil** (239/579-0151) and **Tiki Jim's** (239/472-0188). All of the shops are located in a few detached buildings that are comfortable and inviting. There's also a pretty good restaurant on-site, in the form of **The Blue Giraffe** (239/472-2525, 9am-9pm daily, breakfast and lunch from $6, dinner from $10).

### The Village Shops

On the western edge of the heart of Sanibel, **The Village Shops** (2340 Periwinkle Way) is a small shopping center with just about 10 businesses. There are boutiques and even a wine shop, **Sanibel Tropical Wines** (239/472-3398), where you can pick up a bottle of fruit-derived vino. Additionally, there's one art gallery, **Watson MacRae Gallery** (239/472-3386), while **Tribeca Salon**

(239/395-3800) is the place to go if you need to get your hair or nails done.

### Other Shops

There are lots of other shops, boutiques, and galleries on Sanibel, and most of them are in the main village area of the island. **Lily & Co.** (520 Tarpon Bay Rd., 239/472-2888, www.lilyjewelers.com, 10am-5pm Mon.-Sat.) specializes in couture jewelry, but the store also offers a range of gifts and cost-accessible jewelry items. The shop and its products are surprisingly full of personality. Book lovers will want to carve out some time to hang out at the comfortable and quirky **Gene's Books** (2365 Periwinkle Way, 239/395-0500, 10am-5pm Mon.-Sat.). And, if you want to get your hands on one of Sanibel's most famous souvenirs—seashells—without bothering to dig around in the sand for your own, **She Sells Sea Shells** has two locations (2422 Periwinkle Way, 239/472-8080, and 1157 Periwinkle Way, 239/472-6991) where you can pick up a wide variety of shell-inspired artwork.

## FOOD
### Breakfast

Nestled into the village-like atmosphere of eastern Sanibel Island, the **Lighthouse Cafe** (362 Periwinkle Way, 239/472-0303, www.lighthousecafe.com, 7am-3pm daily, main courses from $8) claims to have the "world's best breakfast." Breakfast here is definitely not "the world's best breakfast," but it's nonetheless pretty popular, resulting in long waits and service that ranges from perfunctory to nonexistent. Morning-meal standards (eggs Benedict, omelets, waffles, etc.) are augmented by a few interesting additions like frittatas and shrimp-and-crab omelets, but, once you finally get a table, you may be more interested in one of the Lighthouse's sake-based Bloody Marys or mimosas, so then you can take your own sweet time.

The quaint and quirky **Island Cow** (2163 Periwinkle Way, 239/472-0606, 7am-9pm daily, main courses from $7) is a great place to grab a great meal any time of day. Breakfast seems to function with a theme of "more is more." Whether it's one of their enormous pancakes, a belt-stretching seafood omelet (which combines shrimp, scallops, and crabmeat, and what seems like a half-dozen eggs and a quarter pound of cheese), or a plate of eggs, grits, and home fries, there's absolutely no way you'll push back from the morning table feeling hungry. The lunch and dinner menus are no less satisfying, with quesadillas, po'boys, pasta, and seafood dishes. Beer and wine are served too, but the beverages of choice come from their dairy bar, which whips up smoothies, milkshakes, floats, and even egg creams.

Just down the street is another good breakfast option, the tiny **Over Easy Cafe** (630-1 Tarpon Bay Rd., 239/472-2625, www.over-easycafesanibel.com, 7am-3pm daily, main courses from $7). There's an outdoor patio that's perfect for an alfresco morning meal (you can even bring your dog). Make sure to try one of their excellent eggs Benedict plates (the shrimp version is amazing), as well as one of the decadent cinnamon rolls, which are as huge as they are popular.

## Seafood

The best choice for seafood raw bar fans would be the **Lazy Flamingo** (1036 Periwinkle Way, 239/472-6939; 6520 Pine Ave., 239/472-5353; 11am-midnight daily, main courses from $10). In addition to freshly shucked oysters and clams, the Flamingo also has a standard selection of fried seafood, conch fritters, sandwiches, salads, and wings.

Another great low-key option for super-fresh seafood is **The Clam Shack** (2407 Periwinkle Way, 239/472-6882, theclam-shacksanibel.com, 11:30am-8pm daily, main courses from $12), which serves up New England-style dishes (lobster rolls, clam bakes, shrimp sandwiches, plus nonstop Boston sports) in a casual and warm environment. Prices are reasonable (especially for Sanibel), and the food is superb.

If you're traveling with kids, **George & Wendy's Sanibel Seafood Grille** (2499 Periwinkle Way, 239/395-1263, www.sani-belseafoodgrille.com, 11am-1am daily, main courses from $11) is a prime spot for some post-beach grub. Not only are kids' meals served on Frisbees that the little ones can take with them, but weary adults can take advantage of a wide selection of beer and wine. The seafood is fresh, and while most of the dishes are unsurprising, there are a few like the grouper Reuben and piña colada snapper that break up the predictability somewhat. Don't overlook the burgers; for a restaurant with "seafood" in the name, George & Wendy's may just do its best work when putting together a plain old hamburger.

For dinner, the seafood preparations at **Gramma Dot's** (634 N. Yachtsman Dr., 239/472-8138, 11:30am-8pm daily, lunch from $9, dinner from $19) are uniformly dependable. Though some may balk at the notion of spending $23 on a plate of coconut shrimp, the prawns used are gigantic and super-fresh, coated perfectly with coconut shavings and served with a rich, sweet pineapple sauce. Scallops, grouper, and mahi-mahi round out the seafood section of the small menu, which also has a few steak and chicken dishes.

## American

Just need a hot dog? Hit up **Schnapper's Hots** (1528 Periwinkle Way, 239/472-8686, www.schnappershotssanibel.com, 11am-4pm daily, from $6), a friendly, no-frills spot that serves franks, burgers, fries, pizza, and fresh ice cream.

## Fine Dining

The best fine-dining option on Sanibel is the perfectly named **Blue Coyote Supper Club** (1100 Par View Dr., 239/472-9222, www.blue-coyotesupperclub.com, lunch 11am-3pm Sun.-Fri., dinner 5pm-9pm Tues.-Sat., main courses from $25). An extension of a members-only restaurant in Fort Myers, the Blue Coyote on Sanibel is open to anyone . . . or at least anyone who's ready to shell out at least $50 on dinner for two. The food—a skillful and modern take on Continental cuisine with standards like beef tenderloin sitting alongside inspired comfort food like a seafood-and-sausage stew—is remarkable for its emphasis on consistency and quality, rather than adventurous flourishes. However, the atmosphere, thanks to a variety of whimsically dark paintings at the club's heart and a friendly and attentive (but not obsequious) staff, ensures that this feels less like your grandparents' stuffy supper club and more like dinner at your artsy chef friend's house.

Despite a name that may conjure images of a classic rock-inspired bar-and-grill, **Sweet Melissa's Cafe** (1625 Periwinkle Way, 239/472-1956, www.sweetmelissascafe. net, lunch 11:30am-2:30pm Mon.-Fri., dinner 5pm-close Mon.-Sat., main courses from $26) is, in fact, one of the best fine-dining options on Sanibel Island. The menu is extensive and varied. Executive chef Melissa Talmage wisely invests her talents in presenting a wide array of nearly 20 tapas-style small plates that allow diners to indulge in anything from a goat cheese crepe and bourbon-glazed pork belly to ricotta ravioli with Kobe beef-cheek sugo (a kind of sauce); even the entrées—of which there are half a dozen—are available in small portions to basically make the entire menu a tasting menu. It's a smart and fantastic way to explore a range of flavors, and, incredibly, Talmage seems to excel at all of the preparations.

## ACCOMMODATIONS

During high season, "budget accommodations" on Sanibel and Captiva is an incredibly relative term. Many places offer incredible values during the scorching summer months, but when the snowbirds descend from November through April, overnight rates go through the roof; at many places, there are minimum stay requirements.

### Under $300

**Anchor Inn** (1245 Periwinkle Way, 239/395-9688, doubles from $229) is a centrally located property with a variety of room options, ranging from basic hotel accommodations and one- and two-room efficiencies to a two-bedroom cottage. Rooms are cute and tidy, with tropical color schemes; the bright-yellow, two-story cottages have sleeping lofts and bedrooms. There's a heated pool and grilling/picnic area.

The tropical foliage that engulfs the **Kona Kai** (1539 Periwinkle Way, 239/472-1001, doubles from $199) does an admirable job at masking the traditional motel feel of this property, and in addition to a handful of regular rooms, there are efficiency and suite accommodations, as well as two small cottages. All of the rooms have garden views, with the exception of the pool cottage, which, logically, overlooks the pool. Furnishings are, ironically, not quite as heavy on the tropical rattan-and-pastels theme that many other properties go for; instead, they're clean and contemporary.

Located right on the beach, the perfectly named ★ **Beachview Cottages** (3325 W. Gulf Dr., 239/472-1202, doubles from $235) is a great, reasonably priced option. A handful of cottages are lined up along a sandy pathway to the beach. These small, 1960s-era lodgings are comfortable and clean, with full kitchens. Although the resort is situated among condos along West Gulf Drive, the Beachview feels like it is its own private village.

Since it's on the Fort Myers side of the Sanibel Causeway, the **Sanibel Harbour Marriott Resort & Spa** (17260 Harbour Pointe Dr., 239/466-4000, www.marriott. com, doubles from $249) is extraordinarily convenient to Sanibel Island (despite the $6 toll to cross the causeway), and is actually closer to Sanibel than it is to downtown Fort Myers. It's a large, well-appointed resort that offers beautiful views of San Carlos Bay and Sanibel Island. Most of the accommodations are in the 350-room hotel, which offers traditional guest rooms and a variety of suites; all of these rooms have private balconies, coffeemakers, mini-fridges, and microwaves, and are decorated in a light, tropical style. Suites range from studio-size (includes a sleeper sofa and a bit more space) to 1,400-square-foot mini-apartments. Condo rentals are also available. The resort features a large spa and fitness facility, five restaurants, an evening dinner cruise, and tennis and golf facilities. The overall atmosphere is one of isolated luxury; you'll have to traverse the bridge over to Sanibel Island to commune with non-guests, as the property at Sanibel Harbour is self-contained.

### Over $300

The ★ **Seaside Inn** (541 E. Gulf Dr., 239/472-1400, www.sanibelcollection.com, doubles from $379) manages to combine a casual, classic beach feel with subtly upscale appointments and highly attentive service, resulting in one of the most luxurious and comfortable places to stay on Sanibel Island. Though built in the 1960s, the inn was completely renovated in the mid-2000s to meet the expectations held by many of the island's well-to-do visitors. The Seaside is a part of the "Inns of Sanibel" family of hotels. From the daily in-room delivery of a continental breakfast (a basket of pastries, fresh fruit, juice, and coffee) to the plush in-room appointments, the Seaside is simultaneously charming and posh. The 32 units are spacious, ranging from standard guest rooms to studio cottages and three-bedroom suites, and they're all decorated tastefully, with muted tropical tones and contemporary furnishings. All rooms have at least a mini-kitchen, and the cottages have full kitchens; DVD players (and a free rental library) and Wi-Fi are also available. More to the point, gorgeous blue waters are right outside your window.

The **Song of the Sea** (863 E. Gulf Dr., 239/472-3181, www.sanibelcollection.com, doubles from $329) is also part of the "Inns of Sanibel" family of hotels, and is positioned to appeal to deep-pocketed visitors who crave charm and personality but don't want to sacrifice luxury and service. The pink-hued resort couldn't scream "romance" any louder, from its quiet, tropical atmosphere to the bottle of wine that greets guests upon arrival. There's a lot to love for couples, without feeling like you've stepped into a champagne-glass whirlpool tub. There are only 30 rooms on the property, and all are comfortable and cozy without being cramped. Tile floors, ceiling fans, and wooden blinds give the rooms a classic tropical vibe, and all the rooms and suites have their own kitchenettes and Wi-Fi.

### Vacation Rentals

As with many small beach towns, one of the

the Kona Kai motel

best lodging options on Sanibel and Captiva is a vacation rental; unlike at many other beach towns, the rentals can climb to astronomically high rates. Still, explore the listings at **SanibelRent** (www.sanibelrent.com), where weekly condo rentals can be found during the winter for as low as $900; house rentals are also available, but only on a monthly basis. **Lighthouse Realty** (www.lighthouserealtyoftheislands.com) also has weekly condo rentals and similarly only rents houses by the month.

## INFORMATION AND SERVICES

The **Lee County Visitor & Convention Bureau** (2201 2nd St., Suite 600, Fort Myers, 239/338-3500, www.fortmyers-sanibel.com) is a great source of information for Sanibel, Captiva, Pine Island, and the barrier islands. The Sanibel & Captiva Islands Chamber of Commerce operates the **Sanibel & Captiva Island Visitor Center** (1159 Causeway Rd., Sanibel, 239/472-1080, www.sanibel-captiva. org), which is the first building you'll see as you come off the Sanibel Causeway onto Sanibel Island.

There are several banks in central Sanibel village, including a **Bank of America** (2450 Periwinkle Way) branch with an ATM, **Bank of the Islands** (1699 Periwinkle Way), and **Sanibel Captiva Community Bank** (1037 Periwinkle Way).

If you didn't stock up on groceries on the mainland (you should have!), there are several nice (if pricey) markets on Sanibel, such as **Jerry's Foods** (1700 Periwinkle Way, 239/472-9300, www.jerrysfoods.com, 6am-10pm daily), which is a gourmet supermarket and deli; **Huxter's Market** (1201 Periwinkle Way, 239/472-2151, www.huxtersmarket.com, 6:30am-9pm daily); and the **Santiva General Store** (6406 Sanibel-Captiva Rd., 239/472-5556, 8am-8pm Mon.-Thurs., 8am-9pm Fri.-Sat., 8am-7pm Sun.).

Bicyclists will find Sanibel Island quite welcoming.

There's a **CVS Pharmacy** (2331 Palm Ridge Rd., 239/472-1719) at the western end of Sanibel village.

## GETTING THERE AND AROUND

The only way to drive onto Sanibel Island is via the Sanibel Causeway, which connects the island to Punta Rassa, just at the western tip of mainland Fort Myers. There's a $6 toll to go onto the island.

You can drive around Sanibel if you want to, but you really should ride a bike. Twenty-five miles of wide, multi-use trails run parallel to the main roads, and unless you're staying on the eastern tip of the island and want to make it all the way to the other end, the flat terrain is optimal for biking. Using a bike for your main mode of transportation also makes parking at crowded beach access points much easier.

# Captiva Island

Captiva is, predominantly, an island of exclusive waterfront residences. There are a few hotels, a tiny downtown area, and one main public beach, but for the most part, Captiva's beauty is largely reserved for Captiva's residents. And that's fine, since it means that for those who do manage to vacation here, you're all but guaranteed a pleasant, relaxing, and completely undemanding stay. With nothing for you to do but luxuriate on the beautiful, white sand of the beach or maybe head out on a kayak excursion, Captiva is blissfully free of distractions.

## SIGHTS

As far as "sights" go on Captiva, there just aren't that many. Beyond the island itself, of course. It's important to remember that this is very much a residential enclave. Visitors are encouraged to live as the locals do. To that end, pretty much the only thing to see is the **Chapel by the Sea** (11580 Chapin Ln., 239/472-1646, www.captivachapel.com), a tiny, historic church nestled among the sea grapes and sand next to the Captiva Civic Center and Library. There's a beautiful, peaceful cemetery with more than a century's worth of history, but the small white church building is exactly the sort of religious outpost that speaks both to the faith of some of Captiva's early Caucasian settlers as well as to the sense of community that has long defined this beautiful island.

## BEACHES
### ★ Captiva Beach

At the northern tip of Captiva Island is **Captiva Beach** (14790 Captiva Dr., 239/472-2472, www.leegov.com/parks, 7am-7pm, parking $5/two hours), a part of **Alison Hagerup Beach Park,** and one of only two publicly accessible beaches on the island. (Although the beach along the main road is, technically, publicly accessible, there is absolutely nowhere to park to actually access it. So, unless you're renting a house nearby, there's no easy way to get to the beach.) The wide expanse of soft white sand is quite popular, but the tiny parking lot has the effect of limiting daily attendance. This is one of the

**SANIBEL AND CAPTIVA**
CAPTIVA ISLAND

Chapel by the Sea is one of the few "sights" on Captiva Island.

most beautiful beaches on either island. Get here early to enjoy the shallow, blue waters or to explore for shells. Despite being a named park—Alison Hagerup Beach Park—the only facilities are portable toilets.

### Blind Pass Beach and Turner Beach

**Blind Pass Beach** and **Turner Beach** (17200 Captiva Dr., 239/395-1860, www.leeparks.org, sunrise-sunset daily, parking $2/hour) are on either side of the bridge that links Sanibel and Captiva Islands; Blind Pass Beach is technically on the Sanibel side, but both are closer to the action in Captiva than in Sanibel. Neither beach is particularly excellent for swimming; the undertow can be quite strong, especially near the bridge. But that same wave activity also makes for some incredible shelling at both beaches. The soft white sand and crisp blue water are absolutely gorgeous, making this a good place for sunbathing and a near-perfect spot for couples to catch the sunset. Fishing is quite popular at both beaches.

### SPORTS AND RECREATION

**Captiva Kayak** (11401 Andy Rosse Ln., 239/395-2925, kayak rentals from $30/2.5 hours, stand-up paddleboard rentals from $30/hr) offers a range of predetermined kayak rental routes, as well as half-day and multiple-day rentals that include car racks. Additionally, they provide two-hour guided tours of the Buck Key kayak trail and sunset kayak tours. Sailboat rentals are also available.

At **YOLO Watersports & Jim's Rentals** (11534 Andy Rosse Ln., 239/472-9656, eight-hour bike rentals from $10, one-hour scooter rentals from $45), you can rent everything from bikes and scooters to golf carts, beach gear, GoPro cameras, paddleboards, coolers, Jet Skis, and more.

### SHOPPING

Given the tiny nature of downtown Captiva, it shouldn't come as much of a surprise that shopping is somewhat limited. However, you'll definitely find yourself browsing the shelves at the **Island Store** (11500 Andy Rosse Ln., 239/472-2374, www.captivaislandstore.com, 8am-6pm Sun.-Thurs., 8am-8pm Fri.-Sat.) at some point during your stay. It's the only grocery on the island, and, given the tastes of many Captiva visitors, you won't be surprised by the great selection of gourmet foods, organic produce, fine wines, and exceptional baked goods. They also sell beer and

the public beach on north Captiva Island

wine (there's a liquor store next door), as well as souvenirs and gift items.

The vividly painted **Jungle Drums Gallery** (11532 Andy Rosse Ln., 239/395-2266, www.jungledrumsgallery.com, 11am-7pm Mon.-Sat.) is also worth checking out (it's hard to miss). With everything from giant bronze sculptures and furniture to delicately handcrafted jewelry and paintings, this gallery emphasizes pan-global visuals, with a focus on works that represent wildlife.

# FOOD
## Pub Grub
**The Mucky Duck** (11546 Andy Rosse Ln., 239/472-3434, www.muckyduck.com, 11:30am-9:30pm daily, main courses from $18) is a basic pub-with-grub place, serving up a somewhat unique combination of seafood platters and traditional English fare. Mucky Duck has an unbeatable location right on the sand. It boasts a fantastic outdoor dining area, with some of the best sunset views in the entire state of Florida, making it something of a must-stop for most visitors to Captiva.

The colorful **RC Otters** (11506 Andy Rosse Ln, 239/395-1142, 8am-10pm daily, main courses from $8) is a smaller, less-touristy spot (which is ironic, considering it's in the heart

of "downtown" Captiva), serving up breakfast, burgers, sandwiches, and fried seafood baskets. There is frequently live music, but the bar scene—though lively—is always well behaved, so families should feel comfortable bringing the kids.

## American
Located at the Captiva Island Inn, **Keylime Bistro** (11509 Andy Rosse Ln, 239/395-4000, 8am-10pm daily, breakfast and lunch from $10, dinner from $22) offers an array of fresh seafood dishes and pasta plates for dinner, sandwiches and salads for lunch, and a standard selection of breakfast dishes. The best way to approach the menu, though, is to focus on the full page of appetizers, which range from seafood (fried shrimp, seafood antipasto, tuna tataki) to nachos, chicken fingers, and fried calamari. The portions on these small plates are generous, and any of them makes a perfect accompaniment to the wide selection of custom cocktails available at the bar.

No visit to Captiva would be complete without a meal at the **Bubble Room** (15001 Captiva Dr., 239/472-5558, lunch 11am-3pm daily, dinner 4:30pm-10pm daily, main courses from $14)—perhaps not so much for the food, but for the sheer insanity of

The whimsical vibe at the Bubble Room extends to its exterior.

the decor. Imagine decades' worth of movie memorabilia, vintage toys, pop culture effluvia, and various kitsch from the 1930s, '40s, and '50s jammed into a restaurant where the servers are dressed as youth scouts and you're halfway there. The Bubble Room is definitely quirky and has played on that reputation for years, but what makes the environment so much fun is the sense that all that crazy clutter is there by accident, and not by design; it doesn't feel like a corporate-designed bit of weirdness, it's just weird. Dishes like the Duck Ellington, the Cluck Gable, and the Salmon Davis Jr. are more fun to order than they are to eat, but they're still quite decent. By far the best thing on the menu is the Bubble Bread, a decadently sweet sticky-bun concoction that is perhaps the best finish-your-vegetables bribe ever invented.

The ★ **Mad Hatter** (6460 Sanibel-Captiva Rd., 239/472-0033, 5pm-10pm Tues.-Sun., main courses from $18) serves a selection of excellent dishes like seared duck breast, truffle-encrusted scallops, and foie gras in a unique environment that melds luxe touches and a whimsical *Alice in Wonderland* motif. Grab a window seat for marvelous sunset views.

**The Green Flash** (15183 Captiva Dr., 239/472-3337, www.greenflashcaptiva.com, 11:30am-9:30pm daily, main courses from $26) can also offer some extraordinary views, thanks to its unusual-for-Captiva second-floor location. However, keep in mind that the windows are facing east, so this isn't a place to head for sunset drinks and dinner. The menu is focused squarely on seafood, with shrimp, crab, and multiple grouper preparations making up the bulk of the dinner menu. (They also serve several veal and pork dishes.) Dinner can be a pretty expensive endeavor, and the food is decent without being remarkable; the Green Flash is a much better bet for lunch, when you can grab a burger, a basket of fried shrimp, or one of the excellent veggie sandwiches for less than $10 while enjoying the view of the boats in Pine Island Sound.

## Mexican

**Cantina Captiva** (14970 Captiva Dr, 239/472-0248, 11:30am-10pm daily, main courses from $10) is the only Mexican restaurant on Sanibel or Captiva, so it really doesn't have to try too hard to be the best. Fortunately, the menu offers a couple of interesting additions to the standard fare found in most Mexican restaurants; be sure to try the tamales, which are wrapped in banana leaves. The basics—tacos, burritos, etc.—are covered, and the chips and salsa, of all things, is one of this place's signature items. The atmosphere and service leave something to be desired, but, again, it's the only Mexican restaurant on Sanibel or Captiva.

## ACCOMMODATIONS
### Under $300

**Jensen's "On the Gulf"** (15300 Captiva Dr., 239/472-4684, www.gocaptiva.com, doubles from $165) is a unique collection of 10 villas, cottages, suites, and beach houses. It has an intimate, boutique vibe. Each room is decorated differently, but all the furnishings are very nice and comfortable. One of the most interesting spots is the "Post Office Sweet," which was originally the Captiva Post Office but is now a semi-private cottage. This is one of the few properties on Captiva that's directly on the beach. The Jensen family also operates the nearby Twin Palm Marina.

**South Seas Island Resort** (5400 Plantation Rd., 866/565-5089, www.southseas.com, doubles from $229) attracts folks who want packaged activities and condo-style accommodations. South Seas feels a bit isolated from the heart and spirit of Captiva, a pretty exclusive and recherché version of a beach town. Still, for families and those who want all their amenities within arm's reach, this is probably a good choice.

It's kind of incredible that you can get a room at a place as charming as the ★ **Captiva Island Inn** (11508 Andy Rosse Ln., 239/395-0882, www.captivaislandinn.com, doubles from $229) for such a reasonable rate, but it is actually possible to book lodgings here during the winter for less than $300. Now, granted, that rate applies only to two tiny "cottages" that consist of a bedroom and a bathroom, but even those cozy accommodations are reflective of the cute personality of the inn. Rooms can be as expansive as the five-bedroom Celebration house or somewhere in the middle (for instance, the pink, one-bedroom Hibiscus Cottage). No matter where you stay, you'll be in an individually decorated and highly unique place on this compound of standalone cottages. On-site, there's a pool and two restaurants, and the beautiful beach is just across the street.

## Over $300

**'Tween Waters Inn** (15951 Captiva Dr., 239/472-5161, doubles from $325) on Captiva has a decades-old past but has been updated to suit the needs of contemporary travelers. The property's history goes back to the 1930s, and though there are more than 100 units, it's the 19 one-, two-, and three-bedroom cottages that exude the most nostalgic ambience. With vibrant paint schemes outside, the interiors of the cottages are decorated in rustic, hunting-lodge tones and are equipped with full kitchens, living and dining rooms, and separate bedrooms. Slightly less expensive are the spacious and contemporary hotel-style accommodations, available as regular rooms and suites. The well-groomed beach is where most folks will spend their day, but other amenities include a large, sparkling pool, tennis courts, and discounted access to the Beachview Golf Club.

## Vacation Rentals

Since Captiva is predominantly residential, one of the best (and most common) ways to visit the island is by renting a house for a week (or longer). In fact, only a handful of places on Captiva rent rooms by the night, so booking a house for an extended stay is definitely the preferred way to visit. Several agencies on Captiva specialize in vacation rentals; contact **Kingfisher** (239/472-2100, www.sanibelandcaptivarentals.com), **American Realty** (239/395-2490, www.captiva-island.com), or **Royal Shell Real Estate** (239/213-3311, www.royalshellrentals.com) to get more information on listings. During the high season, availability is severely limited, and rental stock is priced accordingly.

**SANIBEL AND CAPTIVA**
CAPTIVA ISLAND

'Tween Waters Inn

## INFORMATION AND SERVICES

The **Lee County Visitor & Convention Bureau** (2201 2nd St., Fort Myers, 239/338-3500, www.fortmyers-sanibel.com) is a great source of information for Sanibel, Captiva, Pine Island, and the barrier islands. The Sanibel & Captiva Islands Chamber of Commerce operates the **Sanibel & Captiva Island Visitor Center** (1159 Causeway Rd., 239/472-1080, www.sanibel-captiva.org), which is the first building you'll see as you come off the Sanibel Causeway onto Sanibel Island.

There's a branch of **Bank of the Islands** (14812 Captiva Dr., 239/395-0248) right next to the post office on Captiva; this branch has a 24-hour ATM. For groceries or pharmacies, you'll need to head back to Sanibel.

## GETTING THERE AND AROUND

The only way to get to Captiva is via Sanibel Island; the two islands are connected by a short bridge.

The downtown area of Captiva is quite walkable; however, that section of the island is really only about two blocks long by two blocks wide. The rest of Captiva has narrow roads with no sidewalks, making it something of a challenge for those on bikes or on foot. Parking is at a premium, so be mindful that you don't park in a private lot, because you will be towed.

# Cape Coral and the Barrier Islands

The canals that were dredged to build the city of Cape Coral in the 1950s are said to comprise the largest network of navigable canals in the world. Still, the best reason to make your way to Cape Coral is if you're on your way to the barrier islands of Pine Island and Cayo Costa. There, the spirit and beauty of Old Florida are in full effect. On Pine Island, there are three separate fishing villages worth exploring; Bokeelia and St. James City feel like traditional docks-and-piers kind of fishing towns, while Matlacha is a truly unique spot that combines the vibrancy of an active artists' community with the sunrise-to-low-tide work ethic of the many fish-boat captains who live and work there.

## CAPE CORAL

Although Cape Coral is one of the largest cities between Tampa and Miami, it feels like a small town that has grown incredibly fast, a fact that's somewhat ironic considering that the entire city's existence is the result of a massive, pre-planned real estate development from the 1950s that brought lots of military retirees to the area. The primary remnant of that development—besides the large number of veterans who call Cape Coral home—is the vast network of navigable canals that define the city. Most of the canals make their way through the city's residential areas and do little to define the environment of the city. In other words, no, you won't feel like you're in Venice when you're here, unless you take into account the abnormally high number of Italian restaurants that thrive in the downtown area. That downtown area is the most charming attribute of the city, and it's one that has been rescued from disrepair by a concerted effort to encourage new and interesting businesses to set up shop in the city's core, rather than in the sprawling expanses of strip malls elsewhere in Cape Coral.

### Sights and Recreation

Be sure to explore the compact, revitalized downtown district and gawk at the city's canals. Nestled among some of the canals is the **Cape Coral Historical Society and Museum** (544 Historical Park Blvd., 239/772-7037, www.capecoralhistoricalmuseum.org, 1pm-4pm Wed., Thurs., and Sun., closed

July-Aug., $2 adults, children free), a small facility with a few exhibits of memorabilia, antiques, and artifacts, as well as a house that gives visitors some idea of how the pioneer settlers lived in the late 19th century. There's also a small rose garden on the premises. The museum is located in the city's Cultural Park, which is also home to a community theater and the Cape Coral Art League.

A great way to get a breather from the sprawl of Cape Coral is to head for **Four Mile Cove Ecological Preserve** (east end of SE 23rd Ter., 239/549-4606, sunrise-sunset daily, free). The 365-acre preserve is a largely undeveloped wetland area, although there is an extensive boardwalk walking trail that allows visitors to get a glimpse of some of the preserve's ecology; it's a great spot for bird-watching. The best way to explore the preserve, though, is in a kayak, which gets you into the brackish waterways that vary from expansive to mangrove-thick. Kayak rentals are available at the park between November and May.

If you're in town with kids during the warm months, you'll definitely want to visit **Sun Splash Water Park** (400 Santa Barbara Blvd., 239/574-0558, www.capecoral.net, call for hours, $20 adults, $18 seniors and children), a 12-acre park with a gigantic tube ride, splash pool, speed slides, a lazy river, and an area designated for little ones. There are almost two dozen different ways to get wet at this municipal park, and although Sun Splash may not be as, uh, splashy as some of Florida's theme-park water parks, it's an affordable and family-friendly way to kill a hot afternoon.

Former Boston Red Sox left-fielder Mike Greenwell is the man behind **Mike Greenwell's Bat-A-Ball & Family Fun Park** (35 NE Pine Island Rd., 239/574-4386, www. greenwellsfamilyfunpark.com, 10am-10pm Sun.-Thurs., 10am-11pm Fri.-Sat., free). If the weather is cooperating—which, in Cape Coral, it probably is—this is a great outdoor park with tons of activities for adults and kids. In addition to the expected baseball elements (eight batting cages), there's also a paintball field, a go-kart track, a miniature golf course, and a small playground. And, if clouds roll in, there's a gigantic indoor arcade. Admission is free, although all of the activities (except the playground) require an additional (though not exorbitant) fee.

## Entertainment and Events

The premiere event on Cape Coral's annual festival schedule is the **Oktoberfest** that is

Welcome to Cape Coral!

put on by the German-American Social Club of Cape Coral during the third and fourth weekends in October. Although the club's grounds are a bit out of town (and, in reality, are more convenient to Pine Island than to downtown Cape Coral), the raucous party is well worth making a (designated) drive to. With three performance stages, the musical entertainment is continuous, and, as the day rolls on, it seems like the dancing is pretty nonstop, too. There are heaping plates of German food, available as both walking-around food (bratwurst, potato pancakes) and as sit-down meals (schnitzel, dumplings), and, of course, lots and lots of beer. Carnival attractions are set up for kids, and there are usually many local vendors selling crafts.

Just a few weeks later, the **Coconut Festival** (Nov.) brings bands (including a national act or two), carnival games, local food and craft vendors, and more to the Sun Splash Festival Grounds (400 Santa Barbara Blvd.).

In July, the **Mangomania** festival is held on the grounds of the German-American Social Club. The Mango Queen is crowned, mango drinks, desserts, and dishes are sold, plants and trees can be bought, and a handful of arts vendors are on-site selling their (mainly non-mango-related) works.

## Food

You'll want to keep to the downtown area when looking for restaurants. There are several good Italian restaurants in the area, ranging from basic, traditional places like **Papa Joe's Italian** (814 Cape Coral Pkwy. E., 239/945-1700, 11am-10pm daily, main courses from $8) to somewhat more inventive takes, like the casual but nice **Ciao Wood-Fired Pizza & Trattoria** (823 SE 47th Ter., 239/471-0033, www.ciaowoodfired.com, 11am-9pm Tues.-Thurs., 11am-10pm Fri., 4pm-10pm Sat., main courses from $10), where you can get excellent wood-oven-baked pizzas made from exceptionally fresh ingredients.

**Iguana Mia** (1027 Cape Coral Pkwy. E., 239/945-7755, 11am-10pm daily, main courses from $7) is a decent choice for Mexican food.

For seafood, **Thirsty's** (4835 Vincennes St., 239/549-6661, 11am-8pm Mon.-Thurs., 11am-8:30pm Fri.-Sat., main courses from $7) serves up some amazing and affordable fresh seafood dishes, in addition to the expected fried-shrimp baskets and a selection of overstuffed sandwiches.

Much more of a bar with great food than a restaurant with a great bar, **Nevermind Awesome Bar & Eatery** (927 Cape Coral Pkwy. E., 239/471-0534, www.nevermind-animalhouse.com, noon-2am daily, main courses from $10) nonetheless manages to be one of the best bars and one of the best restaurants in Cape Coral. With a relaxed and welcoming vibe (it is a bar, after all), the atmosphere is definitely decadent, with a menu featuring a wide array of excellent burgers (lamb, Kobe beef, and more), interesting small plates (a super-spicy spring roll, fresh hummus), surprising sides (brussels sprouts with your burger?), and rich desserts. Add to that a bar staff skilled at making craft cocktails and you've got a recipe for an excellent one-stop night on the town.

Outside of the main downtown area is one of the few vegetarian spots in Cape Coral, **Loving Hut** (1918 Del Prado Blvd. S., 239/424-8433, 11:30am-2:30pm and 4:30pm-8pm Mon.-Fri., noon-4pm Sat., main courses from $8). Loving Hut is a global chain of vegan restaurants that specializes in fried meat substitutes and proselytizing on behalf of Supreme Master Ching Hai, a spiritual leader from Vietnam with a global following. Eating here is an undoubtedly unique experience, but vegans will welcome the availability of a menu designed just for them.

## Accommodations

**The Westin Cape Coral Resort at Marina Village** (5951 Silver King Blvd., 239/541-5000, www.marinavillageresort.com, doubles from $279) is a 19-story, condo-style resort that's one of the latest—and certainly the most luxurious—additions to the Cape Coral lodging scene. Located at the Tarpon Point Marina (which means you're surrounded by some gorgeous, beachless waterfront), Marina Village very much feels like an isolated pocket of luxury, with upscale restaurants and, obviously, a marina. The resort itself is very nice, with upscale touches to the decor, and amenities include two outdoor pools, a spa, and two restaurants. There are also tennis courts, a boccie ball pitch, and even a nature trail. You can rent kayaks or bikes from the resort as well. Rooms are stylish and well-equipped, with flat-screen TVs and nicely appointed bathrooms; one- and two-bedroom suites come with full kitchens and floor plans that are more like apartments than hotel rooms.

The **Dolphin Key Resort** (1505 Miramar St., 239/945-0060, www.dolphinkeyresort. com, doubles from $119) is a nice option, giving visitors a relaxed, semitropical vibe in the heart of downtown Cape Coral. The hotel itself is a basic, motel-style setup, with rooms that look out over a central pool area that's lushly landscaped. The on-site tiki bar is loads of fun, and all the rooms are clean and up-to-date.

**Hideaway Waterfront Resort & Hotel** (4601 SE 5th Ave., 239/542-5812, doubles from $79) is a much more budget-oriented option. Amenities consist of a heated pool and a canal-side deck area. The 20 rooms—available as basic rooms, kitchenette rooms, or full-kitchen suites—are tidy and reasonably comfortable.

# PINE ISLAND
## ★ Matlacha

The tiny fishing village of Matlacha is one of the coolest places in Florida, and residents and regulars definitely appear to know that. Somehow managing to combine Old Florida charm—it is, before all else, a fishing village—and a deep undercurrent of kooky creativity, Matlacha is the Florida that so many Floridians desperately wish still existed throughout the state, a Florida that's defined by its natural surroundings, with residents who intimately engage with those surroundings, both for commerce and for art. There seem to be as many artists as anglers, and, to this writer at least, that's exactly the right sort of balance a Florida town needs.

The buildings that have been erected are something of an architectural hodgepodge, ranging from reconstituted cracker cottages operating as hotels or bait shops to brightly painted block buildings that could house art galleries and restaurants; it's admittedly a little visually chaotic. This chaos is related to Matlacha's status as a historic district: The

The vibe in Matlacha is decidedly quirky.

village sprouted up in 1927 when the first bridge was built to connect the mainland to Pine Island.

Matlacha is definitely the kind of place that, once you visit it for half a day, you may very well decide that you could see yourself living here for the rest of your life. And good luck with that; the population seems fixed at just about 700 people, mainly because there's no room for any additional housing. Which is another argument for why Matlacha is one of the coolest places in Florida.

## SIGHTS AND RECREATION

The main activity in Matlacha is to stroll the galleries or rent a kayak. Try **Gulf Coast Kayak** (4530 Pine Island Rd., 239/283-1125, www.gulfcoastkayak.com, kayak rentals from $35/half-day, stand-up paddleboard rentals from $25/hour) if plying the waters is on your agenda.

## SHOPPING

There are at least a half-dozen art galleries in the tiny town of Matlacha. **Island Visions Gallery** (4643 Pine Island Rd., 239/282-0452, www.island-visions.com), **Lovegrove Gallery & Gardens** (4637 Pine Island Rd., 239/283-6453, www.leomalovegrove.com),

and **Frills Gallery** (4608 Pine Island Rd., 239/283-0192) are some of the best. However, **Bert's Pine Bay Gallery & Gifts** (4332 Pine Island Rd., 239/283-1335) is definitely the most Matlachan of them all; nestled in a converted cottage right on the water (the back porch is great for sunset-viewing), the gallery features the work of more than 30 local artists, with jewelry, crafts, paintings, and more.

## FOOD

If you're getting an early start on Matlacha, try **Perfect Cup** (4548 Pine Island Rd., 239/283-4447, 7am-3pm daily, main courses from $6), which (unsurprisingly) serves great coffee, as well as a selection of fresh breakfast dishes, including gigantic omelets. Later, after you're done browsing the shops and art galleries, you'll want to grab a bite to eat, and in Matlacha, that means you'll be eating some seafood. One of the best bets is **Bert's Bar & Grill** (4271 Pine Island Rd., 239/282-3232, 11am-9pm daily, main courses from $7), a tin-roofed watering hole that serves some of the freshest seafood in this part of the state. **Andy's Island Seafood Market** (4330 Pine Island Rd., 239/283-2525, 11am-9pm daily, main courses from $9) and the **Olde Fish House** (4530 Pine Island Rd., 239/282-9577,

Lovegrove Gallery & Gardens

10am-8pm daily, main courses from $11) are both excellent choices as well. For a menu that goes a little beyond seafood, try **Sandy Hook Fish & Rib** (4875 Pine Island Rd., 239/283-0113, 11am-9pm daily, main courses from $7), which is on the southern end of Matlacha, right as you're about to exit the pass onto the main part of Pine Island.

## ACCOMMODATIONS

If you're looking to spend the night in Matlacha, your options are limited, but decent. There are waterfront rooms, and then there are rooms that are actually on the water. The nine rooms at the **Bridgewater Inn** (4331 Pine Island Rd., 239/283-2423, www.bridgewaterinn.com, doubles from $149, three-night minimum stay required during peak season) are built on a dock, with front porches that dangle your feet right over the waters of Pine Island Sound. It's a pretty phenomenal location, and the rooms themselves, while certainly not the most luxurious you've ever stayed in, are spacious, comfortable, and modern. Opt for the larger suites at the end of the dock (#2 and #3), as they provide exceptional panoramic views.

The rooms at the cozy **Knoll's Court Motel** (4755 Pine Island Rd. NW, 239/283-0616, www.knollscourtmotel.com, doubles from $109) are of the more traditional "waterfront" variety, with a spacious, grassy area separating the main motel building from the water and motel dock. The rooms are either efficiency suites or two-bedroom units, all of which have full kitchen setups, making this a great spot for extended stays (monthly rates from $2,600 are available). Decor and fixtures are a couple of decades out of date, but everything is tidy and well-maintained. **Serenity Bay Cottages** (4824 Pine Island Rd., 408/561-8041, www.serenitybay.webs.com, doubles from $110) is fairly similar, with a pleasant waterfront area and basic, efficiency-style rooms.

The rooms at the **Bayview Bed and Breakfast** (12251 Shoreview Dr., 239/283-7510, doubles from $169) are decorated more like residential bedrooms than they are hotel rooms, but the "bed-and-breakfast" atmosphere is more due to the pinks and pastels used for decor, rather than a traditional B&B house-stay. Nonetheless, the Bayview offers incredible views of the water and the local wildlife, with free docking for canoes and kayaks.

## Pine Island Center

The obviously monikered village of Pine Island Center is home to the island's police and fire departments, a library, a public park with tennis courts and a swimming pool, and one of the few gas stations on the island. The **Museum of the Islands** (5728 Sesame Dr., 239/283-1525, 11am-3pm Tues.-Sat., 1pm-4pm Sun., $2 adults, $1 children) is a small facility that focuses primarily on the early Calusa residents of the island, with a selection of reproductions of art, pottery, and tools. There's also a collection of shells, a taxidermied boar's head, a portrait of George Washington created from nearly a half-million glass beads, and, most oddly, an early-20th-century horse cart filled with dolls. Yeah, it's a pretty unusual museum.

If you're refueling your car in Pine Island Center, you might want to consider refueling yourself as well; the brisket and other barbecue dishes at **Saltwater Smokehouse** (10251 Stringfellow Rd., 239/282-8811, www.saltwatersmokehouse.com, 11am-9pm daily, main courses from $8) are definitely worth digging into.

## St. James City

St. James City technically takes up almost all of the southern half of Pine Island, but outside of a few residential and agricultural enclaves along Pine Island Boulevard, there's not much to see until you get to its fishing-village heart at the very southern tip of the island.

### SIGHTS AND RECREATION

One thing definitely worth exploring is the **Pine Island Flatwoods Preserve,** a 730-acre ecological preserve that's about halfway between Pine Island Center and the marinas of St. James City. The preserve is predominantly pine flatwoods, and there are ample opportunities for wildlife viewing along a circuitous mile-long hiking trail; there's a trailhead (6351 Stringfellow Rd., 239/707-8251, www.conservation2020.org) with a small parking lot.

A little closer to St. James City is the **St. James Creek Preserve** (4344 Stringfellow Rd., 239/533-7456, www.conservation2020.org), on the bay side of Pine Island, thick with mangroves and pine flatwoods. The wildlife viewing is also quite exceptional, and the St. Jude Nature Trail—about a mile-long loop trail—will take you through it. The pastoral seclusion of this trail is something of an ironic treasure; it is built along a roadbed that was being constructed as a tourist-focused parkway with restaurants and entertainment, one that would lead to a skybridge that would connect Pine Island and Punta Rassa (where the Sanibel Causeway connects Sanibel Island to the Fort Myers mainland). One can only imagine how completely that would have altered the low-key complexion of St. James City, but thankfully, it never came to fruition.

Anglers and boaters are the folks who will find St. James City most appealing, as there are several marinas that open up to the Gulf waters. However, the friendly, isolated vibe is something that's well worth taking in on its own.

## FOOD

You won't find much in the way of gourmet eats in St. James City—and that's just fine. The **Ragged Ass Saloon & Starboard Grill** (3421 Stringfellow Rd., 239/282-1131, www.raggedasssaloon.com, 7am-10pm Mon.-Sat., 7am-9pm Sun., main courses from $9), however, will have you covered for just about all your needs, whether you need a cheap and hearty breakfast, sandwiches and burgers for lunch, or a meat-and-three (or fresh fish) for dinner. The outdoor bar area is right along the water and is not just a perfect place for a drink with a view, but also a prime spot to hear some incredible stories from the locals who have (or haven't) brought in a catch for the day. Offering a very similar experience—but with one fewer profanity puns in the name, and at the more isolated southern end of the island—is **The Waterfront Restaurant** (2131 Oleander St., 239/283-0592, www.waterfrontrestaurant.com, 11am-9pm daily, main courses from $10). Make sure to grab a table on the outdoor deck, which sits right

the waterfront in St. James City

alongside the canal. **Woody's Waterside** (3051 Stringfellow Rd., 239/283-5555, 11am-10pm daily, main courses from $9) is another great choice for waterfront dining and drinks, and like everything else in St. James City, it's definitely not fancy, but it's definitely fun. Live music and craft beer on tap complement an array of burgers, sandwiches, and fried seafood baskets; the outdoor, tiki-bar-style "dining room" is a great place to watch the sunset. Speaking of tiki bars, **Low Key Tiki** (3135 Stringfellow Rd., 239/282-8454, 11am-10pm daily, main courses from $8) is a laid-back, canal-side bar with cheap drinks, decent burgers, and ice-cold beer. If you're staying in a place with a kitchen and want to cook up a fresh catch that you didn't catch yourself, head to **The Fish House** (2153 Palm Ave., 239/283-0601, 10am-3pm daily), where you can get fish, shrimp, and other seafood right off the boat for incredibly reasonable prices.

## ACCOMMODATIONS

If you want to stay a night, **The Two Fish Inn** (2960 Oleander St., 239/283-4519, www. twofishinn.com, doubles from $109) in the heart of St. James City has extremely affordable rates for their five suites, which are cute and comfortable, and perfectly outfitted for those who have come to the island to fish. The owners of the Two Fish also operate the tiny and tidy **Southernmost Inn** (2061 Oleander St., 239/283-4519, www.southernmostinnof-pineisland.com, doubles from $119)—which, unsurprisingly, is located in a predominantly residential area at the south tip of the island; these four suites are also quite nice (if not luxurious), backing up to a canal that leads right into the bay. **Waters Edge Motel & Apartments** (2938 Sanibel Blvd., 239/283-0515, www.thewatersedgemotel.com, doubles from $120) features clean one-bedroom and efficiency-style apartments overlooking a swimming pool in a motel-style setup, with free boat dockage (for full-size boats and even kayaks). Although all of the above-listed accommodations are available for extended

visits (and offer considerable discounts for monthly stays), if you're looking to stay a little longer in a more traditionally residential setting, **Pine Island Realty** (239/283-0909, www.pine-island.com) can help with long-term vacation rentals. If you brought your own hotel, you can park it at the **Pine Island Resort KOA** (5120 Stringfellow Rd., 239/283-2415, www.pineislandkoa.com, tent sites from $40/night, RV sites from $72/night, one-room cabins from $69/night).

## Bokeelia

With 2,000 permanent residents, Bokeelia is the biggest town on Pine Island. Most of the town is given over to condo complexes.

### SIGHTS AND RECREATION

The real heart of the town is at the northern-most tip, the site of the century-old **Bokeelia Fishing Pier** (8421 Main St., 7am-5pm daily).

For those not interested in fishing, the **Calusa Heritage Trail** (13810 Waterfront Dr., 239/283-2157, www.flmnh.ufl.edu/rrc, $7 adults, $5 seniors, $4 children) is about a mile or so away in Pineland; the trail is less than a mile long, but it's dotted with informative signposts and exhibits that provide a good historical look at the area's earliest native settlers, as well as a shell mound. The trail is the public face of the Randell Research Center, which maintains more than 60 acres of archaeologically important land and is dedicated to researching the history of the Calusa in the area.

You can also board a water taxi in Pineland at the **Pineland Marina** (13921 Waterfront Dr., 239/283-3593, www.pinelandmarina. com) via **Island Girl Charters** (239/633-8142, www.islandgirlcharters.com, charters depart every two hours 7am-5pm, $26 adults, reservations recommended) to North Captiva and Cabbage Key or **Tropic Star** (239/283-0015, www.tropicstaradventures.com, charter boards at 9am and returns at 1pm or 3:30pm, $35 adults, $25 children, reservations recommended) to Cayo Costa.

## FOOD

Unsurprisingly, seafood will be your best dining bet in Bokeelia, and restaurants like the **Lazy Flamingo** (16501 Stringfellow Rd., 239/283-5959, www.lazyflamingo.com, call for hours, main courses from $12), at the marina, and **Capt'n Con's Fish House** (8421 Main St., 239/283-4300, 11am-9pm daily, main courses from $16), near the pier, do a great job serving up the freshest catches of the day.

## ACCOMMODATIONS

The **Beachouse Lodge** (7702 Bocilla Ln., 239/283-4303, www.beachousefl.com, doubles from $130) has five rooms (three suites, a standard guest room, and a penthouse) that are quite nice, and the location right on the southern end of Charlotte Harbor is gorgeous. (However, please be mindful that, although there is a beach, it's just a small patch of sand along the seawall, and not designed as a swimming beach.)

The beautiful **Tarpon Lodge** (13771 Waterfront Dr., Pineland, 239/283-3999, www.tarponlodge.com, doubles from $160) is in isolated Pineland, and though there's not much around besides the marina, the quiet locale and historic feel of this circa-1926 lodge make it an ideal spot for a relaxed and romantic getaway. The on-site restaurant is excellent.

# CAYO COSTA AND THE BARRIER ISLANDS
## ★ Cayo Costa State Park

**Cayo Costa State Park** (north of Captiva, 941/964-0375, 8am-sunset daily, $2) is all there is to La Costa Island, and that's just fine. The island (and the park) is only accessible by private boat or via the **Tropic Star Ferry** (13921 Waterfront Dr., Pineland, 239/283-0015, www.tropicstaradventures.com, daily departures at 9:30am, with returns at 1pm and 3pm, round-trip ferry $35 adults, $25 kids), which departs from the Pineland Marina on Pine Island. There are nine miles of beautiful, white-sand beaches at the park, and snorkeling is fantastic just offshore. There are 30 tent campsites ($22/night), 12 cabins ($40/night, but they are nearly impossible to reserve, given the park's popularity), and boat camping is also available ($20/night). The entire island is incredibly rustic, with facilities limited to a few public restrooms, outdoor showers, and a concession stand that sells insect repellent and sunscreen. In addition to beachcombing on the impossibly soft and sugary sand, visitors to Cayo Costa can also explore

Bokeelia Fishing Pier is a popular destination for anglers looking for solitude.

more than five miles of hiking trails that wind through hardwood hammocks and mangrove swamps.

## Cabbage Key and Useppa Island

Both Cabbage Key and Useppa Island are private islands accessible only by boat. Cabbage Key mainly comprises the **Cabbage Key Inn & Resort** (239/283-2278, www.cabbagekey. com, doubles from $199), an Old Florida beauty, with six rooms in the main inn and seven freestanding cottages. For the privacy and beauty afforded, it's almost impossible to believe that nightly rentals are so reasonably priced, but reasonably priced they are, and although you may find that you're sharing the island with boating day-trippers during the sunny hours, by the time night falls, Cabbage Key feels like it's all yours. The on-site restaurant serves three meals daily, and there are nature trails and boat rentals available.

## INFORMATION

The **Lee County Visitor & Convention Bureau** (2201 2nd St., Fort Myers, 239/338-3500, www.fortmyers-sanibel.com) is a great source of information for Pine Island and the barrier islands. The **Greater Pine Island Chamber of Commerce** (3640 SW Pine Island Rd., Matlacha, 239/283-0888, www. pineislandchamber.org) offers information on local businesses, lodging, and food.

## GETTING THERE AND AROUND

The barrier islands are geographically close, but not exactly easy to navigate between. The downtown core of Cape Coral is easily accessible from I-75 via a toll bridge; Pine Island is accessed via Pine Island Road, which cuts an east-west path across the northern part of Cape Coral's suburbs. Cayo Costa, Cabbage Key, and Useppa Island are only accessible by boat; **Captiva Cruises** (239/472-5300, www. captivacruises.com, reservations essential) offers daily cruises from Captiva Island that can take visitors to all three of these islands.

# Naples

The Naples area has, without a doubt, some of the wildest and most beautiful swathes of natural land in the state, ranging from swamps and rivers to isolated coastline and barrier islands.

The white sand and blue waters of the beaches here are often unsung, although they easily rival (and, in some cases, outshine) some of the more famous and well-regarded beaches in the state. Although one of the more popular outdoor pastimes around here is the decidedly down-to-earth thrill of riding in a swamp buggy, this part of the state is known more for being a winter home to wealthy retirees and those who strive to be wealthy retirees.

The city itself is quite pretty, with a beautiful and historic downtown area, a charming waterfront location, and gorgeous public beaches. But when the city swells with snowbirds between November and May, Naples's gallery and cultural scene explodes, and getting a table (or even a barstool) at one of historic 5th Avenue's many stylish eateries is a challenge that's not for the faint of heart (or wallet).

Although the art galleries and boutiques of downtown Naples provide wonderful, walkable window-shopping year-round, some of the best sights Naples has to offer are actually outside of that central core. Nature preserves and wildlife areas abound just outside of town, and longtime locals are eager to show them off to adventurous visitors. Even within city limits, Naples's beaches, with their white, powdery sand, are some of the best (and most underappreciated) in all of Florida. The Naples Zoo and the Baker Museum are both exceptional and accessible. In other words, Naples is a city that certainly reveals part of its personality on the surface, but once you get past that initial impression, there's a lot more that is worth exploring.

## HISTORY

As is the case throughout much of Florida, the history of the Naples area can be traced to a very rich man with the vision (and the means) to get a whole lot richer. In the case of Naples, that man was Baron G. Collier. Collier

---

**Previous:** 5th Avenue South in Naples; Naples Botanical Garden. **Above:** Lowdermilk Park & Beach.

Look for ★ to find recommended sights, activities, dining, and lodging.

# Highlights

★ **Old Naples:** The heart of Naples is in these 10 square blocks of chic boutiques, art galleries, and upscale restaurants. The architecture is charming, the window-shopping is fantastic, and the people-watching is unsurpassed (page 173).

★ **Baker Museum:** Naples is an arts town, to be sure. So it shouldn't be surprising that the city boasts a beautiful and well-curated art museum stocked with both classics and stunning modern art (page 174).

★ **Naples Zoo at Caribbean Gardens:** No other zoo in Florida is as attractive and welcoming. The lushly landscaped grounds are instantly calming and a joy to walk through (page 175).

★ **Naples Botanical Garden:** What began as little more than a community garden has become an impressive and expansive destination for plant and flower lovers. More than 600 different species of plants are presented in distinct garden environments (page 176).

★ **Corkscrew Swamp Sanctuary:** The more than 11,000 acres of absolutely unspoiled natural habitat are a permanent home for dozens of birds and other wildlife. During the winter, its winged population explodes as other birds make their way here to escape the northern cold (page 177).

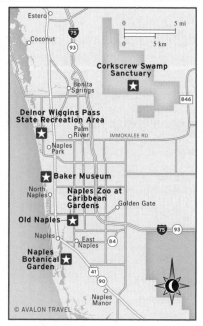

★ **Delnor Wiggins Pass State Recreation Area:** The most secluded and gorgeous stretches of sand can be found just a few miles north of downtown Naples. Soft white sand and blue waters on one side and dense mangrove thickets on the other provide plenty of natural space (page 179).

# Naples

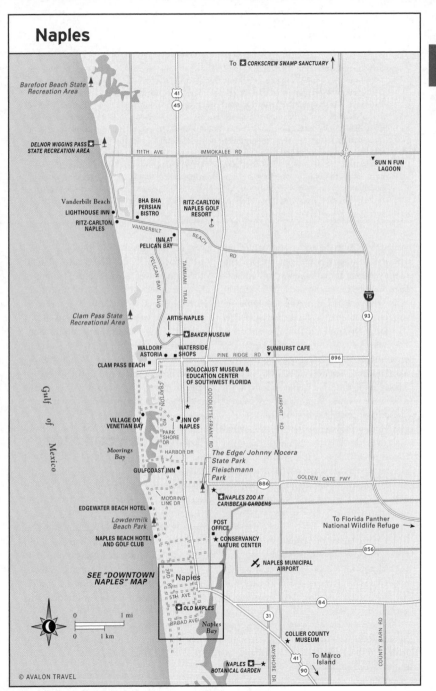

To ★ CORKSCREW SWAMP SANCTUARY ↑

Barefoot Beach State Recreation Area

41
45

DELNOR WIGGINS PASS ★
STATE RECREATION AREA

111TH AVE     IMMOKALEE RD

▼ SUN N FUN LAGOON

Vanderbilt Beach
LIGHTHOUSE INN ●
RITZ-CARLTON, ●
NAPLES

BHA BHA PERSIAN BISTRO

RITZ-CARLTON NAPLES GOLF RESORT

VANDERBILT     BEACH     RD

INN AT ●
PELICAN BAY

PELICAN BAY BLVD

TAMIAMI TRAIL

75

93

Clam Pass State Recreational Area

ARTIS-NAPLES
★ ★BAKER MUSEUM

WALDORF ● WATERSIDE
ASTORIA     SHOPS

PINE RIDGE RD     SUNBURST CAFE

896

CLAM PASS BEACH ■

HOLOCAUST MUSEUM & EDUCATION CENTER OF SOUTHWEST FLORIDA

Gulf

of

Mexico

CRAYTON RD

GOODLETTE-FRANK RD

AIRPORT RD

★

VILLAGE ON ●
VENETIAN BAY

● INN OF NAPLES

PARK SHORE DR

Moorings Bay

HARBOR DR

The Edge/ Johnny Nocera State Park

GULFCOAST INN ●

Fleischmann Park

GOLDEN GATE PWY

886

MOORING LINE DR

★ ★NAPLES ZOO AT CARIBBEAN GARDENS

EDGEWATER BEACH HOTEL ●

Lowdermilk Beach Park

POST OFFICE

To Florida Panther National Wildlife Refuge →

NAPLES BEACH HOTEL ●
AND GOLF CLUB

★ CONSERVANCY NATURE CENTER

856

✈ NAPLES MUNICIPAL AIRPORT

SEE "DOWNTOWN NAPLES" MAP

Naples

5TH AVE

31

84

0     1 mi
0     1 km

★OLD NAPLES

BROAD AVE

Naples Bay

COLLIER COUNTY ★ MUSEUM

BAYSHORE DR

COUNTY BARN RD

41

To Marco Island

NAPLES ★ ★
BOTANICAL GARDEN

90

© AVALON TRAVEL

# Snowbirds

Snowbirds are common throughout Florida. The annual migration of northern and Midwestern retirees utterly changes the composition and personality of southwest Florida. For the most part, it's easy to delineate the difference between "eastern" snowbirds and "western" snowbirds: The retirees who make their way down I-95 from New York and New England generally winter in the Miami area, and the ones from the Midwest—Chicago, Michigan, Ohio—come to the Gulf Coast via I-75. Of course, there are some exceptions, and Marco Island is one of them: The island's mid-1960s development was spearheaded by the Deltona Corporation, which had extensive experience developing and marketing communities along the east coast of Florida to clients in New York and New England. Still, for the most part, the Naples area and most of the other areas covered in this guide are preferred by those from Rust Belt states. So, during "season," when the population explodes with a combination of well-to-do retirees and pensioners, the area can feel more like a colonial outpost than "true Florida."

visited the area in the early 20th century and saw what was then a sleepy winter resort community. Naples at that time was tiny and isolated, despite the development undertaken by some other very rich men who bought the entire town in the 1880s, built the Naples Pier (bolstering the trade and fishing economies), and helped establish the Naples Hotel as a premier cold-weather destination for wealthy Northerners. There was no easy way to get to Naples at the time, but Collier saw how railroad access was transforming the east coast of Florida (and making Henry Flagler a very rich man), and went about petitioning the government to let him build the Tamiami Trail. After Collier pitched in more than $1 million of his own money for the project, the Trail—the only paved highway linking Tampa and Miami via Sarasota, Fort Myers, and Naples—opened in 1926. In return, the state named Collier County after him.

The opening of the Trail also served to open up Naples, and over the next decades, the city became a prime tourist destination, marketed as an optimal place for retirees from the northern and Midwestern U.S. states to spend their pensions.

Another Collier—"Captain Bill" Collier (no relation)—helped establish Marco Island. Although this Collier was nowhere near as rich as Baron, his founding in 1896 of a small

hotel on the island (now the Olde Marco Inn) helped make the island accessible for fishers and adventurous boaters. Not much more happened on Marco Island until 1962, when the Miami-based Deltona Corporation saw the massive potential of the island as a residential community. Deltona's development defined the island as it is today—pleasant and unassuming—and their marketing to New Yorkers and New Englanders helped establish Marco Island as a wintertime nesting spot for a species of snowbird not typically found on Florida's west coast.

## PLANNING YOUR TIME

Take a day to hit one of Naples's beautiful beaches, and devote another to exploring the isolated natural beauty of Corkscrew Swamp Sanctuary or the Florida Panther National Wildlife Refuge. You can soak in plenty of downtown Naples's upscale vibe by dining in one of the restaurants on 5th Avenue South and strolling the sidewalks afterward.

Sights like the Naples Zoo at Caribbean Gardens and the Baker Museum are best explored if you have plenty of time to spare; the zoo on its own warrants at least a day. Head down to Marco Island for a day, making sure to stop in the charming fishing village of Goodland for lunch and a beer.

# Sights

## ★ OLD NAPLES

To get a real feel for Naples, the best place to start is **Old Naples** (public parking garages located at 400 8th St. S. and off 6th Ave. S., between 5th and 6th Aves.). Along 5th Avenue and 3rd Street South, there are numerous shops, galleries, and cafés that evoke a sense of tropical luxury that's unique in Florida. It's decidedly upscale, reflecting the sensibilities of the annual migration of moneyed snowbirds who flock to the area from the frigid Midwest every winter. Window-shoppers and art lovers will find plenty to capture their interest in the boutiques and galleries that are housed in dozens of century-old buildings, and the tree-lined sidewalks are eminently stroll-able. **Naples Trolley** (239/262-7300, www.naplestrolleytours.com, 9:30am-5:30pm daily, $25 adults, $13 children over 4, free reboarding) runs throughout downtown Naples, with stops along 5th Avenue South and 3rd Street South, as well as in Tin City and other locations.

## TIN CITY

Thanks to its location on a stretch of the Gordon River, and a history that dates back to its role in the early 20th century as the area's hub for its maritime and transportation industries, **Tin City** (1200 5th Ave. S., 239/262-4200, www.tin-city.com) is much more interesting than your average suburban shopping center. So named for the tin-roofed, waterfront buildings that used to house fishmongers, oyster shuckers, boat repair facilities, and other businesses that catered to a thriving fishing industry, Tin City is currently home to more than two dozen stores that range from jewelry shops and clothing boutiques to gift shops and art galleries. The two waterfront restaurants provide some excellent vistas of the still-busy waterway. A **History of the Waterfront Museum,** a one-room museum on-site, gives some perspective on how much (and how little) this slice of historic Naples has changed. A block away, set just back from the waterfront, is the **Dockside Boardwalk** (1100 6th Ave. S., www.naplesboardwalk.com), a smaller version of Tin City.

Tin City is at the waterfront heart of Old Naples.

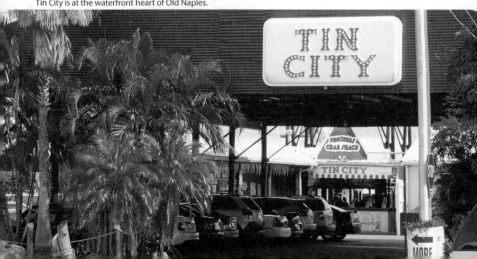

# Downtown Naples

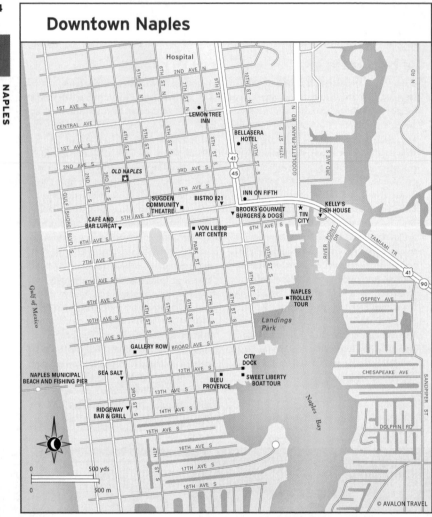

## TOP EXPERIENCE

## ★ BAKER MUSEUM

For a city with such a strong reputation as a place to view and purchase fine art, it's not surprising that the **Baker Museum** (5833 Pelican Bay Blvd., 239/597-1111, 10am-4pm Tues.-Sat., noon-4pm Sun., closed July-Oct., $8 adults, $6 children) is such an impressive facility. Formerly known as the Naples Museum of Art, the building is beautiful, a three-story, 30,000-square-foot modern jewel located at **Artis—Naples** (the same grounds that house the Naples Philharmonic), with imposing metal gates designed by Albert Paley. The museum's permanent collections focus on modernism and sculpture, and seasonal exhibits are notably well curated, with a balance of modern works from around the globe and more predictable fare. Photography, sculpture, and design work also figure prominently in the museum's ethos, making for an art experience that's somewhat surprising in such a buttoned-down city.

## HOLOCAUST MUSEUM & EDUCATION CENTER OF SOUTHWEST FLORIDA

The **Holocaust Museum & Education Center of Southwest Florida** (4760 Tamiami Trail N., #7, 239/263-9200, www.holocaustmuseumswfl.org, 1pm-4pm Tues.-Sun., $8 adults, $3 students 12-18, free for students under 12 with parent/guardian approval) has its roots in, of all things, a middle-school classroom project that, in 2001, was expanded into a full-fledged museum. There are more than 1,000 period artifacts in the museum, many of which are personal items from Naples residents who either survived the Holocaust or were part of the Allied liberation of the concentration camps. The very first thing you see, though, before you even enter the museum, is probably the most striking: In 2007, the museum acquired a WWII-era boxcar, just like the ones the Nazis used to transport humans to concentration camps. Although the museum is very careful to stress that this particular boxcar may not have been used to move human freight, the very thought of it is an appropriately chilling and humbling prologue to the museum's exhibits. (The boxcar is often used as a traveling exhibit, so it may or may not be present at the museum.) Knowledgeable docents are available to help guide visitors through the museum collection.

## ★ NAPLES ZOO AT CARIBBEAN GARDENS

The 45-acre **Naples Zoo at Caribbean Gardens** (1590 Goodlette Rd., 239/262-5409, www.caribbeangardens.com, 9am-5pm daily, $22.95 adults, $21.95 seniors, $14.95 children, children under 3 free) is an impressive combination of a conservation-minded zoo and a relaxed, informative botanical garden. Originally founded in 1919 as just a garden, the property is enfolded with stately palm trees and tropical foliage that enhance the immersive, natural experience; this experience is further amplified by the fact that the scores of animals on display are often no more than a few feet away from visitors at any given moment. From lemurs and lions and leopards to parrots, porcupines, and panthers, the zoo has an impressive, but not too expansive, array of animals, all housed in a relatively modern and very clean and comfortable environment. This zoo is one of my favorites; the shady pathways,

the Baker Museum

the casual, animal-centric attitude of its design, and the breathtakingly beautiful array of plants make coming here very calming, giving visitors the right mindset they need to take in the pro-conservation message the zoo is trying to impart.

## CONSERVANCY NATURE CENTER

Reopened in 2013 after extensive renovations, the **Conservancy Nature Center** (1450 Merrihue Dr., 239/262-0304, www.conservancy.org, 9:30am-4:30pm daily Jan.-Apr., closed Sun. May-Dec., $14.95 adults, $9.95 children 3-12, children under 3 free) is operated by the Conservancy of Southwest Florida (a rescue, rehabilitation, and education organization) and features an interpretive center with interactive exhibits and 150 animals, boat cruises in their lagoon, and extensive access to a large nature preserve on the property. The renovations have resulted in a space that's incredibly attractive and welcoming, as well as more explicitly connected to the Naples Zoo next door; however, they have also thankfully done little to diminish the rescue-and-release mission, and the animal hospital is still the heart of the operation.

## ★ NAPLES BOTANICAL GARDEN

The **Naples Botanical Garden** (4820 Bayshore Dr., 239/643-7275, www.naplesgarden.org, 9am-5pm daily, $14.95 adults, $9.95 children 4-14, children under 3 free) got its start back in the mid-1990s, as something of a community project spearheaded by local volunteers, and, over the years, it has experienced considerable evolution and growth. In fact, in 2007, the garden closed for nearly a year and a half to undergo extensive renovations and expansion. When it reopened in 2009, Naples Botanical Garden was the second-largest botanical garden in Florida, with 160 acres of plant life representing more than 600 different species of flora in seven distinct garden environments. The Florida Garden is, obviously, dedicated to native Florida plants. The artful design of the Asian Garden, with its combination of beautiful flowers and tasteful architecture, makes it one of the best spots on the entire property. There's also a children's garden, where junior planters can get their hands dirty and burn off whatever excess energy they accumulated while you were investigating the plants and flowers in the other areas of the park. And, on some days (call for days/hours), you can even bring your dog to the

Naples Botanical Garden

# Florida Panthers

When Congress passed the Endangered Species Act in 1973, one of the first animals listed as endangered was the Florida panther. A puma subspecies that used to abound in North and South America, the Florida panther is related to mountain lions, cougars, and catamounts; however, it's the only extant example of the species currently remaining in the eastern United States. In 1989, the panther population in Florida had precipitously fallen to only a few dozen animals, a situation brought about not so much by human predation as by habitat loss; the fast-growing South Florida region that these panthers used to freely roam has, over the past century, experienced such rapid and unchecked growth that the main Florida panther habitat is now the **Florida Panther National Wildlife Refuge** near Naples. Although the panther population has rebounded somewhat over the past two decades, thanks to captive breeding programs and the protection offered by the refuge, there are still fewer than 100 wild panthers left. It's a situation that will be difficult to remedy, as the 26,400 acres of the refuge are somewhat limiting to a species in which the male typically can lay claim to up to 200 square miles of territory.

garden; additional admission is $4.95, and all dogs must be current on shots and registration.

## COLLIER COUNTY MUSEUM

The actual "museum" part of the **Collier County Museum** (3301 E. Tamiami Trail, 239/252-8476, 9am-4pm Mon.-Sat., free) is interesting enough, with displays and exhibits documenting the area's past from prehistory to the present. Considerable attention is given to the Calusa tribe and other regional Native American tribes. However, it's the five-acre grounds around the museum that make it an interesting destination. The beautiful property houses two historic cottages, a re-created Seminole village, a beautiful garden of native plants, and even a Sherman tank. It's unique, engaging, and free.

## FLORIDA PANTHER NATIONAL WILDLIFE REFUGE

Don't arrive at the **Florida Panther National Wildlife Refuge** (13233 SR-29 S., 239/658-6163, sunrise-sunset daily, free) expecting to see any panthers. The endangered cats have had these 26,400 acres allocated to just them for the safety of both the public and the panthers. There are, however, two hiking trails for the public. The Leslie M. Duncan Trail is a short, wheelchair-accessible trail that loops for one-third of a mile through a hardwood hammock. The other, unnamed trail is longer (1.3 miles) and, though well-marked, is unimproved and can get quite muddy; still, as fewer people make their way along this trail, wildlife is much more likely to be seen.

**TOP** EXPERIENCE

## ★ CORKSCREW SWAMP SANCTUARY

The **Corkscrew Swamp Sanctuary** (375 Sanctuary Rd. W., 239/348-9151, http://fl.audubon.org/corkscrew-swamp-sanctuary, 7am-5:30pm daily Oct. 1-Apr. 10, 7am-7:30pm daily Apr. 11-Sept. 30, $10 adults, $6 full-time college students with photo ID, $4 students 6-18, children under 6 free) is about an hour or so from downtown Naples, all the way at the end of a road at the end of a road at the end of a road that's off a rural highway. If getting away from the hustle and bustle is your goal, this is the place to do it. But, even if that's not what brings you out here, the voyage to Corkscrew is well worth it. Maintained and operated by the National Audubon Society, the sanctuary covers more than 11,000 acres of completely unspoiled land that, given its isolation and ecological diversity, is a perfect bird-watching spot.

During the winter months, scores of bird species make their way here to escape the northern chill, and this is one of the country's main breeding grounds for endangered wood storks. Bird-watchers will spot herons, egrets, owls, and a wide variety of wading birds, as well as quite a few alligators. The swamp is only accessible via a 2.5-mile boardwalk, which, though circular, offers two distinct routes through the swamp. Benches and "pull-off" areas are dotted along the boardwalk, in case you want to rest or set up a place to get the most out of your binoculars or zoom lenses. Stepping onto the boardwalk out of the visitors center (which has an exhibit area, coffee shop, and the sanctuary's "living machine," which helps process waste water), one can almost immediately feel the sense of calm and silence that permeates the swamp, a feeling that will only be interrupted by the occasional bird call that echoes loudly throughout the property. It's a truly stunning place.

# Beaches

The beaches are fantastic. Large expanses of soft white sand open onto calm, blue Gulf waters, as a constant, easy breeze flows off the water. They're very nearly perfect, and the citizens of Collier County know it. Though the beaches are certainly welcoming to visitors, it's worth noting that many of the parking lots aren't: All the "good" spots are reserved for residents; visitors are left to fight over spots usually a block or so away from the beach entrance. (And yes, you will be towed if you park illegally.) Still, ample metered parking is available, both in lots and along Naples's Gulf Shore Boulevard. Most spots are ticket-metered, meaning you go to an automated booth near your parking spot, buy a ticket (usually $2.50 per hour or $8 per day), and place it on your dashboard.

## GULF SHORE BOULEVARD BEACHES

The most centrally located public beaches in Naples are along Gulf Shore Boulevard. **North Gulf Shore Boulevard Beach** (81 Seagate Dr., sunrise-sunset daily, $2.50/hour parking) is close to the Village on Venetian

the peaceful boardwalk in Corkscrew Swamp Sanctuary

parking). A block south of the pier, the waves break as high as they're going to in this part of the state (which is to say, not very high at all), drawing determined boarders. The beach area in between the pier and the surfing area is pleasant, though it can get a bit congested on holidays and during the summer. On a late spring weekday, though, this is one of the best places for a relaxing day at the beach.

## VANDERBILT BEACH

It's almost impossible to believe that the parking lot at **Vanderbilt Beach** (280 Vanderbilt Beach Rd., 239/254-4000, 8am-sundown daily, $8 parking) can hold more than 150 cars. It seems like no matter when you get there, the lot is nearly full. This is, without a doubt, a very popular beach. And for good reason. The crystal-blue waters are among the most beautiful of Naples's beaches, and the white sand is packed a little tighter along the waterfront, making it more amenable for all-day sunbathing. Still, get here early if you want to find a place to park and access the beach easily, and plan on making a full day of it; there are plenty of shops and restaurants within walking distance.

## ★ DELNOR WIGGINS PASS STATE RECREATION AREA

Situated on a small barrier island a few miles north of downtown Naples, the **Delnor Wiggins Pass State Recreation Area** (11100 Gulf Shore Dr., 239/597-6196, 8am-sundown daily, $6 per vehicle) offers a rustic and semi-natural beach environment. Though quite popular, the park is also quite large; once you pay your entrance fee, you simply drive down the road until you find an appealing spot, pull over, and park. On the east side of the road are 80 acres of mangrove swamps, and on the west is one of the more beautiful beaches in the area, on which, if you get there early enough, you can stake out a spot all to yourself. It can get quite crowded around sunset.

Delnor Wiggins Pass State Recreation Area

Bay, and situated between two giant condominium complexes. There's a bit of a walk from the 38 available parking spaces to the beach entrance, but once on the beach, you should immediately start walking north for one of the more isolated beach experiences in town; just a few steps past the condos, it becomes almost deserted.

There is no such quietude to be found at **Lowdermilk Park & Beach** (257 Banyan Blvd., sunrise-sunset daily, $2.50/hour parking), perhaps the most popular of all the beaches in Naples. The central location and abundant facilities (playground, restroom/shower facilities, picnic areas, a volleyball court, and over 100 parking spaces) draw huge crowds almost every day, and in the summer, you can wind up elbow-to-elbow with other sun-worshippers. Still, the beach itself is gorgeous, and the waters warm and beautiful.

Surfers and anglers head for the **Naples Municipal Beach & Fishing Pier** (25 12th Ave., sunrise-sunset daily, $2.50/hour

# CLAM PASS BEACH

Lots of beaches in Florida offer boardwalk access from their parking areas to the beach. In many cases, this is to help folks navigate some rough terrain, or to help protect the fragile dunes that often line the coast. These boardwalks are usually pretty short. So, after parking in the spacious lot for **Clam Pass Beach** (410 Seagate Dr., 239/254-4000, 8am-sundown daily, $8 parking), I declined the offer of a ride from the trams that shuttle visitors between the lot and the beach. Considering both the relative age and relative expectations of comfort of many tourists in Naples, I figured this was a touch of luxury that I had no need to avail myself of. I figured wrong. The boardwalk at Clam Pass Beach is an attraction in and of itself, winding through marshy mangrove swamps, crossing a river, and cutting through a forest before finally—*finally*—depositing you at the actual beach. The boardwalk is 3,000 feet long, which doesn't seem that long, but a half-mile nature-trail walk when you're expecting a quick few steps to the beach is the sort of thing that makes you start to resent nature's beauty after a while. So, consider yourself forewarned.

Once you get to the beach, the first thing you'll encounter is a restaurant and bar operated by the Naples Grande Beach Resort, complete with open-air seating and the incredibly tempting smell of grilling burgers. From the patio area, you can make your way down to the beach itself, which is definitely one of the quietest and most isolated within city limits.

the scenic boardwalk at Clam Pass Beach

# Sports and Recreation

## SUN N FUN LAGOON

Few county governments have the fiscal means to construct a water park for their residents, but the **Sun N Fun Lagoon** (15000 Livingston Rd., 239/252-4021, 10am-5pm daily in summer with extended evening hours on Fri., 10am-5pm Sat.-Sun. the rest of the year, $13 visitors 48 inches and taller, $6 visitors under 48 inches tall) is evidence of Collier County's robust tax base of millionaires and multi-millionaires. Although the foreclosure crisis may have hit this part of Florida particularly hard, this park opened in 2006 in North Collier Regional Park, when the area was exploding with real estate development (and the attendant property taxes). Kids will doubtless enjoy the four pools, five water slides, and various other soaking attractions, while adults may just shake their heads in wonder at the government largesse. The non-wet parts of North Collier Regional Park include soccer fields, a large playground area, and a fitness complex.

## SWAMP BUGGIES

All those luxury cars, high-end boutiques, and five-star boîtes can't mask the fact that Naples is right next door to some pretty huge swamps. And there's no better way to get around those swamps than on a swamp buggy. These monstrous, open-air vehicles with giant tires and roaring engines were invented in Naples as hunting vehicles, but with the banning of hunting in the Everglades, resourceful drivers figured out something else to do with them. If you want to experience some swamp buggy fun, head out to **Captain Steve's Swamp Buggy Adventures** (22903 SR-29, Jerome, 239/695-2773, 7am-9pm daily, $97.50 adults for a half-day tour, children under 12 free). Located about a half hour east of Naples, right near the boundary of the Big Cypress National Preserve, Captain Steve's will take you out into the wild-and-wet in a buggy. The rides are more geared to exploration rather than muddy adventure, so you'll have to count on wildlife sightings and the occasional near-encounter with an alligator to get your adrenaline rush.

## GOLF

Naples is called the "Golf Capital of the World" for good reason; there are more than 80 courses in the immediate area, and driving down U.S. 41, one almost feels like the entirety of Collier County outside of downtown Naples has been given over to fairways and retirement communities filled with golfers. However, many of those courses are private, which means visitors are relegated to hitting up an old-timer at the bar for an invite or making their way to one of the handful of decent public courses in the area.

Thankfully, those publicly accessible courses are impressive in their own right. Two of the three courses at **Lely Resort Golf & Country Club** (8004 Lely Resort Blvd., 239/793-2600, greens fees $35-167) are open to the public: Flamingo Island is a straightforward Robert Trent Jones Sr. course (7,171 yards), and the Mustang course (7,217 yards) was designed by Lee Trevino with lots of water hazards. **Quality Inn Golf Resort** (4100 Golden Gate Pkwy., 800/277-0017, greens fees $25-75) used to be known as the Golden Gate Golf Club but has since changed hands to the discount hotelier; the course has 18 holes and 6,570 yards.

The two Greg Norman-designed courses at **Tiburon Golf Club** (2620 Tiburon Dr., 239/594-2040, greens fees $170-280) are pricey, but this club, which is home to both the LPGA Tour's CME Group Tour Championship in November and the PGA Tour's QBE Shootout in December, is situated on an 800-acre, full-feature resort, and the courses are routinely rated highly by guests who pony up the money to play them.

# TENNIS

There are two fantastic publicly accessible tennis facilities in Naples. The city-operated **Arthur L. Allen Tennis Center** (239/213-3060, www.allentenniscenter.com, $13.75 for 90 minutes of play) is located in **Cambier Park** (755 8th Ave. S., 239/213-3058) and has a dozen lighted Har-Tru courts. Unlike many municipal courts, the ones here are very well maintained and actually seem to exceed the standards held by many private and club courts. The additional touch of using chickees (stilt houses built open on all sides and thatched) for shaded sitting areas—rather than an awning off the side of the fence—is pretty nice. Cambier Park also has a great wooden playground, if you're toting your kids along with you.

The **Pelican Bay Community Park Tennis Facility** (764 Vanderbilt Beach Rd., 239/598-3025, $10.60 for 90 minutes of play) is in a somewhat exclusive residential area, but it also offers up usage of its excellent courts to the visiting public. Although community residents get first dibs at court reservations, guests can still often get a reservation on one of the eight Har-Tru courts, especially in the late spring and summer. Both of these tennis centers offer round robins, lessons, and clinics, and they host multiple tournaments throughout the year.

# SAILING

Many of the people doing the sailing around Naples are doing so on their own boat. However, there are numerous opportunities for guests to enjoy the nautical life. **Naples Sailing Adventures** (239/354-0305, www.naplessailingadventures.com, call for rates) will design a custom charter package for you and your family aboard the *Beula Lee* (which departs from the City Dock, 880 12th Ave. S.). Whether the trip is purely for relaxation (the boat has three staterooms, two bathrooms, and a kitchen) or built to teach basic sailing skills, there are full- and half-day charters available.

Likewise, **Sailboats Unlimited** (Naples City Dock, 880 12th Ave. S., 239/649-1740, www.sailboatsunlimited.com, charters from $50/person) offers instruction, rentals, and crewed charters ranging from two hours to a full day, with seven different boats to choose from.

# BIKING AND SKATING

Naples may not seem like a very bike-friendly town, especially with the wide gash that the super-busy Tamiami Trail cuts through town. However, there are pretty wide sidewalks along most of the city's major thoroughfares, and in some parking-limited places like Old Naples and the area around Vanderbilt Beach, a bike is definitely the best mode of transportation. If you haven't brought your own, **Naples Cyclery** (813 Vanderbilt Beach Rd., 239/566-0600, http://naplescyclery.com, generally 9am-6pm Mon.-Sat., noon-5pm Sun., rentals from $14/five hours), just south of downtown, and **Big Momma's Bicycles** (850 Seagate Dr., 239/734-7734, http://bigmommasbicycles.com, 9am-6pm daily and by appointment, rentals from $5/hour), near Pelican Bay on the north side of town, both offer a wide selection of rentals; and, if you did bring your own, they offer service, too.

If you or your teenager brought a skateboard along for the trip, **Fleischmann Park** (1600 Fleischmann Blvd., 239/213-3020, free) has a great skate park attached to it: **The Edge/Johnny Nocera Skate Park** (10am-8pm Tues.-Fri., noon-8pm Sat., noon-4pm Sun., nonresident rates from $20/day) has multiple wood and concrete ramps, streetskate imitations, and a deep bowl. The rest of Fleischmann Park has basketball and racquetball courts, baseball and football fields, a playground, and a small but fun splash plaza connected to a playground.

# SPAS

The spa at the **Ritz-Carlton** (280 Vanderbilt Beach Rd., 239/538-3330, treatments from $185) is, unsurprisingly, one of the best in the city, with treatments ranging from massages and facials to eco-friendly pedicures. The downtown spa at **The Inn on Fifth** (699 5th Ave. S., 239/403-8777, treatments from $120) also has aromatherapy treatments, reflexology therapy sessions, facials, and body wraps.

# Entertainment and Events

## NIGHTLIFE

Most of Naples's nightlife takes place in bar-and-grill type places and sports-bar settings like the **Foxboro Sports Tavern** (4420 Thomason Dr., 239/530-2337, www.foxboro-tavern.com, 11am-1am daily, no cover). There are also a few spots like the **Old Naples Pub** (255 13th Ave. S., 239/649-8200, 11am-10pm Mon.-Sat., noon-9pm Sun., no cover) and **The Village Pub** (4360 Gulf Shore Blvd., 239/262-2707, 11am-10pm Mon.-Sat., noon-9pm Sun., no cover) that serve decent pub grub but mainly function as drinking establishments. **Shane's Cabana Bar** (495 Bayfront Pl., 239/732-6633, 11am-2am daily, no cover) is a neat spot to grab a drink, as it's little more than a bar, a roof, and some barstools, situated right on a relatively untrafficked northern portion of Naples Bay. Shane's has great happy hour specials and friendly bartenders, although its relative status as one of Naples's few "real" bars means that it's often hard to grab a stool.

For an upscale take on the "Naples nightlife" experience, you should put on your best outfit and head for the decadent cigar bar **BURN by Rocky Patel** (9110 Strada Pl., 239/653-9013, www.burnbyrockypatel.com, 2pm-2am daily, no cover); in addition to cigars, BURN also offers craft beer, wine, and craft cocktails in a boisterous atmosphere.

## PERFORMING ARTS

For those interested in the performing arts, the **Naples Community Players** perform a mix of crowd-pleasing musicals, kid-friendly fare, and even some more modern fare at the beautiful **Sugden Community Theater** (701 5th Ave. S., 239/263-7990, www.naplesplayers.com). Ballet, classical music, and Broadway productions are performed at **Artis—Naples,** home of the **Naples**

Sugden Community Theater presents performances by the Naples Community Players.

**Philharmonic** (5833 Pelican Bay Blvd., 239/597-1900, www.thephil.org).

## FESTIVALS AND EVENTS

Unsurprisingly, many of Naples's high-profile annual events are centered around art. Most occur during the peak of snowbird season, like the **Naples New Year's Weekend Art Fair,** the **Downtown Naples Festival of the Arts** (Apr.), and the twice-yearly **Naples Masters Art Festival** (Jan. and Mar.).

Beyond those, the trapped-in-amber vibe of the **Old Florida Festival** during November is a must-see for history buffs. Taking place on the historic grounds of the Collier County Museum, the Old Florida Festival divides the grounds up into "camps" populated variously by Native American tribes, Spanish settlers, British soldiers, Civil War fighters, pioneers, and more; the result is a look at the many different phases of progress that Florida has seen throughout the years.

During the last two weeks of October, as the city prepares for the seasonal influx of snowbirds, the Naples **CityFest** brings a wide variety of art, dining, music, and shopping events to the downtown area, as well as seasonal stuff like trick-or-treating. It's less a festival in the traditional sense than a rolling, multiday celebration that highlights the city's charms. The **Stone Crab Festival** is part of CityFest, and it's also worth noting that this may be the only festival in the country where a swamp buggy parade—now in its sixth decade—is a focal point of a municipal party.

# Shopping

TOP EXPERIENCE

## ART GALLERIES

Naples is famous for its high-end art scene, and the area in and around downtown is thick with galleries showcasing a wide variety of work. Along Gallery Row on 5th Avenue, well-known galleries like **New River Fine Art** (600 5th Ave. S., 239/435-4515, 10am-5pm Mon.-Sat., extended hours in winter) display masterworks from the likes of Dalí, Miró, Renoir, and more, alongside modern pieces from Frederick Hart, M. L. Snowden, Henry Asencio, and others, making it one of the most notable (and expensive) galleries on the Row. The **Four Winds Gallery** (658 5th Ave. S., 239/263-7555, 10am-5pm Mon.-Sat., extended hours in winter) takes a different approach, with carvings, jewelry, pottery, and other examples of modern Native American art, with an atmosphere that's both reflective and respectful of its artistic focus.

**Shaw Gallery** (761 5th Ave. S., 239/261-7828, www.shawgallery.com, 10am-6pm Mon.-Thurs., 10am-9pm Fri.-Sat., noon-5pm Sun.) has been a mainstay on 5th Avenue for more than two decades and specializes in sculpture, glass art, and paintings. It represents nearly 40 local, regional, and national artists. Although most of the art is both incredible and impressive, some of it is a little different from the standard offerings (the giant Tim Tebow action painting, for instance); such occasional deviations from the norm shouldn't be held against Shaw, which is generally quite well regarded in the community.

**Gallery One** (770 5th Ave. S., 239/263-0835, www.galleryonenaples.com, 10am-6pm Mon.-Wed.,10am-9pm Thurs.-Sat., noon-6pm Sun.) offers a standard selection of paintings, ceramics, and sculpture, most of which is quite good. One thing that sets Gallery One apart from many of the other 5th Avenue galleries is its focus on Judaica. More than a half-dozen Judaica-focused artists working in multiple media have their work on display.

A block south of 5th Avenue is the **Von Liebig Art Center** (585 Park St., 239/262-6517, 10am-4pm Mon.-Sat., $5 adults, $2 children) at the Naples Art Center, which combines exhibitions and gallery displays of the work of more than 400 local and regional artists. A little farther south, on 3rd Street between Broad and 12th Avenues is another concentration of galleries. The **Darvish Collection of Fine Art** (1199 3rd St. S., 239/261-7581, 10am-5pm Mon.-Sat., limited hours in summer) is the second-oldest gallery in Naples; it focuses on 19th- and 20th-century artists.

## DOWNTOWN NAPLES

Interspersed among all those art galleries and cultural sites are high-end (and not-so-high-end) shops. From candles and furniture to dog treats and Christmas ornaments, there is a wide variety of shops offering numerous ways to dispose of whatever disposable income you may have with you. **Julie's of Naples** (533 5th Ave. S., 239/434-9761, www.juliesofnaples.com, 10am-6pm Mon.-Sat., noon-5pm Sun.) is a friendly, fashion-forward women's boutique, with highbrow casual wear, jewelry, and accessories. **Anthony Verderamo** (800 5th Ave. S., 239/403-7772, 10am-5pm Mon.-Sat.) specializes in luxe, custom-made gold jewelry that's as notable for its personal artistic touches as it is for its high-end appeal.

## THE VILLAGE ON VENETIAN BAY

The **Village on Venetian Bay** (4300 Gulf Shore Blvd., 10am-6pm Mon.-Sat., noon-6pm Sun.) is an upscale, open-air mall, home to more than 50 stores, as well as a handful of restaurants and art galleries. The waterfront location makes it a bit more scenic than your average mall, and although there's a bit of an upscale tilt to most of the businesses, there are accessible shops as well.

Men's and women's clothing stores like **Diane's Fine Fashions** (239/213-4202), **Simply Natural** (239/643-5571), and **Teruzzi** (239/263-2252) dominate the offerings, along with a few decor-and-accessories shops and five (!) jewelers. The six restaurants—most of which are pretty high-end—and a Ben & Jerry's easily put to shame any regular old mall's food court.

## WATERSIDE SHOPS

**Waterside Shops** (5415 Tamiami Trail N., 239/598-1605, www.watersideshops.com, 10am-7pm Mon.-Sat., noon-6pm Sun.) is definitely a shopping experience in keeping with the area's upscale clientele, but instead of ultra-high-end boutiques, the stores—**Apple** (239/254-4240), **Louis Vuitton** (239/254-0456), **Nordstrom** (239/325-6100), **Saks Fifth Avenue** (239/592-5900)—are quite a bit more familiar. And, thankfully for those on a tighter budget, there are also quite a few accessible stores like **Gap** (239/598-1175) and **Pottery Barn** (239/593-3772), along with mall standards like **Starbucks** (239/596-8300), and more locally oriented shops like **The Beach House of Naples** (239/598-4144). Waterside is a multi-building mall, with an open-air pavilion at its heart, making it quite a bit less stifling than one might expect from a mall (and the valet parking available). Even if you're not actually in the mood to buy anything, the accessibility and atmosphere make a visit enjoyable in and of itself.

# Food

## BREAKFAST

There are two decent spots to grab a morning bite in the arts district downtown. The appropriately monikered **Third Street Cafe** (1361 3rd St., 239/261-1498, 6:30am-3pm Mon.-Sun., main courses from $6) has basic breakfast fare served in a pleasant environment (during lunch, they welcome larger crowds for their deli selections). Even if you can't be bothered to make the walk, fear not, as the Third Street Cafe also delivers.

**Jane's Cafe** (1209 3rd St., 239/261-2253, 8am-5pm Mon.-Sat., 8:30am-4pm Sun., main courses from $3) is a small, European-style café (complete with a beautiful outdoor dining area) that specializes in pastries and lighter breakfast bites, as well as impressive omelets and a few vegetarian options.

The fine folks at Naples Cyclery are available to help get you onto a bicycle rental; or, if you brought your own, they can perform maintenance or repairs on it. They're also available to fill up your personal combustion engine with **Fit & Fuel** (819 Vanderbilt Beach Rd., 239/514-3333, http://naplescyclery.com, 6:30am-5:30pm Mon.-Fri., 6:30am-2:30pm Sat., 7:30am-2:30pm Sun.), a small café attached to the bike shop where you can get fully caffeinated on fresh espresso or brew coffee before or after your ride.

The specialties at the comfortable and bright **Sunburst Cafe** (2340 Pine Ridge Rd., 239/263-3123, www.sunburstnaples.com, 7am-3pm daily, main courses from $5) are its coffees. Espresso drinks are the focus, and the place has clearly positioned itself as a coffeehouse first and a restaurant second. However, that doesn't at all diminish the quality of the food served. Homemade pastries and crepes are excellent, as are the items on an expansive traditional breakfast menu that includes omelets, eggs-and-bacon dishes, French toast, pancakes, and more; breakfast is served all day, alongside a lunch menu that focuses on light sandwiches and salads.

## AMERICAN

You can get your burger cooked in dozens of different ways at **Brooks Gourmet Burgers and Dogs** (330 9th St. S., 239/262-1127, www. naplesburgers.com, 11am-9pm Mon.-Sat., main courses from $6), a fact that is endlessly trumpeted throughout this great restaurant. In addition to artery-challenging monsters like a Donut Burger (cheese and bacon and a half pound of beef in between two glazed doughnuts) and the Todd's Way (a burger topped with fried egg, bacon, and two kinds of cheese), there are some more refined options, such as the Greek (red onion, feta, olives, tomatoes, and Greek dressing) and one topped with fresh pesto and goat cheese. They also have an array of similarly decadent hot dogs and sandwiches, but with so many ways to truly get a burger prepared "your way," why bother? There's also a great selection of beer to wash it all down with.

I-75 connects Naples to the Midwest and cuts right through the heart of Ohio, bringing a large number of visitors from the area. Therefore, it shouldn't be surprising that when the Cincinnati institution known as **Skyline Chili** (710 9th St. N., 239/649-5665, www. skylinechili.com, 11am-7:30pm Mon.-Sat., 11am-3:30pm Sun., main courses from $5) was looking to expand beyond the Buckeye State, they chose to open an outlet here. Sure, you can get a wrap or a salad, but what would be the point when the rich, steaming chili Skyline is known for can be delivered atop a hot dog or even as part of a spaghetti dish?

## NEW AMERICAN

**Citrus** (455 5th Ave. S., 239/435-0408, 11am-10pm daily, main courses from $15) offers gorgeous alfresco dining and an extensive menu of fresh seafood dishes. But that could be said about a good number of restaurants in downtown Naples. What sets this place apart is its casually upscale vibe, along with an amazingly extensive beer menu. While it may not present itself as a gastropub, Citrus almost certainly is one, as the food is excellent and innovative without being precious, served in an atmosphere that's pleasant but not fussy. Flash-fried whole hogfish served atop a bed of jasmine rice is one of the specialties; although whole fish is sometimes difficult to navigate gracefully, the hogfish's crispy outside easily opens up to reveal chunky, semisweet flesh. And, thankfully, since the atmosphere isn't all that uptight, nobody will notice (or care) as you pick your way through it.

While a lot of restaurants on 5th Avenue can coast by simply combining sky-high menu prices with the benefits of their location, it's always refreshing to find a spot in this area of town that is obviously working hard to be great at what it does. While the menu at **Bistro 821** (821 5th Ave. S., 239/261-5821, www.bistro821.com, 5pm-10pm daily, main courses from $27) is certainly not inexpensive, the combination of attentive and friendly service, excellent atmosphere, and top-notch food makes it well worth the expense. There's an emphasis on fresh seafood—sea bass, snapper, shrimp—but it's typically prepared with flair, often with a bit of an Asian influence. However, American staples such as meat loaf (yes, meat loaf) also get treated well by the kitchen. A great (and affordable) way to explore the Bistro's menu is to take advantage of their "pick two or three" option, which gets you and your dining companion two (or three) half entrées and a side for a greatly reduced price; often, there will be specials that combine a pick-two with a special selection from the restaurant's extensive wine list.

Wine is one of the specialties at **Ridgway Bar & Grill** (1300 3rd St. S., #101, 239/262-5500, www.ridgwaybarandgrill.com, 11:30am-9:30pm daily, main courses from $18), an intimate and beautiful establishment in downtown Naples. The wine list is *huge*, with over 600 selections, more than a dozen of which are served by the glass. It's not just the vino that sets Ridgway apart, though. The menus are impressive, featuring a standard selection of meat, seafood, poultry, and pasta dishes that are prepared with fresh, locally sourced ingredients. Veal chops, snapper piccata, and braised short ribs may not sound too special, but the kitchen is thoughtful in their preparations. Those selections are complemented by a great array of comfort foods like meat loaf, chicken potpie, and fish-and-chips. Ridgway also offers two "simple" menus of seafood and meat, which allow you to select your steak or fish and then add a side from choices like fried green tomatoes, ratatouille, grits cake, and other down-home specialties. If you're having trouble squaring "extensive wine list" with "fried green tomatoes," then the friendly, food-focused vibe at Ridgway may not be for you; however, those who enjoy indulging in kitchen-table standards prepared with flair and care will find a lot to love.

There are few instances in this guide where you'll be advised to head out of the heart of a city to eat at a strip mall, but, north of downtown, tucked into a mall between a Subway and a mattress store is **The Local** (5323 Airport Pulling Rd. N., 239/596-3276, thelocalnaples.com, 11am-9pm Tues.-Sun., main courses from $10), a farm-to-table experience that manages to be one of the best restaurants in town, despite its inconvenient location. Lots of vegetarian and gluten-free options, ultra-fresh seafood, soups, decadent chef-driven pork and poultry preparations, as well as an incredible wine list and a casual, laid-back vibe (the bar is actually a pretty great place to watch the game and have a decent beer and some great, non-wing food) make The Local the kind of place that would be a no-brainer for an urban environment, but it's a pleasant surprise on the outskirts of Naples.

## STEAK

Naples is definitely a steaks-and-chops kind of town, and the **Pewter Mug Steakhouse** (12300 Tamiami Trail N., 239/597-3017, www.pewtermug41.com, lunch 11am-2pm

Mon.-Fri., dinner 4:30pm-10pm daily, main courses from $16) is one of the more popular (and populist) places in town to get a well-cooked slab of meat. The atmosphere is a bit old-fashioned, the portions are quite large, and the copious salad bar will help appease any guilt you may have about indulging in one of their 16-ounce prime ribs.

**Andre's Steakhouse** (2800 E. Tamiami Trail, 239/263-5851, 5pm-9pm daily, main courses from $26) is a distinctly more upscale experience, with a dark and romantic dining room. Steaks are served New York-style, coated in butter and plated with sides like creamed spinach and asparagus.

The modern and stylish **Cafe Lurcat** (494 5th Ave. S., 239/213-3357, www.cafelurcat.com, 5pm-10pm Mon.-Thurs., 5pm-11pm Fri.-Sat., 5pm-9pm Sun., main courses from $19) has an expansive menu that adds fresh fish and seafood selections to a solid selection of steaks and chops. The European atmosphere is reflected in unusual menu choices like buckwheat crepes, brie and pickled figs, and even a few Asian-inspired preparations.

If your idea of great steak is "lots of it," then definitely head out to the Pelican Bay area and **Martin Fierro** (13040 Livingston Rd., 239/300-4777, www.martinfierrorestaurant.com, 11am-9pm daily, main courses from $12). This Argentine steakhouse emphasizes both quantity and quality, and although it should definitely not be confused with the Brazilian steakhouse experience of waiters bringing endless plates of meat, the portions are substantial, and the *parrilladas* selections—which combine several different cuts on one plate—are an incredible value. Be aware, this is a place that takes meat seriously, so you'll be able to get tripe, sweetbreads, and blood sausage as well as more typical selections like short ribs, filet mignon, skirt steak, and more.

## SEAFOOD

**Kelly's Fish House** (1302 5th Ave. S., 239/774-0494, http://kellysfishhousediningroom.com, 4:30pm-10pm daily, main courses from $17) is the oldest seafood restaurant in Naples, a badge of honor that could result in lazy service and bland, assembly-line dishes. Instead, this no-nonsense eatery has made a legend of itself not just by lasting a long time, but by serving ultra-fresh seafood in traditional grilled/broiled/fried fashion. You can get raw bar treats like oysters and clams, along with expertly prepared takes on standards like shrimp, grouper, and crab, as well as a limited selection of chicken and steak dishes. The wood-paneled walls and kitschy, nautical bric-a-brac make it clear that Kelly's isn't going to try to impress you with its modern styling, but the quality (and pricing) of the food and the waterfront views more than make up for any such "shortcomings."

On the other hand, the hyper-stylized (and hyper-stylish) **USS Nemo** (3745 Tamiami Trail N., 239/261-6366, www.ussnemorestaurant.com, lunch 11:30am-2pm Mon.-Fri., dinner 5pm-9:30pm daily, main courses from $18) prides itself on delivering an exceptional atmospheric experience that, with blue-tinted windows covered by porthole-like contraptions and a bar that looks like a submarine galley, is intended to make you feel as if you're underwater. Thankfully, the food lives up to the decor, with a focus on super-fresh preparations that are highly influenced by an Asian fusion approach. Sampler platters come in bento-box-type plates, and appetizers include tuna *tataki* salad and shrimp tempura.

The **Yabba Island Grill** (711 5th Ave. S., 239/262-5787, www.yabbaislandgrill.com, 5pm-10pm Sun.-Thurs., 5pm-11pm Fri.-Sat., main courses from $16) combines fresh and inventive seafood dishes prepared with a modern flair with a casual, beachside-bar vibe. Occasionally, the delicate plating and exotic cocktail concoctions get a bit too cute for their own good, but the Yabba is far from pretentious and manages to be mellow and fun while serving up excellent and individual dishes.

If you don't mind getting your seafood in a strip mall (and you shouldn't!), Naples has two options definitely worth checking out. **Steamers** (5317 Airport Pulling Rd., 239/593-3388, 11am-10pm daily, main courses from $9) has a no-frills atmosphere and is a decent option for casual, New England-style seafood with the family. Fried baskets are the main draw (make sure to get the onion rings). There are a few freshly grilled options, as well as lobster rolls, soft-shell crab, and more. **Grouper & Chips** (338 9th St. N., www.grouperandchips.net, 239/643-4577, 11:30am-9pm Mon.-Sat., main courses from $16) definitely lives up to its name, as fried fish and chips is one of the specialties at this casual, hole-in-a-strip-mall location. But don't let the name or the tiny space fool you; these guys also serve other notable dishes, including incredible catch-of-the-day fish tacos, blackened grouper, and even a heartwarming bouillabaisse.

The national upscale seafood chain **Trulucks** (698 4th Ave. S., 239/530-3131, http://trulucks.com, 5pm-10pm Sun.-Thurs., 5pm-11pm Fri.-Sat., main courses from $31) also has a location in Naples.

But, for a more local-oriented upscale seafood experience, head directly to ★ **Sea Salt** (1186 3rd St. S., 239/434-7258, www.seasaltnaples.com, lunch 11:30am-3pm daily, dinner 5pm-10pm daily, main courses from $22), a stylish downtown restaurant that specializes in innovative takes on the fresh seafood that abounds in the Naples area. The dining room is a little crowded, but beautiful; still, request patio seating (or even an indoor table near the patio) to have a little more breathing room. (Conversely, if you're feeling like splurging, go ahead and book the chef's table and get right in the middle of the action in the kitchen.) Organic and local ingredients are the focus on the menu, which changes with somewhat regular frequency. Unique among seafood-oriented spots is an extensive antipasto menu, complete with a half-dozen charcuterie selections as well as raw oysters, carpaccio, cheese, olives, and shrimp cocktails. Making selections from that menu alone would make an evening at Sea Salt memorable, but there's also fresh pasta, high-end beef preparations, and limited (but select and specialized) seafood options. The artful preparations at Sea Salt—not to mention the restaurant's overall aesthetic—make it clear that although their seafood selections may not be numerous, they are where the restaurant's heart is.

## FRENCH

Somewhat surprisingly, the best French restaurants in Naples tend to be focused on home-style, classic French preparations rather than upscale, fine dining. That's not to say that these restaurants are cheap, but they are accessible, with dishes that are authentic, comforting, and well prepared. **Bleu Provence** (1234 8th St. S., 239/261-3410, www.bleuprovencenaples.com, 5pm-10pm daily, main courses from $16) makes it fairly explicit with its name that its specialties are its Provençal dishes, and the combination of seafood (mussels and scallops, especially) and Mediterranean flavors (tajine chicken and couscous) hits the spot. The menu also includes traditional dishes like steak tartare, veal chops, sweetbreads, and duck confit, as well as more locally inspired options like sesame tuna. Bleu Provence also serves up some fantastic steak frites.

**Escargot 41** (4339 Tamiami Trail N., 239/793-5000, www.escargot41.com, 5:30pm-10pm daily, main courses from $19) obviously has a soft spot for snails, and the menu is topped off with more than a half-dozen different escargot preparations. A few French-inspired beef, poultry, and seafood dishes provide the main bulk of the entrées, but if you focus on the escargot and the excellent selection of hors d'oeuvres (foie gras, pâté, salmon *fumé*), you can piece together a far more adventurous and exciting meal. The strip-mall exterior belies a dining room that's beautifully decorated and elegant without being stuffy.

Crepes, quiches, sandwiches, and salads are the main attraction at **Cafe Normandie** (3756 Tamiami Trail N., 239/261-0977, www.cnnaples.com, lunch 11am-3pm Mon.-Sat., dinner 5pm-10pm Mon.-Sat., main courses from $13), which is definitely the most casual

# Florida Stone Crabs

Stone crabs are abundant all along the coast of the Gulf of Mexico, down to the Keys, and then back up the Atlantic Coast to North Carolina. However, the stone crabs that are prevalent along the southwest coast of Florida and in the Keys are known as Florida stone crabs, rather than Gulf stone crabs. Although any stone crab claw is highly prized in kitchens throughout the world, Florida stone crabs have a reputation as being both sweeter and meatier than Gulf stone crabs. Stone crabs are harvested in Florida between mid-October and mid-May, and during that time, visitors to the area can avail themselves of some of the freshest crab claws around. (Frozen? Don't bother.) Stone crabs are incredibly abundant along the Gulf Coast between Naples and Key West, and although demand has spiked in recent years, this fishery is still regarded by conservationists as a viable source for the crabs. During harvest season, crabbers head out on boats and launch crab pots baited with pigs' feet and other scavenge-y delights, and, upon returning, haul the crates to the boat and check for crabs with claws of legal length (2.75 inches minimum, about half the length that a mature stone crab claw can grow to), break the claw off at the "knuckle" so it can regrow, and then toss the now-amputated crab back into the water to grow another. It sounds brutal, and it is, but it's not a death sentence: a study of the practice determined that "only" 28 percent of the crabs who had a claw amputated died. Feasting on stone crab while in the area during harvest season is nearly mandatory, and during Naples's **Stone Crab Festival** in October, if you don't try at least one of these succulent, meaty claws—dip it in mustard, it's better than butter!—you're truly missing out.

of all of Naples's French restaurants. The café atmosphere is comfortable and friendly, and the kitchen is deft at dishing up an extensive selection of classic French comfort food at reasonable prices. This approach has made the Normandie a popular lunch spot, but it shouldn't be overlooked as a dinner option; although the menu is a bit richer in the evening hours, the focus—with dishes like beef bourguignon, veal stew, and roasted chicken—is still on home-style cuisine.

## LATIN

**Agave** (2380 Vanderbilt Beach Rd., 239/598-3473, http://agavenaples.com, 11:30am-9pm Mon.-Wed., 11:30am-10pm Thurs.-Sat., 11am-8pm Sun., main courses from $15) is a relatively new midscale Tex-Mex place near Vanderbilt Beach. The menu includes a few dishes like bison chili and fresh ceviche rounding out the expected selection of quesadillas, tacos, tamales, and entrée-style chicken and beef plates. Agave specializes in what they call "plates on fire," which is basically an amped-up presentation of fajitas. Imagine if your local Mexican place served fajitas on a mobile cart, and prepared them tableside in a semi-theatrical, teppanyaki-inspired manner. Fun to watch? Sure, if you're not the one waiting to eat. Agave also offers tequila and margarita flights, and has an ample selection of top-shelf tequilas.

**IM Tapas** (965 4th Ave. N., 239/403-8272, www.imtapas.com.com, 5:30pm-10pm Mon.-Thurs., 5:30pm-11pm Fri.-Sat., 5:30pm-9pm Sun., tapas from $8) not only serves an expansive menu of hot and cold tapas with more than two dozen selections (including ostrich carpaccio, spicy octopus, and *morcilla* blood sausage, among other surprises), but also dishes up awesome paella and *fideuà* (a pasta dish similar to paella) for those who want to eschew small plates for some family-style indulgence.

Another exceptional tapas option is **Lamoraga** (3936 Tamiami Trail N., 239/331-3669, www.lamoragarestaurant.com, 11:30am-10pm Mon.-Fri., 5pm-10pm Sat.-Sun., tapas from $8), which tacks a sushi bar onto their tapas experience, making it a great place for small-plate explorations.

## JAPANESE AND THAI

Most popular with the birthday crowds that descend on the teppanyaki tables for the food-grilling show, **Fujiyama** (2555 9th St. N., 239/261-4332, www.naplesfujiyama.com, 5:30pm-10pm Mon.-Fri., 5:30pm-11pm Sat.-Sun., main courses from $15) also has one of the area's better sushi bars. On the north side of town, near Vanderbilt Beach, a similar, though pricier, teppanyaki and sushi place is **Daruma Steak and Seafood** (241 Center St. N., 239/591-1200, www.darumarestaurant.com, 5pm-10pm daily, main courses from $14).

A more dedicated sushi experience can be had at **Tokyo Sushi** (3743 E. Tamiami Trail, 239/775-3388, 11am-10pm daily, main courses from $9). It's in a strip mall and also offers a carry-out menu.

The conveniently located **Sushi Thai Too** (898 5th Ave. S., 239/430-7575, http://sushithaitoo.com, 11:30am-10pm Sun.-Thurs., 11:30am-11pm Fri.-Sat., main courses from $8) may not have the most creative name, but the super-fresh sushi and largely authentic Thai fare they serve speak for themselves. Stylish and modern interior decor suits the somewhat up-ladder prices on the menu, and service is exceptional.

## MIDDLE EASTERN

**Bha Bha Persian Bistro** (847 Vanderbilt Beach Rd., 239/594-5557, www.bhabhapersianbistro.com, lunch 11:30am-2:30pm Tues.-Sat., dinner 5pm-9pm Tues.-Thurs. and Sun., 5pm-10pm Fri.-Sat., main courses from $18) has proven to be something of a hit. With an inventive and modern take on Persian and Mediterranean classics, Bha Bha's core menu items won't be unfamiliar to those experienced with the fragrant citrus- and saffron-infused dishes of Turkey, but the Persian influence brings in fruit flavors like currant and apricot. Meat is the focus of the menu, especially lamb and beef, and preparations lean heavily on sauces and marinades. Food is a little pricey, but it's important to keep in mind that you're getting a dining experience that's far beyond your standard falafel-and-hummus take on Middle Eastern food.

However, if that's what you're looking for, you can get a straightforward selection of inexpensive gyros, falafel, pitas, and chicken dishes at the low-key **Falafel Grill** (336 9th St. N., 239/213-0883, www.falafelgrille.com, 11:30am-9pm Mon.-Sat., main courses from $9).

## VEGETARIAN AND VEGAN

There aren't a whole lot of vegetarian options in Naples, but **True Food Kitchen** (5375 Tamiami Trail N., 239/431-4580, http://truefoodkitchen.com, 11am-9pm Mon.-Thurs., 11am-10pm Fri., 10am-10pm Sat., 10am-9pm Sun., main courses from $12) succeeds not only by being a rarity but also by being uniformly satisfying. Featuring vegetarian, vegan, and gluten-free fare—along with a broad selection of "healthy" proteins like grass-fed beef, chicken, shrimp, and salmon—in a spacious and bright location, this national chain manages a seasonally rotating menu, but you can count on decent, fresh food year-round.

# Accommodations

## $50-100

Budget accommodations, especially during the winter, are fairly hard to come by in Naples. The **Sea Shell Motel** (82 9th St. S., 239/262-5129, doubles from $99) is somewhat dated, but it's clean, reasonably well maintained, and close to downtown.

## $100-200

The **Naples Courtyard Inn** (2630 9th St. N., 239/261-3870, http://naplescourtyardinn.com, doubles from $109) is not part of the Marriott chain; rather, this brightly painted and semitropical motel has a selection of recently redecorated rooms. Most of the rooms are standard motel rooms (some of which are adjoining), but there are also a handful of one-bedroom suites with kitchenettes.

Each of the rooms at the **Lemon Tree Inn** (250 9th St. S., 239/262-1414, www.lemontreeinn.com, doubles from $159) is individually decorated, which means you could end up with a plain hotel room with a gorgeous four-poster bed, or a gorgeous room with a plain bed. The best room is the St. Croix Suite, with a separate entrance, two bathrooms, kitchenette, and hardwood floors. All the rooms open up to the courtyard and have mini-fridges and microwaves. There's a pool on-site, which is where the daily continental breakfast is served.

The ★ **Gulfcoast Inn** (2555 Tamiami Trail N., 239/261-6046, http://gulfcoastinnnaples.com, doubles from $139) is a fantastic budget option, especially in the off-season. Located just behind a country club and just a five-minute walk to the beach, the inn offers surprisingly spacious rooms with kitchenettes and free Internet access. Some rooms have tile floors and are tropically decorated. All rooms overlook the large pool area and the poolside bar. There's also a Japanese restaurant on the property.

The **Lighthouse Inn** (9140 Gulf Shore Dr., 239/597-3345, doubles from $135) is showing its age, but in a good way. It's a basic cinder-block motel, with super-clean and comfortable efficiencies and apartments that are some of the least expensive decent accommodations near Vanderbilt Beach. Amenities are spartan—there's a small heated pool, and your room has a television but no telephone—but given the price and the Lighthouse's excellent location (and the fact that you've probably got a mobile phone anyway), who cares? There are only 15 rooms, and they get booked incredibly early during high season.

It bills itself as a "boutique family resort," and it's hard to argue with that self-assessment of ★ **Inn of Naples** (4055 Tamiami Trail N., 239/649-5500, www.innofnaples.com, doubles from $179). Though not located particularly close to anything, it's not exactly far away from anything either, and despite the fact that it's situated on the busy Tamiami Trail, having swampy Sugden Park out its back door gives it a surprisingly secluded feel. Inside, the property reflects a recent renovation, with fresh, bright paint and up-to-date appointments masking decades-old hotel architecture. All rooms have private balconies and flat-screen TVs; in addition to hotel-style accommodations, there are a few one- and two-bedroom suites.

The **Inn at Pelican Bay** (800 Vanderbilt Beach, 239/597-8777, www.innatpelicanbay.com, doubles from $199) is just off the Tamiami Trail, in a massive planned community area north of downtown. It's a few blocks away from beautiful Vanderbilt Beach, and also located quite conveniently to the Baker Museum and Artis—Naples. The inn is actually more of a standard hotel—100 rooms are spread across the four floors of two wings. Everything is quite nice and new. Amenities include a heated outdoor pool and a 24-hour fitness center, and all the clean and freshly decorated rooms have flat-screen TVs and mini-fridges. If you crave consistency and predictability in a hotel but would like to get away from chains, this is a good option.

The **Park Central Hotel** (40 9th St. N., 239/435-9700, www.naplesparkcentral.com, doubles from $159) is a small hotel with only 30 rooms, with a convenient location just a few blocks away from the action on 5th Avenue. All of the rooms are uniquely decorated, and their tile floors give them a spacious feel that belies their somewhat smaller square footage. The rooms are quite nice—with flat-screen TVs, Internet access, wet bars, and new furnishings—and the hotel's heated pool and lounge make it comfortable and relaxing. And, given those amenities and the hotel's location, the rates are something of a bargain.

## $200-300

Perfectly located on 5th Avenue downtown, the historic ★ **Inn on Fifth** (699 5th Ave. S., 239/403-8777, doubles from $279) combines boutique-style intimacy with top-shelf grandeur. The 76 surprisingly large rooms and 11 decadent suites are all decorated in a style that's not too ostentatious, with pillow-top bedding and nice touches like free Wi-Fi and iPod docks; the suites have whirlpool tubs and balconies. There's a beautifully landscaped pool in the back, and one of Naples's best spas is on-site. The Inn on Fifth is an incredibly popular choice, and it's a challenge to get a room on off-season weekends and pretty much any time during season; make sure to reserve early.

Right on Naples Bay is the thatched-roof **Cove Inn** (900 Broad Ave. S., 239/262-7161, www.coveinnnaples.com, doubles from $229). As far south on 9th Street as one can go without falling into the water, the inn's location is its prime attraction, but the clean, spacious rooms are a good value. There are mini-kitchens in the hotel rooms and full kitchens in the suites, and each room in this condo-hotel reflects the individual decorating choice of its owner. Accordingly, some of the rooms are hilariously chintzy, while others are just stocked with the typical array of pastels and pelicans.

Also located downtown (but somewhat closer to the Tin City area) is the **Bellasera** (221 9th St. S., 239/649-7333, www.bellaseranaples.com, doubles from $249). Rooms are spacious, condo-style accommodations, with contemporary, upscale furnishings and luxurious touches that range from DVD players to marble countertops in the kitchen. Studio suites (regular hotel rooms) have refrigerators

The Inn on Fifth is a great lodging option in downtown Naples.

and a king-size bed, while the larger one-, two-, and three-bedroom suites have full kitchens and, in some cases, laundry rooms.

## OVER $300

Upscale lodging options abound in Naples, and although quite a few of the well-heeled types head directly for the **Ritz-Carlton Naples Resort** (280 Vanderbilt Beach Rd., 239/538-3330, www.ritzcarlton.com/naples, doubles from $429), there are several other impressive and luxurious places to stay in Naples. And though wrangling one of these plush beds during high season can be something of a challenge, off-season rates for those prepared to wilt in the summer humidity are surprisingly manageable at most of them. This Ritz-Carlton is right next to Vanderbilt Beach, so in addition to all of the typical amenities of a Ritz, guests are treated to easy access to one of the most beautiful beaches in Florida. Also on-site are four tennis courts, a luxe pool with cabanas, several cool nature-based kids' programs, and a game room stocked with Wii, Playstation, and Xbox consoles.

Guests at the Vanderbilt Beach Ritz also have privileges at the 36-hole Tiburon Golf Course, but serious luxury-minded duffers will want to book a room or suite at **The Ritz-Carlton Golf Resort** (2600 Tiburon Dr., 239/593-2000, doubles from $379), which, though just a few blocks away from the main Ritz beach resort, puts guests right on top of those two Greg Norman-designed courses. The golf resort is a bit smaller, though still far from intimate, with nearly 300 rooms and five restaurants. A good bit of the hotel's real estate is given over to conference facilities, and the vibe is definitely more wheel-and-deal than it is kick-back-on-the-coast. Of course, it's still incredibly luxurious—this is a Ritz-Carlton. (Worth noting: Guests at each resort have reciprocal privileges at the other.)

If you can't decide between the Ritz's luxurious beach resort or the Ritz's luxurious golf resort—or you don't feel like shuttling between the two—then **La Playa Beach & Golf Resort** (9891 Gulf Shore Dr., 239/597-3123, www.laplayaresort.com, doubles from $449) may be able to cover all your bases. Located just north of the Ritz-Carlton's beach resort, La Playa shares the same beautiful stretch of sand that is Vanderbilt Beach, albeit in a somewhat more secluded section. La Playa only has one 18-hole course, but the Robert Cupp-designed course is gorgeous. Rooms are spread across multiple buildings, including two towers; request a beachfront room in the Gulf Tower for incredible views and easy access to the beach. Rooms in the Bay Tower are also luxurious, but located across the street from the main resort; you'll get a decent view in upper-floor rooms, but you'll be somewhat away from the main action. The best rooms, though, are the 850-square-foot one-bedroom suites, which are not only huge and stylish but also beachfront. All of the rooms at La Playa are airy and bright, decorated in a comfortably luxurious style that's tropical without being pastel-drenched and offering all the amenities one would expect from rooms bearing such astronomical tariffs. The resort has two restaurants, a tiki bar, a spa, and a fitness center.

With an excellent location that's very close to central Naples yet still feels out of the way (it's located in a predominantly residential area), ★ **The Naples Beach Hotel & Golf Club** (851 Gulf Shore Blvd. N., 239/261-2222, doubles from $329) is probably my favorite place to stay in all of Naples. And I'm not just saying that because they let me stay there free for one night. I'm saying that because the hotel combines Old Florida charm, 1950s glamour, and modern luxury in a way that manages to be friendly and accessible. Family-owned since it opened in 1946, the Naples Beach Hotel & Golf Club is a little out of step with similarly outfitted resorts in the city. There's no sense of corporate gloss, and instead guests are treated to a collection of buildings that appear on the surface to have little to do with one another. The original hotel building looks like a fishers' motel, one tower very much gives away its origins in the 1970s, while still another looks like an Art Deco apartment building. It may not be visually consistent on the outside, but all of the rooms share the same spacious, casual-tropical atmosphere and fresh decor. And, thanks to the fact that all rooms are decorated with prints by famed Everglades photographer Clyde Butcher and ceramics by Naples artist Jim Rice, it's clear that there's a real effort to keep the resort tied to its local roots. Yes, it's pricey (but there's no resort fee!), and no, the pool may not be as massive or glamorous as the one at the Ritz, but the sunsets can't be beat, and the friendly staff manages to make everyone feel welcome and pampered. All rooms have flat-screen TVs, wet bars, and mini-fridges, and guests can avail themselves of the golf course (across the street; it's the oldest in Naples) and the ample spa facilities.

**The Escalante** (290 5th Ave. S., 239/659-3466, www.hotelescalante.com, doubles from $429) is a boutique hotel that feels like a boutique hotel. The atmosphere manages to cross Mediterranean decor and a Key West-inspired tropical vibe, and it does so in a location that's right in the heart of Old Naples. The Escalante only has 11 rooms on its property, and all of them have some sense of individuality. There are two suites, a standalone villa, and eight small standard rooms, which either have a private patio or open up to the garden and pool area. The on-site restaurant, Dish, is equally intimate and exceptional.

For those looking for elegant beachside accommodations, the Hilton-owned **Edgewater Beach Hotel** (1901 Gulf Shore Blvd., 888/564-1308, doubles from $479) is an excellent option. All the rooms are recently updated and well maintained. The property,

though family-friendly and perfect for a beach vacation, is nonetheless quite classy, with lavish, modern decorations. Guests can get guest privileges (spa, tennis, swimming pools) at the nearby Waldorf Astoria, which, though a bit fancier than the Edgewater, is a property where it's more difficult to get a discounted rate.

For those looking for elegant beachside accommodations, the **Edgewater Beach Hotel** (1901 Gulf Shore Blvd., 888/564-1308, www.edgewaternaples.com, doubles from $479), part of the upscale Opal Collection group of hotels, is an excellent option. All the rooms are well maintained and up-to-date. The property, though family-friendly and perfect for a beach vacation, is nonetheless quite classy, with lavish, modern decorations. Guests can get privileges (spa, tennis, swimming pools) at the nearby Naples Grande Beach Resort, which is a bit fancier than the Edgewater but more difficult to get a discounted rate at.

However, if you want to splurge, the **Naples Grande Beach Resort** (475 Seagate Drive, 239/597-3232, www.waldorfastorianaples.com, doubles from $329) will gladly accommodate you. There are 15 tennis courts, a Rees Jones-designed golf course, and a Golden Door spa. The 474 rooms are modern and well maintained, and they all feature balconies, flat-screen TVs, minibars, and all of the luxe amenities one would expect when staying in an upmarket resort. If you're *really* looking to splurge, go ahead and lay out for one of the 50 suites; rather than just being super-sized rooms, the suites are located in bungalows.

# Information and Services

## VISITOR INFORMATION

The **Naples, Marco Island, Everglades Convention & Visitors Bureau** (www.paradisecoast.com) has an information center downtown (800 5th Ave. S.) with infinitely helpful staff. You can pick up brochures and maps there, as well as make hotel reservations and get information on local events.

## MEDICAL AND EMERGENCY SERVICES

**NCH Healthcare System Downtown Naples Hospital** (350 7th St. N., 239/436-5151) is the main hospital in the area; NCH also operates **NCH North Naples Hospital** (11190 Health Park Blvd., 239/552-7000), which is in the Pelican Bay/Vanderbilt Beach area. Both hospitals have 24-hour emergency rooms. There are more than two dozen branches of national chain pharmacies located throughout Naples, including **Walgreens** and **CVS,** and prescriptions can also be filled at many **Publix** grocery stores.

## POST OFFICES

The downtown **Naples Post Office** (860 6th Ave. S., 239/262-3351, 8:30am-5pm Mon.-Fri.) is convenient to almost all of the main sights in central Naples, and there are nearly 10 other branches scattered between Marco Island and Bonita Springs.

## INTERNET ACCESS

Free Wi-Fi access is available at many cafés, bars, and restaurants in Naples, including chains like McDonald's and Starbucks, as well as the **Collier County Library** (downtown branch, 650 Central Ave., 239/262-4130, 9am-7pm Mon.-Thurs., 9am-5pm Fri.-Sat.).

## BANKS

The banks most well represented in the Naples area are **Wells Fargo, SunTrust, Regions Bank,** and **Fifth Third,** each of which has several branches with ATMs in town. ATMs are also available at **Publix** supermarkets.

# Getting There and Around

## GETTING THERE

The main airport in the area is **Southwest Florida International Airport** (RSW, 11000 Terminal Access Rd., 239/590-4800, www.flylcpa.com) in Fort Myers. It's serviced by most major American carriers, including Southwest. Another option is to fly into Fort Lauderdale-Hollywood International Airport (FLL), which would require a two-hour drive along the toll stretch of I-75 known as Alligator Alley.

I-75 ends its north-south route through the middle United States in Naples, where it takes a sharp turn toward the east and Fort Lauderdale. Also running through Naples is the scenic Tamiami Trail (U.S. 41), which connects Tampa and Miami via the Everglades.

**Greyhound** offers bus service into the **Central Park Bus Terminal** (2699 Davis Blvd., 239/774-5660, www.greyhound.com, 8:15am-10:30am and 1:30pm-5pm Mon.-Sat.).

## GETTING AROUND

Public transportation in Naples, via the county government's **Collier Area Transit** (CAT, 239/252-8192, www.colliergov.net, $1.50/trip or $4 for a day pass) is extremely limited, focused primarily on the Tamiami Trail and outlying areas.

You'll definitely need a car, and parking can sometimes be a challenge. Please keep in mind that beach parking passes purchased from meter boxes are only valid for beach lots.

# Marco Island

While you're on Marco Island, you're never very far from water, whether it's the Gulf, the Marco River, the bays that separate Marco from the mainland, or the scores of canals throughout the island's center. All that water explains why the island was so attractive to its earliest settlers; the coastal Calusa Indians were here during pre-Columbian times.

Until the mid-1960s, it was a sleepy, isolated fishing village that, as far as most Floridians were concerned, was just past the edge of nowhere. As development in West Florida barreled southward in the 1950s and 1960s along I-75, some prescient real estate developers saw Marco Island as a potential gold mine, and began marketing it as a long-term destination for retirees from New York and New England.

Today, No Trespassing signs can be found dotting the landscape, and the two best beaches are strictly reserved for residents. Still, slivers of Old Florida remain in the personality (and personalities) of the small fishing community of Goodland, a vibrant and friendly place. The accessible beaches of Marco Island, including Tigertail Beach, are some of the most beautiful in all of Florida.

In the more historical area of Olde Marco, one can get a feel for Marco's low-key, pre-development past. A quick boat ride out to Keewaydin Island provides an isolated and undeveloped slice of natural beauty, and, by availing oneself of the many charter boat tours available at most of Marco Island's marinas, it's possible to get a sense of both the physical beauty and natural isolation of this part of the Florida coast.

## SIGHTS
### Olde Marco

Olde Marco was an island that was home to little more than a fishing village until the mid-1960s, when a full-fledged real estate boom turned it into a preferred destination for retirees from the northern and Midwestern United States. However, the spiritual remnants of that fishing village are still present in Olde Marco, which is basically the area of Marco Island north of Collier Boulevard. Here, the houses are smaller, high-rises are few and far between, and the vibe is more personable and inviting.

The main sight is the **Rose Marina** (951 Bald Eagle Dr., 239/394-2502, www.marcoriver.com, 7am-7pm daily). Several tour boats operate out of the marina; the best is **Marco Island Princess Tours** (951 Bald Eagle Dr., 239/642-5415, www.themarcoislandprincess.com, 7am-7pm daily, cruises from $38.95), which offers various sightseeing cruises of the Ten Thousand Islands area and the Gulf.

## Marco Island Historical Museum

One of the few actual attractions on Marco Island, the **Marco Island Historical Museum** (180 S. Heathwood Dr., 239/642-1440, 9am-4pm Tues.-Sat., free) is a small museum with a few exhibits. Its emphasis on the island's early history extends to its very design, which mimics that of a Calusa Indian village. Inside, photos and displays track the island's evolution from prehistoric times through agricultural growth and, of course, the mid-1960s real-estate boom that defines its current character.

## Isles of Capri

Okay, there's really no specific reason to visit **Isles of Capri** (SR-951, north of Marco Island), as it's really not much more than a residential area, mainly frequented by anglers and boaters. Purely a result of a real estate developer's fantasy, the four islands provide something of an alternative reality for what could have become of Marco

# Marco Island

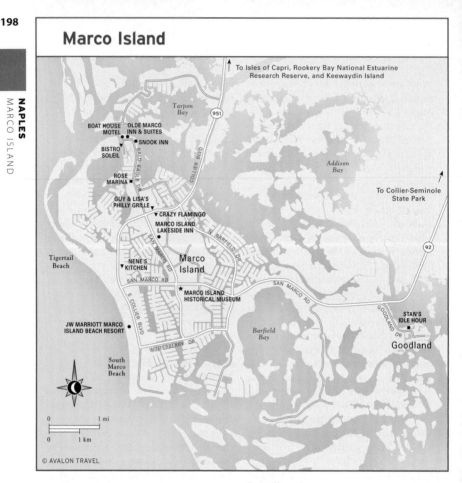

Island. The atmosphere is rustic and down-to-earth, with an emphasis on quiet, natural surroundings. Mangroves surround the islands, palm trees sway over the low-slung houses, and the most active businesses are a handful of restaurants and bars, the latter of which seem to exist primarily in chickee huts (stilt houses built open on all sides and thatched). The Isles are well worth a visit, but don't come expecting to see anything; visitors with a mind to slow down and relax will be pleased with the low-key vibe.

## Goodland

Another nice place to take in an Old Florida vibe is the tiny town of Goodland, located on the southeast corner of Marco Island. It's primarily a fishing village, and one can easily imagine all of Marco Island having the same mellow, friendly vibe of this cozy community. There's not much going on here—the annual **Mullet Festival** in late January/early February is the biggest event in town, and the main business is **Walker's Hideaway Marina** (604 E. Palm Ave.)—but that's the way the few residents of this one-square-mile town like it. Stop in for lunch and a beer at the bayside **Stan's Idle Hour** (401 Papaya St., 239/642-7227, 11am-9pm Tues.-Sat., 11am-7pm Sun.) and party like the locals do. You'll wonder why anyone would choose to live elsewhere on Marco Island when a convivial community like this is so close by.

## Rookery Bay National Estuarine Research Reserve

Located between Naples and Marco Island, the **Rookery Bay National Estuarine Research Reserve** (300 Tower Rd., 239/417-6310, www.rookerybay.org, 9am-4pm Mon.-Sat., closed on Sat. May-Oct., $5 adults, $3 children, children under 6 free) is a mangrove estuary that is home to more than 150 different species of birds and other wildlife. The Environmental Learning Center at the entrance of the reserve is quite large, but most of the 16,500 square feet are given over to working research labs and classrooms. The two-story area taken up by the actual visitors center isn't really worth the price of admission, as it contains only a few interactive exhibits and a large aquarium. The best way to get a feel for the wildlife within the reserve lies outside the air-conditioning; every Wednesday and Saturday, the facility offers guided kayak tours that take you out into the mangroves and waterways for two hours (10am-noon, $35, preregistration required), giving you an up-close look at the quietly vibrant ecosystem.

## BEACHES

There's no easy public beach access facility for those who aren't staying on Marco Island. In fact, the main beach is called "Resident's Beach" (it, as well as Sarazen Park South Beach, is reserved for Marco Island residents), and most of the other strips of sand are cordoned off by the towering condos and five-star hotels. Still, if you're willing to cough up $8 to park, **Tigertail Beach** (400 Hernando Dr., sunrise-sunset daily) is more than worth it. Isolated from the parking lot by dunes and a tidal lagoon, it's absolutely beautiful, with long, empty stretches of sand that beg you to wander along them for hours.

**South Marco Beach** (S. Collier Blvd., north of Winterberry Dr., sunrise-sunset daily, free) has basic facilities: a 70-space parking lot and bathrooms. There are a number of hotels right around South Marco Beach, so it can get rather crowded. Still, it's a pretty beach, with a tree-lined sidewalk getting you

alligators at Rookery Bay National Estuarine Research Reserve

there and tons of seashells in the sand. The water is clear and calm, and dolphin sightings are fairly frequent, especially in the winter months.

**Keewaydin Island** (sunrise-sunset daily, free) located in Rookery Bay and part of the Rookery Bay National Estuarine Research Reserve, has a beautiful, naturally pristine beach, but this island is only accessible by boat. There's a tremendous amount of ecological activity, and the beach is monitored on a daily basis for sea turtle activity; nests will be marked, so as to avoid being disturbed by human visitors. And, for a beach that's not terribly easy to get to, there are a whole lot of human visitors. Boaters come down from Naples and up from Marco Island to anchor and party, or to swim ashore and sunbathe on the white sand.

## SPORTS AND RECREATION
### Boating

Because this is an island, boats are a pretty popular way to get to and from Marco Island. For land-based visitors, **Rose Marina** (951 Bald Eagle Dr., 239/394-2502, www.marcoriver.com, 7am-7pm daily) is definitely worth checking out, as it's home to a good

number of charter boats that provide tours, sunset cruises, and other waterborne adventures; the marina itself offers boat rentals from $205/half-day. For those with their own boat, the titular **Marco Island Marina** (1402 N. Collier Blvd., 239/642-2531) is well equipped and centrally located, with 122 slips ranging in size from 40 to 110 feet. Daily slip rates are from $2.57/foot October-April and from $2.06/foot May-September. In addition to expected facilities like showers and restrooms, the marina also caters to long-term anchorage, with a pool and exercise room, laundry facilities, and cable TV and Wi-Fi connections. Small-craft boaters can avail themselves of the ramps at the **Collier Boulevard Boating Park** (909 Collier Ct., 239/252-4000, sunrise-sunset daily); there are no marina facilities, but the park's location provides easy access to the most popular waterways around Marco Island.

### Golf and Tennis

Perhaps unsurprisingly, there's plenty of golfing to be found on Marco Island. Also unsurprising: Almost none of it is accessible to the public. There are two private clubs on the island, leaving only the **Marco Island Marriott** (400 S. Collier Blvd., 239/394-2511,

the bridge to Marco Island

www.marcoislandmarriott.com) as an option for those who aren't willing to shell out the big bucks for an annual club membership. And, even in that case, the Marriott's two courses are "resort-private," which means that if you're not staying at the hotel, or you're not a guest of someone who is, you won't be playing.

For tennis players, the island is a bit more accommodating. The municipal **Racquet Center** (1275 San Marco Rd., 239/394-5454, 8am-9pm Mon.-Fri., 8am-2pm Sat.-Sun., court rental $20/hr) has eight lighted courts: two clay and six Har-Tru. Additionally, there are two racquetball courts.

# ENTERTAINMENT AND EVENTS
## Nightlife
There are a couple of combo-style bars on Marco Island. **Bombay Liquor** (695 Bald Eagle Dr., 239/389-9100, 3pm-1am daily) is a liquor store with a (pretty quiet) bar called Martini's upstairs, while the **Old Marco Pub** (1105 Bald Eagle Dr., 239/642-9700, www.oldmarcopub.com, 4pm-10pm Mon.-Sat.) is a fairly straightforward restaurant with a bar area (beer and wine only) that's got a little bit of rock 'n' roll flavor.

With superb bay views and a laid-back (at least for Marco Island) atmosphere, the **Dolphin Tiki Bar** (1001 N. Barfield Dr., 239/394-4048, 11am-10pm daily) is a pretty mellow place to wind down your day. Happy hour is a hoot, thanks to the unique combination of drop-in tourists, seasonal snowbirds, and locals.

Sports-bar enthusiasts should head for the **Sand Bar** (826 E. Elkcam Circle, 239/642-3625, 7am-2am daily) to catch the big game. It's worth noting that a handful of retired athletes live on Marco Island, and their occasional presence, as well as a mix of locals, makes this a good place to get a feel for the "real" Marco Island. Also worth noting: The bar opens at 7am.

Tucked away in an easy-to-miss strip mall is the **Marco Island Brewery** (1089 N. Collier Blvd., 239/970-0461, www.

marcoislandbrewery.com, 11:30am-midnight daily), which pours a small but satisfying selection of its own beers. With indoor/outdoor seating and a tremendous amount of real personality, it's one of the best and most welcoming places on the island.

## Festivals and Events
Goodland's **Mullet Festival** is held every year on the weekend before the Super Bowl (because who wants to watch the Pro Bowl anyway?). The fine folks at the raucous and down-home Stan's Idle Hour seafood restaurant (and bar!) celebrate the local anglers who bring in mullet from the surrounding waters with bands, a beauty pageant (which names the "Buzzard Lope Queen"), and lots and lots of smoked and fried fish.

The **Marco Island Seafood and Music Festival** in March is both more refined and less focused than the Mullet Festival. The festival draws thousands of folks (nearly 10,000 in recent years) to Marco Island's Veterans Park (403 Elkcam Circle) for a weekend of food and music. Of course, there are dozens of folks selling seafood—freshly prepared, naturally—as well as typical festival fare like pizzas, sandwiches, and hot dogs. The music tends toward the adult-pop end of the spectrum. This festival can get really crowded, and jostling for a seat underneath the enormous "dining tent" can sometimes be a challenge. Still, it's definitely worth checking out. The profits go toward local charitable organizations.

# FOOD
## Seafood
★ **Stan's Idle Hour** (221 Goodland Dr. W., 239/394-3041, www.stansidlehour.net, 11am-10pm Mon.-Sat., main courses from $15) is an institution on Marco Island, except it's not really *in* Marco Island. Located in the decidedly more friendly and personable fishing village of Goodland, Stan's feels less like a seafood-oriented bar-and-grill than it feels like a community center for longtime locals. The chickee-styled outdoor stage is a great place to

meet and mingle (and drink), but the dining room is equally character-rich and friendly. The menu is heavy on the standards—fried, grilled, and steamed seafood—but frog legs and catfish are just a couple of the things that make it clear that Stan's is not gonna be the place you come to for a white-linen dining experience. The oysters are incredible, and it should go without saying that pretty much any seafood dish you order is going to be incredibly fresh.

Of course, oysters were the original "raw" food, and **The Oyster Society** (599 S. Collier Blvd., 239/394-3474, 4:30pm-10pm Sun.-Thurs., 4:30pm-10:30pm Fri.-Sat., main courses from $16) definitely will remind you of that with their fresh, stylish presentation of an extensive selection of fresh, seasonal oysters, as well as sushi and other raw bar options. The cooked-food menu ranges from simple seafood and steak dishes to decadent bouillabaisse, rack of lamb, and more. An extensive and well-curated craft cocktail menu and a modern but welcoming vibe round things out.

The **Snook Inn** (1215 Bald Eagle Dr., 239/394-3313, www.snookinn.com, 11am-10pm daily, main courses from $10) provides a much more casual seafood joint vibe, but with much better prices, much better food, and some tremendous views of the Marco River. The seafood sandwiches are great (get the fried grouper), and the chickee bar is a fantastic, family-friendly place to hang out. If you're in the mood to cook at your own place, you won't get anything much fresher than the fish and Gulf shrimp available next door at **Lee Be Fish Co.** (350 Royal Palm Dr., 239/389-0580, 11am-10pm Tues.-Sat., main courses from $10); they also offer a selection of fish sandwiches and platters available for takeout or for dining in their outdoor courtyard.

Another good option for enjoying seafood (and a few beers) in a super-casual environment is **Crazy Flamingo** (1035 N. Collier Blvd., 239/642-9600, 11am-1:30am daily, main courses from $10), which is more of a dive bar with food, but the food is definitely a few notches above your standard pub grub. Don't plan on having a fine-dining experience, but if you're looking for a great way to while away an afternoon with drinks and decent food, this Marco institution is a safe bet.

## Southern

The best breakfasts (and some pretty good lunches, too) on Marco Island are served at ★ **Nene's Kitchen** (297 N. Collier Blvd., 239/394-3854, www.neneskitchen.com, 7:30am-2pm daily, main courses from $6). It's a little surprising that Marco Island residents and visitors have continually supported such a low-key and unpretentious place, but the Southern-style food is the kind of stuff that's hard to resist. The French toast is nearly legendary, but it's Nene's biscuits and gravy that should be the signature dish; thick gravy with massive chunks of sausage drenching perfectly baked biscuits—it's the sort of breakfast that consigns you to a mid-morning food coma, but hey, you're on vacation. Portion sizes are ridiculously huge.

## American

For some great burgers, head to **Philly Grille** (1000 N. Collier Blvd., #15, 239/394-2221, www.philly-grille.com, 11am-2pm and 5pm-9pm Mon.-Sat., main courses from $6). There are a ton of different sandwiches on the menu, and several of them are pretty distinctive (try the lobster BLT). And yes, they serve up a pretty decent Philly cheesesteak. But it's the burgers—thick and perfectly grilled, with a stunning array of condiment combinations—that should bring you here. Guy and Lisa offer everything from gruyère cheese to onion jam as additions to their burgers, and while you are certainly welcome to craft your own concoction, the pre-built burgers on the menu should set you straight. They also have flatbread sandwiches, salads, and some great sides. Everything is fresh, thoughtfully prepared, and served without pretense. If you're here during high season, prepare to wait awhile for your lunch.

## Fine Dining

Located in Olde Marco inside the Olde Marco Inn & Suites, ★ **Bistro Soleil** (100 Palm St., 239/389-0981, www.bistrosoleil.net, 5pm-10pm Mon.-Sat., main courses from $21) is one of the most splurge-worthy dining experiences on Marco Island. The restaurant itself is decidedly unstuffy, and the servers are exceptionally attentive. A wide range of European dishes—lamb, foie gras, and more—are complemented by stunning preparations of local seafood, all of which is served in an atmosphere that splits the difference between Old Florida charm and Old World style.

For a lighter approach to upscale dining (that's actually more "bistro" than Bistro Soleil), **Verdi's** (243 N. Collier Blvd., 239/394-5533, www.verdisbistro.com, 5:30pm-9:30pm Mon.-Sat., main courses from $15) is an excellent option. Although quite pricey, the menu is exceptional and creative with lots of fresh seafood, prepared in unique ways using seasonal and international touches. With Asian, European, and classic American influences, Verdi's offers everything from egg rolls and meat loaf to prime rib and crispy duck, all served in a friendly, classy atmosphere.

## ACCOMMODATIONS
### $100-200

It may be somewhat hard to believe, but Marco Island has more than its fair share of affordable accommodations. Many of them are in the Olde Marco area (good!), and most of them manage to have enough character and personality to balance out whatever they may be lacking in amenities (great!).

★ **Marco Island Lakeside Inn** (155 1st Ave., 239/394-1161, www.marcoislandlakeside.com, doubles from $179) is a cozy and friendly small hotel located a bit of a hike from the beaches, but situated right on Lake Marco. Maybe it's because its location isn't terribly convenient, but the renovated rooms are a total bargain. All the rooms are suites, and all are decorated in a pleasant, clean style that's modern without being stylish, and tropical without being corny. Most of the suites are one-bedroom suites that sleep four, but there are also studio suites that sleep two and a couple of two-bedroom suites that sleep up to six people. All of the spacious suites have flat-screen TVs and DVD players, as well as full kitchens and dedicated dining areas. The property has a heated pool with great lakefront views and a relaxing courtyard area.

The **Boat House Motel** (1180 Edington Pl., 239/642-2400, www.theboathousemotel.com, doubles from $132) is a no-frills, family-owned, two-story motel right on the Marco River. It's a small motel, with just 20 rooms, a private dock, and a small swimming pool overlooking the river. However, also on the property are three condos that require three-night minimum stays; these one-bedroom units are much more spacious than the motel rooms and offer full kitchens. Still not enough space? There's also a full house for rent on the property. The Gazebo House is a modern and comfortable two-bedroom house right on the river—literally, it's on a dock—offering great water views from nearly all of the rooms.

The **Marco Resort & Club** (1202 Bald Eagle Dr., 239/394-2777, www.marcoresortandclub.com, doubles from $135) is a small timeshare condo property with incredibly reasonable rates. It's during the off-season that daily rentals of these condos become more available; most of the rest of the year, a five-day minimum rental period is required. Formerly a motel, the resort doesn't quite fit the standard definition of a "timeshare condo resort," with its smaller rooms and outdated decor, but it's a clean and cute property, with a heated pool, laundry facilities, a boat dock, and free Wi-Fi.

### $200-300

**Olde Marco Island Inn & Suites** (100 Palm St., 239/394-3131, www.oldemarcoinn.com, doubles from $279) is perfectly located right in Olde Marco. With a history that goes all the way back to 1883, the inn today has a considerably classier clientele than the folks who stayed in Captain Bill Collier's Inn in the late 18th century for "a dollar a day, bring your own meat." Still, this isn't a stuffy place to stay; rooms are all condo-type suites, in one-bedroom and two-bedroom variations. All have full kitchens and comfortable living spaces. There are also penthouse suites for those with larger groups or planning on longer stays. Rooms are all quite comfortable and modern, and the property has a gorgeously landscaped courtyard area with a pool. Also on-site is Bistro Soleil, one of Marco Island's best restaurants.

## Over $300

Although it boasts nearly 100 rooms, the **Marco Beach Ocean Resort** (480 S. Collier Blvd., 239/393-1400, doubles from $399) valiantly strives to give its mammoth property a more intimate, boutique-style feel. It's not always successful, especially since the imposing exterior looks like a standard chain hotel or condominium. Still, the service is personal and the rooms—which are all one- or two-bedroom suites—are spacious and private. Many have excellent water views. All the rooms are decorated in a muted, modern style and are quite comfortable. The resort is, as one would expect from its name, right on a beautiful stretch of beach, and amenities include a pool, spa, and fitness center. Golfers who stay here can have an outing arranged to the nearby Fiddler's Creek course near Rookery Bay.

The **JW Marriott Marco Island Beach Resort** (400 S. Collier Blvd., 239/394-2511, www.jwmarco.com, doubles from $429) is the elephant in the room of Marco Island accommodations. It is nearly impossible to miss, with its two massive buildings of guest rooms towering over the middle of Collier Boulevard in the heart of Marco Island's beach area. Beyond its size and incredible location, this property provides the familiar luxe style of the JW Marriott brand and the assurance that everything—from your room to the pools to the beachside amenities—will be a little nicer than it needs to be. For those visitors who fear getting lost in their own hotel, this may be a property to avoid; in addition to those two

huge towers of rooms, the Marriott also has a warren of other buildings filled with suites (all of which have private patios), ballrooms, boutiques, a spa, a fitness center, and lots more.

## Vacation Rentals

Many visitors to Marco Island choose to settle in for the entire season or for at least a week or so during the season. And although there are plenty of nightly accommodations available, it does seem that most folks avail themselves of longer-term rentals. During the off-season, many of these rentals are available for shorter-term rentals; some are even available with nightly rates. Both **Horizons Rentals** (239/394-8677, www.mymarcorental.com) and **White Sand Getaways** (239/285-8661, www.whitesandgetaways.com) manage rentals for a wide variety of properties across the island, ranging from condos to relatively more personal houses in the more residential areas of Marco.

# INFORMATION AND SERVICES
## Visitor Information

The offices for the **Naples, Marco Island, Everglades Convention & Visitors Bureau** (2800 Horseshoe Dr., Naples, 239/252-2384, www.paradisecoast.com) are in central Naples. However, on Marco Island, the privately run **Marco Island Chamber of Commerce** (1102 N. Collier Blvd., 239/394-7549, www.marcoislandchamber.com) is a good source for information on local businesses.

## Services

Several banks have branches in downtown Marco Island, including **SunTrust** (950 N. Collier Blvd., 239/642-6688), **Bank of America** (614 Bald Eagle Dr., 239/642-6565), **Fifth Third Bank** (1818 San Marco Rd., 239/394-7737), and **Wells Fargo** (977 N. Collier Blvd., 239/389-3000).

There are two clean, well-stocked **Publix** grocery stores on Marco Island, one in the central part of town (1089 N. Collier Blvd.,

239/642-2202) and one on the eastern side, en route to Goodland (175 S. Barfield Dr., 239/394-3371). There is also a **Winn-Dixie** (625 N. Collier Blvd., 239/393-0843) grocery store. For stocking up on gourmet foodstuffs, head to **Paradise Seafood & Gourmet Market** (721 Bald Eagle Dr., 239/394-3686).

The Winn-Dixie and Publix stores have pharmacies where you can get prescriptions filled, and there are also two **Walgreens** (1100 N. Collier Blvd., 239/389-2888, and 1800 San Marco Rd., 239/394-5303) on the island, as well as a **CVS** (676 Bald Eagle Dr., 239/394-4181).

For medical care, there is an urgent care facility at the **Marco Healthcare Center Campus** (30 S. Heathwood Dr., 239/394-8234). The closest hospital is **Naples Community Hospital** (350 7th St. N., Naples, 239/436-5000) in downtown Naples.

## GETTING THERE AND AROUND

The only way to get to Marco Island is in your car. From Naples, it's about a half-hour drive, via the southbound Tamiami Trail and then Collier Boulevard, which takes you right onto the island.

There is no public transportation on Marco Island, but it's pretty bikeable. You can rent bikes and scooters from **Island Bike Shop** (1095 Bald Eagle Dr., 239/394-8400, http://islandbikeshops.com, 9am-6pm Mon.-Sat., 10am-3pm Sun., bike rentals from $12/day, surrey rentals from $20/hour, scooter rentals from $25/hour). This is definitely recommended, as parking is at a premium pretty much everywhere on the island.

# The Everglades

# The Everglades are huge. There's a whole lot of natural beauty to absorb here, and almost all of it can be explored and enjoyed in relative peace and quiet.

There's a small creek behind an elementary school in Orlando that is as inconspicuous as they come. But the trickle of Shingle Creek is the humble origin of one of the world's most treasured wetland ecosystems. Those headwaters merge into the Kissimmee River, which flows into Lake Okeechobee, which discharges into the Everglades, a vast expanse of marshes, swamps, islands, forests, and the waterways of mainland Florida's southernmost points. Comprising essentially all of the wetlands and prairies south of Lake Okeechobee and sandwiched between Naples in the west and Miami in the east, the area covers nearly 4,000 square miles. Despite the best efforts of voracious real estate developers, most of the Everglades remain wild. Although decades of agriculture, drainage, attempts at "taming" the land, and nearby population growth have dramatically (and, in some cases, permanently) altered the ecosystems for the worse, sentiment has solidified among regular Floridians that this is an area worth preserving, and more and more efforts are being undertaken to reverse the damage done.

## PLANNING YOUR TIME

It's important to keep in mind that, basically, what you're here to see is a relatively undisturbed swamp, along with the various ecosystems within it. This means that facilities are few and far between, and access to the heart of the park is largely limited to what you're able to see from within a small boat. For that reason, people usually have to decide between undertaking a backwater adventure or availing themselves of the easily accessible visitors centers inside the park. The visitors centers not only provide maps and guidance but also provide relatively populous landmarks that help to ensure you won't be unintentionally spending the night in the swamp. Under all circumstances, you should make sure your car's gas tank is topped off, you've brought in plenty of water, sunscreen, and bug repellent, and that you make every effort to ensure that no members of your group wander off on their

---

**Previous:** Clyde Butcher's Big Cypress Gallery; alligators near Oasis Visitor Center. **Above:** the Skunk Ape Research Headquarters.

Look for ★ to find recommended sights, activities, dining, and lodging.

# Highlights

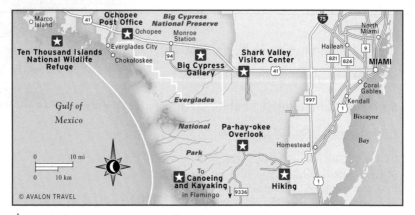

★ **Ten Thousand Islands National Wildlife Refuge:** The 35,000 acres of undeveloped swamps, marshland, and waterways are perfect for adventurous types willing to get their feet wet (page 211).

★ **Ochopee Post Office:** At 61 square feet—just enough room for a clerk and a tiny bit of equipment—it's the smallest fully operational post office in the United States (page 218).

★ **Big Cypress Gallery:** Clyde Butcher's photographs of the Everglades are world-renowned. His gallery is a place to buy everything from prints to books to coffee mugs (page 219).

★ **Shark Valley Visitor Center:** The most popular of all the area visitors centers, Shark Valley offers tram rides, a bike trail, and other ways to gingerly experience the 'Glades firsthand (page 221).

★ **Pa-hay-okee Overlook:** This short boardwalk gives you stunning vistas without hours of backcountry walking (page 226).

★ **Hiking:** The Royal Palm Visitor Center is the starting point for two of the Everglades' most popular trails, **Anhinga Trail** and **Gumbo Limbo** (page 227).

★ **Canoeing and Kayaking:** From the southernmost point on the Florida mainland, boat excursions allow unparalleled access into some remote and unspoiled waters of Florida Bay (page 227).

# The Everglades

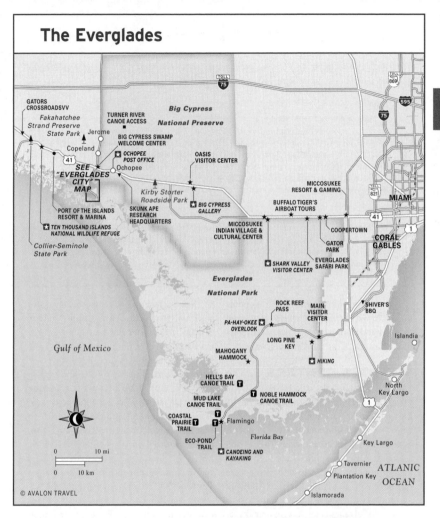

own; all that swamp can start to look the same after a while.

If you're coming to the southern Everglades via Florida City and Homestead, you'll need to dedicate a full day to making the 30-something-mile journey from the park's entrance all the way to the far reaches of the Flamingo Visitor Center. This will give you time not only to take in the multiple stops along the way, but also give you time to return and get back to civilization before nightfall.

## FEES AND PERMITS

It costs $25 to access Everglades National Park in a vehicle via any of the visitors centers; this fee is per vehicle. Pedestrians and bicyclists can enter for $8. This admission fee allows entrance for seven consecutive days. Annual passes cost $40. There is no entrance fee for Big Cypress National Preserve. Campground fees vary depending on the site, but typically are in the $16-20 range, with the exception of the sites near Flamingo that have electrical hookups (those cost $30).

# Two Days in the Everglades

Thanks to the limited points of access available to enter the Everglades, this vast park can be neatly, though superficially, explored in two days.

## DAY 1

If you're camping, plan on staying at **Monument Lake Campground,** which is about half-way between Miami and Naples. This will allow you to spend the two halves of your first day exploring sites on either side: **Everglades City** and **Chokoloskee** to the east, **Shark Valley Visitor Center** and Clyde Butcher's **Big Cypress Gallery** to the west.

If you're not camping, try and book the **cottage at Clyde Butcher's Big Cypress Gallery** or get a room in Everglades City at **Ivey House,** a great lodge-style hotel that can also help arrange canoe/kayak rentals.

## DAY 2

The next day, wake up early and head to the southern area of Everglades National Park near Florida City. Book a room in **Homestead** and plan on spending the entire day taking in the park's vast wilderness, whether by hiking along popular trails like the easily accessible **Anhinga Trail** and **Gumbo Limbo Trail,** or exploring the 16-mile **Turner River Loop** bike trail.

Permits are required for fishing; no hunting is allowed in either park. Pets are allowed in both parks; however, they are typically prohibited on any of the trails or waterways.

## VISITORS CENTERS

Visitors centers are located throughout the Everglades. These centers are staffed by knowledgeable National Park Service staff who can provide information, insight, and directions, and check in campers and hikers into the park. Also: the centers have bathrooms and air-conditioning! All visitor centers are free once park admission has been paid, and you can pay the admission fee at any visitor center. The visitor centers are staffed at specific hours during the day, but the parks are technically open 24 hours a day.

There are two visitors centers in Big Cypress National Preserve, the **Oasis Visitor Center** (52105 Tamiami Trail E., 239/695-1201, www.nps.gov/bicy, 9am-4:30pm daily, free) in the eastern part of the preserve and **Big Cypress Swamp Welcome Center** (33000 Tamiami Trail E., 239/695-4758, www.nps.gov/bicy, 9am-4:30pm daily, free), which is in the western portion of the preserve, near the park boundary.

There are four visitors centers in Everglades National Park. The **Gulf Coast Visitor Center** (815 Oyster Bar Ln., 239/695-3311, www.nps.gov/ever, 9am-4:30pm daily, free) is located in Everglades City and provides watercraft access to the Ten Thousand Islands area. The **Shark Valley Visitor Center** (36000 SW 8th St., 305/221-8776, www.nps.gov/ever, 9:15am-5:15pm daily) is closer to Miami, but is still along the Tamiami Trail. In the southern portions of the Everglades, which will also likely be accessed by visitors coming from Miami, the **Ernest Coe Visitor Center** (40001 SR-9336, Homestead, 305/242-7700, 9am-5pm daily, $10 per vehicle, $5 for pedestrians/cyclists) is located at the main entrance of the park; it's also known as the Main Visitor Center. The **Flamingo Visitor Center** (1 Flamingo Lodge Hwy., 941/695-2945, building open 24/7, staffed 9am-5pm Apr.-Oct., 8am-5pm Nov.-Mar.) is much farther to the southwest, at the main park's road terminus.

## PLANTS AND ANIMALS

The main reason people set foot within the vast expanses of the Everglades is to get a look at wild, natural Florida. And the 'Glades do not disappoint. Of course, the one animal instantly associated with the area is the American alligator, which is not only a large beast (some grow up to around 16 feet) but also a stealthy predator. Some backwater boaters are frequently surprised when they discover that they've paddled within inches of one of these prehistoric marvels. Gators tend to hug the shoreline and prefer the cover of mangroves, so spotting them can sometimes be a challenge. One can also see American crocodiles in the Everglades; however, they tend to be found only in the southernmost area around Flamingo.

Birds are the most abundant animal type in the Everglades. Dozens of species call the 'Glades home, including spoonbills, wood storks, egrets, and bald eagles. During migration season, dozens more non-native species can be seen as well.

Mangroves and sawgrass all but define the plant life of the Everglades. It seems that if you're not hemmed in by the dense thickets of the former, you're being confronted with an endless, uninterrupted expanse of the latter. However, slash pine trees and saw palmetto trees are also quite common, as are tiny pockets of hardwood hammocks that house an abundance of animal life, such as raccoons, rabbits, and deer. And, of course, anyone who's seen the movie *Adaptation* knows South Florida and the Everglades are perfect growing areas for orchids. Almost 50 different species of the fragile, beautiful flowers grow throughout the 'Glades.

# The Everglades via Naples

The Everglades don't actually start until you're halfway across the state from Naples. However, as soon as the city's suburbs begin retreating into your rearview mirror, a landscape nearly as expansive and wildly natural begins to quickly unfold. As you head eastward into the Everglades, you'll encounter the grassy marshes of the Ten Thousand Islands National Wildlife Refuge, and the swampy forests of Big Cypress Bend and the Collier-Seminole State Park. However, most importantly, you'll almost immediately begin experiencing the vast openness and seemingly infinite calm of this part of the state. Herons and egrets are more common than cars, and buildings can be spaced miles apart from one another. Even though the transition from the upscale shops and restaurants of Naples is certainly gradual, it's nonetheless shocking not just how completely different this part of the state is from the rest of Florida, but also how unique it is on this planet. And, this is just the beginning.

## SIGHTS
### ★ Ten Thousand Islands National Wildlife Refuge

The entirety of the **Ten Thousand Islands National Wildlife Refuge** (3860 Tollgate Blvd., Ste. 300, 239/353-8442, www.fws.gov/floridapanther, sunrise-sunset daily, free) is massive, covering more than 35,000 acres of mangrove swamps, tiny keys, grassy marshes, and tropical hardwood hammocks. Nearly all of those acres are completely undeveloped. In fact, the only signs of human life here are a short, rough hiking trail that's about a mile long, and a two-story observation tower that provides some stunning panoramas of the marshlands. This tower and trail are easily accessed via a parking lot right alongside the Tamiami Trail, just as you enter the wildlife refuge area heading east from Naples. The other, oh, 34,990 acres are best explored by hikers, hunters, anglers, and boaters. There are boat launches that get you into the refuge's waterways in the tiny fishing village of Goodland (near Marco Island) and at the **Port of the Islands Resort & Marina** (525

Newport Dr., 239/389-0367), just on the edge of the refuge. Primitive camping can be done on the coastal beach areas that are only accessible by boat. Hunting is limited to about 4,000 acres of the refuge, and even there, it's restricted to ducks and coots only.

## Collier-Seminole State Park

**Collier-Seminole State Park** (20200 Tamiami Trail E., 239/394-3397, www.floridastateparks.org, 8am-sunset daily, $5 per vehicle, $2 pedestrians and bicyclists) is a great way to take in the natural offerings of the Everglades in a way that allows both for independent exploration and somewhat more structured sightseeing. There are more than 7,000 acres of mangrove swampland in the park, and there are several biking and hiking trails that can give you a taste of that vastness. There is also a 13-mile-long kayaking trail that takes you through a mangrove forest along the Black Water River. Camping is incredibly popular here (especially during the cooler months when the weather is less oppressive and the mosquitoes are less overwhelming). There are 120 tent and RV campsites with water, power, and restrooms, as well as two small primitive campsites, one of which is only available by boat. It's worth checking out the nightly campfire circle/slide show, where park rangers teach about the local wildlife.

## Fakahatchee Strand Preserve State Park

The long and narrow swath of land that makes up the **Fakahatchee Strand Preserve State Park** (137 Coastline Dr., 239/695-4593, www.floridastateparks.org, 8am-sunset daily, $5 per vehicle, $2 pedestrians and bicyclists) is a beautiful and largely inaccessible piece of the Everglades. The 100 square miles of forest is four times longer than it is wide. It is primarily a slough that may look like a swamp but is actually a slow-moving, freshwater river. In the mucky ground of the strand grow an astonishing number and variety of plant life, including more orchids and bromeliad species than anywhere else in North America, as well as native royal palm trees and bald cypress trees. In fact, this is one of the only places in the world where both of these trees grow together. All that flora means lots of fauna, such as terrapins, alligators, and bears. Even a few stray Florida panthers have been spotted in the area, along with, of course, voluminous numbers of bird species, including the roseate spoonbill. Given the less-than-solid swamplike terrain, navigating

an observation tower in Ten Thousand Islands National Wildlife Refuge

# Indian Villages

As you drive along the Tamiami Trail through the Everglades, you'll come across signs marked "Indian Village." Off to one or another side of the road (usually the northern end), there will be a chickee hut (or a concentration of several), and they will often be behind a privacy fence. Please be aware that these are private residences of local members of the Miccosukee and Seminole tribes, and you should refrain from photographing the residences or the people within. If you're interested in the public face of the local Native American tribes, the Miccosukee tribe welcomes visitors to the **Miccosukee Indian Village & Cultural Center** (Mile Marker 70, Tamiami Trail, 305/552-8365, www.miccosukee.com, 9am-5pm daily, adults $8, children $5, children under 5 free, airboat rides $16). This facility is geared toward tourists, complete with alligator wrestling and airboat rides.

takes you on a nearly mile-long path through the deepest part of the slough, where you can see much of the flora and fauna mentioned. This boardwalk is an absolute favorite among visitors to the Everglades.

## FOOD AND ACCOMMODATIONS

There are not too many places to eat or stay in this part of the Everglades, and in fact the **Port of the Islands Resort** (25000 Tamiami Trail E., 239/394-3005, http://poiresort.com, doubles from $99) is the only hotel around for miles. The harbor view from the marina is exceptional. The hotel's location makes access to the waters of the Ten Thousand Islands National Wildlife Refuge incredibly easy. Although this resort's restaurant is closed during the summer, many of the rooms are efficiencies with small kitchens. Alternatively, the closest (and, honestly, only) restaurant is just down the road at **Gators Crossroads** (19800 Tamiami Trail E., 239/393-4116, noon-8pm daily, from $8). It's a basic bar-and-grill with great burgers and a preferred stop of motorcyclists making their way through the 'Glades.

the Fakahatchee Strand can be kind of tough on foot. However, there is a fantastic boardwalk trail located at Big Cypress Bend that

# Everglades City and Chokoloskee

Everglades City is the biggest city in the Everglades, but that's not to say it's big. Were it a town along a busy road, you could blink and miss it, as it's only got about a dozen roads and just about twice that many businesses. It's an outpost in the truest sense of the word, established as a marina and fishing village by the hardy souls who explore the waters in and around the Ten Thousand Islands. Chokoloskee is even smaller. It is a literal end-of-the-road community that's seldom visited by outsiders but is adored by the anglers who call it home.

## SIGHTS
### Museum of the Everglades
The **Museum of the Everglades** (105 W. Broadway, 239/695-0008, www.colliermuseums.com, 9am-5pm Tues.-Sat., free) is home to several well-curated permanent exhibits that do a marvelous job of illustrating just how difficult life was for settlers in this area throughout the years. Focusing primarily on the southwestern region of the Everglades, this museum packs plenty of information and perspective into its well-designed exhibition space and a nicely designed art gallery. The physical struggles and environmental challenges that have confronted everyone from the earliest Native Americans to contemporary

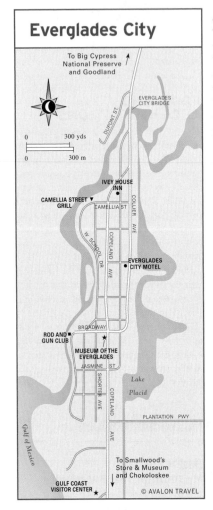

## Everglades City

easy access to some largely inaccessible areas. This particular center gives visitors access to the waterways and tiny islands of the Ten Thousand Islands. Via the park's boat tours and canoe rentals ($32/day), you can make your way through the 99-mile Wilderness Waterway Trail. The guided boat tours are done on pontoons that hold about two dozen passengers. Well-versed naturalists lead the tours and put the array of flora and fauna into perspective. The center's main building also has some interesting nature exhibits, information on Everglades National Park, and picnic areas.

### Smallwood's Store & Museum

Located at the end of a rutted dirt road that, itself, is off the end of an isolated residential street, **Smallwood's Store & Museum** (360 Mamie St., 239/695-2989, www.smallwoodstore.com, 10am-5pm daily Dec.-Apr., 10am-4pm Fri.-Tues. May-Nov., $2) is an authentic, turn-of-the-20th-century trading post, situated on stilts above a sandy beach on Chokoloskee Bay. The site is pretty amazing, as it's where the earliest settlers to the area traded with local Native Americans and managed to learn how to survive in this unforgiving wilderness. The memorabilia here helps tell that story. The near-isolation of the location provides all the background illustration you could need.

## SPORTS AND RECREATION
### Airboat Rides

Airboat tours are an incredibly popular—and super-fun—way to see the Everglades. But, given the delicate ecosystems here, it's quite hard to unreservedly recommend this method of touring. It's not only quite loud and disruptive but also polluting and potentially destructive to plant life as well. As such, airboats aren't allowed within the confines of Everglades National Park and the Ten Thousand Islands National Wildlife Refuge. However, airboat operators are plentiful outside the parks' boundaries. If this

residents are nicely illuminated, and show that, unlike many other places in Florida where human development has tamed Mother Nature, the Everglades are one place where she fights back quite a bit harder.

### Gulf Coast Visitor Center

Like the rest of the visitors centers throughout Everglades National Park, the **Gulf Coast Visitor Center** (815 Oyster Bar Ln., 239/695-3311, www.nps.gov/ever, 9am-4:30pm daily, free) is designed to give visitors relatively

# Marjory Stoneman Douglas

Douglas worked tirelessly for the protection of the Everglades.

The Everglades are often referred to as "the river of grass." That designation comes from a landmark 1947 book by Marjory Stoneman Douglas, *The Everglades: River of Grass*. Until Douglas's book was published, most people perceived the Everglades as a useless wasteland of swamps that needed to, at least, be tamed, and, if possible, paved over. And, for a few decades both before and after her book, that was the primary act of engagement by the government and developers in south Florida. Dredging, draining, canal digging, rerouting, and all other manner of attempts to bring the 'Glades under control were utilized. But Douglas was adamant—and correct—in her assertions that the Everglades was an active and vital (if slow-moving) river that should be protected and respected as much as the Mississippi. Although the book itself was a semi-scholarly work, its impact was profound among the general public, thanks mostly to Douglas's tireless advocacy for protection and restoration of the Everglades, a cause she championed until her death in 1998 at the stunning age of 108. Although the Everglades still suffers undue abuse at the hands of agriculture and development interests, there are now substantial speedbumps in place to prevent the area's wholesale destruction. Change is slow and somewhat modest, but without Douglas, it's likely that the Everglades wouldn't have even survived the 1950s.

is the way you choose to explore the area, **Captain Doug's Family of Airboat Tours** (www.captaindougs.net) can take care of you. Captain Doug is Doug House and has been operating airboat tours in the 'Glades since the early '80s, and although he's retired, he lends his legacy and reputation to his son's operation: **Captain Mitch's Airboat Tours** (www.captainmitchs.com/), as well as his son-in-law's: **Captain Bruce's Original Everglades Airboat Tours** (www.evergladescity-airboattours.com/). Mitch handles grassland tours, while Bruce specializes in mangrove waterway tours; rates are typically the same (about $40 for adults, and $20 for kids) so if you can't decide which is the right tour for you, you can call 800/282-9194 for guidance.

## Canoeing and Kayaking

Canoe rentals are available at the **Gulf Coast Visitor Center** (815 Oyster Bar Ln., 239/695-3311, www.nps.gov/ever, 9am-4:30pm daily, $32/day), but you may have better luck at some of the private operators in the area, as these rentals run out quickly during peak season.

**North American Canoe Tours** (107 Camellia St., 239/695-3229, http://evergladesadventures.com) operates out of the Ivey House Inn. Their daytime, sunset, and overnight tours (from $124/day for non-Ivey House guests) have a decidedly eco-friendly bent and can be done in either kayaks or canoes. Rentals ($35/day for non-Ivey House guests) are also available.

**Shurr Adventures** (360 Mamie St., 239/695-2576, http://shurradventures.net, kayak trips from $80) focuses on kayak tours through the diverse ecosystems of the Ten Thousand Islands. They also offer a backcountry mangrove tour.

## Fishing

There are numerous fishing charters available in the area. **Everglades Kayak Fishing** (239/695-9107), **Capt. Tony Polizos** (239/695-2608), and **Capt. Nick Varallo** (239/695-2536) operate out of Everglades City. Despite what they'd have you believe, most of these charters are essentially the same, offering anglers the opportunity to choose between flats and deep-water fishing excursions that will yield cobia, redfish, tarpon, and snook,

among others. Most charters are geared toward small groups (2-5 people) and prices typically begin around $350 for a half day of fishing. If you have specific needs, it's always best to call the captain before booking.

## Aerial Tours

An exciting way to see the Everglades is by air. **Wings-Ten Thousand Island Aero Tours** (650 E. C. Airpark Rd., 239/695-3296, http://wingsaerotours.com) offers flights ranging from 20 to 90 minutes; you'll cruise in an Alaskan floatplane over the sawgrass and swamps at a low enough altitude to see a good bit of wildlife. It's not up close and personal, but it's quite exhilarating.

## FOOD
### Everglades City

If you're in Everglades City and hungry for anything besides seafood or swamp food, you're going to be out of luck. Thankfully, there are a handful of spots that can fry up water creatures with the best of 'em. The **Camellia Street Grill** (208 Camellia St., 239/695-2003, 11am-10pm daily, from $10) is probably the best, with some quirky decor, great riverfront views, a friendly staff, and some incredible homemade sangria. The

There is an abundance of wildlife at Everglades National Park.

restaurant at **The Rod and Gun Club** (200 Riverside Dr., 239/695-2101, http://everglades-rodandgunclub.com, 11am-9pm daily, lunch from $13, dinner from $21, cash only) is a great choice as well, as it serves up excellent seafood, steak, and sandwiches in a classic Old Florida environment.

## Chokoloskee

This small fishing village's main restaurant isn't a seafood shack or a diner, but a friendly and cute Cuban restaurant. The **Havana Café of the Everglades** (191 Smallwood Dr., 239/695-2214, https://havanacafeoftheev-erglades.com, 7am-3pm Sun.-Thurs. and 7am-8pm Fri.-Sat. Oct.-mid-Apr., from $8) serves breakfast, lunch, and dinner menus that include a selection of Cuban classics and American standards. On a (relatively) cool winter day, the outdoor patio is a great place to relax while you eat.

## ACCOMMODATIONS
### Everglades City

Many of the accommodations in Everglades City evoke the atmosphere of a classic fish camp. **The Rod and Gun Club** (200 Riverside Dr., 239/695-2101, http://everglades-rodandgunclub.com, doubles from $110) is the fanciest of the bunch with more of a relaxed, hunting-lodge vibe.

The rustic cabins and cottages at ★ **Ivey House** (107 Camellia St., 239/695-3299, http://iveyhouse.com, doubles from $115) are even less glamorous, but the staff here is remarkably friendly and quite helpful. The on-site charter and rental service makes it something of a one-stop shop for those embarking upon a backcountry adventure.

For more standard accommodations, the motel-style lodgings at **Everglades City Motel** (310 Collier Ave., 239/695-4224, www.evergladescitymotel.com, doubles from $90) are a good option.

### Chokoloskee

The four very basic rooms at the waterfront **Parkway Motel & Marina** (1180 Chokoloskee Dr., 239/695-3261, www.park-waymotelandmarina.net, doubles from $99) are just about your only option for an overnight stay in Chokoloskee.

## INFORMATION AND SERVICES

The folks at the **Naples, Marco Island, Everglades Convention and Visitors Bureau** (239/225-1013, www.paradisecoast.com) are a great resource for information and planning tips. They can be reached over the phone or online, but have no public office.

## GETTING THERE

Everglades City is located about five miles south of the Tamiami Trail (U.S. 41) via County Road 29. It's about a 45-minute drive from Naples to Everglades City. The only way to get to Chokoloskee is via County Road 29 through Everglades City; the road changes names from County Road 29 to Collier Avenue, to Copeland Avenue, to Smallwood Avenue. The road terminates in Chokoloskee.

## Ochopee and Big Cypress National Preserve

© AVALON TRAVEL

# Big Cypress National Preserve

Although not technically part of the Everglades, the nearby Big Cypress Swamp covers an equally impressive 720,000 acres, most of which are under the protection of the Big Cypress National Preserve, which was the first property in the national park system to be designated as a national preserve. As with Everglades National Park, human access is limited by the terrain, but it's far drier than the 'Glades (relatively speaking), and visitors will find that much more of the park can be used for camping, hiking, and hunting. Ochopee is the only real town along this stretch of the Tamiami Trail.

## SIGHTS AND RECREATION

### Big Cypress Swamp Welcome Center

The **Big Cypress Swamp Welcome Center** (33000 Tamiami Trail, Ochopee, 9am-4:30pm daily, free) has a small wildlife exhibit and a brief movie about the history and natural beauty of the preserve. This is where you need to be if you want to pick up maps, register with rangers, or pick up a camping or Off-Road Vehicle permit.

### ★ Ochopee Post Office

A post office? Yes, a post office. **Ochopee Post Office** (38000 Tamiami Trail E., 10am-4:15pm Mon.-Fri., 10:15am-11:30am Sat.) is the smallest post office in the United States. This tiny building is only 61 square feet. Although there's not much more inside than a desk, a scale, a computer, and a chair for the (necessarily) good-spirited clerk, that's enough for it to act as a fully functional post office for the few permanent residents of Ochopee.

### Skunk Ape Research Headquarters

While cryptozoologists and Bigfoot hunters

have typically focused their efforts on the forests of the Pacific Northwest, there's a legend in southwest Florida about the "Skunk Ape"—a very Bigfoot-like creature—that has persisted since the 1960s. Although reports have been sporadic and inconsistent throughout the years, it seems that the biggest differentiator for the Everglades version of the Bigfoot is its powerful and quite nasty odor. Hence the "Skunk Ape" moniker. Brothers Dave and Jack Shealy head up the **Skunk Ape Research Headquarters** (40904 Tamiami Trail E., 239/695-2275, www.skunkape.info, 7am-7pm daily, adults $5, children under 5 free) in Ochopee. They gather the evidence about Skunk Apes and present it to visitors to make up their own minds. Unsurprisingly, they also sell quite a few T-shirts, bumper stickers, and other Skunk Ape-related memorabilia items. The Shealys also run a campground, a Miss Skunk Ape contest, and Skunktoberfest. A stop here is an essential voyage into classic, kitschy Floridiana. Just be careful!

## Kirby Storter Roadside Park

Lots of folks pull off of the Tamiami Trail at **Kirby Storter Roadside Park** (U.S. 41/Tamiami Trail, between H. P. Williams Roadside Park and Monument Lake Campground, sunrise-sunset daily, free) to avail themselves of the restrooms and picnic tables. However, going just a little bit farther into the park along the boardwalk trail is an incredibly rewarding experience. The approximately half-mile-long boardwalk provides fantastic views of the cypress swamp and the vast expanses of marshlands that make up the Big Cypress Preserve. Bird-watching is excellent, and there's a small chickee hut about halfway down the trail that provides respite from the sun.

## Oasis Visitor Center

The **Oasis Visitor Center** (52105 Tamiami Trail E., 239/695-1201, www.nps.gov/bicy, 9am-4:30pm daily, free) is the second of two visitors centers in the Big Cypress National Preserve, and, like the Big Cypress Swamp Welcome Center, it has sparkling-clean restrooms, helpful park rangers, and a couple of small educational and art exhibits inside the (blissfully) air-conditioned main building. A big draw for Oasis is the roadside boardwalk, which sits above a narrow canal with some resident alligators and cormorants, making for some good photo opportunities.

## ★ Big Cypress Gallery

A stop into **Clyde Butcher's Big Cypress Gallery** (52388 Tamiami Trail E., 239/695-2428, www.clydebutchersbigcypressgallery.com, 9:30am-4:30pm daily, free) should be an all-but-essential part of anyone's Big Cypress itinerary. Located just a half-mile west of the Big Cypress Oasis Visitor Center, the gallery displays Butcher's stunning black-and-white photography, and covers nearly a half-century of amazing visual documentation of wild and natural Florida. As the property is also home to Butcher's studio, odds are he'll be around and more than willing to provide visitors to the area plenty of insight into his work. Every Saturday at 11am, weather permitting, there are guided swamp walks on the property behind the gallery. Also worth noting: There's a bungalow available for overnight stays, which is just about the only place to spend the night in the area if you didn't bring camping gear.

## Turner River Canoe Access

One of the best (and safest) places to put in your canoe or kayak in this part of the Everglades is the **Turner River Canoe Access** (entry point at U.S. 41 west of Turner River Rd., 239/695-2000, www.nps.gov/bicy). However, even non-boaters find this park a good spot to stop, as there's a boardwalk nature trail. For those who don't even want to get out of their car, the Turner River Loop Drive is one of the better scenic drives in the Everglades.

### HIKING TRAILS

There are three primary and well-marked hiking trails within the preserve, all of which are part of the Florida Trail. The most popular is the 6.5-mile trail that connects Loop Road in the south and U.S. 41. During the winter, when the bugs are more tolerable and the ground is dry, this trail can get busy. The vast expanses of prairie still make it feel quite isolated. There's a much longer and more challenging trail with a trailhead at the visitors center, which winds nearly 28 miles through slash pine copses, hardwood hammocks, and lots and lots of dry prairie land.

## SCENIC DRIVES

One of the biggest draws in Big Cypress is a drive along the 27-mile **Loop Road** (off U.S. 41/Tamiami Trail, just at the Miami-Dade County line). The well-marked and generally smooth road makes its way through dense forest canopies filled with dwarf cypress and slash pine trees. The pastoral setting is as relaxing as the frequent wildlife-spotting is invigorating. The drive along the shorter **Turner River Loop,** a 16-mile loop that starts at H. P. Williams Roadside Park (U.S. 41 and Turner River Rd.), is a great option for bird-watchers, as the open spaces and watering areas are popular with migrating (and native) bird species.

## FOOD

**Joanie's Blue Crab Cafe** (39395 Tamiami Trail E., 239/695-2682, http://joaniesbluecrab-cafe.com, 11am-5pm daily, from $12) is the best restaurant in Ochopee (granted, it's one of only two restaurants in Ochopee). Still, Joanie's is an essential stop, and the food is good. The small menu focuses on true swamp fare, with frog legs, fried gator, garlic blue crabs, Indian fry bread, and a few other dishes. Everything on the menu is excellent, and portions are huge. The bar does incredible business serving up ice-cold beer and live music to weary travelers and hardworking locals.

The other restaurant in Ochopee is **Tippy's Big Cypress BBQ** (39025 SW 8th St./U.S. 41, 305/559-6080, www.tippysoutpost.com, 7am-11pm Mon.-Thurs., 6am-midnight Sat.-Sun.,

hours highly variable), which isn't much more than a chickee hut with a smoker and a couple of tables, but the barbecue is excellent, served with a limited selection of sides.

## ACCOMMODATIONS

Non-camping accommodations in this area are pretty much limited to the **Swamp Cottage & Bungalow** (52388 Tamiami Trail E., 239/695-2428, www.clydebutchers-bigcypressgallery.com/swamp-cottage, from $295) at Clyde Butcher's Big Cypress Gallery. They offer two standalone two-bedroom houses with an incredible, immersed-in-the-swamp atmosphere. Please keep in mind that reservations for either can be something of a challenge.

If you've brought your own camping gear—whether it's a tent or an RV—you'll have a much better selection. The **Skunk Ape Headquarters Campground** (40904 Tamiami Trail E., 239/695-2275, www.skunkape.info, tent camping $20/night, RV camping $25/night) is the most mainstream of the bunch and also the kitschiest. It's a pretty typical roadside campground. To get a slightly wilder experience, the **Burns Lake Campground & Backcountry Access** (check in at Oasis Visitor Center, no phone, Aug. 29-Jan. 6, $16/night) has a dozen or so primitive campsites surrounding Burns Lake (which should really be called Burns Pond). It can feel a little busy in the camping area since it's so wide-open, but campers can easily make their way into the vast expanses of flatwood hammocks just behind their campsites. **Monument Lake Campground** (check in at Oasis Visitor Center, no phone, Aug. 28-Apr. 15, $16/night) offers a similar setup, although it has real restrooms, a cold-water shower, and picnic/barbecue facilities. It's also the site of the 1936 Seminole Conference, where Florida's governor met with Seminole tribe leaders in an attempt to offer them aid.

## GETTING THERE

Ochopee is situated right along the Tamiami Trail (U.S. 41), about 35 miles (30 minutes) east of Naples, 8 miles (about 10 minutes) from Everglades City, and 10 miles (about 15 minutes) from the eastern boundary of Big Cypress.

# Everglades National Park via Miami

This part of the Everglades is often the only part of the Everglades that many visitors see. Since it's so close to Miami, tourists make the short drive here for a day trip. The airboat operators and kitschy "alligator wrestling" shows of the Miccosukee tribe are unique to the area and give a glimpse of the vast natural expanses. For a deeper look, visit the popular Shark Valley Visitor Center and discover some of the lesser-traveled canoe and kayak trails.

## SIGHTS AND RECREATION

### ★ Shark Valley Visitor Center

For many visitors—especially those coming from Miami—a trip to the Everglades means a beeline to the **Shark Valley Visitor Center** (36000 SW 8th St., 305/221-8776, www.nps. gov/ever, 9:15am-5:15pm daily; park admission $25 for seven-day automobile pass, $8/person on bike or foot). By far the most developed and the busiest of all the park's visitors centers, Shark Valley is right on the busy Tamiami Trail that links downtown Miami and Naples. Paying the gate fee gets you into the center (and the rest of Everglades National Park). You'll have to pay additional money for the tram rides ($19 adults, $12 children) and bike rentals ($8/hour). The center offers boat cruises, guided walking tours, and two-hour tram tours. A popular 15-mile bike trail loop originates here, and bikes can be rented right where the trams depart. Shark Valley offers a sort of one-stop-shopping for the Everglades experience. Due to the crowds, you should definitely arrive early, as the parking lots can fill up pretty quickly. Also, reservations for tram tours can and should be made in advance.

### Miccosukee Resort & Gaming

For those who like to gamble, the **Miccosukee Resort & Gaming** (500 SW 177th Ave., 305/222-4600, http://500nations.

Florida wetland at Everglades National Park

com, open 24 hours daily) awaits you. This hotel and casino has a 32-table poker room and a deafening assortment of more than 1,900 slot machines. In keeping with its original roots as a bingo hall (the only type of gambling the state of Florida used to allow the Native American tribes to offer), there's a ridiculously huge "high-stakes" bingo room with more than 1,000 seats. It's far less upscale than the gaming resorts operated by the nearby Seminole tribe. Those with an aversion to cigarette smoke should know that the air recirculation system leaves quite a bit to be desired.

## Airboat Rides

Just outside the boundaries of the Everglades National Park, there are several airboat tour operators. Lots of tourists from Miami make their way here to experience the Everglades. Airboats are loud and can be disruptive and potentially an ecological hazard. However, they are also a blast to ride in and their usage is just as much a real part of the Everglades as fried gator tails and the Skunk Ape. Of all the tourist-friendly airboat outfits on the eastern edge of the park, **Coopertown** (22700 SW 8th St./U.S. 41, 305/226-6048, www.coopertownairboats.com, 8am-6pm daily, tour

tickets: adults $22, children 7-11 $11, children under 7 free) is the most interesting, since it's a fish camp that dates back to 1945. It is possibly the oldest continuously operating business in this part of the Everglades, and you should definitely see it while you have a chance; the National Park Service bought the property and gave the original owners a 10-year-lease through 2026, leaving its fate beyond that date unknown. Other airboat operators in the area include **Buffalo Tiger's Airboat Tours** (29701 SW 8th St., 305/559-5250, www.buffalotigersairboattours.com, 9am-5pm daily, airboat rides from $50 for adults, children 6-10 $10, children under 6 free), **Gator Park** (24050 SW 8th St./U.S. 41, 305/559-2255, www.gatorpark.com, 9am-5pm daily, adults $22.99, children $11.99, admission includes park admission, airboat ride, and wildlife show), and **Everglades Safari Park** (26700 SW 8 St., 305/226-6923, www.evergladessafaripark.com, 9am-5pm daily, tour tickets adults $25, children 5-11 $12, children under 5 free). If you come prepared with the knowledge that it's going to be a loud, crowded, half-hour boat ride, taking an airboat tour through the swamp can certainly make for a memorable morning.

Airboats are a popular way to get around the swampy areas of the Everglades.

## FOOD

There are restaurants at **Coopertown** (22700 SW 8th St./U.S. 41, 305/226-6048, www.coopertownairboats.com, 8am-6pm daily, $8) and **Everglades Safari Park** (26700 SW 8th St., 305/226-6923, www.evergladessafaripark.com, 9am-5pm daily, $8) that serve standard burgers-and-fries fare with an expected selection of gator tail and frog legs. Of the two, Coopertown is definitely the best, with an authentic Old Florida vibe that comes from being around since the 1940s. Everglades Safari Park is a little more modern, with a more specific emphasis on airboat rides.

## ACCOMMODATIONS

The **Miccosukee Resort** (500 SW 177th Ave., 305/222-4600, www.miccosukee.com, doubles from $99) is just about the only place to overnight in this part of the Everglades. Although the focus here is on the casino, the rooms are decent enough, if dated. If you're continuing on to Miami, the closest lodgings are some chain hotels near the Dolphin Mall, including a **Courtyard by Marriott** (11275 NW 12th St., Miami, 305/994-9343, www.marriott.com, doubles from $169), which is clean and well-kept, but not particularly interesting.

## GETTING THERE

It's 40 miles (less than an hour) from South Beach to the Shark Valley Visitor Center. It's a 75-mile drive to get from Naples to Shark Valley via the Tamiami Trail (U.S. 41), which takes about 90 minutes.

# Everglades National Park via Homestead

There are vast expanses of the Everglades to the south of the Tamiami Trail (U.S. 41). The southern portions of Everglades National Park offer visitors incredible opportunities for canoeing, kayaking, and other sorts of exploration. These areas aren't as easily accessed as the northern and western portions of the Everglades. Once you're in this part of the 'Glades, it's all Everglades National Park, so all of the (limited) facilities are operated by the park.

Thanks to the lack of civilization, this region presents some of the most idyllic and isolated ways to experience the Everglades. With multiple canoe trails, hiking trails, and camping facilities, this area is geared toward outdoor activities, so visitors can fully appreciate the wild expanses of the Everglades.

## FLORIDA CITY

The last outpost of civilization you'll experience before heading into Everglades National Park is Florida City, a tiny little town that most people breeze through on their way to the Florida Keys. It's not much more than a few gas stations and a 24-hour Starbucks, but as you head west off of U.S. 1 toward the Everglades, you'll see that Florida City has a little more to offer than just a spot to refuel between Miami and Key Largo.

### Everglades Alligator Farm

You're going to see a lot of signs for **Everglades Alligator Farm** (40351 SW 192nd Ave., Homestead, 305/247-2628, www.everglades.com, 9am-6pm daily, $19.50 adults, $14.50 children, airboat rides additional cost) on your way to Everglades National Park. You can't fault the folks at Everglades Alligator Farm for doing whatever they can to lure people down a very long dirt road (past a giant prison) to check out their collection of alligators and snakes. The crew here does a great job of providing a couple of hours' worth of entertainment by hosting entertaining shows. There are three snake shows and three alligator shows every day, as well as gator feedings at noon and 3pm. They allow guests to wander the grounds and feed the lounging gators food that is accessible from 25-cent gumball machines.

Visitors can also take hourly airboat rides into the waterways. These rides don't go into Everglades National Park, as airboats are prohibited within park property. Despite how loud, disruptive, and polluting they are, airboats are as much an essential part of Florida as palm trees and oranges. If it seems like an appealing way to speed through the swamps, by all means, go for it.

If you hang around the farm long enough to get hungry, there's a tiny concession where you can grab a freshly grilled burger—a hamburger, not a gator burger.

## Everglades Outpost Wildlife Rescue

The primary mission of **Everglades Outpost Wildlife Rescue** (35601 SW 192nd Ave., Homestead, 305/247-8000, www.evergladesoutpost.com, 10am-5pm Fri.-Tues., $10 donation requested) is the rescue and rehabilitation of exotic animals. Although it's not a tourist attraction per se, the Outpost welcomes visitors (and donations) as it attempts to raise awareness. Visitors are welcome to tour the facilities and observe the range of animals currently being cared for. Due to the rescue-and-release nature of the Outpost's mission, the exact population varies. You may be able to see a tiger, a lemur, or a parrot, or you may end up seeing a donkey or a camel. Regardless of the wildlife you encounter, the energy and enthusiasm of the volunteer staff here is infectious enough that you may end up "adopting" one of the patients here by way of helping to provide the funds needed for their continued care and relocation.

# VISITORS CENTERS
## Ernest Coe Visitor Center

The **Ernest Coe Visitor Center** (40001 SR-9336, Homestead, 305/242-7700, www.nps.gov/ever, 9am-5pm daily, $25 per vehicle for seven-day pass, $8 per person for pedestrians and cyclists), also known as the Main Visitor Center, is at the main entrance to the park. It is therefore the most popular of all the visitors centers, as well as the most expansive and well-staffed. If you've never been to the 'Glades, this is an ideal place for a park ranger to give you tips on navigating the park, and there are also some excellent exhibits that detail the flora, fauna, and history of the Everglades. The admission fee you pay at the main entrance gate here grants you entrance to the entirety of the Everglades National Park.

## Royal Palm Visitor Center

The **Royal Palm Visitor Center** (four miles west of the park entrance on Main Park Rd., 305/242-7700, 8am-4:15pm daily, admission included with park entrance fee) is the starting point for two of the park's most popular walking trails: the Anhinga Trail and the Gumbo Limbo Trail. The 0.8-mile-long **Anhinga Trail** is thick with visible wildlife. You'll almost certainly see alligators and, in the winter, dozens of species of birds, including the trail's namesake, which will likely be spotted using its long neck to assist it in hunting for fish. Park rangers offer an hour-long guided walk along this trail. The **Gumbo Limbo Trail** is half as long. Instead of wading through swampy marsh grass, walkers along this trail will be strolling through a lush hardwood hammock. Both of these trails are well maintained and wheelchair accessible. Aside from the trails, on-site rangers, and clean restrooms, there is little else at this center.

## Flamingo Visitor Center

About an hour south of the park's main entrance, and at the end of the park's main paved road, is the **Flamingo Visitor Center** (1 Flamingo Lodge Hwy., 941/695-2945, www.nps.gov/ever, building open 24/7, staffed 9am-5pm Apr.-Oct., 8am-5pm Nov.-Mar., admission included with park entrance fee). Flamingo feels like a weird outpost of civilization in a wildlife area. There's really not much here for the casual tourist besides the imposing visitors center and the marina, but it feels like a bustling metropolis compared to the still and quiet throughout the rest of Everglades National Park.

In addition to an educational area inside the center, there's a marina from which you can take **boat tours** ($32 adults, $12 children) of Florida Bay or rent canoes or kayaks ($16/ two hours, $30/day) to take on the beautiful, mangrove-thick **water trails.** The short **Eco Pond Trail** (0.5 mile) here is pleasant and wheelchair accessible. For boaters, Flamingo is often just the beginning of a journey, as it's from here that you can set off into the waters of Florida Bay and its numerous tiny keys for some real explorations. You can buy beer and Moon Pies at the marina.

The visitor center is staffed intermittently mid-April through December, and so does not have regular visiting hours.

## MAIN PARK ROAD

There's not a whole lot of proper sightseeing within Everglades National Park, but the National Park Service has done a good job at balancing visitors' desires to see *something* with the low-impact mission of the park itself. The result is a handful of minimally equipped

pullovers along Main Park Road where you can walk along a boardwalk, have a picnic, or just stare off into the vast expanses of the Everglades. There's only one road in and out of Everglades National Park, which means you're going to pass by all of these anyway, so take time to check them out.

## Long Pine Key

**Long Pine Key** is a great stop about four miles along Main Park Road for biking, hiking, and picnicking. It's also a very popular campsite. The unnamed 14-mile loop bike trail takes you through slash pine and prairies, but there's not a whole lot of shade. Hikers and day-trippers should head for the (also unnamed) half-mile multipurpose trail, which offers a similarly diverse look at the area's ecology. There are picnic tables in the shade, and clean and well-maintained restroom facilities.

## Rock Reef Pass

The sign just before **Rock Reef Pass**, about 11 miles along Main Park Road, reminds you just how flat and near-swampy this part of the state is. It states, Elevation: Three Feet. This is practically mountainous for the Everglades, as much of the area is actually at or below sea

Your first stop in Everglades National Park when coming from Homestead will be the Ernest Coe Visitor Center.

Ernest F. Coe
1866 • 1951
er of Everglades National Park

# Big Sugar and the Everglades

Almost half of the sugar consumed in the United States comes from cane fields growing in and around the Everglades. Thanks to rich, organic peat deposits, sugarcane farming has a long history in the area dating back to the late 19th century. However, since the 1960s, a comingling of industrial agriculture, poor government planning, and rampant development have conspired to devastate the ecosystems that make up the 'Glades. For years, the term "Big Sugar" referred to the web of plantation-style sugar growers throughout the area who worked together to set prices and controlled the line of production from field to refinery with an iron fist. Now, though, "Big Sugar" basically means two companies, Fanjul Corp. (operated by the Fanjul family, and comprising Domino Sugar, Florida Crystals, and other brands) and U.S. Sugar. Even if the names have changed, the game has remained the same.

The power wielded by Big Sugar has resulted in immense damage to the Everglades, both from chemical runoff of fertilizers and pesticides and also from years of damming, dredging, and water-redirection projects undertaken by the U.S. Army Corps of Engineers and the South Florida Water Management District in order to make the region arable and, in many cases, open for residential development. (And that's to speak nothing of the economic impact of having thousands of plantation-wage workers in the employ of a single industry.) Those projects have starved the Everglades of the one thing it needs to survive: a constant flow of water. The results have been predictably devastating, and that devastation has become one of the signature issues of the Florida environmental movement. However, those calls have gone largely unheeded, greeted with complex and incredibly expensive half-measures that seek to chip away at the problem without offending the Fanjuls or U.S. Sugar.

In 2008, Governor Charlie Crist proposed a purchase and shutdown of U.S. Sugar by the state of Florida. Although this move would help the huge company in the short term, it was a dramatic and major move to help the Everglades in the long term. The proposal has been reworked and stripped down in the intervening years to further favor the sugar industry while doing little in the way of actively healing the Everglades. There's still hope among Florida environmentalists that bits and pieces of the deal will eventually happen in a helpful way. But what one day looked like hope for an Everglades free of the sugar industry has now been transformed into a more pragmatic return to trying to contain the damage this industry wreaks on one of America's most important natural treasures.

level. The high altitude of Rock Reef Pass makes for a unique ecological combination of pine forest and marshes filled with dwarf cypress trees. There's a very short boardwalk here that allows you to get out into areas that alternate between tinderbox trails in the dry winter and foot-deep swamp in the summer rainy season.

### ★ Pa-hay-okee Overlook
Situated at 12.5 miles down Main Park Road, the elevated boardwalk at **Pa-hay-okee Overlook** is considerably longer than the one at Rock Reef Pass (about 750 ft). It offers much more magnificent and expansive vistas onto the grassy infinity of the Everglades. It's also much more popular. So, during the

busy season, there is the distinct possibility of a packed parking lot and cattle-chute movement along the boardwalk. This seldom actually happens, though, but for the most quietude and the best chance of having these beautiful views to yourself, make sure to get here early in the day. This boardwalk is wheelchair accessible.

### Mahogany Hammock
**Mahogany Hammock,** which is about 20 miles along Main Park Road, offers another boardwalk-through-the-'Glades experience. Although this particular loop trail (0.5 mi) is quite short, the density of mahogany trees (and the shade they provide!) makes it unique and a nice, quick stop. Mahogany's boardwalk

rewards visitors who look up into the mahogany canopy, where they're likely to see migratory birds.

# SPORTS AND RECREATION

## ★ Hiking

Everglades National Park offers a variety of different hiking experiences, from easily accessed, elevated boardwalks and quick, shaded loops to more challenging and lengthy forays into the more ecologically imposing areas of the park.

The two trails at the **Royal Palm Visitor Center** (four miles west of the park entrance on Main Park Rd., 305/242-7700, 8am-4:15pm daily, admission included with park entrance fee), the **Anhinga Trail** (0.8 mi) and **Gumbo Limbo** (0.4 mi), are by far the most popular non-boardwalk trails in Everglades National Park, and not just because they're the closest to the main entrance. Both trails manage to be easily navigable while taking hikers through the stunning variety of the Everglades' terrain. Even during the hottest summer months, you're likely to see a decent array of wildlife (especially alligators). During the winter months, bird-watching is incredible. If you have to pick, take the Anhinga Trail; even though this easy loop trail is just under a mile long, it provides a great (if quick) look at some great natural beauty.

Other quick and gorgeous trails include the mangrove-lined, waterfront **Bayshore Trail** (2 mi), which starts at Flamingo Campground, and the **Eco-Pond Trail** (0.5 mi), a loop of bird-watching heaven, which starts from the Flamingo Visitor Center.

Hikers looking for something more challenging will want to explore the **Coastal Prairie Trail** (5.6 mi), which starts from Flamingo Campground and is such a tough slog that park rangers discourage casual visitors from taking it on. The campground at the end, at Clubhouse Beach, is well worth the struggle through muck and brush that it takes to get there. Another good trail for experienced hikers (and those unafraid to

spend the majority of their hike under the brutal Florida sun) is the walk along the **Old Ingraham Highway** (22 mi). This used to be the main park road, until Main Park Road was built in the 1960s. It's wide and fairly well-graded, making it a popular trail for bicyclists as well. The trailhead is near Royal Palm Visitor Center.

Hikers should always be prepared with sunscreen, lots of water, and bug repellent, and should always be on the lookout for venomous snakes. In the summer, mosquitoes and other flying insects can make hiking a challenge.

---

**TOP** EXPERIENCE

## ★ Canoeing and Kayaking

By far, the best way to experience the Everglades is in a boat. Canoe and kayak rental opportunities abound, and there are several boat trails throughout the park. While many rental agencies offer guided tours, the quietude of solo exploration has its advantages. By all means, unless you're hauling a lot of gear, a kayak is far better suited to the narrow waterways of the 'Glades, as you'll appreciate the navigational flexibility when making your way through a dense thicket of mangroves. Also, for overnight boaters, several Seminole-style chickees (stilt houses built open on all sides and thatched) throughout the park provide an elevated and roofed camping area right on the water.

Experienced boaters will want to explore the 3-6 miles of twists and turns of **Hell's Bay Canoe Trail,** a challenging run that announces its intentions with a comically difficult put-in and a trail that can take up to six hours to navigate completely; oddly, it's quite popular! Another challenging trail is the eight-mile **West Lake Canoe Trail,** which runs mainly through open waters but also takes boaters through some impressive (and occasionally claustrophobic) mangrove tunnels. There are easier options, too: **Nine Mile Pond Trail** is only 3.5 miles long (the pond it's named after is nine miles from the former site of a visitors center) and is well-marked, guiding paddlers through mangrove tunnels and several wider marshes. It's best explored during the summer, when water levels are higher. Even easier is the two-mile loop of the **Noble Hammock Canoe Trail,** which only takes about an hour to traverse. The **Mud Lake Canoe Trail** is also very popular, as it is close to the Flamingo Visitor Center and quite short.

Serious canoers and kayakers will want to plan their Everglades adventure around exploring the **Wilderness Waterway.** The trail is 99 miles long and gets boaters into some of the most isolated and beautiful areas of the Everglades. Running along the western edge of the 'Glades along Cape Sable, from Flamingo all the way north to Chokoloskee, this part of the Everglades is known as the Ten Thousand Islands. Some of the waterway is in Everglades National Park, while some of it traverses through Ten Thousand Islands National Wildlife Refuge. There may not be 10,000 islands, but it sure does seem like it. The vast majority of the small outcroppings of scrub and sand are tiny, although some of them house chickee huts for overnight camping. Make sure to have up-to-date nautical and tide charts, as some parts of the waterway are nigh-unnavigable without them. Information on specific put-in points is available at Ernest Coe Visitor Center.

If you don't want to do the entire 99 miles, shorter one- and two-night trips can be planned. Consult with a ranger at one of the park's visitors centers first. If you decide to take on the whole thing, be advised that even under the best conditions, this is a hugely challenging affair that can take more than a week to complete.

From Flamingo, boaters can also explore the waters of **Florida Bay** and its numerous keys. Canoers and kayakers probably don't want to go any farther than the chickees on **Shark Point Key,** as the open water of Florida Bay can be daunting, and the density of islands decreases noticeably past here, but

Canoe trails abound in the Everglades, and Hell's Bay is one of the best.

there are also chickees far out in the bay on Little Rabbit and Johnson Keys.

Canoe and kayak rentals within the park are limited to concessionaires operating at the **Flamingo Visitor Center** and the **Gulf Coast Visitor Center** (near Everglades City). Canoe rates range from $20 for two hours to $38 for an eight-hour day; kayak rates range from $45/day for single kayaks to $55/day for tandem kayaks. There are additional rental opportunities near the park, such as at **Ivey House** in Everglades City, which rents canoes for $35/day and kayaks for $49-$65, depending on the type of kayak. Likewise, no tour guides are headquartered within park boundaries, but dozens operate close by, and **Everglades Adventure Tours** (40904 Tamiami Trail, Ochopee, 800/504-6554, two-hour canoe tours from $89/person) is one of the best.

## Hunting

Hunting is illegal within Everglades National Park, but there are several private hunting preserves in the area. **Everglades Adventures** (28965 Obern Rd., Clewiston, 863/983-8999, www.huntsflorida.com) is one of the largest.

## FOOD

There are a number of decent restaurants in Homestead. **Shiver's Bar-B-Q** (28001 S. Dixie Hwy., 305/248-2272, http://shiversbbq.com, 11am-10pm daily, from $7) is something of a local legend, having served up excellent ribs, pulled pork, and chicken since 1950. Another fantastic option to grab a great meal is **Chefs on the Run** (10 E. Mowry Dr., 305/245-0085, noon-8pm Tues.-Sat., from $9), a cozy, table-service spot in "downtown" Homestead that serves up a great array of fresh and hearty Cuban, Caribbean, and even Asian and Vietnamese dishes. As the name implies, the food here is chef-driven, so while the high-variety menu may seem inconsistent, the dishes are almost always excellent.

Closer to the main entrance of Everglades National Park in Florida City is ★ **Robert Is Here** (19200 SW 344th St., Homestead, 305/246-1592, www.robertishere.com, 8am-7pm daily Nov.-Aug.). While it's not a restaurant per se, it's undoubtedly the best place to eat anywhere near the park. Starting out as little more than a far-flung produce stand, it's an essential stop for locals and tourists alike to stock up on fresh fruits, vegetables, snacks, and milkshakes that almost make the drive worth it on their own. Try the key lime milkshake for a quintessential South Florida delicacy. Robert is justifiably proud of his wide selection of hard-to-find "weird tropical fruit" like lychee, guanabanas (soursop), sapotes, starfruit, and tamarind. You can pick up jams and jellies as well as gift baskets and a decent selection of grab-and-go snacks for the road. There's also a petting zoo, but this is probably the only place in Florida where a live emu is the third (or fourth) most interesting reason to visit.

## ACCOMMODATIONS
### Hotels

There are a handful of decent and inexpensive hotels in downtown Homestead that provide relatively quick access to the Everglades. Of them, the **Hotel Redland** (5 S. Flagler Ave., 305/246-1904, www.hotelredland.com, doubles from $99) and the **Floridian Hotel** (990 N. Homestead Blvd., 305/247-7020, doubles from $75) are the best. The Redland is situated in a beautiful, historic building and feels more like a bed-and-breakfast than a typical hotel. The Floridian is a fairly standard, clean, and comfortable motel that looks like some conscientious local owners took over from a national chain, updating its amenities (there's a sparkling pool and decent Wi-Fi) and keeping the property well-maintained. There are also a number of budget motel chains with locations in the area.

### Camping

Camping with a camper, tent, or in a chickee is your only choice for staying within the park's boundaries. There are two easily accessible campgrounds within Everglades National Park, both of which welcome tent campers and RVs. During the summer rainy season, the National Park Service typically allows camping for free, but the sites get quickly waterlogged.

In the eastern portion of the park, **Long Pine Key Campground** (approx. six miles from park entrance, 305/242-7700, $16/site, $30 group site) has 108 drive-up sites and one group site. Restrooms, water, and RV dump stations are available, but there are no showers. Sites are available on a first-come, first-served basis.

**Flamingo Campground** (reservations 877/444-6777, $16/site, $30 group site) is the largest and most popular campground in this part of Everglades National Park, with 234 drive-up sites, 40 walk-up single sites, and 3 walk-up group sites. Its popularity is due to its proximity to the Flamingo Visitor Center. The end-of-the-road isolation of this part of the park has considerable appeal. This campground may feel busy or even a little overcrowded (especially over the winter holidays), but just a quick walk or bike ride away puts you in some of the most pristine natural quietude you've ever experienced.

There are also 47 backcountry campsites, ranging from chickees along the Wilderness Waterway and in Florida Bay to "beach" sites in Cape Sable and standard ground sites, which are only accessible by boat. Wilderness permits are required for all backcountry camping ($10 processing fee, plus $2 pp/day camping fee). The three beach sites at Cape Sable are the largest, accommodating around 150 people. They're as beautiful as they are rustic and are often uncrowded. Call 305/242-7700 for more information on backcountry campsites.

## GETTING THERE

It's about 35 miles (30 minutes) to get to Homestead and Florida City from Miami, and then another 15 miles (30 minutes) west into the park.

# Background

# The Landscape

## GEOGRAPHY

There are three formal geographical regions in the state of Florida, two of which make their way in some fashion to the areas covered in this guide. The **Atlantic Coastal Plain** extends all the way north to Cape Cod, Massachusetts, and encompasses the entirety of Florida's east coast. It's an area defined by low, flat topography and features like sandy beaches, scrub-flecked ranchlands, the swamps of the Everglades and Big Cypress, and the marshy wetlands of central Florida. This region of the state connects seamlessly to the **East Gulf Coastal Plain** that runs along Florida's west coast. In the south-central part of the state, this region shares the swampy characteristics of the 'Glades and Big Cypress; however, the Gulf beaches see far less wave action from the gentle Gulf of Mexico, resulting in powdery, white-sand beaches that are quite legendary. In the Panhandle is the third distinct and formal geographic region, the **Florida Uplands,** which resemble the pine forest landscapes of the American South and are home to what little elevation the state has to offer.

## CLIMATE

This part of Florida really only sees two seasons: oppressive and pleasant. Summer lasts a little longer in south Florida (mid-March to mid-October) and has a tendency to be dizzyingly humid and hot with daily thundershowers. But as a reward for sweating it out for half the year, south Floridians enjoy a picture-perfect other half, with an autumn/winter/spring season that sees consistent sunny, warm, and dry days with highs in the mid-70s to low 80s and lows clicking in comfortably around 60 every night. Though some nights can get a little chilly and there are a handful of days when a light jacket might be necessary to ward off a cool, mid-50s breeze, south Florida's weather between Halloween and Valentine's Day is about as perfect as one could hope for.

The official season for Atlantic **hurricanes** is June through October, but the peak of activity is usually in August and September. The Florida Keys and south Florida are most often in the direct path of the storms that form in the Atlantic basin. Although almost every region of Florida has been impacted by a hurricane (most notably in 2004, when an unprecedented four hurricanes hit the state, including three that crossed the normally untouched central Florida region), it's the Keys and south Florida that generally assume they'll be hit. And for good reason: Florida is a hurricane magnet and when the storms do hit, they hit quite hard. The city of Punta Gorda was almost completely leveled when the 2004 storms hit.

## ENVIRONMENTAL ISSUES

Florida's environmental issues can be distilled into one simple word: growth. In a state with a relatively young history that has most of its roots in its development as a tourist destination, Florida's ecology has been the victim of unplanned and unchecked development throughout the last century. Until very recently, environmental concerns took a very distant backseat to the demands of real estate speculators, construction interests, and the tourism industry. Entire portions of the state's most singular ecological treasure, the Everglades, were drained, dredged, and built upon to satisfy the expansion of south

---

**Previous:** boats docked along the Peace River in Punta Gorda; the Ca' d'Zan in Sarasota.

Florida's suburbs and the needs of the mighty sugar industry. Coastal development has demolished dunes, and even the seemingly inhospitable "Palmetto Prairie" in the south-central portion of the state is beginning to experience far-flung suburban residential developments.

Beyond the impact of development on the state's ecology, the fast-growing state has spread out in all directions, resulting in low-density cities surrounded by dozens of commuter towns. The net effect is a deeply entrenched car culture and endless miles of roadways surrounded by cookie-cutter subdivisions that eat into land that was previously agricultural or undisturbed homes for wildlife. While there are still great swathes of untamed land in Florida, those areas are slowly being eroded by development.

# Plants and Animals

## TREES

To the surprise of many, southwest Florida isn't just home to swaying palm trees and orange groves. Scrub pines and slash pines are common throughout the region's midsection. Along the coastline, mangroves are quite prevalent, and black mangroves can soar up to 50 feet in height. Some unique native Florida trees include West Indian mahogany trees, which can be found in southern Florida and the Keys, and pond apple trees that grow in the state's swamps. Of course, the state is most commonly identified with palm trees, but the massive coconut palms that indicate "tropical vacation" to so many people are, though common throughout the state, not a native tree. The true Florida palms are the equally tall sabal palm trees. Cypress trees abound in the swampy areas of the state.

## FLOWERS

The official flower of Florida is the orange blossom. For the early part of the 20th century, a drive through the orange groves of central and southern Florida as the fragrant flowers bloomed was one of the high points of a vacation to the state. Of course, the tropical and subtropical climate means an abundance of gorgeous flowering plants can be seen almost year-round. "Invasive" species like bougainvillea, jasmine, gardenias, birds of paradise, and oleander have taken their place alongside native beauties like mistletoe and the puffy-flowered sweet acacia to make the state one of the most beautifully and naturally landscaped parts of the country. Note: Though somewhat common throughout the Everglades, wild orchids cannot be collected as they are protected by law.

## MAMMALS

Florida is home to two unique and endangered mammal species, the Florida panther and the tiny Key deer, both of which have come quite close to extinction in recent decades. Preservation efforts have been effective in keeping the species around, but the drastically limited numbers of both animals mean that there's still quite a bit of work to be done. Somewhat more common are bobcats, which are smaller than panthers and can be seen in this region's hardwood swamps and hammocks. The two mammals you're almost certain to see while here are armadillos and opossums.

## SEALIFE

Pods of bottlenose dolphins are easy to spot from shore—especially in coves and bays like Charlotte Harbor—and, farther out to sea, it's possible to see pilot whales. Offshore snorkelers are blessed with an abundance of coral reefs and the attendant schools of colorful tropical fish that live in and around them. However, the most iconic of all of Florida's water creatures is the West Indian manatee.

# Manatee Preservation

As they like to inhabit the same waters that Florida's many boaters enjoy recreating on, manatees face their single biggest threat from the propeller blades of fast-moving boats. Injuries sustained by contact with boats have resulted in thousands of manatees dying in a most gruesome fashion. Even manatees that aren't struck by a boat's propeller have been threatened by the deleterious effects of fishing gear (nets, hooks, etc.) that they swallow while feeding on sea grasses and algae.

Federal law prohibits harming a manatee (they are currently listed as being "vulnerable to extinction"), which has resulted in something of an uneasy standoff on Florida's waterways. Boaters feel they have every right to roam the rivers at whatever speed they feel is appropriate and safe, while wildlife officials have gone to great lengths to cap speed limits on large stretches of water in the hopes of giving manatees an opportunity to avoid colliding with the boats. While the majority of boaters are respectful of the regulations and empathetic to the manatees' plight, a 2017 study by the U.S. Department of the Interior that found the sea cows' position to be improving led many to note that such improvement was grounds for relaxing the regulations.

These gentle "sea cows" feast on the mangrove leaves, algae, and turtle grass that's common throughout Florida's waterways, and the warm waters of this region's rivers are among the manatees' preferred spots for wintering and mating.

## BIRDS

Florida is one of the best places in the United States for bird-watching. In addition to the numerous native species (kites, ospreys, spoonbill herons, scrub jays, and even bald eagles call the state home throughout the year), the original "snowbirds" were the scores of northern species who make their winter homes in the state. Any of the dozens of nature preserves in the state are ideal for bird-watching in the winter, but perhaps the best year-round is the J. N. "Ding" Darling National Wildlife Refuge on Sanibel Island.

Palms and sand epitomize Florida landscapes.

## INSECTS AND ARACHNIDS

This part of the state can be dense with blood-sucking mosquitoes, particularly during the summer. Though coastal breezes make the bugs less of a problem in many spots, the swampy inland areas are an absolute haven for mosquitoes, and you'll almost certainly have a few that will be feasting on your platelets.

## REPTILES AND AMPHIBIANS

Florida's most famous reptile is, of course, the alligator. If there's a body of water in Florida, it's likely home to at least one gator. The Everglades, certainly, are thick with them, but even lakeside residences in urban Naples and Sarasota have been the sites of alligator encounters. These animals are obviously incredibly dangerous, so one should use all due caution while in or near any freshwater area in Florida.

Venomous snakes are also common, both native species like the diamondback rattler and foreign breeds that have been "liberated" into the swamps and forests of the state. These dangerous species are far outnumbered by the ranks of nonvenomous snakes, though, and king snakes and black snakes are quite prevalent.

The most common reptiles are lizards and geckos, which can be seen skittering about during the day, sunning themselves, and chasing down food. They seldom grow to any great size, and most are less than six inches long. Salamanders are also bountiful.

# History

## ANCIENT CIVILIZATION AND EARLY HISTORY

The first residents of Florida were Paleo-Indians who moved into the peninsula around 12,000 BC. These tribes were largely nomadic, following their food sources around the state. The first permanent settlements weren't established until around 5000 BC, when Early Archaic groups established fishing villages along the Gulf and Atlantic Coasts. Between that time and around AD 500, these groups began segmenting into the distinct regional groups that would give way to Native American tribes, which had a cultural identity similar to that of the Mississippian peoples. The major tribes in Florida were the Ais (along the mid-southern Atlantic Coast), Apalachee (mid-Panhandle), Caloosahatchee/Calusa (southwestern Gulf Coast), Mayaimi (around Lake Okeechobee), Tequesta (current Miami-Dade County), and Tocobaga (middle Gulf Coast). The Timucua people lived throughout central and northeastern Florida, but were connected more by a common language than by cultural traits. The Seminole tribe didn't develop until the late 18th century, when members of the Creek nation began migrating into Florida from Georgia and Alabama as a result of an internecine conflict; their numbers included members of other, far-flung tribes as well as freed African American slaves. The Miccosukee tribe also migrated to Florida in the late 18th century, and its members are related to the Seminoles due to shared Creek lineage, but they speak a different language and originally hail from Tennessee.

## COLONIALISM

Juan Ponce de León, on the hunt for the legendary Fountain of Youth, landed on the east coast of Florida on April 2, 1513. This is widely considered to be the first European landing in Florida, although Ponce de León claimed to have met an Indian who already spoke Spanish. The land was named "La Pascua Florida" (the flowery Easter) in honor of the date on the religious calendar. Spanish exploration of Florida continued in earnest for the next half century, although attempts at settlements were continually thwarted by native tribes who wanted nothing to do with these interlopers. The first European settlement in what is now the United States of America was in Pensacola, but it only lasted for two years (1569-1571). The Spanish had better luck with the establishment of St. Augustine in 1565, which is now regarded as the oldest city in the continental United States and was the point from which the Spanish began launching Catholic missions throughout the region.

However, by this time, the Spanish exploits in Florida had gotten the attentions of other European powers. French explorers Jean Ribault and René Goulaine de Laudonnière founded Fort Caroline near modern-day Jacksonville, and the British launched an ill-fated expedition to colonize the area that never even made it across the Atlantic. This left the French and Spanish to duke it out for the next half century, all the while contending with assaults from native tribes. English settlers finally began arriving in the mid-17th century, although they were migrating south from colonies in Carolina and Virginia.

By 1702, though, the English government took a much more concerted interest in Florida, and Colonel James Moore banded together with the Yamassee tribe to attack the Spanish fort at St. Augustine. Although the attack failed, it signaled the beginning of the end of unilateral Spanish rule over Florida. The French captured Pensacola in 1719, extending their sovereignty from Louisiana, and the British continued their attacks on St. Augustine and other Spanish outposts in north Florida, finally wresting control of the region from Spain in 1763. The outbreak of the Revolutionary War diverted Britain's attention from Florida, and Spain was able to regain control of Florida in 1783. However, this last reign was both unenthusiastic (there were no settlements or missions established) and temporary (the Adams-Onís Treaty of 1819 ceded control of Florida to the United States in exchange for all claims that the United States had to Texas).

American control brought organization to the frontier land. The separate colonial states of East Florida and West Florida were merged and the capital was established in Tallahassee (midway between the two former states' capitals of Pensacola and St. Augustine). Migration of Americans from the north soon began in earnest. Early settlers were greeted none too warmly by Native American tribes. In particular, the Seminoles had grown

The Miccosukee Indian Village & Cultural Center preserves history and draws tourists in the Everglades.

# Florida Crackers

Some of the original American pioneers in Florida began arriving as early as the 1760s, when Great Britain began a brief stint as the controlling colonial force in the region. These men and women staked out inhospitable territory, greeted by clouds of mosquitoes, acres of scrub, and thousands of hostile Native Americans. Nonetheless, these pioneer families were able to establish cattle ranches and sparse agricultural settlements in the state. Many of Florida's most notable citizens, from former governor Lawton Chiles to astronaut/senator Bill Nelson, can trace their families' roots back to these daring and resilient settlers.

There's some debate as to why these pioneers were referred to as crackers, though. Some tales have the origin of the term pointing to the cowboys' usage of bullwhips to herd cattle, the "crack" of the whip being something of a clarion call, while others place it in a more pejorative sense. The Spanish colonialists in the region maintained that their towns were, of course, the height of civilization and that these hard-edged interlopers were not only culturally inferior, but also spiritually lacking. The term *quáquero* (a transliteration of "Quaker") referred to any Protestant but was used with particular animosity toward these American settlers.

increasingly powerful in between the colonial powers' tugs-of-war and had increasingly irritated the leaders of Southern states by providing refuge to escaped slaves who had made their way to Seminole land. This, among other conflagrations, ignited the Second Seminole War (the first happened when Spain had control of Florida), which wound up being the costliest and bloodiest war in history between the United States government and a native tribe. The war lasted nearly seven years (1835-1842) and ultimately resulted in the permanent establishment of the expansive Seminole Reservation as well as the exodus of thousands of Native Americans out of Florida and into Oklahoma.

## STATEHOOD AND THE CIVIL WAR

Florida became the 27th state in 1845, and not too long afterward, it experienced considerable upheaval, first with the three-year Third Seminole War and then with its adoption of the Ordinance of Secession in 1861, which saw it separating from the United States along with the rest of the Confederate States of America.

Given the state's considerable history of violent shifts in control, it's somewhat surprising just how small of a role Florida played in the Civil War. The only major battle was the Battle of Olustee near Lake City, a Confederate victory in early 1864 that resulted in nearly 300 deaths, 2,000 wounded soldiers, and a decision by the Union that battles in Florida were strategically unnecessary to win the war. Although they continued to maintain naval blockades around the state in order to prevent supplies from flowing northward, there was little effort by the Union army to retake Florida.

## TURN OF THE 20TH CENTURY

After the Civil War, modern Florida's history began in earnest, with developers and speculators descending upon the state and kickstarting a real estate boom and the beginning of Florida's tourism industry.

Along the east coast of Florida, Henry Flagler, an original partner with John D. Rockefeller in Standard Oil, bought up several regional rail lines and connected them to the main arteries of the rest of the United States. In the process, he began heavy investment in hotels and infrastructure projects. Eventually, the Florida East Coast Railway extended all the way from Jacksonville to Key West, with several of Flagler's notable hotels—the Ponce de León (St. Augustine), the Royal Poinciana

(West Palm Beach), the Palm Beach Inn (now the Breakers, Palm Beach), and the Royal Palm Hotel (now the site of the DuPont Plaza Hotel, Miami)—conveniently providing lodging for customers of the railroad.

On Florida's west coast, Henry Plant was busy buying up small rail lines to connect them to other rail lines he had purchased at bargain-basement, postwar prices in Savannah and Charleston. Eventually, the Atlantic Coast Line Railroad had Florida operations that extended from Jacksonville and Fernandina Beach in the northeast to Tampa and St. Petersburg in the southwest of the state. Like Flagler, Plant smartly constructed a destination-worthy hotel along his lines: The Tampa Bay Hotel is, today, the site of the University of Tampa, but its unique and slightly ostentatious Moorish/Spanish design still marks it as one of the area's more unusual sights.

As tourists began pouring into the area, so did real estate developers, some of whom had visions of turning Florida into a modern and sophisticated state. Most of them, however, saw the swamps and scrublands as a piggy bank ready to be raided. Acres and acres of land were sold by speculators to gullible northern investors sight unseen, who then intended to resell the property at a profit to those folks ready to move to America's new promised land. (Sound familiar?) As Florida's tourism industry kicked up its own marketing and promotional efforts, the paradisiacal images of orange groves, palm trees, and blue seas were amplified by the potential dollar signs promised by real estate investors. While hundreds of thousands of people did move to Florida and establish several of its major cities, many more simply turned around and went back north when they discovered that the little slice of heaven they had purchased was little more than a patch of cabbage palms infested with mosquitoes and unbearable heat and humidity. The boom finally went bust in mid-1925, a deflation that was compounded by a devastating 1926 hurricane in Miami and the 1929 stock market crash.

# WORLD WAR II

Like the rest of America, Florida was highly dependent upon the military-industrial complex for its struggle back to prosperity after the Great Depression. As Florida's agony was compounded by the effect of the real estate bust, it had a lot further to go to climb back than many of its other Southern neighbors. Thankfully, the state offered flat terrain and expansive stretches of coastline that were particularly conducive to the needs of the Air Force and the Navy's aviation program. Several bases were established in Florida during this time, including Eglin Air Force Base (in the Panhandle), MacDill Air Force Base (in Tampa, currently the home of U.S. Central Command), and the Naval Air Station Jacksonville (which, incidentally, is near the site where a submarine manned by eight Nazi spies came on shore at Ponte Vedra Beach).

Postwar, Patrick Air Force Base and Cape Canaveral were chosen to be the site of the military's missile-launch facilities, a development that quickly led to the initiation of the "Space Race" and the build-up of Cape Canaveral as the home of NASA.

# CONTEMPORARY TIMES

Florida's contemporary history is deemed by many to have started on the day in 1971 when the Walt Disney World Resort opened. For it was on that day that the state was transformed from a somewhat quirky land of beaches, swamps, and roadside attractions into one of the world's foremost tourist destinations. While the impact was felt most immediately in the central Florida region, it also upped the ante throughout the state when it came to attracting tourists. However, cities in Florida faced other issues and events aside from growing tourism. Miami struggled with the impact of waves of Cuban immigration throughout the 1960s and again in the 1980s, the latter period being a population explosion that would have been difficult enough to deal with even if Miami hadn't seen its economy falter and its crime rate skyrocket due to drug violence. Jacksonville and Fort Myers had extensive issues with segregation as late as the 1980s, and cities like Tampa and Fort Lauderdale witnessed their urban cores explode as suburban sprawl irrevocably altered their geographic and cultural identity.

Still, through it all, people just keep coming to Florida. Even the economic crisis of 2008, which, again, hit Florida disproportionately hard due to rampant speculation, has been viewed as a temporary setback. After all, the lure of blue skies, gentle breezes, and swaying palm trees is eternal.

# Government and Economy

## GOVERNMENT

Like most U.S. states, Florida has three branches of government: an executive branch (headed by the governor), a judicial branch (headed by the Florida Supreme Court, which has seven justices on the bench), and a legislative branch (consisting of the 120-seat House of Representatives and the 40-seat Senate). The state government does most of its business while the legislature is in session, which is for one 60-day period beginning in March; often, though, special sessions are called in order to complete unfinished business. Locally, the main county governments in this region are Sarasota, Manatee, Lee, and Collier.

As anyone who watched the 2000 presidential election recount can attest, Florida is somewhat schizophrenic politically. In geographical terms, the vast majority of Florida is Republican, but its more densely populated urban areas lean more liberal. In southwest Florida, however, the calculus is a little less predictable, and for the most part, this area of Florida tends to be quite conservative in its politics. Naples resident Rick Scott was elected Florida's governor in 2010 thanks to the support of the ultra-conservative Tea Party wing of the Republican Party and was reelected in 2014 in a faceoff with a former governor (Republican-turned-Independent-turned-Democrat Charlie Crist . . . again, Florida politics are unique!), and it's safe to say that his brand of corporation-friendly politics is well regarded in this part of the state. The vast rural areas down here are also quite friendly toward social conservatives. Nonetheless, Sarasota is something of a liberal oasis in the region, thanks to the presence of the New College and Ringling College of Art & Design communities.

## ECONOMY
### Agriculture

To many people's surprise, Florida has an extensive history as cattle-ranching territory. Most of the middle of the peninsula, from south of Orlando to north of Lake Okeechobee, is given over to dairy and beef pastures; as recently as 2011, Florida was ranked 10th in the U.S. in number of beef cows. Although that ranking has been increasingly threatened as residential development encroaches upon grazing lands, when one is driving through southwest Florida, that high placement is far from surprising. Massive tracts of undeveloped land here are given over to nothing but ranches.

In and around the Everglades, sugar is the number-one crop. The environmentally intensive methods used to harvest and process sugarcane have enacted so much damage to the local ecosystem that the state government has offered to buy out the U.S. Sugar conglomerate in hopes of rescuing the 'Glades.

### Industry

Florida's main industry, by an exponential factor, is tourism, which is estimated to bring in almost $60 billion a year. Agriculture closely follows, and, during years of real estate boom, the construction industry in Florida is one of the nation's busiest, and one of the main engines of economic growth in southwest Florida. When the economy contracted during the Great Recession, construction jobs all but disappeared from the state, and this region was hit particularly hard.

## Distribution of Wealth

Florida is a defiantly middle-class state; with personal income of around $30,000 per capita, the state is ranked 18th in the United States. It's also, like many of its Southern neighbors, a defiantly anti-labor state. There wasn't a minimum wage in Florida until 2004, and the state is considered a "right-to-work" state (meaning employment can be terminated at any point for any reason, which, in turn, means that collective bargaining and union membership are all but irrelevant). There is no personal income tax in Florida, homeowners receive a "homestead exemption" on their personal property tax bill, and food and medicines are exempt from an already low 6 percent sales tax. This has been one of the primary economic drivers of the state's high post-retirement population, as retirees can relocate from the industrial, high-tax North and live out their days paying relatively little in taxes. Throughout the state there are pockets of extreme poverty and pockets of extreme wealth, and in this part of the state, one can find the two extremes butting up against one another. Generally speaking, though, this is one of the wealthier regions of Florida, and also the one with the most obvious levels of income disparity.

# People and Culture

## DEMOGRAPHY

Florida is the third most populous state in the United States, with approximately 20.6 million people calling the state home. The state's population growth has slowed considerably since a migration boom in 2005 made it the fifth fastest-growing state in the country; today, it's estimated to be about the 30th fastest growing. The most densely populated areas are within the Miami/Fort Lauderdale, Tampa, and Orlando regions, while there are parts of the Panhandle that have population densities of less than one person per square mile. In southwest Florida, one of the last parts of the state to be settled, population densities aren't quite that low, but the region is still fairly lightly populated. The biggest cities—Naples, Sarasota, and Fort Myers—are still quite small in comparison to other cities in Florida, and their outlying areas are dominated by sprawling suburban areas that segue into barely populated ranchland.

The largest racial group in Florida is a varied mix of non-Hispanic Caucasians, who make up approximately 60 percent of the state's population. In southwest Florida, that group makes up nearly 80 percent of the population. While Hispanic communities with roots in Cuba and Puerto Rico are quite prevalent in central and southeast Florida, those populations are about half as large in this region. There is a somewhat larger black population in Fort Myers than in other similarly sized cities in Florida; while the majority of the black population in the Panhandle and north Florida claims direct ancestry from Southern slave states, the black population in southwest Florida tends to trace its roots to Afro-Cubans who engaged in trade in the region, as well as a not-insubstantial number of retirees and transplants who migrated from northern industrial states.

## RELIGION

Baptists, Methodists, and other Protestant faiths make up nearly half of the religious affiliation of Florida residents, and nearly a quarter of the state's population is Roman Catholic. The state's Jewish residents total about 5 percent of the total population.

## LANGUAGE

English is the predominant language in Florida, with more than three-quarters of the state's school-age children using it as their first language at home. However, given the cultural diversity of the state and the large population of immigrants from Latin America, Spanish is widely spoken, and many government documents are available in both English and Spanish. All Florida educators must be certified in teaching English for Speakers of Other Languages (ESOL).

## THE ARTS

Pop Art legend Robert Rauschenberg split his time between New York City and a home studio on Captiva Island for years, and from 2003 until his death in 2008, he worked solely from Captiva. Frank Swift Chase, one of the founders of the Woodstock Artists' Association, also founded the Sarasota School of Art, and taught there occasionally for more than a decade.

The same things that drew these famous artists to the region (namely, the weather) still contribute to the area's artistic reputation. Naples is renowned for its gallery and collector scene, and during the winter—when wealthy snowbirds descend to escape the cold weather in the northern United States—the city is the site of dozens of art shows, sales, and auctions. Of course, the quality of the art doesn't quite approach the global modernism of, say, Miami's Art Basel, but it's still well esteemed.

The preeminent artist in the region is doubtlessly Clyde Butcher, whose photos of the Everglades and other stunning examples of Florida's natural beauty have made him one of the country's most respected art photographers. Butcher's Big Cypress Gallery is a must-visit while in the Everglades. Even if your visit doesn't bring you near there, his work is essential to gaining a greater understanding of not just this area, but the whole of Florida.

Farther north, the Ringling College of Art & Design in Sarasota is one of the preeminent visual arts schools in the Southeast, and not only do its faculty and graduates contribute mightily to Sarasota's cultural scene, but also the school's forward-looking approach helps keep the galleries and graphic design firms in the area well-stocked with the work of many modern, interesting artists.

the Van Wezel Performing Arts Hall in Sarasota

# Essentials

# Transportation

## AIR

The international airports in Miami (MIA) and Orlando (MCO) are two of the busiest in the country, and are serviced by all major and most minor American and international carriers. Although these airports are more than two hours away from the region, it's often easier to find more flight options at lower costs. The same applies—but to a somewhat lesser degree—to Tampa Bay International (TPA), about an hour north of Sarasota.

However, the region has poured considerable expense and promotional effort into positioning its own airport, **Southwest Florida International Airport** (RSW, 11000 Terminal Access Rd., 239/590-4800, www.fly-lcpa.com), in Fort Myers. Although considerably smaller than any of the three previously mentioned options, it does offer a respectable range of daily flights from most major hubs in the United States and a handful of international flights as well. Low-cost carriers such as Southwest, Frontier, JetBlue, and Spirit service RSW, in addition to legacy carriers like Delta, United, and American. There's also the smaller—though growing—**Sarasota-Bradenton International Airport** (SRQ, 6000 Airport Circle, Sarasota, 941/359-2770, www.srq-airport.com), which straddles the border of Sarasota and Bradenton and is served by Delta, American, United, Jet Blue, Air Canada, and Allegiant.

## CAR

I-75 connects Florida's west coast to Atlanta, Knoxville, Cincinnati, Toledo, and Detroit and enters the state south of Valdosta, Georgia. From there, it shoots down the middle of the state via Gainesville and Ocala before heading west through Tampa Bay, Sarasota, and Naples; in Naples it makes a hard east turn toward Fort Lauderdale via the northern section of the Everglades.

U.S. 41 (the Tamiami Trail) runs from Miami—through Naples, Fort Myers, Venice, and Sarasota—to Tampa and northward into the midsection of the state on a path roughly parallel to I-75.

All major car-rental agencies have offices in the region's airports as well as city offices in Naples, Sarasota, and Fort Myers. Many of them frequently offer specials for Florida visitors, but even without such discounts, car-rental rates in Florida are some of the least expensive in the country. This is good because, given the dearth of public transportation and the lack of population density throughout most of Florida, you will almost certainly be driving.

## TAXI

Most of the regions covered in this book have at least one taxi service, though in some of the barrier island towns, it may be one guy with a car. Larger cities generally do have ride-sharing services like Lyft and Uber operating. Keep in mind, though, that almost all of these regions are fairly well spread out, so taxis and ride sharing will only be economical if you're keeping your travel within a central urban core.

## TRAIN

The closest Amtrak station to the area is in Tampa, and it offers connecting bus service to Fort Myers and Sarasota.

---

**Previous:** It's easy for kayakers to find waterways in the area; Alligators are everywhere in southwest Florida.

## BUS

**Greyhound** (www.greyhound.com) has bus service into Bradenton, Fort Myers, Naples, and Port Charlotte.

## BOAT

There are four major cruise ports in Florida, and all of them—Miami, Fort Lauderdale (Port Everglades), Tampa, and Port Canaveral—are less than a three-hour drive from the region. Marinas dot the entire Atlantic and Gulf coastlines; the Coast Guard's 7th District is responsible for the Atlantic Coast, Keys, and lower Gulf Coast.

# Sports and Recreation

## OCEAN SPORTS

The calm, blue waters of the Gulf of Mexico make for wonderful beachgoing. They're also ideal for casual snorkeling. While there are far fewer reefs here than in the Keys or on the Atlantic Coast, there are still a few decent opportunities for good snorkeling, such as in the beautiful, fish-friendly Point-of-Rocks on Siesta Key. Sailing, whether you're docking your own boat at one of the many marinas or chartering one for the day, is also fantastic in the region.

## CANOEING AND KAYAKING

The best place for small boating in Florida is throughout the backwaters and slow-moving rivers of the Everglades, as a trip there combines the meditative pastoralism of a canoe trip with the ever-present danger of being swallowed by an alligator. The Myakka and Peace Rivers also offer ample opportunities for long explorations via small boats. Some of the best kayaking can be found in the smaller waterways that are so prevalent in the area, such as the mangrove trails in Sarasota and the canals around Rookery Bay.

Boating is popular in Florida.

# FISHING

Florida is one of the most popular fishing destinations in the United States, due both to the miles and miles of rivers and lakes throughout the inland area and the seemingly infinite possibilities for deep-sea fishing off the shoreline. Saltwater anglers enjoy heading out into the open ocean for tuna, kingfish, marlin, and mackerel; backwater fishing among the mangroves can yield tarpon, mangrove snapper, snook, and more.

# HIKING

There are fantastic trails throughout the Everglades and the Myakka River State Park near Sarasota. The terrain throughout the region is almost completely flat, so most hiking here is done in the service of nature watching (particularly to check out migratory birds in the winter) or sheer endurance-testing during the hot summer months.

# GOLF

There are almost 1,500 golf courses in Florida, and nearly 200 of them are located between Sarasota and Naples. Unfortunately, unlike in the rest of the state, the vast majority of the courses in this region aren't public courses. However, the public and municipal courses here are still quite beautiful and challenging, and they tend to have reasonable greens fees. Many hotels, especially in golf-loving Naples, have their own courses—or access to a good course is included in your room tariff. Keep in mind that at many of the courses mentioned throughout this guide, tee-time reservations are not only mandatory but also should be made as far in advance as possible, especially during the winter.

# Food and Accommodations

The selection of local restaurants, diners, boîtes, cafés, rib shacks, fish camps, and other sundry dining options listed throughout the book should hopefully provide all but the fussiest eaters with some excellent options. However, I also understand that sometimes nothing beats picking up a bag of groceries and whipping up something on your own in your kitchen-equipped hotel room. And although I've gone out of my way to not include chain restaurants and fast-food peddlers in this guide, I also am fully aware that driving through this strip-mall-dotted area sometimes requires a grab-and-go meal so you can get back on the road. To that end, I've included a small list of grocery stores and fast food options that should serve you well while in Florida.

## FOOD
### Grocery Stores

The Lakeland-based **Publix** chain of grocery stores is a Florida institution and for decades was something of a secret that we kept to ourselves. The stores have a strong emphasis on customer service (they'll take your groceries to your car and cannot accept tips for doing so) and have undertaken a great expansion of their organic and all-natural selections. Many stores have full delis and bakeries, as well as a wide selection of ready-made meals and side dishes. The quality is uniformly excellent.

If you can't find a Publix (and I can't imagine why you couldn't; the chain has more than 700 stores in Florida), Naples and Sarasota each have **Trader Joe's.**

### Fast Food

The Gainesville-based **Sonny's BBQ** is omnipresent throughout Florida and much of the rest of the American South, and their barbecue is far better than you might expect. The Cuban and Caribbean fare one can pick up in the drive-through of a **Pollo Tropical**—which specializes in grilled chicken dishes, rice and beans, plantains, and other Latin

American comfort food—is always a good and reasonably healthy option.

## ACCOMMODATIONS
### Pricing
Accommodation pricing in this book is based on peak (or near-peak) pricing of the least expensive room for two people for one night, based on rates listed by the hotel. While rates can vary wildly—often as much as 300 percent between winter peak and summer slow seasons—using this as a baseline does allow you to get a comparative picture between properties. You'll notice that some rates are extraordinarily high, and yes, there are situations where you may end up paying $649 a night for a luxe hotel room, but in most cases, early booking (and off-peak planning) can provide substantial discounts.

### Services
Both Airbnb and VRBO offer short-term rentals throughout the region, but their availability/legality is highly varied and regulated, especially in smaller, waterfront communities where, ironically, such lodging is often the only accommodation available. Often, these rentals (especially for whole-house/condo rentals) don't provide a notable economic savings over nearby hotels, so usually the choice is one of preference, not of value. Some areas allow one-night rentals of private residences, others enforce a minimum of three nights, while still others insist on monthly or even seasonal stays; sometimes these rules will vary even between a municipality's neighborhoods! In my experience, the tonier and more residential the neighborhood, the more likely it is that shorter stays will be prohibited, while highly trafficked areas are more likely to allow quick trips. Generally, both Airbnb and VRBO listings will reflect local legalities, so don't be surprised if your dream spot won't allow you to book a two-night visit.

# Travel Tips

## VISAS AND OFFICIALDOM
### Entering the United States
Non-U.S. citizens will need the following for entry into the country:

- a valid passport (make sure it's valid for at least six months beyond your travel date)

- a valid visa or visa waiver (check with the U.S. Embassy or Consulate to find out if your country is one of the 38 with whom the United States has a reciprocal agreement on visa waivers; otherwise, you'll need to apply for a tourist visa in advance at your local embassy or consulate)

- a return ticket or proof of sufficient funds to support yourself

Contact the U.S. Embassy in your country for further details, as enforcement of restrictions has tightened up considerably since September 11, 2001. You can also consult the U.S. Immigration and Citizenship Services online (www.uscis.gov).

### Entering Florida
The primary restriction on entering Florida from Georgia or Alabama is that the importation of nonnative produce, livestock, and plants is tightly monitored. If you have any of those items in your vehicle, you need to check in at the Agricultural Inspection Station at the state line.

## ACCESS FOR TRAVELERS WITH DISABILITIES
Along with California, Florida is one of the leaders in making public places accessible to people with disabilities. Even the beaches and nature trails have wheelchair access, and visitors who are hearing-impaired or blind will find that most of the major attractions have

# Festival and Events Calendar

There are numerous and varied festivals throughout the year in southwest Florida, and the bulk of them occur during prime snowbird season. During the summer, it really is just too hot to bother with being outside. The following is a list of some the premier events that occur annually; for more details on each of these, as well as a broader listing of each city's festival events, consult the individual chapters.

## JANUARY
The **Naples New Year's Weekend Art Fair** is just one of several excellent art festivals that occur in Naples during the height of the winter cultural season.

## FEBRUARY
The city of Fort Myers honors its most famous part-time resident, Thomas Edison, with the **Edison Festival of Light** (throughout February, with most activities occurring over the third weekend), a monthlong celebration that includes weekends with live music, craft shows, a parade, and even a bed race.

Every weekend before the Super Bowl, the small fishing village of Goodland (near Marco Island) hosts the rambunctious and friendly **Mullet Festival.**

## MARCH
The **Old Florida Festival** in Naples is a must-see for history buffs. The grounds are divided into "camps" populated variously by Native American tribes, Spanish settlers, British soldiers, Civil War fighters, pioneers, and more; the result is a look at the many different phases of progress that Florida has seen throughout the years.

For almost a quarter century, the **Sanibel Shell Fair & Show** has drawn beachcombers and shell aficionados to the island. Taking place over three days at the Sanibel Community House, there's an outdoor fair with shell-themed crafts and vendors; inside, there's a show ($3 admission), where rare shells, jewelry, and juried exhibits are on display.

## APRIL
One of the best—and most quietly heralded—film festivals in Florida is the **Sarasota Film Festival,** which routinely picks up accolades as one of the better regional film festivals in the country.

## MAY
The **Siesta Key Sand Sculpture Contest** has been featured on several cable travel shows, and for good reason; the soft white sand at Siesta Key packs quite well but is also malleable enough to allow for considerable detail. These are no ordinary sandcastles.

## OCTOBER
Sarasota's **Ringling International Arts Festival** is a relatively new event, but it has quickly established itself as a premier event for cutting-edge arts, music, dance, and theater.

the technology to make them not only accessible but enjoyable. Although there may be some locations that are less accessible than others (particularly some historic buildings), by and large, travelers with disabilities will find Florida both accommodating and welcoming.

# TRAVELING WITH CHILDREN

At its core, Florida is a family-friendly destination. Although there are numerous opportunities for adults to indulge themselves in grown-up activities and sophisticated pursuits, every major city in the area has at least a few attractions expressly designed to capture the interest of children. Quite a few resorts in the region have lodgings designed with families in mind, ranging from multi-bed suites to full, apartment-style lodging. However, I've found that when traveling with kids for an extended time in one locale, it's probably a much better option to explore rental homes. Kids' menus are commonplace in all but the most upscale restaurants.

## WOMEN TRAVELING ALONE

Women traveling alone in Florida should exercise the same caution they would in any major city; however, women should feel comfortable traveling anywhere throughout the state.

## SENIOR TRAVELERS

Florida is among the most prepared states in America when it comes to the needs of senior travelers. Some destinations, like Naples, seem to have been expressly designed for them, in fact. Almost every attraction and hotel offers discounted rates for senior citizens, and Florida's sizable population of retirees guarantees that activities and dining options designed for older visitors are available statewide.

## GAY AND LESBIAN TRAVELERS

As a rule, Florida is generally quite tolerant, and with the rare exception of some of southwest Florida's more rural areas, gays and lesbians should encounter no problems traveling throughout the area.

The **International Gay and Lesbian Travel Association** (IGLTA, 800/448-8550, www.iglta.org) is a great resource for information on gay- and lesbian-friendly accommodations and businesses throughout the world, and maintains an online-accessible database.

# CONDUCT AND CUSTOMS
## Behavior

Florida is considerably less courteous than its Southern neighbors to the north. Unsolicited greetings are usually frowned upon, and smiles are seldom yielded without provocation. People here drive like they're the only person on the road, and the odds are pretty low for someone to voluntarily hold the door open for anyone. However, "less courteous" doesn't necessarily equal "rude." Floridians tend to have a laissez-faire approach to most everything: That extends to their interactions with other people, resulting in a seemingly blinkered unawareness that falls away as soon as someone is determined to actually need assistance. Otherwise, they're going to stay out of your business and would hope that you would do the same for them.

## Dress

Florida is generally very laid-back. Most restaurants don't have dress codes and people tend to leave the house dressed as casually as they can get away with. Of course, business meetings, formal gatherings, and a handful of Naples's top-notch, five-star restaurants require getting dressed up, but beyond that, a clean shirt, some sort of pants or shorts, and a pair of shoes are about all you need to gain admittance to most places. At the beach, flip-flops and shorts are fine just about anywhere, and anywhere else, slacks and a collared shirt would be considered getting cleaned up to go out.

## Smoking

Smoking in restaurants and public buildings is prohibited, and in private, outdoor spaces like botanical gardens, it's highly restricted. The only indoor space you're able to legally light up in Florida is in a bar or nightclub, although more and more have begun enacting no-smoking policies.

# Hurricanes

The official season for Atlantic hurricanes is June through October, but the peak of activity is usually in August and September. The Florida Keys and south Florida are most often in the direct path of the storms that form in the Atlantic basin.

If there is a hurricane warning announced for the area you're vacationing in, you need to leave immediately. Don't let nay-saying locals sway your decision with talk about how "it wasn't so bad the last time" or "it'll curve away like they always do." The terror of 70 mph (or higher) winds is an entirely different experience when you're not watching it on the Weather Channel, and even storms with midrange winds can often bring flooding downpours that are incredibly dangerous. Despite their best efforts, hurricane trackers are usually wrong, or at least not completely right, and these storms are large and unpredictable. Don't be a hero, don't be a know-it-all, don't be brave. Just leave. The state will (hopefully) still be here when you come back.

## HEALTH AND SAFETY
### Sun Protection

One of the biggest health problems people encounter in Florida is sunburn. The long-term health effects of a brutal sunburn are potentially pretty serious. The sun here is tropical, and while you're soaking up the ocean breezes, you're unlikely to notice just how badly you're getting burned. Use sunscreen and lots of it.

That same sun can affect you in other ways, namely in the form of heatstroke. Make sure to drink plenty of water during the day and especially while engaged in outdoor activities.

### Insects

Mosquitoes and stinging insects like bees and wasps are quite common throughout Florida. People with allergies to the latter should consult their doctor before coming to the state and pack a dose or three of strong antihistamines. About the only thing you can do to avoid getting bitten by a mosquito is to pack some insect repellent; if you're heading into any of Florida's state parks or backwaters, its inclusion should be mandatory. The importation of the mosquito-borne Zika virus from Latin America hit Florida quite hard, and, although municipalities throughout the state have since upped their mosquito control programs, vastly reducing the population of these insects, mosquitoes (and, theoretically, Zika-carrying mosquitoes) are a fact of life in Florida. However, we do know that, as of late 2016, there are no "active" Zika zones in Florida, which means no areas of active transmission.

### Wildlife

Snakes and alligators are also common; the former are most often encountered in wilderness areas, but in the case of gators, you should assume that any natural body of water larger than a mud puddle will likely have an alligator in it. If you see one, don't stand, don't gawk, don't tease: Just get yourself, your children, and any pets away from the site as quickly and quietly as possible.

# Information and Services

## VISITOR INFORMATION

For in-depth information on specific locations, you should consult the local visitors centers or tourism bureaus listed in each chapter. However, for information on the entire state, contact the hardworking folks at the state's tourism marketing board **Visit Florida** (888/735-2872, www.visitflorida.com). They can provide maps, trip-planning tools, and information on hotels and attractions.

## MONEY
### Currency

The U.S. dollar is the coin of the realm throughout Florida. Currency exchange facilities are available in all of the state's major international airports—Miami, Orlando, Tampa, and Fort Myers. However, since this region of the state is not as flush with international travelers as Miami and Orlando, you may have to utilize a bank's services to exchange funds.

## Banks and ATMs

Major U.S. banks are well represented throughout the region: Bank of America, SunTrust, Wells Fargo, and Chase branches are quite easy to find, as are a number of regional and state banks and credit unions. These banks also have ATMs at their branches, as well as many freestanding ATMs in heavily touristed locations. Independent ATMs can also be found at many attractions, bars, and convenience stores; however, these often carry exorbitant fees. Many grocery stores and pharmacies accept ATM debit cards and will give cash back (usually up to around $50 or $100 at a time) with purchase, at no additional fee.

## Credit Cards

Visa and MasterCard are widely accepted everywhere from food trucks to gas stations; many places also accept American Express. Diners Club and Discover cards are

A storm rolls through the Everglades.

sometimes accepted, but their usage is far less common.

## Taxes

The statewide sales tax is 6 percent. Many counties and municipalities levy additional "local option" sales taxes, ranging from 0.5 to 2 percent, on top of the state tax. Hotel taxes range from 9 to 12 percent, in addition to sales tax on the room rate.

## Tipping

For the most part, gratuities and service charges are not included on bills, although in some instances (tourist-heavy restaurants, especially) you should check your bill first, especially if you are part of a large group. A 15 percent tip is considered the baseline tip for acceptable service, although 20 percent for restaurant bills and cab fares and $1 per drink on bar tabs is far more common; $1 per bag is normal for hotel porters.

# COMMUNICATIONS AND MEDIA
## Internet Access

Broadband Internet is available throughout Florida, although many rural areas have limited access. Many hotels offer wireless Internet access, if not in guest rooms, then at least in public areas. Coffee shops and bakeries like Starbucks and Panera Bread have Wi-Fi as well.

## Telephones

In most Florida locales, 10-digit dialing is standard, meaning the area code must be dialed before the main number. Pay phones are all but nonexistent. Cell phone coverage, however, pretty much blankets the state. In all but the most remote areas, you'll be able to get at least a couple of bars on your phone—even in the heart of the Everglades. AT&T, T-Mobile, Sprint, and Verizon have towers all over the state, as well as dozens of stores and service centers in most major cities.

## Media

There are five major television markets in Florida—Jacksonville, Miami/Fort Lauderdale, Orlando/Daytona Beach, West Palm Beach/Fort Pierce, and Tampa/St. Petersburg/Sarasota. Each market carries the four U.S. networks (NBC, CBS, ABC, FOX) as well as PBS, Univision, Telemundo, and community programming.

Radio in Florida features the standard assortment of rock, pop, country, and public stations on the FM dial and talk and sports on the AM dial.

# Resources

## Suggested Reading

### NONFICTION

Burt, Al. *The Tropic of Cracker*. Gainesville: University of Florida Press, 1999. Former *Miami Herald* columnist Al Burt did Florida natives a great service when he wrote *The Tropic of Cracker*. By reminding readers that the state would be nothing without the farmers, homesteaders, and pioneers who made this swamp livable (or at least bearable), Burt draws a bright line between the warm, organic, and occasionally quirky heart of Florida's traditional residents and the hucksters and opportunists who have sought to exploit the state for a quick buck.

Carlson, Charlie. *Weird Florida*. New York: Sterling, 2005. While nearly every state in the Union has its own weird sites and stories, Florida undoubtedly has more than most. Charlie Carlson has done a great job in collecting and organizing the weirdest and most wonderful, and for those looking for a sort of alternate-reality tour through the Sunshine State—or simply looking for a good chuckle—this book is essential reading.

Douglas, Marjory Stoneman. *The Everglades: River of Grass*. New York: Rinehart & Company, 1947. This seminal treatise on the Everglades was originally assigned as a piece on the Miami River for Rinehart's "Rivers of America" series; instead, Douglas's research took her to the vast waterways and swamps of the Everglades, where she found a diversity of flora, fauna, and delicate ecosystems that was wholly unique and under threat from nearby development. By all accounts, Douglas's evocative and accessible writing in *River of Grass* laid the foundation for the contemporary conservation efforts underway in the 'Glades, as she painted a portrait of a natural area that was a distinct national treasure, worthy of protection.

Gannon, Michael. *Florida: A Short History*. Gainesville: University Press of Florida, 2003. Histories of Florida, both comprehensive and condensed, abound. None, however, are as compelling and engaging as Gannon's 190-page narrative. Cramming five centuries of discovery, exploration, exploitation, and growth into an easy-to-read and stylistically enjoyable tale, Gannon's book dusts away the dry studiousness of most history texts and presents the state itself as the main character in an epic tale.

Pittman, Craig. *Oh, Florida!* New York: St. Martin's Press, 2016. Florida's reputation as the weirdest state in the Union may be well-deserved (see: Florida Man), but it's also somewhat misunderstood. Pittman's background as a newspaper reporter helps put it into context, threading history with more recent news to paint a picture of a state that has always been a magnet for grifters and dreamers alike, and showing how the state's uniqueness has impacted not just its residents but the rest of the country and world. As Pittman likes to say, if there's a piece of strange or scandalous news somewhere, there's almost always a Florida connection.

# FICTION

Hiaasen, Carl. *Tourist Season.* New York: G. P. Putnam's Sons, 1986. Carl Hiaasen's first book may not be his best—that honor has to go to 1991's *Native Tongue*—but the template the author set out here for his books is unmistakable and revolutionary in terms of Florida literature. Hiaasen has a reporter's knack for weaving a story out of multiple threads of corruption, crime, and craven carnality, and he does so with a steady dose of wry humor. Hiaasen's work is nuanced; he's one of the few authors to capture the insanity, beauty, depravity, and deep-seated weirdness of the Sunshine State, though he is clearly in love with Florida and uses each of his novels to jab at the moneyed interests that threaten to pave over it entirely.

Smith, Patrick. *A Land Remembered.* Sarasota: Pineapple Press, 1996. Smith's sprawling novel covers more than a century of Florida history, told from the perspective of three generations of the MacIvey family. From the Civil War and the early 20th-century land boom (and bust) on through the massive wealth amassed by "Old Florida" families through the 1960s, the book tends to get lost in its melodramatic sweep. But it captures and crystallizes the growth and change of the state.

White, Randy Wayne. *The Man Who Invented Florida.* New York: St. Martin's Press, 1993. In the wake of Carl Hiaasen's success with telling the story of Florida from a slightly off-kilter (and ultimately more realistic) perspective, a number of other Florida writers found themselves getting attention. Randy Wayne White is one of the most prolific and, thankfully, also one of the best. White's "Doc Ford" adventures (of which *The Man Who Invented Florida* is the third, best, and strangest) take place on Florida's Gulf Coast, which lends the proceedings more of a swampy, backwoods-noir feel, but the crimes and current issues at play keep the books from being standard potboilers.

# Internet Resources

## GENERAL INFORMATION

**Visit Florida**
**www.visitflorida.com**
Operated by the state's tourism board, this site is rich in content. In addition to basic information on many of the state's attractions, as well as weather reports and event calendars, Visit Florida also offers trip-planning tools, blogs, video features, and reservation services. While the site is unflinchingly positive about everything (of course), it's surprisingly informative and an excellent resource if you're in the initial stages of planning a trip.

## NEWSPAPERS

*Naples Daily News*
**www.naplesnews.com**
The *Naples Daily News* focuses on Collier County, with supplementary coverage of Charlotte County and Lee County (including Marco Island, the Everglades, Cape Coral, and Bonita Springs).

*The News-Press*
**www.news-press.com**
There's considerable crossover in the coverage of the *Naples Daily News* and the Fort Myers-based *News-Press*. The *News-Press* covers Fort Myers, Fort Myers Beach, and Estero.

*Sarasota Herald-Tribune*
**www.heraldtribune.com**
The largest newspaper in southwest Florida obviously focuses on the Sarasota area, but it also covers news in Bradenton and Venice. Their entertainment-focused subsite, http://

ticketsarasota.com, is a good resource for arts, music, and events information. Each of the bigger cities covered in this guide claims a reasonably sized daily newspaper. Of them, the *Sarasota Herald-Tribune* is the best.

## PARKS AND CAMPING
### Florida State Parks
### www.floridastateparks.org
This is a fantastic resource for every possible bit of information you could need on any of Florida's 160 state parks.

### National Park Service
### www.nps.gov/state/FL
This site offers information on all 10 of the national parks in Florida, with hours, seasons, entrance fees, and other vitals.

### Reserve America
### www.reserveamerica.com
Many of the state, national, and privately owned RV parks in Florida utilize Reserve America to process campground reservations.

# Index

# List of Maps

# Photo Credits

# MAP SYMBOLS

| | | | | | | | |
|---|---|---|---|---|---|---|---|
| ≡≡≡ | Expressway | ○ | City/Town | ✈ | Airport | ⌕ | Golf Course |
| ≡≡≡ | Primary Road | ◉ | State Capital | ✗ | Airfield | 🅿 | Parking Area |
| ≡≡≡ | Secondary Road | ⊛ | National Capital | ▲ | Mountain | ⬟ | Archaeological Site |
| ------- | Unpaved Road | ★ | Point of Interest | ✦ | Unique Natural Feature | ▮ | Church |
| —— | Feature Trail | • | Accommodation | | | | Gas Station |
| - - - - | Other Trail | ▾ | Restaurant/Bar | ⚑ | Waterfall | | Glacier |
| ·········· | Ferry | ■ | Other Location | ▲ | Park | | Mangrove |
| ≡≡≡ | Pedestrian Walkway | Λ | Campground | ▯ | Trailhead | | Reef |
| ▥▥▥ | Stairs | | | ⛷ | Skiing Area | | Swamp |

# CONVERSION TABLES

°C = (°F - 32) / 1.8
°F = (°C x 1.8) + 32
1 inch = 2.54 centimeters (cm)
1 foot = 0.304 meters (m)
1 yard = 0.914 meters
1 mile = 1.6093 kilometers (km)
1 km = 0.6214 miles
1 fathom = 1.8288 m
1 chain = 20.1168 m
1 furlong = 201.168 m
1 acre = 0.4047 hectares
1 sq km = 100 hectares
1 sq mile = 2.59 square km
1 ounce = 28.35 grams
1 pound = 0.4536 kilograms
1 short ton = 0.90718 metric ton
1 short ton = 2,000 pounds
1 long ton = 1.016 metric tons
1 long ton = 2,240 pounds
1 metric ton = 1,000 kilograms
1 quart = 0.94635 liters
1 US gallon = 3.7854 liters
1 Imperial gallon = 4.5459 liters
1 nautical mile = 1.852 km

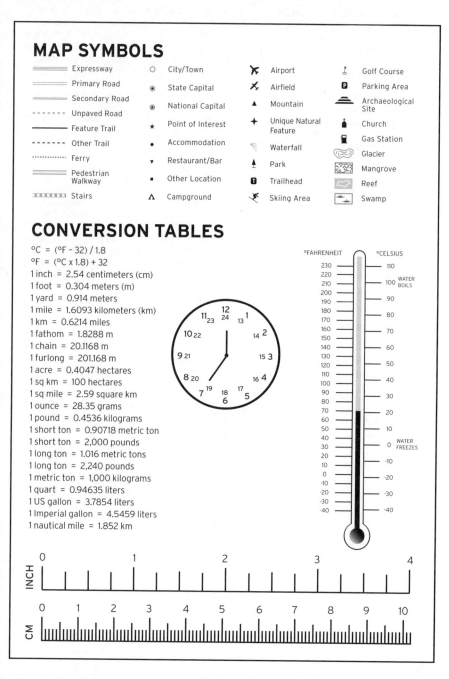

## MOON SARASOTA & NAPLES

Avalon Travel
Hachette Book Group
1700 Fourth Street
Berkeley, CA 94710, USA
www.moon.com

Editor: Rachel Feldman
Series Manager: Kathryn Ettinger
Copy Editor: Linda Cabasin
Production and Graphics Coordinator:
  Suzanne Albertson
Cover Design: Faceout Studios, Charles Brock
Interior Design: Domini Dragoone
Moon Logo: Tim McGrath
Map Editor: Kat Bennett
Cartographer: Karin Dahl
Indexer: Greg Jewett

ISBN-13: 978-1-64049-265-3

Printing History
1st Edition — 2013
3rd Edition — September 2018
5 4 3 2 1

Front cover photo: the Ca' d'Zan in Sarasota ©
  Jennifer Wright / Alamy Stock Photo
Back cover photo: Crescent Beach on Siesta Key ©
  Alinalemay | Dreamstime.com

Printed in China by RR Donnelley